In this unique and very special book, Shelley A. Riggs and Laura E. Captari provide the definitive systemic guide to working with trauma. The authors build on the foundation of a clearly articulated multisystemic understanding of trauma that is deeply ingrained in relevant research. They draw from the best of evidence-based practice to help the reader learn to shape helpful case formulations and intervene in the context of trauma. Filled with practical advice and evocative illustrative cases, the authors brilliantly bridge evidence-based practice and clinical wisdom. This book should be read by every clinician and therapist in training who works with or plans to work with trauma.

—**JAY LEBOW, PhD, ABPP,** CLINICAL PROFESSOR, THE FAMILY INSTITUTE AT NORTHWESTERN UNIVERSITY, EVANSTON, IL

This text is a timely addition to the literature on systemic and communal healing practices for trauma-impacted individuals and families. It contributes new ways to conceptualize trauma and its impact on others and the reciprocal role played by trauma in its relational and cultural contexts. The authors make explicit how the family system, even intergenerational "ghosts," can affect the occurrence of trauma and serve to further traumatize or as a healing resource.

—**CHRISTINE A. COURTOIS, PhD, ABPP,** CONSULTANT/TRAINER IN TRAUMA PSYCHOLOGY AND TREATMENT, LEWES, DE; AUTHOR, *HEALING THE INCEST WOUND: ADULT SURVIVORS IN THERAPY*; COEDITOR, *TREATING COMPLEX TRAUMATIC STRESS DISORDERS (ADULTS)*; AUTHOR, *IT'S NOT YOU, IT'S WHAT HAPPENED TO YOU: COMPLEX TRAUMA AND TREATMENT*

This book provides a much-needed integration of systemic family and couples theory and practice with traumatic stress assessment and treatment. The impact of psychological trauma on family systems, and the vital importance of understanding family systems dynamics, is brought to life with vivid case studies and an illuminating overview of treatment models from both fields. The authors have provided a unique resource for both preprofessional trainees and practicing professionals on how to be both systemic and trauma-informed.

–JULIAN D. FORD, PhD, ABPP, PROFESSOR OF PSYCHIATRY AND LAW, UNIVERSITY OF CONNECTICUT, STORRS; PAST PRESIDENT, INTERNATIONAL SOCIETY FOR TRAUMATIC STRESS STUDIES; AND FELLOW OF THE AMERICAN PSYCHOLOGICAL ASSOCIATION

SYSTEMIC TREATMENT OF

TRAUMA-IMPACTED FAMILIES:

A CLINICIAN'S GUIDE TO ASSESSMENT,

FORMULATION, AND INTERVENTION

Fundamentals of Clinical Practice With Couples and Families

Best Clinical Practices for Treating Families in Juvenile and Criminal Justice Systems
Corinne C. Datchi

A Systemic Approach to Behavioral Healthcare Integration: Context Matters
Nancy Breen Ruddy and Susan H. McDaniel

Systemic Treatment of Trauma-Impacted Families: A Clinician's Guide to Assessment, Formulation, and Intervention
Shelley A. Riggs and Laura E. Captari

SYSTEMIC TREATMENT OF TRAUMA-IMPACTED FAMILIES:

A CLINICIAN'S GUIDE TO ASSESSMENT, FORMULATION, AND INTERVENTION

SHELLEY A. RIGGS AND **LAURA E. CAPTARI**

AMERICAN PSYCHOLOGICAL ASSOCIATION

Published by
American Psychological Association
750 First Street, NE
Washington, DC 20002
https://www.apa.org

Order Department
https://www.apa.org/pubs/books
order@apa.org

Typeset in Charter and Interstate by Lumina Datamatics, India

Printer: Gasch Printing, Odenton, MD
Cover Designer: Mark Karis

Library of Congress Cataloging-in-Publication Data

CIP data has been applied for.
Library of Congress Control Number: 2025050603

ISBN 9781433839382 (paperback)
ISBN 9781433839399 (epub)
ISBN 9781433850097 (pdf)

https://doi.org/10.1037/0000487-000

Printed in the United States of America

10 9 8 7 6 5 4 3 2 1

To my brother, who set me on this path,
and my mother, who showed me the way.

—SHELLEY A. RIGGS

To C.W., whose steady love has buoyed me amid life's tragedies,
and E.R. and C.T., who beckon me to savor life's tiny wonders.

—LAURA E. CAPTARI

Contents

Foreword

As war begets war, trauma can beget trauma. If you believe that the impact of a person's traumatic experience ripples over generations and across relationships, you already know that trauma is best viewed through a systemic lens. If you include parents or other family members in your efforts to help children heal from trauma, you are no stranger to systemic thinking. There are multiple ethical, scientific, and clinical arguments for a systemic clinical practice (Harway et al., 2012). However, the best argument may be found in human nature itself: We are inextricably connected with one another and with the natural world.

But our connections are complex: reciprocal, dynamic, meaningful, and nested within multiple relational contexts. Only a systemic framework can capture this complexity. Among health service psychologists, only the specialty of couple and family psychology (CFP) conceptualizes and treats problems within this relational matrix. Fortunately, mental health practitioners are increasingly considering trauma from a systemic perspective, and they are beginning to use systemic interventions to help survivors. *Systemic Treatment of Trauma Impacted Families: A Clinician's Guide to Assessment, Formulation, and Intervention* marks a tremendous leap forward in this direction, as it presents a systemic, evidence-based approach to helping individuals, families, and communities affected by traumatic events.

There are four ways in which this book is unique among other textbooks on trauma. First, authors Riggs and Captari expertly integrate CFP concepts and science with trauma psychology, highlighting how families affect and are affected by individual and collective responses to trauma. The authors succeed in braiding their knowledge and expertise in both systems and trauma to create a compelling whole that is more than the sum of its parts.

Second, the book draws on the shared CFP base of evidence-based concepts and strategies (i.e., "common factors"), rather than focusing on a single evidence-based model for understanding and treating people affected by trauma. This choice is important because many clinicians (a) draw on diverse sources to select treatment strategies likely to be successful and with which they feel comfortable (Lebow, 2014), (b) work with culturally and clinically heterogeneous populations for which a particular evidence-based treatment model may not have been tested, and (c) may not have the resources to devote to the extensive training required by an evidence-based model. Additionally, the common factors approach may make treatment more accessible to clients given the lag between research advances and clinical applications.

Third, the authors offer inspiring breadth in their coverage of relevant material, attending to different types of trauma (including collective trauma), multiple competencies, and various evidence-based models. For example, the authors focus on both foundational competencies (e.g., individual and cultural diversity, scientific knowledge and methods, ethical legal standards and policy, and reflection/self-awareness/self-care) and functional competencies (e.g., assessment, intervention, evidence-based practice, consultation, and advocacy). This comprehensive presentation of competencies is important because many clinicians who apply a systemic framework do so inconsistently or in a piecemeal fashion; for example, they may apply a systemic lens to assessment but not to intervention (Celano, 2018).

Fourth, the authors' liberal use of realistic case material allows readers to understand how systemic theory, concepts, and strategies can be practically applied in clinical situations, in the context of a specific family and community. That is, the case illustrations breathe life into the systemic model. Readers will learn how a systemic lens informs the assessment and treatment of families affected by neglect, foster home placement, intimate partner violence, alcoholism, suicide, homelessness, and/or racism.

This book is an important resource for clinicians from diverse mental health disciplines, as well as for students and trainees entering the field. Although the authors focus primarily on competencies defined for CFP, psychologists from other specialties will find the book relevant to their clinical work, in part because the same competencies are applicable for all health service psychologists. Clinical social workers, professional counselors, pastoral counselors, psychiatrists, and psychiatric nurse practitioners will also find the material useful. In short, this book is recommended for any clinician who provides mental health services to people who have experienced trauma.

There is no better time for a book on systemic approaches to treating trauma. Exposure to traumatic events is distressingly common among both youth (Swedo et al., 2024) and adults (Swedo et al., 2023). Parenting has become so stressful that the Office of the Surgeon General (2024, Chapter 1) has issued a public health advisory about the impact of modern stressors on parents' mental health and well-being. Sadly, humans will continue to experience traumatic events despite advances in technology and health care. In fact, traumatic experiences will become more common and intense as we face the global existential crisis posed by climate change. Deemed a "threat multiplier" by the Center for Naval Analysis Analyses (CNA) Military Advisory Board (2007), the climate crisis has the potential to increase downstream dangers such as extreme weather events, pandemics, famine, mass migration, and political instability or conflict. In this context, mental health clinicians have an essential civic responsibility. Our legacy as a species may well depend not only on our success in limiting global heating, but also on our recovery from climate-related traumas and injustices.

—*Marianne Celano, PhD, ABPP*

Series Preface

Couple and family therapy represents a specialty area of clinical practice in the mental health professions. In 2022, an estimated 75% and 33% of psychologists worked with couples and families, respectively (Norcross et al., 2023). The percentage of time they devoted to these treatment formats was 13% for marital therapy and 4% for family therapy (Norcross et al., 2023). Future projections suggest that the field of couple and family therapy will grow 16% between 2023 and 2033 (Bureau of Labor Statistics, U.S. Department of Labor, n.d.). This reflects the increasing demand for couple and family practitioners that understand the link between mental health and relational functioning and that are trained to successfully address the common challenges of couple and family relationships.

We, the editors of this book series, are board-certified couple and family psychologists involved in research and clinical activities with diverse individuals, couples, and families. We have at least 20 years of experience in the specialty of couple and family psychology, as couple and family practitioners, scholars, and educators. We have trained and supervised graduate students and clinicians to work with couples and families in various settings, including university clinics, community-based mental health agencies, and criminal justice systems. Couple and family psychology is a core dimension of our professional identity, and systems thinking is the primary conceptual lens that guides our professional activities.

We have created this book series to support competency-based education and training for specialty practice with couples and families at the graduate, postgraduate, and postlicensure levels. Our goal is to highlight the distinctive knowledge and skills that are required to work effectively with diverse couples and families. We seek to showcase best practices in the treatment of couples and families, based on the most current research in psychology and psychotherapy.

The series consists of short books that discuss specialty assessment, case conceptualization, intervention, and consultation for clinical practice with couples and families. The books are written by field experts and designed to be clinical guides. They provide comprehensive summaries of the specialty knowledge needed to work with specific clinical populations and mental health concerns. They also demonstrate how to use the specialty skills to treat specific populations of couples and families in various settings.

The focus on using a systemic theoretical framework is a common thread that links the books together. The key concepts and principles of systems theory are used to organize knowledge about couples and families and to discuss treatment decisions. Systemic thinking emphasizes a holistic approach to clinical practice. It calls for the ability to see the person in interaction with their context and to observe how the dynamic factors in and around the person influence each other, the progression of clinical problems, and the course of treatment.

The focus on specialty competencies is also a common thread that links the books together. These are the specialty competencies for professional practice with couples and families endorsed by the American Board of Couple and Family Psychology (2022). The Board has recognized 16 competencies that represent the systemic knowledge, skills, values, and attitudes of couple and family psychology. A detailed discussion of each of the competencies, their components, and behavioral anchors can be found in Stanton and Welsh's (2011) seminal book.

Professional competence is both an outcome of education and training and an ethical imperative to protect the welfare of the public (Stanton & Harway, 2019). The term refers to clinicians' overall suitability for the delivery of mental health services. Competence is context specific: Different clinical settings and populations require different kinds of expertise (Falender & Shafranske, 2017). Developing competence is a dynamic and ongoing process of learning rather than an endpoint.

Competencies are interrelated sets of knowledge, skills, attitudes, and values that are observable and measurable (Celano, 2019). They are grouped into two categories: (a) foundational and (b) functional. Foundational competencies (e.g., the capacity to engage in self-reflective practice, knowledge, and application of ethical standards) are a prerequisite for the development of functional competencies (knowledge and skills used to work with clients); they are the basis for all professional activities, including assessment, diagnosis, conceptualization, intervention, consultation, research and evaluation, supervision and teaching, and administration and management.

Competencies for clinical practice with couples and families require specialty education and training at the doctoral, postdoctoral, and/or postlicensure stage. The Couple and Family Psychology Specialty Council, which represents three organizations (American Board of Couple and Family Psychology; American Academy of Couple and Family Psychology; and American Psychological Association Division 43, the Society for Couple and Family Psychology), has adopted education and training guidelines for model doctoral, internship, postdoctoral, and postlicensure programs in couple and family psychology (Riggs et al., 2020). These guidelines follow the taxonomy developed by the Council of Specialties in Professional Psychology (2021) and specify the didactic and experiential components necessary for developing different levels of competence in clinical practice with couples and families.

The majority of doctoral psychology programs in the United States provide some exposure to couple and family psychology, most often through a survey course that focuses on it (Stanton & Harway, 2019). However, exposure is not sufficient to develop competence in the specialty. The American Board of Professional Psychology (n.d.) recommends additional postgraduation experiences to demonstrate appropriate specialty education and training, for example a predoctoral internship with a track in couple and family psychology; a postdoctoral residency with 30% to 50% of supervised practice with couples and families; at least 25 hours of postgraduation continuing education, specific to couple and family psychology; and at least 25 hours of specialty supervision by a board-certified couple and family psychologist.

This book series is intended to expand access to specialty education in clinical practice with couples and families. It is designed for a diverse audience of mental health practitioners with different levels of training and experience. Graduate students and postdoctoral fellows will find it useful to increase their understanding of systemic thinking, assessment, case conceptualization, and intervention with couples and families and to support their application of systemic principles in the treatment of clinical problems. Seasoned clinicians—psychologists, social workers, counselors, and marriage and family therapists—will also find the series useful to keep current of new practice developments and to build on their specialty knowledge and skills.

Systemic Treatment of Trauma Impacted Families: A Clinician's Guide to Assessment, Formulation, and Intervention is another essential volume in the series. The demand for trauma-focused psychological services has increased from 51% to 64% from 2020 to 2022 (American Psychological Association, 2022a). Trauma and stress-related disorders follow anxiety and depression as the most common reasons for seeking psychotherapy. This book describes the foundational knowledge and skills needed to treat the sequelae of trauma from a systemic perspective. It examines how trauma-related dynamics manifest in family relationships and are transmitted across generations. It also emphasizes the importance of recognizing the intergenerational transmission of resilience and adaptation. It defines and illustrates the application of systemic competencies that enable clinicians to perceive the patterns of trauma-related family interactions, to formulate innovative hypotheses about the nature of the clinical problem, and to adapt treatment to meet the unique needs of trauma-impacted families. Finally, it underscores the critical advocacy role of mental health professionals in driving systems-level change to promote trauma-informed interventions across mental health care, education, and broader social settings.

—Corinne C. Datchi, PhD, ABPP
Anthony Chambers, PhD, ABPP
Series Editors

Acknowledgments

This book would not have been possible apart from the generosity, support, patience, and unwavering dedication of many in our lives. First and foremost, we would like to express heartfelt gratitude to our families, without whom we would've possessed neither the time nor resolve to stay the course in completing this effort. We want to acknowledge and honor the many teachers, supervisors, mentors, and colleagues who have shaped our perspectives in approaching trauma healing through a systemic lens. Their wisdom, groundedness, and creativity echo across these pages. We also thank our students and supervisees, whose commitment to learning and passion for this work enliven us—what a gift to be students and teachers to each other! In addition, we would like to express appreciation to APA, as well as Corinne Datchi and Anthony Chambers, for the opportunity to contribute to this book series, and to Marianne Celano for her helpful and detailed feedback in the book's development. Finally, we want to honor the courage of the individuals, couples, and families we have had the opportunity to work with in psychotherapy across the years. You have taught us so much about the healing potential of relationships after trauma, and how the natural order of things is to grow and develop beyond despair.

SYSTEMIC TREATMENT OF

TRAUMA-IMPACTED FAMILIES:

A CLINICIAN'S GUIDE TO ASSESSMENT, FORMULATION, AND INTERVENTION

INTRODUCTION

A Systemic Lens as Vital for Trauma Treatment

Children don't get traumatized because they are hurt. They get traumatized because they're alone with the hurt.

—GABOR MATÉ (BENAZZO & BENAZZO 2021)

The book in your hands is the result of 5 years of planning, writing, editing, and feedback in order to develop a concise clinical guide applying a systemic lens to the broad sequelae of trauma in families. Most of us as psychotherapists enter professional practice with essential clinical skills to conduct individual therapy, but have little to no training in systemically oriented assessment and intervention (Kaslow et al., 2005). A systemic lens takes as a starting point that mental health distress—and sources of strength, resilience, and growth—are inextricably intertwined with the dynamics of family relationships, environment, and social context (Celano, 2018). In this book, we explore how such interaction processes can both contribute to trauma and be a vital source of healing.

Systemic therapies often involve working with multiple family members (e.g., a couple, parent–child dyad) and/or close coordination with others who are significant in the lives of trauma-impacted individuals (e.g., extended

https://doi.org/10.1037/0000487-001
Systemic Treatment of Trauma-Impacted Families: A Clinician's Guide to Assessment, Formulation, and Intervention, by S. A. Riggs and L. E. Captari

family networks, school personnel). However, throughout this book, we use the terms *couple and family* and *systemic* alongside each other to highlight how such therapeutic work is not defined by intervention modality. A systemic perspective is relevant whether you work primarily with individuals, couples, families, and/or groups, and whether you are a psychologist, psychiatrist, social worker, counselor, couple and family therapist, or other clinician. It goes well beyond who is present for a particular session and is rooted in what you are paying attention to as well as how you are intervening.

When it comes to working with trauma in clinical settings, even those of us lucky enough to have had a graduate course in this area may be underprepared to meaningfully address the nuances of assessment and treatment (American Psychological Association [APA], 2015a; Henning et al., 2022; Kumar et al., 2022), particularly considering how the effects of trauma ripple across families, communities, and generations. Increasing attention to this public health concern—well beyond posttraumatic stress disorder alone—highlights the critical importance of trauma-informed and -responsive care in routine practice (Magruder et al., 2017). Trauma-informed care is rooted in an emphasis on safety and collaboration, recognizing that traumatized individuals are vulnerable to further harm and iatrogenic outcomes. Trauma-responsive care goes further by tailoring treatment to each patient's experience and needs in real time, necessitating high levels of attunement and flexibility. Rather than being solely oriented by questions such as "What type of trauma occurred?" or "What's the diagnosis?" we must more deeply consider, "What has this individual, couple, or family endured—and how does it live on both inside of and between them?"

GAPS IN TRAINING AND AVAILABLE CARE

Many clients and their family members have experienced trauma, with wide-ranging sequelae that include constricted or reactive relational patterns as well as complex symptom presentations. Yet, given that couple and family therapy and trauma therapy are not well integrated, most of us are left to "put the pieces together." Perhaps what initially looked like a child therapy case has necessitated supporting parents in addressing their own unresolved trauma as part of strengthening the parent–child relationship. Or maybe individual adults with histories of trauma keep bringing into session conflicts arising in their romantic relationship or family. One way or another, we often find our way to a more systemic formulation via the complexities arising in our cases. This can unwittingly lead to treating trauma as an "accidental family therapist" (Wise & Gomez, 2018). It can be extremely challenging to hold in mind and meaningfully apply these distinct streams of knowledge in real time, especially amid anxiety-provoking and high-stakes clinical situations ... where our own nervous systems can easily get "hijacked" by relational dynamics of dysregulation or disengagement.

For many therapists, clinical situations that challenge individually oriented conceptualizations and interventions compel them to learn more about working with couples, parents, siblings, grandparents, and other family constellations. Yet, research suggests that this "piecing it together as you go" approach can be haphazard; on average, psychotherapist effectiveness has not been found to improve across one's career, with evidence of either nonimprovement beyond internship or slight deterioration effects (Tracey et al., 2024). Of note, this trend is not clearly related to the difficulty of one's cases. What are the public health implications of this for traumatized populations? Gaps in our ongoing development as clinicians—and in the effects on routine clinical practice—are sobering and can limit clients' possibilities for accessing evidence-based care that promotes holistic trauma healing. As Henning et al. (2022) noted,

> The disparity between the need for clinicians who can provide safe and effective treatment for individuals with trauma-related conditions and disorders, and the availability of such professionals, is great and ever-increasing. This is especially problematic due to the high number of mental health clients whose clinical picture is related to current or past traumatic events and experiences. (p. 372)

We argue that integrating the wisdom of systemic thinking in working with trauma-impacted clients and families is an ethical necessity as part of addressing this disparity. In line with the importance of practicing within the boundaries of our competence (American Association for Marriage and Family Therapy, 2015; American Counseling Association, 2014; APA, 2017b; National Association of Social Workers, 2021), it behooves us as mental health professionals to intentionally seek out postgraduate training and supervision when we experience a gap between our training and the competencies necessary to provide specialty care. While this book is insufficient on its own, and should be supplemented, we hope it serves as a springboard by sparking increased attention to and momentum in approaching the treatment of trauma beyond the individual psyche.

THE PURPOSE AND SCOPE OF THIS BOOK

Our experience has been that trauma therapy training tends to focus largely on individual intervention, and that training in working with couples and families often does not adequately prepare clinicians to address trauma-related dynamics that surface in relationships and across generations. Thus, practitioners may end up developing competencies in one area but not the other (i.e., trauma or couple/family) and are often left to do the integrative work in their real-time practice. Many excellent books and manuals already exist that comprehensively cover the vast body of available trauma research, provide in-depth guidance on particular types of trauma or clinical presentations, and detail how to conduct therapy sessions using specific approaches. The same could be said of resources for readers who want to take a deep dive into couple and family therapy. Thus, we do not try to replicate these or provide comprehensive reviews of the literatures on trauma science or family systems. Furthermore, we do not have the space to discuss every possibility or complication that may arise in either trauma-focused[1] or family therapy—never mind the intersection between them! Acknowledging this, we provide references throughout for readers who are interested in consulting such resources for more in-depth information and guidance.

What you can expect from this read is an introduction to and application of core systemic principles and practices, providing a holistic and nuanced—but often overlooked—metatheoretical perspective to working with trauma in the family system. This book offers an accelerated primer on systems theory as applied to trauma-related assessment, formulation, and treatment. Rather than focusing on one treatment approach or modality, we describe the unique challenges and potential of systemically oriented interventions to help people heal from trauma and develop richer, more rewarding relationships with family and kinship networks. Systems theory functions as a valuable metatheory that provides a broad conceptual framework for working with couples and families impacted by trauma. As such, this book does not offer a step-by-step approach to assessment and treatment, but instead introduces systemic concepts and processes, as well as specialty skills and techniques that clinicians can apply to their own assessment and psychotherapy practices with traumatized clients. The focus here is on developing systemic capabilities (Fraser & Greenhalgh, 2001; Kaslow et al., 2022) that will enable you to learn about and "see" the reciprocal patterns in family interactions and the interconnectedness of trauma in family systems, to use all of your clinical knowledge and experience to generate innovative clinical hypotheses and interventions to assist in relational healing processes, and to flexibly adapt your established professional competencies to the unique needs of trauma-impacted clients and their families.

[1] We use the term *trauma-focused* throughout this book to capture the broad array of psychological assessment and intervention strategies that address the multidimensional impacts of potentially traumatic stressors on mental health.

Drawing from almost 40 years of combined clinical work, research, teaching, and ongoing theorizing (plus our own lived experience as children, siblings, partners, parents, and now a grandparent!), we synthesize key systemic principles and practices relevant to clinical practice with children, couples, and families. We speak from experience having worked in intensive in-home, inpatient, community mental health, college counseling, private practice, Veteran's Affairs, and educational settings, where we have provided and supervised individual, child–parent, couple, family, and group therapy. We find working systemically as therapists to be invigorating, sometimes hard and frustrating, and at many times humbling and awe-inspiring as we partner with families in activating healing processes.

As part of a larger series applying specialty professional competencies to working with couples and families, this clinician's guide aims to fill some of the aforementioned gaps for therapists keen to develop or enrich their clinical competencies in helping couples, families, and communities who have been individually or collectively affected by trauma. This book is also relevant for mental health professionals who work mainly with individual clients but want to bring a more systemic lens and formulation to trauma-focused treatment. We do not blithely propose couple or family modalities as THE answer; as we will discuss, in traumatized family systems, there may be multiple clinically appropriate reasons to not include certain members in treatment. Whether you primarily interact with a single member of a family system, members of a particular subsystem (e.g., couple, siblings), entire families, dyads within a kinship network (e.g., friends or colleagues), or a larger milieu (e.g., school, community), gaining a comprehensive understanding of trauma and systems can elucidate important details that deepen your understanding of what is happening and change how you approach trauma intervention. Our experience has been that once you "see" systemic dynamics, it is hard to "unsee" them! Given the reciprocal nature of relational dynamics and family processes, systemically oriented treatment can help both support individual trauma healing of the involved members and create the conditions for change in a couple or family's ways of relating, regardless of who is physically in the therapy room. Thus, applying systems theory to trauma treatment enables us to work flexibly and creatively to meet each client, couple, or family where they are at.

ORGANIZATION OF THIS BOOK

This book is organized into seven interrelated chapters that cover foundational knowledge and skills for treating the sequelae of trauma from a systemic perspective. Each chapter begins with a brief illustrative vignette (amalgamated or fictitious) that sets the stage for reviewing relevant theory and research, with a focus throughout the book on practical application to real-world clinical practice with individuals, couples, and families. We attend equally to each leg of the stool of evidence-based practice, namely, knowing the empirical evidence and mechanisms of change underlying diverse treatment approaches, developing clinical wisdom and greater competency in couple and family intervention, and personalizing treatment in light of each client's or family's culture and preferences (APA, 2021). To enhance understanding and application of systemic concepts and strategies, we integrate an amalgamated case study of the fictitious Garcia family in detail across several chapters to show what systemic assessment, case formulation, treatment, and consultation might look like in practice. While illustrative, this case captures only one of many different types of family constellations, clinical presentations, and courses of treatment; thus, we invite readers to consider how to apply systemic principles and concepts creatively in light of their own specific workplace context, populations served, and clients' presenting concerns.

To begin, Chapter 1 describes key systemic principles and concepts relevant to trauma work, such as subsystems, organization, power and control, communication, cohesion and autonomy, boundaries, alliances and coalitions, conflict, and role reversal. Zooming out beyond individual symptomology, we orient readers toward relationships and processes between and among individuals where the sequelae of trauma—for example, patterns of fight, flight, freeze, and/or fawn—often live in the family system. Recognizing that many clinicians operate as "accidental family therapists" due to the relevance of such concerns arising in professional practice, ongoing learning and professional development is critical in order to provide the best possible clinical care (Wise & Gomez, 2018). Foundational competencies for working with couples and families are discussed, including attention to family and life cycle diversity, as well as unique ethical and legal considerations.

Building on this, Chapter 2 grapples with the question of what constitutes trauma and explicates an intersubjective, multidimensional, and holistic understanding that moves beyond Criterion A events[2] and also attends to covert, cumulative, community-based, intergenerational, and collective experiences. We distinguish traumatic stressors external to the family system (which may impact one or more family members) from those within the system (wherein one or more family members perpetrates against others), and consider the interplay between these areas. Attention is also paid to the intergenerational

[2] Criterion A events are those that meet the definition required as part of diagnosis of acute stress disorder or posttraumatic stress disorder in the *Diagnostic and Statistical Manual of Mental Disorders* (*DSM-5*; American Psychiatric Association, 2022).

transmission of family strengths, resilience, and adaptation, being mindful to conceptualize traumatized families as a group of living, hurting, whole people—not a bundle of symptoms or dysfunctional patterns. This chapter also introduces trauma-specific competencies that are distinct from generalist training as a mental health practitioner.

Chapter 3 applies the three-legged stool of evidence-based practice to working systemically with traumatized populations, integrating the best available scientific evidence with clinical expertise and responsiveness to each family's values and preferences. We explore underlying common factors in systemic intervention, then offer readers a tour of treatment approaches in three areas: (a) models specifically designed to involve family members in the treatment of trauma, (b) established couple/family treatment approaches that have been adapted for trauma, and (c) established individual approaches for treating trauma that can be enriched through a systemic formulation. In light of growing evidence that treatment responsiveness and collaboration matters more in real-world settings than fidelity to any one particular intervention model, this chapter offers a metatheoretical perspective that brings into focus common factors and mechanisms of change, equipping readers to integrate multiple frameworks to meet each client's unique needs throughout treatment.

Assessment is a foundational competency for clinical practice across disciplines (Accreditation Council for Graduate Medical Education, 2023; APA, 2018; Commission on Accreditation for Marriage and Family Education, 2021; Council for Accreditation of Counseling and Related Educational Programs, 2024; Council on Social Work Education, 2022), yet most training focuses on evaluating individuals, not dyads or families. Chapter 4 delves into the process of assessing complex interactions between intrapersonal, interpersonal, and contextual aspects of family systems, with attention to both the diverse sequelae of trauma and members' strengths and resilience. This chapter discusses the added value of systemic assessment, as well as key areas to assess, who to include, and the selection and administration of assessment measures. An in-depth case study of the Garcia family is introduced to illustrate these areas and provide applied examples of instrument selection and documentation for systemically oriented assessment. Readers are encouraged to consider the unique ways that such an assessment might be embodied in their clinical context.

Chapter 5 guides readers through the process of systemic formulation, treatment planning, and intervention, using the case of the Garcia family. This chapter delineates how systemic assessment informs case formulation and subsequent treatment decisions. Although systems theory is typically applied to couple and/or family therapy, a systemic perspective can be incorporated into a variety of treatment modalities (e.g., individual, dyadic, family, group) and use multiple methods of delivery (e.g., psychoeducation, coaching/consulting, psychotherapy). In this chapter, we describe the process of organizing and beginning systemic treatment with multiple family members, then provide an overview of common techniques utilized in couple and family therapy that may be useful in trauma intervention. A case formulation and treatment plan are presented for the Garcia case, along with key clinical moments in the course of family therapy.

Traumatized families interact with larger systems, including school, community, legal/court, health systems/hospitals, religious organizations, and government agencies, and far too often fall through the many cracks existing between, and sometimes within, these systems. Considering this, Chapter 6 explicates the salience of ongoing consultation and interdisciplinary/interprofessional collaboration with other providers and involved parties (e.g., school teachers/counselors, pediatricians, psychiatrists, legal advocates), tying this in to the Garcia family's needs and context. Beyond psychotherapy alone, we explore the potential of community-based intervention in cases of widespread trauma to address and ameliorate long-term risks through activating culturally and spiritually embedded strengths. This chapter also discusses mental health professionals' role in advocacy in order to facilitate systems-level changes in mental health care, educational systems, and society at large.

Finally, Chapter 7 explores unique challenges and opportunities for therapists working systemically with individuals and families impacted by trauma. We discuss the self-of-the-therapist and the complex countertransferences that are part and parcel of this sort of clinical work. Readers are invited to reflect on their own identities and personalities, developmental histories, personal experiences of trauma, and how all this informs their therapeutic stance and presence in cases of both similarity to and difference from clients. Considering risks for secondary and/or vicarious trauma and the influence of contextual/organizational factors on therapists' well-being, we propose the need for building systems of care, rather than the primary emphasis being on self-care. This chapter highlights the importance of our ongoing personal and professional development as part of resilience building.

IDENTIFYING YOUR CONTEXT AND NEEDS

In this book, we argue that a systemic lens is vital to clinically formulate and meaningfully address how the sequelae of trauma often take root and propagate within relationships and across family systems, creating or exacerbating members' mental health distress:

> If we do not understand and integrate the shaping power of institutions, social norms, economic systems, oppression, and privilege alongside the profound influences of family and community, we will not fully understand trauma or how to heal from it. We will not understand how to prevent it. (Haines, 2019, p. 11)

Considering our own embeddedness as members of families who are impacted by institutions and social norms, we invite you to take a moment to consider your own context and needs:

- What aspects of clinical work with family members (whether they are actually in the room or discussed by a client) do you find most challenging? Most intriguing?
- In providing psychological care to trauma-exposed populations, what are you particularly curious to learn about? Anything you find confusing?
- How might your own intersectional identities and social location inform how traumatized families perceive and experience you as a clinician?
- What experiences and/or relational dynamics in your own family of origin (and creation, if relevant) tend to overlap with types of clients you are working with? What countertransference do you notice getting activated in you in session?

How you answer these questions can offer guidance about where to focus as you engage with this material, given the specifics of your contextual knowledge and experience. Our hope is that you find this book to be a catalyst that sparks your development and engages you in the lifelong journey of moving toward greater competency in helping families heal, find resilience, and thrive.

1 FAMILIES AND SYSTEMIC CONTEXTS

Key Concepts and Competencies to Facilitate Trauma Work

The family is a microcosm of the world. To understand the world, we can study the family: issues such as power, intimacy, autonomy, trust, and communication skills are vital parts underlying how we live in the world.

—VIRGINIA SATIR (1988, P. 11)

"It's no use. It always falls apart. Everything good goes away." Thirteen-year-old Sammie, a biracial girl whose feistiness is readily apparent, speaks with indignance. Yet, her voice hints at the pain she carries.

Sammie's adoptive mother, Kim, shares that she and her wife, Ronnie, are considering dissolving the adoption "if Sammie doesn't start listening and respecting us as her *parents*." Kim explains that Sammie becomes emotionally reactive on a daily basis, screaming "I hate you ... you're not my mom," throwing things, and threatening to run away. She continues, "I've found bloody razors in the bathroom, and she reeks of pot when she gets home from school ... but when we try to talk to her, she just gets sullen and defiant."

This chapter contains a composite case vignette drawn from multiple clients and fictitious aspects. Details have been substantively changed to protect confidentiality.

https://doi.org/10.1037/0000487-002
Systemic Treatment of Trauma-Impacted Families: A Clinician's Guide to Assessment, Formulation, and Intervention, by S. A. Riggs and L. E. Captari

Kim and Ronnie have responded to these challenging behaviors by grounding Sammie, pulling her out of extracurriculars, taking away her phone, and trying to put her in time-out. Most recently, they sent the family dog Max—whom Sammie had connected deeply with—to live with an extended family member as a "consequence."

Sammie lets out an exasperated sigh. "Why can't you just leave me the f—k alone? You're always on my case!"

As the tension escalates in the intake, you as the therapist struggle a bit to keep your clinical bearing. Sammie has worked with a variety of individual clinicians, receiving both trauma-focused cognitive behavioral therapy and dialectical behavior therapy, with little progress. Given the intense conflicts between Sammie and her adoptive parents that frequently end in a stalemate, they have been referred to work with you. It seems that some sort of family intervention is warranted . . . but where to start? You try to remember what you learned in that family therapy course in graduate school. For starters, you suggest meeting separately with Sammie and her adoptive parents to build rapport and gain further information.

Sammie is initially guarded but begins to open up as you express curiosity about her life and her story. She loves rap music, hip-hop dancing, and art, and identifies several friends at school whom she enjoys spending time with . . . "if they'd ever let me out of the f—king house!" she rolls her eyes. She describes bouncing between foster homes with her siblings after their mother died of an overdose when she was eight. She doesn't elaborate on what home life was like with her biological parents, but it sounds like she was often left for long periods of time—sometimes days—to care for her siblings, who were then a baby and a toddler. "I can make a mean mac-n-cheese," she smiles ruefully.

Following several failed family reunifications with their father, parental rights were terminated, and her younger brother and sister, Benji and Ava, were quickly adopted. "That was so tough," Sammie chokes up. "I'd do anything for them to have a better life, but we don't get together much anymore, since they're out of state."

"Nobody wants a teenager," she laments. "I got my hopes up with Kim and Ronnie, but I just keep messing up. I can never be good enough for them. The other day, Kim packed her suitcase and told me and Ronnie she was leaving."

Surprised by this new information, you wonder about attachment dynamics in play and the accumulated strain on Kim and Ronnie's relationship that you want to explore further. When you meet with the couple, Kim describes pursuing adoption and how they both felt really good about giving a foster child a home.

"We wanted a kid so badly," Ronnie shares, "I don't know, I guess I just thought that if we truly loved her—unlike her birth parents [you note her disparaging tone]—that would heal her. But it's not working. And it just boils my blood the way she talks to Kim ... if I'd done that growing up, I would've gotten slapped across the mouth."

Kim chimes in, "I'm not sure I—she wants to be part of this family." You make mental note of the slip. "Can you help her?" Ronnie asks you in desperation.

The complex relational dynamics between Sammie, her siblings, biological parents, and adoptive parents—and let's not forget the dog, Max—leave your head spinning. There is far more going on in this family than meets the eye, and you hear so much in what has been shared: a well-meaning couple with little awareness about complex trauma, presuming that love can heal all; attachment-laden ultimatums being made; and a marriage possibly on the rocks ... not to mention possible discrimination against LGBTQ+ couples and parents. A host of ambiguous losses that may have not been grieved—the death of Sammie's biological mother, the absence of her father, and the current minimal contact with her siblings. A child whose behavior testifies to being in survival mode, to huge gaps in socioemotional development, to missing her siblings. She is terrified of being known and terrified of being alone. She is waiting for it to all fall apart ... just like it always has in her short life.

This vignette underscores the complicated reality that individual family members' psychological and relational challenges often interact with each other, and that failing to attend to these links can jeopardize treatment effectiveness. The book in your hands is designed for mental health professionals and those in training who seek to develop greater competence in clinical work with couples and families affected by trauma, as well as those who want to bring a more systemic lens to individual trauma treatment. To begin our journey, this chapter highlights important applications and extensions of profession-wide competencies when working with couples and families who have experienced trauma. Specifically, we discuss additional factors systemic practitioners must consider, such as diversity of family form and life cycle, as well as unique ethical and legal issues when working clinically with more than one person at a time. Perhaps most importantly, the chapter provides an overview of key principles and concepts from family systems theory and research. Emphasizing the importance of context and interpersonal interactions, systems theory expands our focus beyond the individual to relational patterns and sequences in which trauma is often instantiated. Buckle up! The following pages will give you an accelerated primer on family systems theory, defining key systemic concepts regarding family dynamics and processes to serve as a foundation we build on in later chapters.

FROM ACCIDENTAL TO INTENTIONAL SYSTEMICALLY ORIENTED THERAPISTS

Competency-based approaches to training and education have been widely adopted across the health professions, including psychology, social work, counseling, marriage and family therapy, and psychiatry. At its core, the competency movement is motivated by an accountability to the public welfare that requires practitioners to be adequately trained and prepared to provide effective mental health care services. In psychology, the competency benchmarks documents (Fouad et al., 2009; Hatcher et al., 2013) delineated essential elements and behavioral indicators for seven "foundational" competencies (i.e., professionalism; reflective practice; scientific knowledge and methods; relationships; individual and cultural diversity; ethical and legal standards and policy; and interdisciplinary systems) and eight "functional" competencies (i.e., assessment, intervention, consultation, research and evaluation, supervision, teaching, administration, and advocacy) across various levels of psychology training. Subsequently, the American Psychological Association (APA, 2015b) published the Standards of Accreditation for Health Service Psychology programs, which identifies discipline-specific knowledge and profession-wide competencies that clinical, counseling, and school psychology training programs must assess and document in order to obtain and maintain accreditation. While these overarching competencies lay the foundation for professional practice in psychology, many other disciplines involved in mental health treatment have established corresponding competencies, as well as unique competencies specific to their values and areas of practice. Thus, we have designed this book with readers from a variety of disciplines in mind because, regardless of your degree or accrediting body, most graduate training does not fully prepare us to provide evidence-based services to families impacted by trauma.

Recognizing this gap, specific competencies as well as training and practice guidelines have been developed for the specialty of couple and family psychology and trauma-focused treatment. Consistent with ethical codes regarding boundaries of competence across mental health professions (e.g., American Association for Marriage and Family Therapy, 2015; American Counseling Association, 2014; American Mental Health Counselors Association, 2020; APA, 2017b; National Association of Social Workers, 2021), these specialty- or population-specific guidelines acknowledge additional professional learning and growth as critical for effective practice within various settings, specialty services, and subpopulations of clients. In addition to the previously mentioned competency benchmarks in psychology (Fouad et al., 2009; Hatcher et al., 2013), we root our discussion throughout this book in several important documents that provide clinical roadmaps and practical reference points, including the New Haven Competency Conference findings (Cook et al., 2014), Clinical Practice Guideline for the Treatment of Posttraumatic Stress Disorder (PTSD) in Adults (APA, 2017a), Guidelines on Trauma Competencies for Education and Training (APA, 2015a), *Specialty Competencies in Couple and Family Psychology* (Stanton & Welsh, 2011), and APA Guidelines on Evidence-Based Psychological Practice in Health Care (APA, 2021). Other informative guidelines have also been produced by various organizations, such as the National Child Traumatic Stress Network, the Substance Abuse and Mental Health Services Administration, and the National Center for PTSD, to name a few. These resources offer guidance around the many complexities of trauma treatment and couple and family intervention, and we encourage interested readers to consult them directly for greater detail.

Here, our aim is to boil down the essence and important takeaways from these lengthy documents in an accessible manner that informs your trauma-informed practice and equips you to be a more intentional systemically oriented therapist. Leading couple and family specialists have critically considered and elaborated on the competency benchmarks to address the unique challenges that can emerge when working with couples and families (Celano, 2019; Kaslow et al., 2005; T. Patterson, 2013; Stanton & Welsh, 2011). While all competencies are salient to couple and family practice, this chapter focuses on essential points of distinction and extension in three foundational competencies for the couple and family specialty in psychology: individual and cultural diversity, scientific knowledge and methods, and ethical and legal aspects. In later chapters, we apply the foundational competency of professionalism (e.g., self-reflection/self-awareness/self-care) and the functional competencies of assessment, intervention, and consultation to systemically oriented trauma work, but for now, you might think about these first three competencies as stepping stones to effectively engage families like Sammie and her adoptive parents.

INDIVIDUAL AND CULTURAL DIVERSITY COMPETENCIES

Highly consistent with a systems theory perspective, APA's (2017c) Multicultural Guidelines delineate a layered ecological model that prioritizes developmental and contextual issues, as well as the intersectionality of identities. In line with how trauma inevitably impacts the self, the model describes the bidirectional nature of self-definition and interpersonal interactions, which are embedded within increasingly expanding ecological levels including family, school, and community; institutional engagement; and the domestic and international climate. Extending well beyond an earlier focus on race and ethnicity in the previous version (APA, 2003), the current guidelines highlight the importance of personalizing treatment based on characteristics such as age, sex, gender identity, sexual orientation, religion/spirituality, language, education, economic class, immigration status, and physical or mental abilities. In addition, couple and family practitioners must take care to attend to diversity of family form, family life cycle stage, structure and organization, family values and worldviews, and historical experiences.

When working with trauma-impacted families, individual and cultural diversity competence for therapists who seek to work systemically includes awareness of cultural influences on the self; knowledge of couple and family interventions for multicultural populations; and consideration of individual, interpersonal, and macrosystemic factors that reciprocally shape the experience of individuals, couples/families, and organizations (Stanton & Welsh, 2011). Training in couple and family practice often involves family of origin work (e.g., genograms, intergenerational pattern analysis) to increase therapists' awareness of their own family and cultural heritage and to identify personal biases and stereotypes learned in their family and community of origin (Celano, 2019; Kaslow et al., 2005). The multicultural orientation framework (D. E. Davis et al., 2018) elucidates the importance of balancing the pursuit of competency with cultural humility and a lifelong commitment to ongoing learning. This includes developing comfort working across differences and seeking out opportunities to attend to each family's cultural context in session as it relates to the therapeutic alliance and all members' treatment goals (more on this in Chapter 6 in this volume).

Increasingly Diverse Family Forms

Conceptions of family have evolved appreciably over the last several generations, at least in part due to increasing societal openness and celebration of the diverse forms that families can take. In the 1950s United States, the "normal" or stereotypical family composition consisted of an employed husband, a stay-at-home wife, their biological children, and possibly extended family members. When looking at the breadth of family forms and cultural backgrounds in present-day American society, one would be hard pressed to identify a "normal" family. Well-functioning and thriving families can take many forms, including the nuclear family unit, single-parent families, couples without children, cohabitating couples, divorced and coparenting families, blended/remarried families, adoptive families, multigenerational families, multiracial/ethnic families, LGBTQ+ couples and families, couples in open relationships, chosen families . . . and the list goes on! When meeting and getting to know clients, it is important to consider who constitutes family from their perspective and whose participation in systems-oriented treatment might be helpful based on presenting concerns and goals (e.g., extended family, members of one's kinship network, or chosen family).

Regardless of a family's composition or form, internal systemic processes associated with healthy family functioning include the presence of clear leadership and differentiated roles, relational maintenance practices, commitment and warmth/affection (often referred to as cohesion/connectedness), openness to emotional expression and change, shared rituals and traditions, collective family goals, effective communication, fun time together as family, and for those who have children, constructive parenting practices (Walsh, 2012b). In particular, a family's flexibility and adaptability to accommodate normal developmental challenges and manage stress are key factors in effective functioning (Olson, 2000; Olson & Gorall, 2003), whereas family rigidity and reactivity can increase the risk that stressful life events are experienced as traumatic.

Intersectional Identities and Cultural Influences

Families' demographic and identity characteristics are best conceptualized through an intersectional lens (Crenshaw, 1989), which can illuminate the overlapping and "complex ways in which identities, inequality, and social justice converge to manifest unique sources of strength and vulnerability" (Curtis et al., 2020, p. 510). Racial, ethnic, and cultural identities influence families by way of their traditions and worldviews, life cycle expectations, occupational choice, attitudes toward therapy, and even their definition of family. Identities that deviate from society's traditional expectations of "normal" can both increase the likelihood of family traumatization and serve as the context for culturally embedded healing practices. Most therapists are familiar with the characteristics of individualistic and collectivist cultures, which differ substantially in their values and views regarding the importance of independence and self-interest versus the prioritization of interdependence, unity, and selflessness in the family or community, respectively. Given that an estimated 25% of Americans are first- or second-generation immigrants (Pew Research Center, 2019), clinicians must be mindful of acculturation processes, which often differ along generational lines and can be a source of strain in a family system when parents who continue to value norms and practices from their country of origin disapprove of their children's adoption of American customs and values.

A majority of Americans (75%) identify as religious and/or spiritual, and 45% belong to a local religious community (Gallup, 2024), which can function as an influential relational context for support across the life cycle, but can also sometimes signify the context for experiences of exclusion or religious trauma (Zaeske et al., 2024). Religion and spirituality, both explicit (e.g., views of suffering, personhood, sexuality, an afterlife) and implicit (e.g., relative valuing of emotions vs. seeing them as "sinful"), can be deeply embedded in the family system by cultural experiences and mores. Religious and spiritual practices can function as a source of strength and meaning, struggle and internal conflict, or perhaps both, depending on the context (Sandage et al., 2020). Moreover, it is often the case that family members have different religious or spiritual perspectives and experiences, which can be a source of tension and conflict, especially in family systems marked by emotional enmeshment and blurred boundaries.

Couples and families whose members hold LGBTQ+ identities often experience minority stress and oppression, not only in society writ large but also within health care settings, which can add additional layers of potential traumatization. LGBTQ+ couples who are raising children often reside in socially conservative areas of the United States, which could be in part due to coming out later in life and having child(ren) with a previous partner; ironically, these areas of the country often have policies that fail to protect and may even impede access to care for LGBTQ+ family members (Gates, 2013, 2015). With this in mind, clinicians should be particularly attuned to issues related to family formation, the coming out process, adoption, navigating co-parenting, and sorting through internal conflicts between sexual identity and certain forms of religion and spirituality (Bigner & Wetchler, 2012).

With respect to sex and gender, early feminist scholars harshly critiqued family systems approaches based on legitimate concerns regarding early emphasis on therapeutic neutrality (i.e., nonblaming stance) and the reciprocal influences in family interactions (Bograd, 1992). As Kaslow et al. (1999) explained,

> Paralleling the developments in American psychology in which feminist theorists and therapists underscored the power imbalances between men and women and highlighted gender differences in various domains of functioning, feminist family therapists brought the same issues to the fore, focusing . . . on marital, parent–child, and larger family relationships. (p. 768)

In cases of family abuse, particularly, attunement to gender roles or stereotypes and issues of power (e.g., women and children as holding less power in society) is critical in order to avoid blaming survivors while minimizing male perpetrators' violence (Saunders, 2003). Contemporary family systems theorists and practitioners have argued for a more complex understanding of causal processes that recognize unequal power and influence among members, particularly in cases of family violence (Lebow, 2005). Mutual participation in a relational interaction that becomes violent does not equate to equal responsibility for the interaction or its outcomes, and systemic therapy grounded in feminist concerns for safety and justice can be a viable treatment option for family violence (Goldner, 1998). More recent work has applied feminist theory to various couple and family interventions, including Satir's growth model of family therapy (Maxey, 2021) and feminist family therapy (Garcia & Johnson, 2019).

Family Functioning in Context

Considering all this, our understanding of each family—and the trauma wounds they carry—must be informed by a careful exploration of their unique social, cultural, and historical contexts. This is incredibly important in order to avoid intervention that unwittingly colonizes families with dominant societal values and norms, especially because the field of family therapy has developed largely within Eurocentric nations in the Global North (McDowell, 2015; Rober & Seltzer, 2010). Although early family models espoused theory-specific views of optimal family functioning, contemporary scholars recognize that what is "optimal" is highly dependent on social and developmental contexts. Rather than conceptualizing family processes as good or bad, per se, it is helpful to consider how these patterns function within the family's ecosystem; functional family processes are workable and promote achievement of family goals without sacrificing member well-being. In contrast, dysfunctional family patterns frequently undermine the family's effectiveness in meeting goals or supporting its members. Family systems theory views individual psychological symptoms in the context of these interaction patterns, connecting one family member's behavior to another's, potentially as both a source and outcome or symptom of dysfunction in the system.

An ecosystemic perspective broadens the view of traumatogenesis to factors outside of the family household as well, such as neighborhood disadvantage and violence, school and health systems, and societal and cultural norms (more on this in Chapter 2 in this volume). As an illustration of the impact of social and cultural norms, immigrant families may present clinical challenges when beliefs or actions that are culturally sanctioned in their country of origin violate norms and expectations held by the dominant culture in their current place of residence. Merali (2002) discussed erroneous judgements that are possible when definitions of "good" and "harmful" parenting derived from the dominant culture are applied to culturally diverse families. She points out that some cultures sanction physical punishment of children or other practices that appear abusive in Western societies, but are intended to benefit children in various ways. When child abuse is suspected, clinicians must balance cultural sensitivity with the child's best interests, considering parental and child perceptions of the culturally sanctioned practice and differences therein, parental intentions, and child outcomes, with the latter taking legal and ethical precedent (Merali, 2002).

Family Life Cycles . . . Not Quite the Game of Life!

Just as individuals develop and change over time, so do relationships, yet trauma within the family system frequently impedes developmental momentum and can result in a sense of "stuckness." A family life cycle framework is helpful in conceptualizing individual and family development, highlighting the interdependence of development-related tasks for each family member and the systemic processes that may facilitate or impede a family's adaptation (McGoldrick & Shibusawa, 2012). Given society's changing norms and expectations (e.g., around education, marriage, parenting), it is important to recognize that life cycle norms and definitions are relative and directly tied to sociocultural and historical context. A family's journey these days is much more iterative and divergent than the milestones captured in the iconic boardgame *The Game of Life*. For example, it would be difficult to argue that norms and expectations for Baby Boomers were/are the same for millennials or Gen Z. Taking a flexible approach that acknowledges these differences, family life cycle processes and stages offer important contextual information about family problems and strengths for therapists to bear in mind as they develop clinical hypotheses. Consideration of time and development allows examination of how different developmental phases and transitions affect individual and family functioning, as well as behavior patterns, through bidirectional interactions and cumulative effects across years and generations. As part of this, it is vital to attend to the developmental stage of each family member—and the family as a whole—at the time a potentially traumatic experience occurs, as this has significant implications for members' recovery trajectory.

The family life cycle has been thoroughly described by McGoldrick et al. (2015), beginning with single adulthood and proceeding to couplehood and sometimes marriage. For those who have children, the transition to parenthood is followed by the stages of having young children, adolescents, and launching adult children. Families in later life face unique challenges related to retirement, health, aging, and loss; many of today's families are simultaneously raising children and caring for their parents, which has been dubbed "the sandwich generation" (D. A. Miller, 1981).

Normative transitions that occur between these life cycle stages involve significant changes in the system, characterized by expansion with the addition of a family member(s), contraction when a family member(s) leaves the system, or realignment/revision of the system to support a member's development or entry or exit into/from the system (McGoldrick & Shibusawa, 2012). As a family attempts to balance stability and change during life transitions, disequilibrium in the system creates both a vulnerability to symptom development and an opportunity for positive change. Family stress and anxiety are often greatest during major life cycle transitions that create a crisis of reorganization involving significant alterations in the family system itself, as well as parallel adjustments to self-organization made by individual family members. Specifically, life cycle transitions often require families to negotiate new rules/boundaries and roles/tasks, changes in power/control, different ways of interacting with members or external systems, and expectations for closeness/autonomy in family relationships. As a result, the definition of family health will differ at each stage of the life cycle. For example, effective functioning in families with infants and young children will look quite different from effective functioning in families with older adolescents or young adult children.

While normative transitions involve expected changes for most families within a specific culture, nonnormative transitions are usually unexpected and statistically less common (Cowan & Cowan, 2012). Although rates for trauma exposure are relatively high globally (Benjet et al., 2016; Kessler et al., 2017), life cycle theory considers most traumatic experiences to be outside of the predictable life course and thus nonnormative. Examples of traumatic experiences that engender nonnormative family transitions include a natural disaster or war that displaces the family from home, or the sudden death of a young child or parent that requires structural reorganization and shifting of family roles. Even when a traumatic event directly affects only one member (e.g., combat, sexual assault), the indirect impact of that event almost inevitably extends into the family system and to other members through systemic processes, such as parenting, spousal relations, boundary shifts, control, and conflict or aggression.

Scholars have referred to the results of this transmission process from one family member to another as vicarious trauma or secondary traumatic stress

(Figley, 1995; McCann & Pearlman, 1990), characterized by cognitive changes and/or the development of traumatic symptoms after indirect exposure to the trauma of a significant family member. Research with samples of Holocaust survivors, combat war veterans, and survivors of rape have established significant links between individual trauma and the downstream psychological or relational functioning of spouses and the next generation of children (Davidson et al., 1998; R. Dekel & Goldblatt, 2008; S. Dekel et al., 2023; Galovski & Lyons, 2004; Greenblatt-Kimron et al., 2025; Perilloux et al., 2012). The intergenerational transmission of trauma represents one's "emotional inheritance" from parents and families passed down from one generation to the next (Atlas, 2022), a process highlighted in Bowenian theory and family therapy (Bowen, 1978). The family cycle of violence (Widom, 1989), an extremely pernicious form of intergenerational trauma transmission, refers to the tendency of children who experienced or witnessed family violence while growing up to then perpetrate or be victimized by violence as adults, repeating violent interaction patterns passed down from previous generations. Family violence is often chronic, severe, and disorganizing to the extent that emotional regulation is deficient across the family system, subsystems, and individual members (J. P. Siegel, 2013).

Some families carry the added legacy of historical or racial trauma originating from their ancestors' collective experience of oppression and/or mass group trauma, such as the Holocaust, slavery, or the colonization of indigenous/native populations (more on this in Chapter 2 in this volume; Brave Heart et al., 2011; H. E. Fitzgerald et al., 2021; Johns et al., 2022; A. T. Lee et al., 2023; Vaughans, 2016). Across trauma situations and populations (e.g., Holocaust survivors, combat veterans, refugees, those impacted by disaster, survivors of child abuse, and interparental violence), exposure to potentially traumatic events and severity of posttraumatic reactions are significant risk factors for family violence, including child abuse and intimate partner violence (Montgomery et al., 2019; Stith et al., 2000; Timshel et al., 2017; Yehuda et al., 2001).

Family life cycle events and family responses during both normative and nonnormative transitions frequently set the stage over time for a ripple of psychological and emotional consequences across the family system. Just as knowledge of normal and atypical child development allows parents and therapists to understand children's behavior at various ages and better intervene when difficulties are encountered, so does knowledge of family developmental stages help therapists conceptualize family adaptation and identify unhealthy patterns that can be addressed and improved, or conversely, potential family strengths that can be leveraged in treatment.

SCIENTIFIC KNOWLEDGE COMPETENCIES

Clinical work with children, couples, and/or families necessitates specialized learning of psychological theory and scientific knowledge (Celano, 2019; Stanton & Welsh, 2011). A systemic epistemology guides a holistic conceptualization of human behavior and relationships that informs comprehensive treatment planning for couples and families. Although students in some mental health disciplines become familiar with systems theory in graduate school (e.g., social work, marriage and family therapy), systems theory is not a standard curriculum element in most psychology graduate programs (Kaslow et al., 2013), with the possible exception of Bronfenbrenner's (1977, 1979) ecological systems theory. This book applies systemic thinking to clinical work with trauma in particular. We highlight here some key systemic assumptions that represent a significant paradigm shift for therapists whose training emphasized individual modalities and the medical model (Stanton & Harway, 2019) . . . that's most of us! In contrast to the Cartesian model of knowledge underlying the individualistic, linear approach common to many scientific fields, systems theory instead focuses on reciprocal interactions in complex systems and subsystems. In the health service professions, a systemic epistemology promotes consideration of individual characteristics and interpersonal systems, as well as ecological and macrosystemic factors that are interdependent and reciprocally influence both individual and group behavior (Stanton & Welsh, 2011).

Systems Thinking 101: Your Clinical Night Vision Goggles

Working with trauma can be messy and complicated. A systemic approach to psychotherapy orients clinicians toward relationships and processes between and among individuals, and tracks diverse clinical outcomes beyond individual symptoms (e.g., changes in attachment, differentiation, family functioning). Rather than detailing the many schools of family therapy, each of which emphasizes various techniques and theory-driven approaches to family problems, we engage systems theory as an overarching metatheory for working with trauma-impacted couples and families that provides a broad conceptual framework with core assumptions and knowledge to explain human behavior and guide research, theorizing, and interventions. This metatheory can direct our attention to specific processes and patterns to understand trauma effects within a family, but it can't necessarily tell us exactly how to make a change to the situation, which will ultimately depend on the many different parts and their interactions within the particular system(s) under consideration.

Developing foundational knowledge of systems theory is in many ways like procuring night vision goggles for therapy! In clinical situations that are murky, dark, and confusing, tracking and formulating what is happening across the family system (and beyond) can bring into focus the underlying patterns and processes fueling symptom distress and impairing relational functioning. Learning to think systemically can catalyze our clinical insight, attunement, and responsiveness in providing evidence-based care to meet the complex needs of clients with histories of trauma. To begin to construct these clinical night vision goggles and "see" the family system, let's survey some foundational concepts and terminology from general systems theory, which we organize around three key principles: wholeness and order, openness, and self-organization/self-correction (Rambo & Hibel, 2013).

First, systems theory considers wholeness and order (Sexton & Stanton, 2016). Systems are cohesive groups of smaller interdependent elements, or subsystems, that interact with one another in a reciprocal, mutually influential manner, as well as with other external systems (see Figure 1.1). As systems of people, families tend to organize hierarchically into subsystems that have certain functions and roles (Minuchin, 1974). While each family is unique, researchers and practitioners delineate four common family subsystems: the spousal/couple subsystem, parental subsystem, sibling/child subsystem, and parent–child dyads. This amalgamation creates a complex system whereby multiple relationships exist at several levels (e.g., individual, dyadic,

FIGURE 1.1. Family Systems and Subsystems

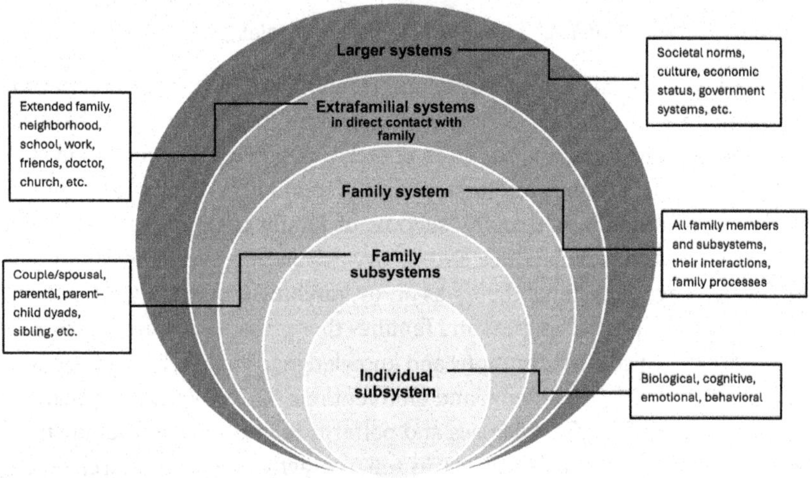

Note. The principle of wholeness and order suggests that family systems are organized hierarchically, with various system levels/subsystems that are distinct but connected to other levels through reciprocal interactions and influences.

subsystem, system-wide interaction patterns), each of which has characteristics that are distinct and may not exist at other levels, but is connected to other levels and relationships within the larger system (Kozlowska & Hanney, 2002). Due to these intricate connections, stress or trauma in one individual or relationship will affect other subsystems and the system as a whole. The family "is greater than the sum of its parts" and the unit under consideration expands to the whole system and its relationships rather than individual family members, who are self-subsystems nested within the larger systems in which they live. This principle has notable implications for understanding trauma's ripple effects across the family system (more on this in Chapter 2 in this volume).

The tendency toward order described in systems theory also pertains to family structure, a term used in two completely different ways in the literature. Some use "structure" to describe a family's demographic composition or form (e.g., intact, single-parent, multigenerational, LGBTQ+-led, etc.; e.g., Murry & Lippold, 2018; Savell et al., 2023). A second meaning, emerging from family therapy, refers to organizational characteristics, such as subsystems, boundaries, hierarchical control/leadership, and relationship alliances or coalitions (Minuchin, 1974). This latter definition will be used throughout this book, while the former will be referred to as family composition or form. Family mapping techniques are useful for assessing family structure, conceptualization/hypothesizing, and treatment planning/formulation (more on this in Chapter 4 in this volume). Families must accomplish a number of tasks, including the maintenance and distribution of resources (e.g., food, shelter, protection), creation of a sense of family identity with shared beliefs and values, regulation of emotional climate, and nurturance and socialization in both family and societal roles (Giuliani, 2016; Walsh, 2012a). Adequate organization and leadership are essential to a family's success in fulfilling these tasks, and the breakdown of this infrastructure leaves its members much more vulnerable to traumatization, both within and beyond the family.

While particular subsystem tasks and individual roles vary by culture and context, the spousal/couple subsystem provides support and intimacy for adult partners and also typically serves an executive function responsible for carrying out system maintenance tasks, establishing generational boundaries, and developing a balance between connection and autonomy in the family system (Hindman et al., 2013). When children are present, the parental subsystem provides guidance, nurturance, and discipline while also managing children's access to family resources. Across cultures, this subsystem frequently includes extended family members and others in caregiving roles for children (Longo et al., 2024). In single-parent households, the parental subsystem also takes on the family's executive tasks, as previously described. In families with multiple children, the sibling subsystem can also provide a context for children to learn about cooperation, competition, negotiation, and conflict management among peers (Dunn, 2002). Individual family members can be part of several different subsystems depending on their roles in the system. For example, in married families with children, a spouse is usually part of both the couple and the parental subsystems, but there are many families where one spouse/partner or parent is often absent (e.g., deployed military spouse) or does not carry out the tasks of one of those subsystems for other reasons (e.g., ill or disabled parent). At the same time, other adults who live inside or outside the home (e.g., grandparent, ex-spouse/biological parent) often contribute to the parental subsystem but may or may not hold executive responsibilities for managing the current family household and its resources.

A second key feature of natural systems is openness. Open systems interact with the environment, so the family's ecological and cultural contexts are central to understanding behavioral patterns (Sexton & Stanton, 2016). Families interact frequently with schools, neighborhoods, faith communities, employers, health care networks, government agencies, and other larger systems. How much information is allowed into or out of the family system can vary, however. Each family establishes implicit rules, or boundaries (Minuchin, 1974), that determine who can have access to the system and what that person can do in or out of the system boundaries. Family boundaries can apply to the whole system, its subsystems, and/or individual family members. The family–environment boundary regulates what external information or persons can enter or exit the family system. Similarly, subsystem boundaries determine who belongs to and has a role or influence in each family subsystem. Generational boundaries reflect expectations regarding interactions between various age cohorts within the family system (e.g., children, parents/adults, grandparents).

Boundaries differ in degree of permeability, ranging from diffuse/weak (allowing most/all information to cross) to rigid/closed (allowing little/no information to cross), with clear/flexible boundaries representing a balance between the two extremes (Minuchin, 1974; Sexton & Stanton, 2016). Diffuse boundaries are often associated with ineffective leadership and inappropriate role reversals, such as parentification or spousification of children. Rigid boundaries are related to poor communication and disengagement of family members. While clear boundaries are typical of well-functioning systems, adaptability in response to environmental or developmental factors is essential to open systems; that is, systems must adapt to circumstances in the ways that are most functional within their specific ecology at their particular stage of the family life cycle (Sexton & Stanton, 2016). As we will explore further in coming chapters, family boundaries sometimes instantiate survival-oriented responses as part of the intergenerational transmission of trauma. For example, rigid boundaries between a family and their environment may be rooted in hypervigilance and high control to minimize outsider threats (think Nemo's dad in the film *Finding Nemo*), whereas diffuse boundaries may occur when parents overcompensate for their own childhood abuse or neglect by being overly accommodating to their children's wishes and functioning as a peer (think Homer in the TV show *The Simpsons*).

With some exceptions where ethical, legal, and moral codes of conduct clearly identify right and wrong (e.g., maltreatment, violence), what is optimal for each family must take into account the function of boundaries and rules for a family, given its resources, context, and developmental needs. In some cases, a rigid family–environment boundary may represent positive adaptation for a close-knit family with young children, particularly in the context of a dangerous neighborhood that threatens the children's safety. On the other hand, a rigid family–environment boundary may be maladaptive for a family with older adolescents living in a relatively safe community, and may instead represent overprotective or overcontrolling parenting practices that contribute to the system's stuckness at a previous developmental stage when closer supervision was needed.

Third, open systems are self-organizing and self-correcting, moving independently toward a dynamic state of equilibrium, referred to as homeostasis (Rambo & Hibel, 2013). Feedback loops are patterns of interaction or communication in the system and are considered the primary mechanism for facilitating or preventing change. Negative feedback loops function to stabilize current patterns or behaviors and prevent change, much as the thermostat in your house monitors and corrects any deviation from the set temperature by kicking on the A/C or furnace. Positive feedback loops, on the other hand, are self-organizing patterns that promote adaptive changes in order to effectively navigate normative and nonnormative transitions (Beavers & Hampson, 2000; Cox & Paley, 1997), or respond to critical incidents that make previous patterns insufficient or unworkable. Dynamic family systems are continuously evolving, adapting, and striving to balance stability and change. Systems thinkers often distinguish between first- and second-order change in families (Davey et al., 2012), and this is particularly salient when considering treatment goals as part of trauma recovery. First-order change involves alteration of individual symptoms and characteristics, but not the structure of the system, thus restoring the original balance although individual roles and behaviors may have shifted.

In second-order change, the system changes qualitatively with respect to the rules and boundaries governing the structure or internal order.

An understanding of feedback loops clarifies the nature of causality in systems, which is circular rather than linear. Rather than asking "why?" and tracing a linear path from cause to effect (A causes B, but B does not cause A), systemically oriented practitioners ask "what?" and "how?" and shift the focus to the relational context, framing a problem as a reciprocal relationship pattern between parts of the system (A influences B, B influences A; Becvar et al., 2023). Moreover, by recognizing the interconnectedness of multiple relationships across system levels (e.g., individual, dyadic, subsystem, system-wide), circular causality means that there is rarely a clearly identifiable beginning or end (Kelledy & Lyons, 2019). Interaction patterns can sometimes become entrenched or "stuck" within the system's ordinary functioning and prevent healthy adaptation. With no definitive start or endpoint in the circular sequence, the systemic concept of circular causality reduces individual blame, promotes shared family responsibility for change, and offers clinicians multiple points in the interactional sequence for potential intervention, with the understanding that change in one part of the interaction cycle will lead to changes in other parts of the cycle and larger system.

When working with families impacted by trauma, a systemic epistemology widens our clinical lens beyond the individual and suggests alternative hypotheses regarding underlying processes that may be hampering family members' functioning. Especially when symptom-focused intervention has had limited success, intervening to create second-order changes at the level of systemic structures and interaction patterns can provide notable momentum in trauma recovery. To deepen this exploration, we now turn our attention to how therapists can track and observe the specifics of these interactions and reciprocal processes.

Family Process and Functioning: Like Thermal Imaging for Therapy

If familiarity with systemic principles functions clinically like night vision goggles, understanding family process and functioning might be thought of as acquiring a trauma-focused thermal imaging camera, which creates pictures based on heat (or, in this case, affect and emotion). Family process encapsulates the emotional climate and various elements characterizing the system's functioning, which develop organically and reflexively as repeated interactions evolve into stable patterns that are largely unconscious and unrecognized by members. While trauma-focused treatment often attends to individual affect, family system models go further by identifying the contributions of numerous family processes, such as cohesion/connectedness and autonomy, flexibility/adaptability, communication, emotional expression, nurturance/support, control, leadership, organization, conflict, rituals and traditions, and family member interaction patterns and relationship quality. Each of these areas has substantial empirical support and could warrant a chapter of its own. Given the focus and scope of this book, we utilize the Circumplex Model (Olson, 2000; Olson & Gorall, 2003) here to highlight key family process dimensions, each of which is relevant in clinical work with families who have experienced trauma.

The circumplex model delineates three dimensions of family functioning: cohesion, flexibility, and communication. Olson (2000) defined cohesion as emotional bonding, positing a continuum of separateness and togetherness that ranges from disengaged, to separated, to connected, to enmeshed. The middle ranges (separated and connected) represent balanced levels of cohesion, whereas the continuum's extremes reflect an unbalanced system that is often problematic. For example, in disengaged systems with very low cohesion, family members are overly independent, with limited bonding and commitment to the family. By contrast, in enmeshed systems with exceedingly high cohesion, family members lack sufficient autonomy and demand absolute loyalty, but also demonstrate a high degree of consensus. As we will see in coming chapters, where family members fall along this spectrum is significantly influenced by their individual trauma histories and can also substantially shape the family's trajectory of functioning following a potentially traumatic experience. Both disengagement and enmeshment have been conceptualized as the result of boundary disturbances (extremely rigid or diffuse, respectively) and are associated with children's externalizing and internalizing symptoms (Jacobvitz et al., 2004; Sturge-Apple et al., 2010). Variables relevant to measuring cohesion include closeness, boundaries, coalitions, decision making, and time together, as well as shared friends, interests, and recreation.

Second, flexibility reflects how a family balances stability and change, focusing on leadership and organization, role stability and sharing, and rules and negotiations (Lebow & Stroud, 2012; Olson, 2000). Similar to cohesion, flexibility is located along a continuum with four levels: rigid, structured, flexible, and chaotic. Structured and flexible relationships are balanced and more functional than the rigid and chaotic extremes. Rigid families are often characterized by a highly controlling leader who makes all decisions, allows little to no negotiation, and implements strictly defined rules and roles. Chaotic families, on the other hand, tend to have very little or erratic leadership, impulsive decision making, and unclear and inconsistent rules and roles.

Readers can likely think of clients where such dynamics interacted with a potentially traumatic experience to exacerbate distress and impairment. All families try to influence or shape members' behaviors and views in some way, ideally in the service of healthy development. Family control processes are evident in rule-making, disciplinary practices, negotiating and decision-making, attempts to change undesirable behavior, and family conflict and violence (Le Poire, 2006). While some degree of control is needed to prevent chaos, there is no question that control and power can also be abused in ways detrimental to many family members, particularly women and children, who are more vulnerable and often considered less important than men within many societies and cultures. Variables relevant to measuring flexibility include leadership, control, task accomplishment, and role performance.

The third dimension of the circumplex model is communication, which, when effective, facilitates the accomplishment of a family's goals (Olson, 2000). Communication has long been recognized by scholars as a key process in couple and family functioning, with contributing factors including empathic listening, speaking for oneself and allowing others to speak, self-disclosure of feelings, clarity of meaning, tracking (i.e., staying on topic), and respect. According to the model, these three dimensions are interrelated in that communication facilitates how cohesion and flexibility manifest in the system. Effective communication processes, including emotional expression and collaborative problem solving, support family adaptation to normative stressors and foster resilience in the face of adversity (Walsh, 2012b). Ineffective and reactive communication, on the other hand, bodes poorly for family adaptation to stress, especially as invalidation and lack of support increase risk for traumatization amid stressful life circumstances (Charuvastra & Cloitre, 2008). When members are unable to clearly communicate their needs and limitations, frustration and conflict can escalate. For example, intimate partner violence has been linked to a lack of problem solving and negotiation, as well as defensive communication patterns, such as blaming, withdrawing, invalidating, and interrupting (Murphy & O'Farrell, 1997; Sabourin et al., 1993).

Building on these dimensions, we now turn our attention to common couple and family "thermal images"—dyadic, triadic, and system-wide interaction patterns, as well as the function or result of such interactions that are critical to track in trauma-focused work. In addition to the balanced, enmeshed, and disengaged relationships that comprise the cohesion dimension of the circumplex model, systems-oriented therapists commonly work with other types of interactions germane to conceptualization and treatment. Within the couple/marital subsystem, "pursuer–distancer" (Fogarty, 1979) or "demand–withdraw" (Christensen, 1988) interaction patterns are important to track. In this type of interaction, a dissatisfied partner "pursues" communication and emotional closeness, while the other member of the couple refuses to negotiate or engage in discussion and "distances" from emotional connection. When the pursuer's efforts to create change fail, the pursuit often escalates to demanding, nagging, or complaining, which are met with further avoidance, rejection, and withdrawal by the distancer. Poor communication and high levels of demand–withdraw interaction patterns have been found in violent couple relationships (Babcock et al., 1993; Berns et al., 1999; Holtzworth-Munroe et al., 1998; Pickover et al., 2017).

Moving to the larger family system, pairs or groups of family members may form alliances that are mutually supportive and work toward common goals, or coalitions intended to work against one or more other family members. Triangles are another family configuration recognized by prominent theorists (Bowen, 1978; Minuchin, 1974), formed through a process of triangulation whereby two family members incorporate a third, often vulnerable, family member to offset anxiety or conflict between the original two. As an example, in cases of parental substance abuse or domestic violence, siblings may form alliances to protect one another and compensate for the loss of support from one or both parents (J. Williams et al., 2016). At the same time, parents may consciously or unconsciously triangulate a child, potentially forming a cross-generational coalition that enlists the child's support and blames the other parent. While the underlying systemic goal of triangulation is usually the reduction of anxiety or conflict between two family members to maintain system homeostasis, the process can take various forms that function and impact family members in different ways.

For instance, parents could "detour" the tension in their couple relationship by focusing excessively on one child in a detouring-supportive manner (e.g., the perfect child, the star athlete, the sick child) or blaming the child for family problems in a detouring-attacking manner (e.g., the scapegoat, the black sheep; Kerig, 2016; Kerig & Swanson, 2010). The systemic function of detouring patterns is often to mitigate interparental conflict and unite the parents in the executive subsystem, increase closeness in the couple relationship, and stabilize the family system (Minuchin, 1974). However, detouring patterns often involve targeted rejection or more subtle exclusion and disregard of nontargeted children (e.g., the average/imperfect or healthy child), which may contribute to the development of resentment, a sense of unfairness, hostility, and externalizing behaviors (Kerig, 1995; Vuchinich et al., 1988). Coe et al. (2020) found that family detouring predicted increases in children's externalizing symptoms, hostile attributions, and peer rejection and victimization across the 1-year transition from kindergarten to first grade. Child behavior problems at 4 years of age, however, did not predict family processes (i.e., detouring, negativity, conflict) at 5 years of age, which challenges the systemic assumption of circular causality. Based on research demonstrating bidirectional effects between child and family functioning with samples of older children and adolescents (Cui et al., 2007; Fite et al., 2006), Coe et al. (2020) speculated that children's influence on family functioning becomes more pronounced as children age and learn new behaviors that affect power dynamics in the family.

In addition, another parent–child triangle involving role reversals is parentification (Kerr & Bowen, 1988), although this pattern could also be considered a cross-generational dyadic alliance for single parents with one child. Parentification can occur when generational boundaries within the family weaken, such that children assume adult roles and parental responsibilities that are age-inappropriate and can interfere with the child's normal development. Unlike clear evidence for the negative effects of coalitions and scapegoating (Coe et al., 2020; Wang et al., 2017), however, findings are mixed regarding parentification. Possible negative effects of role reversal on children include internalizing and externalizing behavior problems, depression, anxiety, low self-esteem, eating disorders, and interpersonal difficulties (Cho & Lee, 2019; Hetherington, 1999; Jacobvitz & Bush, 1996; Jacobvitz et al., 1999; Rowa et al., 2001; Van Loon et al., 2017; Wang et al., 2024). On the other hand, potentially adaptive effects of parentification might be positive parent–child and sibling relationships, better mental health, less alcohol and tobacco use, resilience, and greater social responsibility (Hetherington, 1999; Khafi et al., 2014; Stein et al., 2007; Tomeny et al., 2017; Tompkins, 2007). These discrepant outcomes may be related to children's perceptions of fairness, the duration of the role reversal, differing cultural values and expectations, or distinct mechanisms and functions underlying various forms of parentification (Cho & Lee, 2019; McGauran et al., 2019; Wang et al., 2024; for a review, see Masiran et al., 2023). The literature distinguishes between instrumental parentification, whereby a child is made responsible for family maintenance tasks (e.g., chores, childcare, grocery shopping; Van Parys & Rober, 2013), and emotional parentification, whereby a child is expected to nurture and care for parents and/or siblings (Boszormenyi-Nagy & Spark, 1973). Emotional parentification may have more detrimental effects, with emotional burdens and lack of parent–child psychological boundaries increasing the risk of poor outcomes (Byng-Hall, 2008a; Haxhe, 2016).

Parentification is a relatively common system response when parents' functioning is compromised and they are unable to effectively manage their parental role and responsibilities. A recent review found parentification to correlate with interparental conflict, alcoholism, single-parent and step-family households, paternal disengagement, maternal helplessness, and family crises that facilitate role reversals (e.g., parental illness, divorce, violence; Masiran et al., 2023). Among families affected by violence, older children frequently care for siblings and victimized parents (Callaghan et al., 2017; J. Williams et al., 2016), and may be more likely to take on additional family tasks or intervene in conflicts if they blame themselves (Fortin et al., 2011; Grych et al., 2004).

ETHICAL AND LEGAL COMPETENCIES

All therapists who work with children, couples, and/or family constellations must attend to unique ethical and legal considerations, and this can feel trickier to navigate when family members' trauma-related presentations include volatility and/or disengagement. Thus, it behooves us to become well-versed in navigating these complexities before we face them in session. The ethical demands of simultaneous treatment of multiple persons can activate personal anxieties that lead some therapists to shy away from everything but individual therapy! And, to be fair, this is an area where being an "accidental" family therapist and figuring it out as you go could have serious unforeseen consequences, given crucial differences in informed consent, record-keeping, and treatment planning. Becoming familiar with the practicalities of family-related ethical and legal concerns can quell anxiety and build confidence in inviting multiple family members into session when this is clinically indicated. Because laws differ from state to state in the United States, it is incumbent on mental health professionals working with children, couples, or families to be familiar with and abide by family law in the jurisdiction in which they practice. We refer readers to the state board that administrates your license for more specifics about state laws pertinent to these areas. Here, we cover key areas to keep in mind.

Informed Consent, Confidentiality, and Secret-Keeping

The ethical and legal doctrine of informed consent dictates that at the outset of treatment, couple and family practitioners must clearly identify who the client/patient is, that is, to whom their primary professional responsibility belongs (Stanton & Welsh, 2011). For example, when a parent brings a child with behavioral problems into treatment, as in the case of Sammie and her parents at the beginning of this chapter, the clinician may identify the client as the child, the parent–child dyad, the family unit, or possibly the parental/spousal dyad in cases where difficulties in the couple relationship are linked to child problems. Any of these options may be appropriate depending on the case, and the decision will guide the choice of treatment modality. Importantly, in working systemically, therapists often employ multiple modalities, including individual, couple, or family interventions, in pursuit of overarching treatment goals. Regardless of the rationale, we must always inform and gain consent/assent from all relevant parties regarding who the primary client is and clarify our relationship with each person involved (APA, 2017b, Standard 10.02). With minors, parental consent is required and assent procedures should be tailored to the child's developmental level to promote the child's active participation in treatment and the therapeutic alliance (Koocher & Daniel, 2012; Lind et al., 2003). Clinicians who treat minors should also clarify custodial arrangements and obtain documentation regarding a parent's right to make health care decisions prior to treatment onset (Barnett & Jacobson, 2019).

When a family unit comprised of multiple individuals is defined as the client, complex ethical and legal questions can arise regarding confidentiality, privilege, secrets, record-keeping, and change of format. As a standard of professional conduct, confidentiality obligates therapists to refrain from discussing clients with anyone, except when noted in the informed consent process (e.g., mandated reporting, treatment team) or with client permission via a signed release of information form (Koocher & Keith-Spiegel, 2008). When working with couples and families, systemically oriented therapists may pivot between meeting with the entire family unit, individual family members, dyads (e.g., parent–child, spouses), or other subsystems (e.g., siblings), depending on what is happening in the system at that moment. At the outset of treatment, clinicians must inform family members about the nature of confidentiality for these different session configurations. Specifically, will the content of individual or dyadic meetings be kept secret or can it be shared with the other members of the couple/family?

Varying opinions have been expressed regarding the pros and cons of secret-keeping in couple and family work. Many therapists adopt a "no secrets" policy, which has the advantages of being straightforward, conceptually consistent with identifying the client as the relationship or system, and reducing the potential risk of inadvertently aligning with one partner through secrecy or accidentally revealing the secret in session (Gottlieb et al., 2008). Yet, this position raises the possibility that critical information will be withheld by a member who is not ready to disclose to other members, potentially jeopardizing treatment effectiveness (T. Patterson, 2013). If practitioners agree to keep secrets, they may obtain more in-depth information, but at the same time they may risk colluding with one family member at the expense of open communication and trust with the other members of the system to whom the clinician is also responsible (Gottlieb et al., 2008; T. Patterson, 2013). While there are certain limitations to each approach, clinicians should establish a clear policy and include this in informed consent documents (Stanton & Welsh, 2011).

Legal Privilege, Record-Keeping, and Changes in Treatment Format

Most ethics codes and state legal statutes are clear regarding psychotherapist–client privilege covering communications and records over the course of individual treatment, but these standards and laws are specific to professional relationships between *two* people and thus have limited applicability to couple and family therapy. Should practitioners maintain one record for the couple or family, referred to as a "comingled record," or keep separate, individual records for each member of the system? Either approach may be acceptable based on practical concerns, ethical guidelines, and third-party reporting requirements, as long as this practice is explained to clients during the informed consent process (APA, 2007). On one hand, therapists may decide to maintain separate clinical records for each party to provide greater confidentiality and legal protection, particularly in cases that bring potential for litigation, such as divorce and child custody, or other situations arising in high-conflict families (McLaughlin, 2017; T. Patterson, 2013). Alternatively, a systems-oriented therapist who wants to document contextually based family interactions and relational interventions can explain their use of comingled records and establish a policy included in the consent form that requires permission from all adult parties to release treatment records (Gottlieb et al., 2008). Because state laws regarding legal privilege vary, it is critical to be well-versed in your state's laws and view of privilege, then describe these in your informed consent forms and as part of orientation to treatment (Stanton & Welsh, 2011).

Ethical issues must also be considered when there is a change of format in treatment, defined as "a circumstance in which the formal definition of the client changes after the initiation of treatment such that the responsibility of the therapist is altered" (Gottlieb, 1995, p. 562). For example, a clinician may begin relational therapy with a distressed couple, then move to individual treatment with one of the partners after a break-up; alternatively, individual therapy with one client may shift to couple therapy after learning that individual problems are directly related to the couple relationship and the client wants to invite their partner into therapy. Of note, such shifts are distinct from inviting a partner or family member in for a single session when this is clearly part of an individual client's treatment goals—for example, to gather additional information or help facilitate a difficult conversation. Doing so can also be one way of bringing a systemic ethos to your clinical practice but does not constitute a shift in modality. Before agreeing to changes in treatment modality, systemically oriented therapists should carefully consider and discuss with existing clients the risks in transitioning from one format to another, such as interference with the original therapeutic alliance, actual or perceived disruption of therapeutic neutrality, or deterioration in previous progress (Gottlieb, 1995). When a clinician anticipates these or other potentially harmful issues, priority must be afforded to the existing client and a referral to a different therapist for other types of treatment may be warranted. If both therapist and client agree to the benefits of a change in format, clinicians must explicitly address questions regarding how to handle private information and revisit informed consent with all those involved (Stanton & Welsh, 2011).

Navigating Divorce, Custody, and Family Violence

Working with trauma-impacted families can increase the risk of legal involvement. Unique ethical issues arise for therapists working in areas such as high-conflict divorce and custody determinations, child protection, and family violence. Forensic practice is a specialty area that requires additional training and experience to meet competency expectations. Due to unique issues and challenges, guidelines have been developed for psychologists who provide forensic consultation (APA, 2013a) and/or conduct evaluations in matters of child protection and custody in family law proceedings (APA, 2013b, 2022). These documents describe common issues encountered and provide guidance for resolving ethical dilemmas. One important distinction that affects ethical and legal responsibility is the identified role of the mental health professional. The therapeutic role of a clinician involves advocacy and support of clients, whereas a forensic evaluator (e.g., custody evaluations) serves as an unbiased third party to evaluate everyone in the family with the goal of providing objective recommendations for the child's best interests to the court (Barnett & Jacobson, 2019).

Whenever therapists become aware of violence or abuse, a number of potential challenges arise, including client safety, mandated reporting, and interactions with the justice system (Murray, 2006). Minimizing risk and maximizing the safety of all family members is the most prominent ethical consideration, so one of the first questions to consider is what type of treatment is ethically appropriate and safe for the family's particular situation? While individual and group therapy are common interventions in situations of family violence (e.g., child abuse, intimate partner violence), a systemically oriented therapist should carefully consider the risks and benefits of family therapy with or without the perpetrator. A thorough assessment that includes both individual and family sessions is necessary to gather essential information before making this determination (Economidis et al., 2023; Keilholtz & Spencer, 2022).

Although couple and family interventions for child maltreatment and intimate partner violence can be effective (Carr, 2025; Karakurt et al., 2016), some situations would qualify for exclusion, including active and severe ongoing abuse. Additional contraindications for therapy with families or couples marked by child or partner abuse include the perpetrator's inability to acknowledge violence is a problem, accept responsibility for behavior, empathize with the victim or listen to alternative viewpoints, or cooperate with professionals and agree to accept help (Bograd & Mederos, 1999; Cooper & Vetere, 2005; Institute of Medicine & National Research Council, 2014). An abuser's problematic substance use, consistent externalization and blaming of others, frequent and substantial psychological abuse, inability to understand relational factors and roles that may be contributing to violence, and a lack of anger control and internal motivation for change are additional factors to consider in formulation and ethical decision making for cases involving family violence (Bograd & Mederos, 1999; Cooper & Vetere, 2006). More on ethical treatment of violence in couples and families is discussed in Chapter 5 in this volume.

The assurance of confidentiality is qualified by ethical and legal exceptions, which attempt to balance individual privacy and protection of clients. Examples of exceptions legally requiring us as therapists to violate confidentiality include a client's imminent suicidal risk and suspected abuse of vulnerable people who are unable to make health decisions and are dependent on others, usually family (Barnett & Jacobson, 2019). As mandated reporters of maltreatment affecting children, elders, and disabled individuals in the United States, mental health professionals are required to report suspected abuse to their state's relevant agency (e.g., Child Protective Services). This involves the concomitant possibility of damage to the therapeutic relationship and the potential that this report could exacerbate family dysfunction and delay improvement, given the often-overwhelmed welfare and justice systems (Dubowitz, 1997). When possible, discussing and collaborating with the client/family prior to making mandated reports respects client agency and can help offset a sense of betrayal. In situations where therapists become aware of a client's homicidal plan and intent, practitioners in some state jurisdictions also have a duty to warn/protect the intended victim(s) in addition to mandated reporting to law enforcement.

SUMMARY AND KEY TAKEAWAYS

This chapter has covered a lot of terrain! We invite you to refer back to these pages as you are trying to understand what is unfolding in a particular family on your caseload—no matter what your current treatment modality is. Our experience as practitioners and supervisors has been that these systemic concepts can be exceptionally helpful in grounding us and illuminating the multifaceted clinical presentations that frequently show up in the wake of trauma. In this chapter, our discussion has focused on three foundational competencies that require additional thought and action when working with couples and families. We argue that a systemic epistemology offers a distinct vantage point from which to approach psychotherapy with families who have experienced trauma, going beyond symptoms alone to track, formulate, and intervene at the level of underlying relational processes and patterns. There are unique complexities about this sort of clinical work, to be sure, yet approaching trauma systemically offers extraordinary potential to catalyze recovery, and growth, in part by activating healing emotional and relational processes within the family that can gain momentum well beyond the therapy room.

As we expand on the question of where to start and what to focus on in the coming chapters, these principles, concepts, and competencies are foundational reference points . . . helping you begin the journey from "accidental" to intentional family therapist. Clinicians who work with couples and families—as well as those who practice systemically in individual therapy—apply research to practice in a variety of ways. Given the presenting problem, client demographics, and the therapist's training, best practices involve selecting and implementing a trauma-informed treatment model that aligns with or can accommodate systemic principles. At times, this will require flexibility in adapting or modifying conceptualizations and techniques (e.g., common factors) to guide clinical interventions to "fit" a particular client's needs (Sprenkle et al., 2013). For example, a systemically oriented therapist who works with children may consult the research findings to help weigh the benefits of child versus family therapy that targets parenting or parent–child interactions for the specific child client. Given the ever-changing nature of family forms, attention to emerging research is particularly important with regard to cultural responsiveness to diverse family contexts, worldviews, and relational norms.

All families experience some level of stress and strain amid life cycle transitions. Crises, unexpected changes, and losses are part of human experience. Yet, importantly, not all such disruptions are experienced as traumatic.

The intergenerational transmission of strengths and resilience is equally important to attend to alongside considerations around intergenerational trauma. Equipped with our clinical night vision goggles and thermal imaging for family systems, in the next chapter we take up the question of what constitutes trauma from a systemic perspective and discuss trauma-specific competencies to prepare us for this work.

2 THE MULTIDIMENSIONAL NATURE OF TRAUMA

An Intersubjective, Systemic Approach to Clinical Competencies

Trauma is not what happens to us, but what we hold inside in the absence of an empathic witness.

—PETER A. LEVINE (2010, P. XXI)

Aisha remembered her childhood as "difficult" and described her family as "dysfunctional" . . . but trauma? Not so much. Sure, her father was emotionally reactive, and Aisha often put herself between him and her mother to try to diffuse potential violence. Sure, the corporal punishment was harsh, sometimes leaving bruises and swelling that she tried to cover with makeup so kids at school would not notice. But, as she saw it, "My parents were under a lot of stress as immigrants" and "I could be a very annoying kid sometimes."

As a young professional whose parents immigrated from India to the United States before she was born, Aisha sought therapy due to panic attacks and challenges in dating. One of Aisha's core organizing schemas was some version of "I end up creating these situations that cause me pain." The astute

This chapter contains a composite case vignette drawn from multiple clients and fictitious aspects. Details have been substantively changed to protect confidentiality.

https://doi.org/10.1037/0000487-003
Systemic Treatment of Trauma-Impacted Families: A Clinician's Guide to Assessment, Formulation, and Intervention, by S. A. Riggs and L. E. Captari

reader might notice Aisha's attempt to find a sense of coherence by framing herself as the "bad" one. The alternative would involve grappling with the complex reality of growing up with an unpredictable father who relied heavily on alcohol to manage his own emotions and frequently became violent, and a mother who didn't intervene. In therapy, Aisha's minimization softens and her relationship to the language of trauma changes. She comes to experience this new framing as incredibly validating, in contrast with hiding and covering for her father's behavior.

Now, imagine instead that you are sitting with Aisha's family, a referral from your colleague who is her individual therapist. In the wake of her father's recent death, the family (Aisha along with her mother and younger sister) is trying to work through a huge rupture that happened at the funeral. As you explore each person's vantage point, you feel Aisha's urgency and clarity in naming the trauma her father perpetuated, and she describes him as a narcissist.

Aisha's mother, Deepti, holds quite a different view: "Life is full of suffering," she reflects. "There's no getting away from that. I did my very best to respond to your father with kindness and to not let his temper get to me." Deepti's worldview frames what she experienced across her 30-year marriage as somewhat expected—not terrifying or incomprehensible. Further, she perceives her response of calm fortitude as virtuous and storing up good karma.

Aisha's 17-year-old sister, Maya, chimes in emphatically. Pulling out her results from an online quiz that can purportedly "diagnose" trauma, she asserts, "This whole family is in denial. We are swimming in trauma. And it's not just dad. Mom, I was so traumatized by what you said at the funeral . . . how dare you gaslight us! And Aisha, it didn't help that you shushed me. I can't trust any of you!"

Like many teens and emerging adults, Maya identifies readily with the language of trauma and uses it in common vernacular.

When working with families in therapy, important questions surface about the intersubjective experience of trauma. How might you thoughtfully engage with such divergence in narratives? Like Aisha, some clients do not (at least initially) label their life experiences as traumatic, but over time may find such an understanding to be validating and healing. The language of trauma may function as an external witness, helping them place blame with whom it belongs and easing the weight of anger and shame that is common among survivors.

Others you may encounter clinically, like Deepti, make meaning of adversity primarily outside of psychological frameworks. Attunement and responsiveness are critical in order to understand clients' diverse standpoints and worldviews, while also not ignoring our clinical intuition about what might be between and beneath a client's self-report. This raises questions about how to differentiate dissociation and denial from cultural and religious perspectives that help support transcendence of suffering. An undifferentiated therapist might fully fuse with Deepti's subjectivity and praise her "resilience," presuming she was not really impacted by the chronic domestic violence she experienced. Yet, such a formulation fails to consider and explore the relational, psychological, and spiritual toll of such experiences, some of which might initially be outside of a client's conscious awareness. Those in the field who frame the sequelae of trauma as posttraumatic stress disorder (PTSD) alone emphasize resilient functioning, but just because someone does not meet criteria for PTSD does not mean that they have not been notably impacted. Indeed, the manifestations of traumatization are vast, and clients presenting with divergent mental health challenges—ranging from depression to addiction and eating disorders—can be understood more holistically by situating current behavior in the context of abuse, maltreatment, and other forms of trauma.

Then there are clients like 17-year-old Maya, who adopt trauma as a central organizing narrative for understanding life. Haslam and McGrath (2020) documented trauma's drastically increasing cultural salience and the semantic "creep" in how the term is being applied. A hashtag on TikTok—#Traumatok—that has accrued nearly half a million posts, frames common human challenges, like being unmotivated, self-critical, and stressed out, as inherent consequences of trauma. In a recent *New York Times* opinion piece, Bennett (2022) quoted cultural critic Natalie Wynn as commenting on dubious applications of the term: "All pain is 'harm.' All 'harm' is 'trauma.' All 'trauma' comes from someone who is an 'abuser.' It's as if people can't articulate disagreement or hardships without using this language" (para. 4). One risk of this outlook on life is a lack of personal responsibility due to an overly simplistic focus on others as harmful, and the self as a helpless victim who is unable to take action toward change. The idea that trauma was once narrowly understood as "shell shock" is a distant memory, and the broad dissemination of ideas about how trauma impacts the psyche and how people can heal offers validation and hope to survivors. Yet, an unintended result may in some cases be concept creep and potential over/misuse (O'Connor et al., 2025).

In this chapter, we bridge the systemic and traumatic by exploring the multidimensional ways families affect and are affected by individual and collective responses to trauma. As dynamic, mutually influential systems, couples and families reciprocally shape each individual's and the entire family's adaptation. We describe a multidimensional understanding of what constitutes trauma intersubjectively, and then invite readers to consider the diverse ways that trauma shows up in families—including perpetration from external forces and/or family members, which may occur as discrete events or chronic conditions. As part of a dual-factor approach to mental health that attends to both suffering and flourishing (Keyes, 2007, 2024), we also explore family strengths and resilience, and build on this by overviewing specialty competencies for trauma treatment.

WHAT IS TRAUMA? FOUR CORE DIMENSIONS

Clinicians do not need to look far to find "trauma-informed" and "trauma-responsive" approaches.[1] Yet, despite heightened attention to trauma in mental health treatment, there remains definitional ambiguity. Trauma is often understood in terms of Criterion A for trauma-and-stressor-related disorders—exposure to events deemed traumatic (e.g., "actual or threatened death, serious injury, or sexual violence") and the ensuing clinically significant distress, in line with diagnostic criteria outlined in the fifth edition of the *Diagnostic and Statistical Manual of Mental Disorders* (*DSM-5-TR*; American Psychiatric Association, 2022, p. 301). Past editions of the *Diagnostic and Statistical Manual of Mental Disorders* also included events that threatened psychological integrity. While it can be clinically useful to demarcate situations that are almost universally traumatizing, this most recent definition has been critiqued for excluding experiences such as "extreme emotional abuse, major losses and separations, degradation or humiliation, and coerced (but not physically violent) sexual experiences" (Briere & Scott, 2015, p. 9). Furthermore, events themselves are only one piece of the puzzle when it comes to what constitutes trauma. In this book, we argue that trauma cannot be reduced to an event, nor is it synonymous with PTSD. Research in complex and developmental trauma illuminates how some individuals and families have never known life without trauma (Danylchuk & Connors, 2023; Harris et al., 2024). Yet, even among the many survivors who do not develop clinical levels of PTSD, their mental, emotional, and spiritual well-being may still be constrained in a variety of ways.

At an individual level, traumatic stress symptoms can take many forms, including intrusive memories (e.g., nightmares, flashbacks); heightened physiological arousal (e.g., hypervigilance, sleep problems); negative mood and emotional reactivity (e.g., irritability, depression, difficulty experiencing positive emotions); changes in cognition, identity, and meaning (e.g., shattered self, negative views of others and the world, spiritual struggles); sense of detachment (e.g., dissociation); and interpersonal difficulties (e.g., reticence to trust, social withdrawal). Beyond trauma- and stressor-related disorders (American

[1] Trauma-informed care is rooted in an emphasis on safety and collaboration, recognizing that traumatized individuals are vulnerable to further harm and iatrogenic outcomes. Trauma-responsive care goes further by tailoring treatment to each client's experience and needs in real time, necessitating high levels of attunement and flexibility.

Psychiatric Association, 2022), trauma survivors often struggle with a variety of mental health challenges, including anxiety and depression, problematic substance use, eating disturbances, sexual dysfunction, and so forth. Unfortunately, many such clients carry a laundry list of diagnoses and receive treatment targeting a particular mental health challenge (e.g., depression, social anxiety) in the absence of a larger trauma-informed and -responsive treatment approach. Understanding trauma cumulatively, systemically, and intergenerationally necessitates broadening and deepening our clinical foci, and throughout this book we emphasize the broad sequelae of trauma. When clinicians conflate "trauma" with "PTSD," they miss many traumatized individuals and their families who present with a plethora of distressing symptoms but do not endorse a particular event as the source. Thus, a more intersubjective and nuanced perspective is needed.

The word "trauma" originates from the Greek root (τραύμα) for "wound," referencing "a piercing of the skin" (Garland, 1998, p. 9). Not unlike the body, the mind too can be seriously injured. Thus, when we speak of psychological trauma, we are referring to the piercing through or severe injury of the human psyche. Such wounding may have been caused both by things that happened that should not have happened—like physical or sexual abuse, domestic violence, or suicide—as well as things that should have happened but did not. The latter designation is often not considered in assessing trauma, despite evidence that emotional neglect and other insidious forms of maltreatment have some of the most profound and long-standing developmental impacts (Captari, 2020; Riggs, 2010; Strathearn et al., 2020). Defining trauma mainly in terms of objective events fails to account for this complexity and ignores each person's—and family's—subjective experience of what is unfolding, which matters profoundly as far as clinical prognosis. We might ask, what constitutes the psychological wounding or "piercing"? Is it the event itself that strikes a blow to the psyche? Perhaps more accurately, it is the subjective experience often inherent within such events, which can live on in the present in various trauma responses. Below, we delineate four interrelated aspects of human experience that coalesce in traumatogenesis, noting considerable coherence between key tenets of early theorists with the current empirical evidence. We find it fascinating that some of the earliest psychological practitioners, such as Freud and Ferenczi, intuited the multifaceted nature of trauma's impacts while working with highly distressed clients, and how many of their original clinical insights have since been confirmed by research.

First, central to the experience of trauma is feeling helpless, overpowered, and/or unsafe in the face of perceived danger—the sense of being at the mercy of greater, malevolent forces. As far back as Freud's seminal writings, traumatization was thought to arise from "an extensive rupture of the [mind's] barrier against stimuli" (Freud, 1920/1955, p. 24) resulting in the "experience of helplessness" (Freud, 1926/1953, p. 81). In such situations, there is a sense of chaos due to breakdown of "the ordinary systems of care that give people a sense of control, connection, and meaning" (Herman, 1992, p. 33). Neuroscientific evidence has borne this out, suggesting a cascade within the human threat response system, which begins with a brief "freeze" to orient to the danger, then activates the sympathetic nervous system toward either flight or fight. If this fails, the body adapts to promote survival through extreme parasympathetic activation (e.g., tonic immobility, collapse; Schauer & Elbert, 2010), resulting in dissociation. Potential threat includes not only physical but also emotional, relational, and existential aspects—as one's subjective sense of being able to "go on being" is often in question (Shengold, 2011). It is important to note that in situations of developmental and intergenerational trauma, there is often a chronic lack of safety, security, control, and agency, rather than a sudden loss of such experiences.

Second and relatedly, trauma includes being flooded by extreme, unbearable affects. This may include terror, horror, shock, disgust, rage, humiliation, shame, and other emotions that exceed one's capacity to cope or regulate. One of the first therapists to attempt in-depth clinical work with severely traumatized clients, Ferenczi (1926) hypothesized that "sudden affect that could not be psychically controlled (the shock) causes the trauma" (p. 129), and Freud (1920/1955) pointed to fright (*schreck*) in particular. Research over the last century has explicated how emotional flooding can alter brain structure and function in the hypothalamic–pituitary–adrenal axis (Karl et al., 2006; Malarbi et al., 2016; Teicher et al., 2016). While changes in physiological arousal, emotion, perception, and attention have potential to be adaptive in the short term, when faced with helplessness and loss of control (i.e., unable to "fight" or "flee"), the body's threat response system "becomes overwhelmed and disorganized" and emotions "persist in an altered and exaggerated state" (Herman, 1992, p. 34). Ongoing overactivation in the hypothalamic–pituitary–adrenal axis can lead to chronic psychological and physical vulnerabilities as well as decreased social engagement, which can be particularly taxing within family and romantic relationships (Porges, 2011).

Third, trauma involves profound aloneness, disconnection, intrusion, and/or misattunement—the absence of coregulation possibilities that might otherwise make the previously described experiences bearable. Ferenczi (1931) poignantly observed that "children get over even severe shocks . . . if [parents are] at hand with understanding and tenderness and (what is most rare) with complete sincerity" (p. 138), whereas "aloneness . . . renders the [situation] traumatic" (Ferenczi, 1932/1988, p. 193). One particularly damaging situation is when the expected source of one's comfort becomes the source of pain (e.g., attachment trauma; Fonagy, 2018; Main & Hesse, 1990). Even when the stressor is outside of one's attachment figures, these relationships play a critical role in whether or not stress rises to unbearable levels. When there is no one to think or feel with, it is much more likely that a situation will be experienced as traumatic. This may be due to physical separation (as in a child who survives in war but whose parents are killed) but is most often a sense of feeling rejected or shut down by those turned to for help. When family members or others in power respond by minimizing (e.g., "stop making such a big deal about it"), denying (e.g., "that never happened"), or blaming (e.g., "it was your fault"), initial distress is compounded (Borgogno, 2019). Institutional betrayal, which is often present amid religious trauma, represents a larger example of this same phenomenon (Christl et al., 2024; Zaeske et al., 2024). The interpersonal fallout of trauma is often a reorientation toward self-protection rather than connection, which creates painful internal double binds between the safety of loneliness and the presumed danger of being known.

Fourth, trauma elicits a sense of incomprehensibility, incoherence, and unspeakability that is both cognitive and existential—what has happened (or is happening) is "unfathomable ... incalculable ... the sense of which one cannot grasp" (Ferenczi, 1932/1988, p. 171). It has been said that whatever can be understood can be endured; as such, what constitutes trauma are those things that cannot be symbolized, thought about, talked about, or integrated within one's psyche: "Trauma is whatever outstrips and disrupts the psyche's capacity for representation or mentalization. Absent the potential for mental representation, these events and phenomena ... remain locked within an ahistorical, repetitive process as potentials for action, somatization, and projection" (H. B. Levine, 2014, p. 214). Neurobiological evidence suggests that glucocorticoids secreted by the brain in response to extreme threat disrupt the formation of episodic memory (e.g., the sense of "being there" in the moment), while procedural, implicit, and bodily memories may be encoded separately from one another (Solms & Turnbull, 2002). The result can be substantial incoherence (e.g., nothing makes sense), meaninglessness (e.g., nothing matters), and discontinuous self-experience (e.g., I feel shattered, or like I don't exist). Things previously taken for granted are called into question, and life may feel fragmented and unpredictable (Janoff-Bulman, 1992; Park, 2022). As meaning-making creatures, humans will often choose painful coherence over incoherence; consider the child who perceives herself as "bad" to avoid the unbearable situation of feeling helpless against "bad" adults (Fairbairn, 1943) or the frightening conclusion that the person they depend on most is also the one who hurts them most.

Taken together, these four areas coalesce in the lived experience of trauma and can offer readers a heuristic frame to understand more deeply what clients have endured and how this may be spilling over into their life currently. For example, this may show up in the ways people feel helpless, unsafe, and lacking agency; at the mercy of overwhelming and chaotic emotions; fundamentally alone in the world, relationally hypervigilant, and preoccupied with fear of abandonment; and splintered or disjointed in their experience of the present moment. Building on this, we now consider how these phenomena can play out within family relationships and interactions, applying the systemic concepts described in Chapter 1 in this volume.

A SYSTEMIC, MULTIDIMENSIONAL UNDERSTANDING OF TRAUMA IN FAMILIES

The family context is an influential factor in whether a highly stressful event is experienced as traumatic and how the process of recovery unfolds. Indeed, systemic factors have been shown to be key mediators between experiencing complex trauma and developing complex PTSD, and thus hold distinct potential as targeted mechanisms of change in treatment (Harris et al., 2024). Families can perpetuate trauma, exacerbating the ensuing suffering, and/or they can support members' healing, minimizing negative outcomes. However, most mental health treatment for trauma is still individually focused. Why might this be? One influential factor could be a lack of clarity and training about how to intervene effectively at a systemic level when working with traumatized families. Common models such as trauma-focused cognitive behavioral therapy (J. A. Cohen et al., 2016) incorporate parents and/or partners as an assumed support, but what happens when these family members are significantly impacted by trauma symptoms themselves, impeding their ability to engage? Or when multiple subsystems (e.g., spousal/partner, parenting, child) within a family are struggling?

One option is to refer each family member or family subsystem to therapy—and a case might be made for this in some instances, such as when couples may benefit from having a separate space to work on their intimate relationship. However, a proliferation of therapies can sometimes result in a splintering of family experience, with multiple clinicians and treatment teams, each aligned with a single family member, that can end up working at cross-purposes. In one case we are familiar with, 18 different professionals across multiple agencies were providing mental health-related services to a single family. Imagine trying to convene a time for case consultation! Are there other possibilities? As summarized in Chapter 1 in this volume, couple and family therapy has a rich history and well-developed clinical literature; however, researchers and clinicians have only recently begun to elucidate the nuances of providing couple or family therapy to traumatized populations (Grove et al., 2020). The hopeful reality is that relational contexts play an important role in how people process acutely stressful events, and normative acute stress responses do not necessarily translate into chronic symptomology.

In today's parlance, the word "trauma" is often used indiscriminately. Thus, it is vital that systemically oriented practitioners distinguish between adverse or injurious experiences and traumatization. Collapsing the two misses the complexity inherent within how each member in the family system, and the system as a whole, navigates this process. There is no single experience of trauma when it comes to a family. Each member's perception and ensuing ways of coping and making meaning are shaped by their life histories, distinct characterological and psychological strengths and vulnerabilities, and available emotional and social resources.

In recent decades, attention to complex trauma has become more widespread, facilitating a nuanced understanding beyond discrete events. Complex trauma refers to multiple, chronic, and prolonged traumatic experiences—often of an interpersonal nature—such as abuse, neglect, or violence, typically occurring during childhood or adolescence (National Child Traumatic Stress Network, Complex Trauma Task Force, 2003). Unlike a single traumatic incident, complex trauma involves repeated harm over time—the combined effects of chronic toxic stress within the context of a family and relational milieu that is reactive, unpredictable, and/or hostile. Complex trauma can also be understood as emerging out of historical and/or current communal trauma, by which children and families who hold marginalized identities and have less access to resources are most vulnerable to polytraumatization. Taken together, trauma-impacted families can easily become traumatizing contexts for development, leading to profound and lasting effects on members' sense of self, emotional awareness and regulation, cognitive schemas, and ways of relating. Concerningly, these combined effects increase risk for experiencing subsequent trauma across the lifespan.

For readers interested in a deeper dive into the latest research and clinical approaches to trauma, we refer to many well-developed texts (e.g., Beck & Sloan, 2022; Briere & Scott, 2025; Ford & Courtois, 2020; Gómez & Hosey, 2025; Monson & Fredman, 2021). Here, we delve into the particular interplay between—and complexity of—how trauma "lives" in the family system. As part of case conceptualization, it is important to consider what traumatic experiences each person in the family may have endured and/or perpetrated. A systemic, multidimensional approach to trauma treatment considers the interwoven aspects of how potentially traumatic stressors (a) may be both external to and within the family system; and (b) may include both singular, acute experiences as well as chronic contexts of suffering and adversity.

We visualize these two components as distinct—but interconnected—axes that reveal a systemic constellation of each family's cumulative trauma burden. Box 2.1 applies this heuristic to the opening vignette of Aisha, Deepti, and Maya. Visual mapping of family trauma is one way to help formulate each family's cumulative burden by plotting the conglomerate of traumatic stressors its members have experienced. Considering intergenerational trauma, this could include both current family members as well as past generations.

BOX 2.1

MAPPING TRAUMA BURDEN ACROSS THE FAMILY SYSTEM

It is important to consider what potentially traumatic experiences each person in the family has endured and/or perpetrated. Plotting this conglomerate creates a helpful visual representation of the system's cumulative trauma burden to refer back to, and is necessarily constrained by clients' self-disclosure. Given survivors' frequent use of minimization and denial to cope—as well as reticence to share personal information with a professional they have just met—practitioners may find it helpful to return to this family trauma map iteratively throughout treatment. To offer an example, we consider Aisha, Deepti, and Maya's family introduced in the opening vignette, including their deceased father/husband, Kabir.

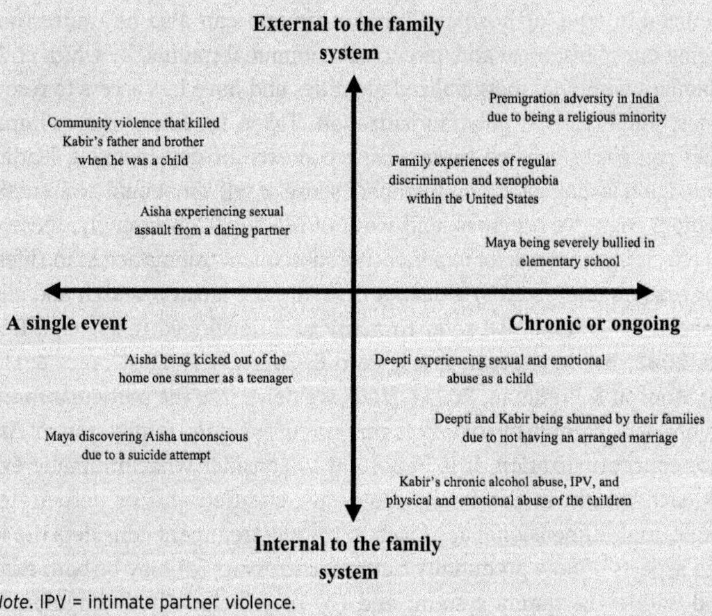

Note. IPV = intimate partner violence.

Beginning in the top left quadrant, we can consider and make note of potentially traumatic events that Aisha, Maya, Deepti, and Kabir have been exposed to external of the family system itself. This includes community violence in the father's (Kabir's) childhood that killed his father and brother, as well as Aisha's experience of sexual assault from a dating partner in college.

Next, moving to the top right quadrant, we can identify and mark any chronic, ongoing potentially traumatic contexts for this family perpetrated by external forces. This includes Kabir and Deepti's notable adversity, due to their minority religious affiliation and financial hardship, which contributed to their decision to relocate. Added to that, the family, like many immigrants, has endured discrimination, racism, and xenophobia in daily life. In addition, Maya experienced severe bullying in elementary school, leading to changing schools.

Turning our attention to the bottom left quadrant, we can then pinpoint and jot down any distinct potentially traumatic events that Aisha, Deepti, and Maya have been exposed to within the family system. In high school, Aisha was kicked out of the home for a summer when she began dating someone her parents didn't approve of. In college, the fallout of Aisha's sexual assault (which the family minimized) led to her dropping out of school and attempting suicide by overdosing. Maya discovered her sister unconscious and called 911, which was terrifying.

Finally, lingering on the bottom right quadrant, we can consider and make note of chronic traumatic relational contexts within the family itself. Central to this is Kabir's chronic alcohol misuse, fueling inter-partner violence and various forms of child abuse, as well as Deepti's failure to intervene. Going back a generation, Deepti experienced emotional and physical abuse from her parents and sexual abuse from an extended family member. Furthermore, both Kabir and Deepti were shunned by their families due to not having an arranged marriage, with resultant loss of extended family support and connection for their children.

Trauma external or internal to the family system can significantly impact individual members, a family subsystem, the entire family, or multiple generations (e.g., historical/ancestral trauma transmitted and enacted across time). We also find it helpful to distinguish between a traumatic experience that one family member lives through (e.g., combat, sexual assault), which may reverberate through the system, as distinct from what occurs at a family level (e.g., a member's suicide, high-conflict divorce involving removal of children) or community level (e.g., police violence, natural disaster, war). Mapping these aspects with regard to a particular case offers a snapshot to refer back to throughout treatment. In our clinical work, we have witnessed time and again how families carrying a greater burden of trauma expend tremendous energy just to survive, often with fewer resources (e.g., emotional, relational, psychological, financial) available to address and work through the aforementioned impacts. This creates significant strain on the family, which can lead to feeling stuck, uniquely "broken," and unsure if things can be different when available mental health interventions fail to consider the larger systemic picture, and thus have limited impact (Goff et al., 2020; Weiling et al., 2020). Below, we describe these areas one at a time for purposes of clarity, although they are closely interrelated.

Trauma External to the Family System

Individual

Individual family members may be exposed to potentially traumatic stressors from a variety of outside sources, including specific contexts such as school (e.g., a child who is severely bullied) or work (e.g., parents exposed to extreme human suffering in their jobs, like health care, first response teams, or the military), and specific relationships such as peers (e.g., a child who is abused by a teen in the neighborhood) or authorities (e.g., a parent who experiences sexual or racial harassment from a landlord, boss, or law enforcement). These situations could involve a time-limited stressor or a chronic, ongoing experience, such as a biracial child growing up in a predominantly White community who is often bullied and ostracized due to their skin tone. Within the well-developed literature on adverse childhood experiences (ACEs), there is growing attention to previously overlooked areas, such as bullying, discrimination, racism, living in an unsafe neighborhood, and experiencing or witnessing community violence (Bernard et al., 2021; Cronholm et al., 2015; SmithBattle et al., 2022).

By directly impacting a single member, individual trauma experiences often have a spillover effect on family dynamics and functioning (Pu & Rodriguez, 2021; Visser et al., 2016). Some systemic therapists might even argue that there is no such thing as individual trauma alone, since traumatized people often act in dysregulated and traumatizing ways toward those closest to them. For example, the effects of a parent's work-related trauma can compromise their ability to emotionally connect and be intimate with their spouse (Knobloch & Theiss, 2012; Tuttle et al., 2018). Spillover to children can occur when traumatized parents model maladaptive coping strategies (e.g., avoidance, numbing), communicate distorted thoughts (e.g., distrust, paranoia), withdraw and become less emotionally available, and/or develop skewed perceptions of children that foster boundary violations (e.g., parentification; Kerig & Alexander, 2012). Over time, a traumatized parent's denial and dissociation can inundate the family system, becoming instantiated in unspoken norms that oblige the rest of the family to also avoid talking about emotions or the trauma. Sometimes, family responses to an acutely stressful event result in additional traumatization to the affected person, fundamentally changing the nature of that relationship. Consider a teenager who is sexually assaulted by a dating partner, and whose parents respond with shaming, victim-blaming, and grounding her. These actions further compromise her sense of agency, fuel distress-inducing narratives, and isolate her from peers who might otherwise be a source of support and coregulation. Thus, the assault itself is only the first "domino" in the resultant psychological and social fallout.

Family

In some instances, multiple (but not all) members of a family system encounter a potentially traumatic stressor from an external source, ranging from isolated incidents (e.g., a car accident) to ongoing realities (e.g., siblings attending a school where exposure to violence is commonplace). Family members not present in the moment may still be indirectly traumatized—for example, not knowing their loved one's immediate whereabouts and fearing for their safety.

Despite living through the same event, however, each person has their own subjectivity. Take, for instance, a mother and young child who are in a severe car accident. It is not hard to imagine how a toddler or preschooler could experience the accident differently from her mother behind the wheel. First, the child has limited language and understanding of how the world works; thus, she has less of a reference point for the shattering and screeching sounds, smell of burning rubber, and seeing her mother bloodied and panicked—it is raw human experience that cannot be understood. In contrast, her mother's subjectivity is likely shaped by perceived sense of control and responsibility to protect her child, which can fuel self-blame. How the mother responds in the moment and talks about it later will inevitably impact the child's subjectivity as well, exemplifying the dynamic influences of family interactions amid acute stress.

In the wake of trauma, it is not unusual for some family members to develop intense emotional bonds with the traumatized individual(s) (Figley & Barnes, 2005; Newby et al., 2000). While this closeness may ease feelings of guilt and vulnerability, overinvolvement and overprotection may interfere with the post-trauma adjustment of the traumatized family member. In particular, those directly impacted by the stressor may be drawn closer in a "trauma bond," creating a highly cohesive subgroup that seeks mutual comfort and excludes other family members (Figley & Barnes, 2005; Galano & Graham-Bermann, 2019). For example, adolescents who experienced a school shooting may want to confide in and spend time with siblings or peers who are fellow survivors, while significantly struggling to relate with parents and other family members. When previously stable family patterns of communication, support, and discipline are disturbed, higher rates of parent–child conflict and discord may ensue (Figley & Barnes, 2005), with negative feedback loops in the system making it difficult to reconnect meaningfully. Especially when multiple members experience states of fight/flight/freeze/fawn, the system may be strained in its ability to coregulate this trauma-related physiology, resulting in compromised family functioning. Members may be increasingly disengaged and the system overly rigid, with an exclusive emphasis on maintaining the status quo and little space for negotiation (Figley & Barnes, 2005). Alternatively, one or more members may hypervigilantly become "trauma symptom managers," overextending themselves to take care of others and anticipate to avoid any potential triggers (Goff et al., 2020; Sherman et al., 2016). Most often, each family member responds uniquely, whether by leaning in or out of these relationships, which can result in a dizzying matrix of reactively charged interaction patterns.

When an entire family endures a traumatic stressor, the structure and foundation of the system is rocked, much like a relational earthquake that shakes and sometimes splinters the existing family infrastructure. Like clinical night vision goggles and thermal imaging, systems theory illuminates the post-trauma reorganization of the family, highlighting potential role shifts, boundary disturbances, and/or communication problems. Often, a traumatic event will alter the family's views around safety and agency, resulting in over-organization, hypervigilance, and control behaviors to counteract the crushing sense of helplessness (Peebles-Kleiger, 2000). In an effort to control external threats, families may try to reestablish homeostasis by developing rigid/closed external boundaries and diffuse/open internal system boundaries (Figley & Barnes, 2005). With little information coming in from the outside world, this situation can spawn an authoritarian hierarchical structure with harsh parenting practices and excessive pressure toward compliance and/or achievement. On the other hand, weak internal boundaries set the stage for overinvolvement, enmeshment, and triangulation, such as when a distressed parent turns to and "spousifies" their child, inappropriately seeking emotional validation and care. When there is a lack of leadership, the family system may become underregulated, resulting in chaos and reactivity.

This unpredictability can be further traumatizing, especially to children. These survival orientations, while adaptive in the acute phases of trauma recovery, are likely to constrain family functioning over time and may cause additional harm to members.

As mentioned previously, family members' subjective experience of the trauma will likely vary significantly based on developmental stage, relationship to power, sense of responsibility, and constellation of strengths and vulnerabilities. Traumatic stressors that impact the family collective often have spillover effects across subsystems as well as other domains of life. For example, family members often respond to a potentially traumatic event in distinct ways based on their own personalities and prior life experiences, which can disrupt communication and set the stage for misunderstanding. Different ways of managing stress and making decisions within the couple subsystem may lead to heightened conflict and may inadvertently spill over into parenting disagreements and inconsistent discipline for children (Galano & Graham-Bermann, 2019). Because adults' emotional resources are often necessarily focused on their own recovery and survival, children may be left to cope with what has happened by themselves, with available supports from peers and teachers often varying by sibling.

Trauma Within the Family System

Tragically, trauma most often stems from within families and related interpersonal contexts (Kessler et al., 2017), whether the perpetrator is a parent, spouse, sibling, extended family member, or another person in one's close kinship network (e.g., cousin, grandparent, religious leader). Decades of ACEs research has documented negative longitudinal impacts on physical, mental, and relational health (Kalmakis & Chandler, 2015). The original ACEs questionnaire targeted 10 areas, namely, abuse (physical, emotional, sexual), neglect (physical, emotional), and challenges in the household (family member with mental illness or problematic substance use, domestic violence, parental separation/divorce, incarcerated relative; Felitti et al., 1998). In family therapy, it is important to remember that you may be interacting with the perpetrator(s) and/or the one(s) victimized, although there are important contraindications for including both in couple or family treatment (see Chapters 1 and 5 in this volume). The context of a close relationship—presumed to be a source of safety—becoming a source of pain compounds the unbearable nature of such experiences. Such complex trauma can include physical, sexual, psychological, emotional, and/or spiritual abuse or neglect,[2] which are often co-occurring, chronic, and interrelated, rather than isolated incidents. In such situations, trauma is deeply engrained in the system within patterns of relating, such that it becomes the "water" that members swim in. Thus, there is presumably little chance of escape, and people often begin to recognize and process such traumas only in adulthood when it is safe to no longer rely on denial and dissociation, and new relational experiences highlight the horrific nature of their upbringing (e.g., what they previously thought of as "dysfunctional" is now understood as traumatic). Even when the perpetrator aggresses against only one member, there are undeniable impacts on other parts of the system. Often, family members' denial and failure to intervene to protect the impacted child are just as traumatizing as the abuse or neglect itself.

Some family systems are aptly described as both traumatized and traumatizing. There are particular complexities involved in cases of cumulative trauma where specific family members or the dysfunctional family system itself represent the origin and sustaining source of ongoing traumatization. How does this come about? Adults often bring into their families of creation the unmetabolized effects of individual histories of abuse, neglect, and maltreatment, sometimes believing such experiences and behaviors to be "normal" (Fraiberg et al., 1975; Lyons-Ruth & Jacobvitz, 2018). High levels of personal traumatization, manifesting in both psychological distress and personality disturbances, fuel friction both within and across family subsystems. For example, spouses/partners may treat each other in emotionally demeaning and abusive ways, with conflict at times rising to the level of physical aggression (Stith et al., 2020). Parents and other adults involved in childcare may similarly take a harsh, punitive approach toward developmentally normative misbehaviors of children. An additional layer of trauma for youngsters in such contexts lies not only in things that happened, but also those that did not—attunement, mentalization, and empathy are often glaringly absent from such families. While distressing to contemplate, it is not surprising, then, that these children often perpetrate harm against siblings and peers or turn aggression on themselves (e.g., suicidal behaviors; Institute of Medicine & National Research Council, 2014). Here, the spillover effect frequently extends beyond the family into other relationships and community networks. Maltreated children are often

[2] While it was initially presumed that child sexual and physical abuse were the most tramatogenic, research has shown the diverse forms that both abuse and neglect can take, as well as their frequent interconnectedness. In fact, more covert forms of psychological/emotional abuse and neglect may have some of the most damaging and widespread developmental consequences (e.g., Captari, 2020; Dye, 2020; Riggs, 2010).

seen as the "identified patient" and referred for—or mandated to attend—treatment (Celano, 2018). Yet, individual intervention, even if trauma-focused, will likely have limited effects unless traumatizing family dynamics are addressed.

In these situations, it is sometimes difficult to know where to begin clinically. You may feel as though wherever you look, you see trauma and its fallout embedded in the family processes we explored in the previous chapter. An entire family system may be operating in hypervigilance mode, whether through fighting (e.g., emotional reactivity, physical aggression), fleeing (e.g., withdrawal, emotional shutdown), freezing (e.g., inability to think or communicate personal needs), and/or fawning (e.g., placating to avoid conflict, compulsive self-sacrifice). Relationships in traumatized families are often marked by disengagement and cutoff or enmeshment and lack of autonomy—neither of which support family cohesion, flexibility, and communication (Galano & Graham-Bermann, 2019). Whether rife with chaos (i.e., lack of stabilizing structure) or extreme control, survival and defense-oriented responses impair family members' ability to reflect, communicate, and collaborate effectively. Therapists trained in individual models of intervention may feel frustrated by how psychotherapy in such contexts seems like a moving target. Freud (1920/1955) noted the human "compulsion to repeat" unresolved trauma in the present rather than "remembering it as something belonging to the past" (p. 12). Wherever family members cannot acknowledge, symbolize, and address their psychological wounds, they are apt to recreate them in the present. Don't get lost in the details and dysregulation! Instead, try to keep a differentiated but open stance as you observe and participate in the family. You might soon notice that you are being recruited into alliances, coalitions, and unspoken family rules; this is incredibly valuable clinical data. Rather than homing in on a single Criterion A event, psychiatric diagnosis, or identified patient, seek to understand how trauma is "living" in the family—and perhaps even being fueled by the system.

What relational and communication patterns keep the family locked in traumatized states? Who holds the power? Who feels powerless? What is it that cannot be named, owned, or integrated? Who carries distress for the family system, and where are trauma-related cognitions and emotions being denied or detoured? Such questions mark a significant departure from many forms of trauma treatment rooted in individual psychology. Expanding to assess and treat the family system opens possibilities beyond individual coping and distress management, which represent first-order change. Rather, by addressing family processes driving traumatization and resultant psychopathology, systems-oriented clinicians can catalyze structural and interactional processes that promote family healing, growth, and evolution (i.e., second-order change;

Grove et al., 2020). Throughout this book, we have included amalgamated and fictional case vignettes to help elucidate the complexities of working with families who have experienced multiple and overlapping forms of trauma; these populations are often at higher risk for therapeutic ruptures and dropout than in cases of isolated trauma (Eubanks et al., 2023; Friedlander & Escudero, 2023).

Ancestral, Intergenerational, and Community Trauma

Attention to family diversity includes expanding our awareness beyond the immediate family unit. Historical trauma often becomes embedded within a family or community culture, identity, and norms, sometimes making it difficult to distinguish what is culture from what is trauma responses (Brave Heart et al., 2011; Rosenthal, 2021). For example, where community infrastructure is upended by violence, civil unrest, or war, families may out of necessity lean heavily on hypervigilance, minimization, denial, isolationism, or emotional suppression in order to survive. Over time, these patterns become instantiated in parenting practices, both supporting survival and constricting children's socioemotional development (e.g., through lack of mirroring, joint attention) across generations (Plant et al., 2018). For example, Beebe et al.'s (2020) research among pregnant women widowed by the September 11, 2001, terrorist attacks on the United States found a sense of "urgent engagement" between these mothers and their babies. The researchers concluded that while vigilant, high-arousal patterns of interacting seemed optimized for "finding" each other, this could also set the stage for intrusiveness and difficulty navigating conflicts and ruptures over time. Given how trauma can shape personality, relationship to emotion, communication styles, and expectations of how the world works (e.g., expecting harm/threat), the spillover of trauma can extend across multiple generations, and it is helpful to elucidate these nuances using tools such as systemic visual mapping of trauma burden as well as family genograms.

Even if conscious links to a particular traumatic event are lost to time, ways of relating to oneself, others, and emotional distress tend to be internalized and passed on. Atlas (2022) aptly noted, "The secrets of the mind include not only our own life experiences but also those that we unknowingly carry with us: the memories, feelings, and traumas that we inherit from previous generations" (p. 17). Using the language of cultural introjects in discussing African American experience in particular, Vaughans (2016) defined this as the "internalization of something without quite knowing why . . . a disturbing amplification of unknown fears" (p. 246). Trauma can be transmitted intergenerationally through multiple avenues, including biological changes (e.g., epigenetic alterations in regulating the stress response; Yehuda & Lehrner, 2018); family schemas and narratives (e.g., the world as a dangerous place, people as untrustworthy; Chou et al., 2023); systemic processes such as those involved in parenting (e.g., coping, communication; M. Fitzgerald et al., 2020; Plant et al., 2018); and collective experiences of a particular group (e.g., colonization, displacement, slavery; Brave Heart, 2003; Brave Heart et al., 2011; Hirschberger, 2018).

Parents' tendencies toward hypervigilance, emotional reactivity, or other trauma reactions stemming from their own life experiences inevitably spill over into their attachment dynamics with their children. Aside from overt forms of maltreatment already discussed, covert second-generation trauma effects embodied in parenting include dissociation and chronic emotional disengagement (Hipwell et al., 2019; Tronick et al., 1978), states of mind that are hostile or helpless, and behaviors that are frightened or frightening (for reviews, see Lyons-Ruth & Jacobvitz, 2018; Turgeon et al., 2022). These unresolved effects of parents' trauma have been linked with disorganized attachment in their children, among other areas of disrupted development; such children experience chronic relational ruptures in the absence of repair and reconnection (Tronick & Gold, 2020). And it is not just a two-generation phenomena. Empirical evidence has traced the sequelae of trauma across four or more subsequent generations, including among Holocaust survivors, families experiencing forced migration, African Americans whose ancestors were enslaved, and populations impacted by genocide, to name a few (Chou & Buchanan, 2021; Giladi & Bell, 2013; Haladjian, 2020; Hicks, 2015; Lev-Wiesel, 2007).

In situations of widespread crisis or disaster, traumatic stressors impact not only an entire family system but also the community they are embedded within. Upheaval of government, communication, and relational networks can further exacerbate the sense of chaos, powerlessness, and unpredictability, isolating families from important sources of support, practical help, and meaning-making (e.g., one's neighborhood, school, religious community). Yet, even amid mass trauma (e.g., shootings, natural disasters, war), some families are more vulnerable to chronic, toxic levels of stress. This was readily apparent in the COVID-19 pandemic, during which some families benefited from flexible work, lack of commutes, and more time with their children, while other parts of the population experienced impossible dilemmas—working in-person jobs that exposed them to infection risk, while simultaneously being responsible for their children's remote schooling, with few childcare options. Disproportionate hospitalizations and deaths among Black, Latinx, and Native American families (Tai et al., 2022) offer one example of how an objective event such as a pandemic may impact a family's functioning—including level of stress, disorientation, perceived helplessness, and losses incurred—in vastly different ways based on race, social location, and socioeconomic status. An ecosystemic orientation encourages us to reflect on significant ecological influences, such as community norms, sociopolitical contexts, and social determinants of health, that shape the differential trauma burden experienced by some families and communities.

Despite being sources of vulnerability and suffering, systemic contexts where trauma unfolds and reverberates are only one part of the clinical picture. In each of the previously described domains, we would do well to also attend to the presence of intergenerationally transmitted strengths and resources—including at individual, family subsystem, family system, and community levels. Thus, we turn our attention to these areas and their relevance in treatment.

FAMILY STRENGTHS, RESILIENCE, AND ADAPTATION

As one client rightly challenged me (LC) early in my career, "When all you ask me about is my trauma, it feels like nothing else about me is real." Part of the complexity of trauma work with families is holding in mind both the family as a whole (e.g., family structure, processes, defenses) and the unique experiences of each member. With all of this to consider, it can be easy to miss the strengths and capacities that have supported survival and adaptation. Dual-factor understandings of mental health distinguish families' well-being and flourishing from simply a lack of distress (Keyes, 2007, 2024); some families may not exhibit significant symptomology but report a sense of languishing—feeling indifferent, empty, and wondering if there is more to life. Furthermore, suffering and flourishing are not mutually exclusive, such that treatment may enable moments of family flourishing even amid deep pain and hardship. Attention to flourishing expands our focus beyond measures of family functioning and satisfaction alone to more holistic indicators, such as meaning and purpose, communal concern, and integrating agency with communion. Only recently has substantive attention been given in trauma treatment to more holistic formulations that center families' culturally embedded strengths and resources as key intervention points; for example, Hicks (2015) advised clinicians to look for "inherited legacies of healing that have manifested as survival, strength, spirituality, perseverance, vitality, dynamism, and resiliency" (p. v).

While resilience is frequently framed as an individual trait (e.g., inner strength and flexibility that enables one to "bounce back"), couple and family psychology expands our focus to dynamic multisystemic processes of resilience that unfold at relational, family, and community levels (Maurović et al., 2020), including kinship networks that families draw support and meaning from, such as religious and spiritual communities (Walsh, 2007, 2015, 2016). From this perspective, resilience is not an inherent trait, but rather an unfolding state of adaptation to systemic disturbances that depends on the interactions between "biological, psychological, social, and ecological systems . . . that help individuals [and families] regain, sustain, or improve their mental well-being" (Ungar & Theron, 2020, p. 441). Research has examined the diverse, multisystemic mechanisms of resilience across development, identifying dynamic constellations of interconnected resources and protective systems that vary by context (Masten et al., 2023). A variety of strengths and processes across family subsystems can buffer negative outcomes of trauma and promote positive adaptation, meaning-making, and posttraumatic growth (see Benzies & Mychasiuk, 2009; Berger & Weiss, 2009; Bhana & Bachoo, 2011; Black & Lobo, 2008; Duncan et al., 2021; Dunst, 2021). Below, we summarize key findings in the literature that systemically oriented practitioners can listen for and help clients capitalize on.

Family Relational Dynamics

Strong family cohesion—involving relationships marked by emotional security, trust, support, and openness—can facilitate resilience in the wake of potentially traumatic stressors (López-Zerón & Blow, 2017). As we have discussed, a central aspect of what makes a circumstance traumatizing is loss of connection, emotional safety, and agency. Thus, secure attachment dynamics in the family system are particularly salient in recovery (Byng-Hall, 2008b). Families who can flexibly utilize relationships with one another as both a safe haven and secure base can more effectively navigate acute stress reactions (Darling Rasmussen et al., 2019). The family attachment network includes each child's relationship with both parents, each child's relationship with any other children, and parents'/spouses' relationship with each other, not to mention children's and parents' relationships with other caregivers and extended family members in the home. A secure family attachment network "enables all family members, of whatever age, to feel secure enough to explore their relationships with each other and with others outside the family" (Byng-Hall, 1995, p. 104). Differentiation of self within the family system enables members to know where they "end" and others "begin," such that there is room for family members' unique perspectives and emotional experiences. This is especially important, given that there is often initially no coherent family trauma narrative; adaptive processing requires appreciation for each member's subjectivity, perspective, and needs, and may include working to create a shared narrative.

Parenting that capitalizes on warmth, responsiveness, and communication—while setting consistent limits—fosters safety, trust, and stability in the family (Gee & Cohodes, 2023). When faced with a traumatic stressor, children who experience their caregivers as optimally attuned and responsive, but not as permissive or intrusive, are better equipped to work through trauma-related emotions and thoughts. Far from "perfect," such parent–child dynamics inevitably involve moments of mismatch and rupture, but these are attended to, such that children learn through experience that relational challenges can be worked through and repaired (Tronick & Gold, 2020). Age-appropriate parental involvement and monitoring of children can also help strengthen cohesion and facilitate micro-opportunities for coregulation and processing. Within the couple subsystem, a sense of partnership, playing to each other's strengths, taking personal responsibility (rather than blaming others or internally collapsing in shame), and building a culture of appreciation all prepare partners to lean in toward each other and collaborate to protect and care for the family in situations of stress and crisis (Schulz et al., 2010).

Norms Around Communication and Emotion

All families have unspoken rules and norms about what can and cannot be talked about, and part of what makes an experience traumatic is systemic denial—it cannot be named and empathically witnessed. Direct, nonreactive, and age-appropriate communication about the potentially traumatic situation can reduce ambiguity and support children's recovery trajectory (Bhana & Bachoo, 2011; Duncan et al., 2021). Providing clarity in the face of ambiguity and threat can significantly downregulate feelings of terror and enable coregulation. How emotion and vulnerability are handled in the family (e.g., overregulated, underregulated) hold import for trauma processing. Emotional awareness, expression, and regulation are all salient here (S. M. Johnson, 2002, 2019a, 1996/2019b). Overregulated systems that shut down emotional expression may fuel members' shame about trauma-related affects (e.g., anger, despair), whereas underregulated systems may struggle to coregulate and reestablish a sense of predictability. Families are more resilient when they can normalize and validate emotional responses, support open discussion around difficult and vulnerable topics, encourage emotional expression within one's window of tolerance (such that both self-regulation and coregulation of trauma-related affects are available), and respect each person's unique needs. In addition, holding space for the full spectrum of human emotion—without cutting off either extreme—can facilitate moments of peace, hope, humor, and joy even amid hardship (Paivio & Pascual-Leone, 2023).

Shared Beliefs, Values, and Narratives

Families are meaning-making systems (Walsh, 2015, 2016). Shared narratives offer a sense of coherence amid disorientation, and at best, these narratives are coconstructed. The appraisals that families make amid acute stress and adversity will significantly influence their collective response and long-term adjustment. For example, while situations deemed to be overwhelming threats are likely to fuel trauma reactions, the belief that challenges may be survived and overcome can fuel vigilant collective action. Cultural resources, such as religion, spirituality, and family values, undergird a sense of hope and meaning in life; it is from this wellspring that family narratives often emerge (Sandage et al., 2020; Trimble, 2018). For example, we might expect a family to respond quite differently based on whether they presume that "good/bad things happen to good/bad people" compared with a family that understands suffering to be an inherent part of life, drawing strength and hope from stories of ancestors who persisted and overcame challenges. The former would likely experience greater disorientation, incomprehensibility, and self-blame (i.e., "I must be a bad person to deserve this"); the latter might focus more on adaptive ways to endure, while accepting what they cannot change. Although trauma can shake or shatter previously held beliefs about the self, others, the world, and the divine, families that possess openness and curiosity are better prepared to reevaluate and expand on previous beliefs, as this helps counter fear and cautiousness.

Family Coping and Systemic Responsiveness

Coping involves attempts to deal with and potentially overcome stressors. This may include both individual and family behaviors and practices that aim to make the situation better, or, at minimum, do not make it worse (Lazarus & Folkman, 1984). In the face of trauma-related affect, families are better equipped to navigate acute stress responses if they can utilize emotion-focused coping strategies like meditation, journaling, or somatic exercises to find soothing and grounding (rather than exacerbating this through displacement or scapegoating). In response to the disorientation, disruptions, and unpredictability that trauma produces, families tend to be more resilient if they can use problem-focused coping to take an active role in responding (rather than high parental control, which may reinforce feelings of helplessness). This may involve working together to brainstorm options, plan, and make decisions about the best course of action (rather than feeling paralyzed and/or turning against each other).

While family members will cope in distinct ways based on their own personalities and life experiences (e.g., needing space vs. wanting to talk), families who seek support and foster a sense of togetherness, as well as those who regularly engage with coping routines and rituals, can help offset the sense of isolation that compounds trauma (Dunst, 2021). Relatedly, members' self-determination and an internal locus of control have been shown to support resilient processes through reinforcing agency (Benzies & Mychasiuk, 2009). At a systemic level, flexibility and adaptability are important qualities, facilitating necessary system-wide adjustments and reorganization in the face of stress. Rather than holding rigidly to previous family norms, or collapsing and withdrawing in the face of overwhelming stress, systemic responsiveness enables families to stay meaningfully connected, negotiate competing demands between individual members and the system as a whole, and identify and make use of available resources (e.g., social capital, spiritual support; Duncan et al., 2021).

Kinship and Community Contexts

Beyond the family system alone, relationships and contexts characterized by support, belonging, and solidarity can facilitate processes of social cohesion (i.e., trust and shared values) and capital (i.e., resources and practical help accessible through relational networks). This includes networks the entire family is part of—such as extended family, chosen family, neighborhood, and religious/spiritual community (Captari & Worthington, 2024)—as well as contexts unique to each member, such as friendships, work, school, and sports teams or other extracurriculars. When faced with stressful and potentially traumatic circumstances, families that feel held and supported by these larger systemic milieus are better equipped to adaptively process and move through adversity and tragedy (Masten et al., 2023). Families that are financially stable, live in safe areas with less crime, and have access to quality schools, childcare, and health care, are more well-resourced and thus less likely to face chronic, toxic levels of stress that may exhaust family resilience processes (Bhana & Bachoo, 2011).

Thus far, this chapter has explored an intersubjective, systemic understanding of traumatogenesis as well as the importance of attending to families' strengths, resources, and culturally embedded healing capacities. Building on this—and in conjunction with the couple and family specialty competencies discussed in Chapter 1 in this volume—we now apply this knowledge to briefly overview several areas identified by key stakeholders in the field where specific clinical skills and expertise are warranted to provide trauma-informed and -responsive clinical care.

SYSTEMIC APPLICATION OF TRAUMA TREATMENT COMPETENCIES

As discussed in the previous chapter with regard to couple and family work, many practitioners also find their way to trauma treatment out of the needs showing up in their clinical practice. In this way, sometimes our clients are our best trainers! A core component of evidence-based practice is an ongoing commitment to developing clinical expertise. Over a decade ago, when competencies specific to trauma intervention were initially developed, American Psychological Association (APA, 2015a) noted that many therapists "ha[d] only a cursory knowledge of trauma science and d[id] not apply evidence-based psychosocial treatments ... consistently, if at all" (p. 17). Since then, trauma science has gained increasing attention within mental health research and practice, recognizing the diverse and intergenerational impacts of trauma that underpin clients' presenting problems, as well as how graduate training alone falls short of fully equipping practitioners for the complexity of such cases (Cook et al., 2011, 2017). Yet, there is much more work to be done here; in our supervision and consultation work, we frequently encounter situations where ineffective or even iatrogenic treatment recommendations have been offered, at least in part, due to failures to conceptualize trauma-related dynamics and underlying developmental impacts. The fallout is that often such clients and families feel uniquely "broken" and lose hope that change is possible. Considering clinicians' core ethical duty to do no harm, this is highly concerning. As one example, 75% of therapists in a recent survey did not feel adequately trained to treat complex trauma (Kumar et al., 2022). This is likely even more so the case when it comes to feeling prepared to address trauma impacts through a systemic lens, although research and theory about couple and family interventions for trauma and trauma-related disorders are rapidly growing (for reviews, see Carr, 2018, 2025; Dorsey et al., 2017; Monson & Fredman, 2021; Suomi et al., 2019).

Despite important advances in the literature in the past decade, it can be difficult for traumatized couples and families who are seeking mental health care to access treatment that aligns with the current evidence base (Brand et al., 2016, 2017; Dorahy et al., 2017). The gap between what we know from clinical research and the routine care that trauma-impacted families receive represents unnecessary human suffering, which this book seeks to reduce. Working skillfully with the sequelae of trauma in psychotherapy necessitates the development of distinct competencies, beyond generalist training. In addition to the foundational knowledge discussed so far, this includes a distinct therapeutic skill set and particular attitudes embodied by systemically oriented practitioners. Drawing on expert consensus findings of the New

Haven Trauma Competency Group (Cook et al., 2014), the APA (2015a) Guidelines on Trauma Competencies for Education and Training delineated 14 core competencies expected for entry level practice in trauma psychology, which represent an important advancement in establishing common ground in the field, agnostic to theoretical approach.

Nine of these competencies cut across all forms of intervention (APA, 2015a), informing how systemically oriented clinicians approach and interact with survivors in any professional context. Notably, these competencies highlight contextual variables consistent with systems theory, including understanding "how trauma impacts a survivor, the family system (including parents and caregivers), community, and organizations" (APA, 2015a, p. 4). To be truly evidence-based, trauma treatment must be tailored in light of clients' (a) intersecting identities, cultural contexts, preferences, and values; as well as (b) developmental lifespan factors such as trauma frequency and duration, age(s) at which the trauma(s) occurred, and length of time since. Moreover, therapists should keep in mind the well-established links of toxic stress and ACEs with negative health outcomes, particularly among marginalized groups, as discussed in this chapter.

It is also critical to approach trauma work with an appreciation for nuance and flexibility, as "effective trauma treatment is inherently complex" (APA, 2015a, p. 8). This could include formulating the case from a systemic perspective (e.g., tracking person–environment interactions), recognizing family members' suffering and resilience, and considering both short- and longer-term outcomes. For example, a teenager experiencing familial abuse may run away from home and use substances to cope, resulting in short-term reprieve as well as additional vulnerabilities. Given the sense of helplessness inherent in traumatization, we must always take care to embody shared decision making and recognize and reinforce clients' strengths and growth. Other cross-cutting competencies address the critical importance of working collaboratively with other professionals or lay responders (more on this in Chapters 5 and 6 in this volume) and attending to the self of the therapist, including awareness of one's own history, values, and vulnerabilities (more in Chapter 7 in this volume). Especially given the dynamic nature of the trauma literature, practitioners should "critically evaluate and apply up-to-date available science on research-supported therapies and assessment strategies" (APA, 2015a, p. 5). One reason we do not attempt a comprehensive review of trauma science here, aside from space constraints, is because of how quickly the research is evolving in this area. We encourage practitioners to seek out recent publications and continuing education training regularly to stay abreast of the latest developments.

In addition to the aforementioned cross-cutting competencies, a number of domain-specific competencies (APA, 2015a) inform therapists' engagement with trauma-impacted couples and families. First, it is incumbent on practitioners to develop core scientific knowledge about trauma, including (a) the epidemiology of trauma exposure and outcomes; (b) interactions between psychological, social, and neurobiological factors; and (c) the contributions of historical, social, and cultural contexts. This chapter has offered a brief, foundational primer that readers can build from, and familiarity with these areas is critical in order to recognize and engage effectively with the diverse sequelae of trauma in clinical settings. Building on this, trauma-focused assessment goes well beyond asking about lifetime trauma histories and reactions in intake, but does include this as a starting point (more on this in Chapter 4 in this volume). We must gain experience and comfort adjusting assessment and psychotherapeutic processes when clients experience dissociation, avoidance, or other trauma reactions in session, rather than forging ahead out of a mistaken understanding that prioritizes treatment fidelity over responsiveness.

Developing and negotiating a strong alliance is the backdrop for engaging with traumatized clients, but is often challenging, as survivors have good reason to be guarded and slow to trust. In therapeutic work with multiple family members, we must hold in mind a complex web of relationships that comprise the systemic therapeutic alliance, which includes the therapist's alliance with each individual and how members perceive each other's relationship with the therapist (Cordukes et al., 2024; Friedlander & Escudero, 2022; Muntigl & Horvath, 2016). It is important to respect the survival-oriented wisdom embedded in clients' cautiousness and reactivity, while inviting authentic interactions that privilege each family member's agency and choice. Working through therapeutic ruptures toward repairing and strengthening the alliance is vital in order to decrease risk of dropout (Friedlander & Escudero, 2022). This necessitates that systemically oriented therapists cultivate empathy, honesty, respect, humility, courage, and patience, while addressing and using countertransference feelings that arise to deepen the treatment. We return to this discussion throughout the book and refer readers to Eubanks et al. (2023) for a more in-depth discussion.

Clinical attunement and pacing are imperative in order to engage trauma-impacted families in treatment effectively, and must be informed by consideration of the type(s) of trauma; potential comorbidities; clients' developmental levels, personality traits, strengths, resources, and preferences; and their recovery environment (e.g., families, communities; APA, 2015a). Rather than simply focusing on delivering an empirically supported protocol, becoming competent in trauma intervention necessitates going much deeper to familiarize ourselves with the key components and mechanisms of change in various therapeutic approaches (e.g., reducing avoidance, regulating trauma-related affects, increasing social connection, facilitating meaning-making; more on this in Chapter 3 in this volume). Considering the specific needs and goals of each particular couple or family, trauma-responsive treatment is an iterative process that involves clinical judgement, collaborative goal-setting, and interventions adapted to evolving needs, which change from moment to moment and session to session. There is growing evidence that therapeutic responsiveness often matters more than fidelity to one particular model (Watson & Wiseman, 2021), and this may be especially the case when working with trauma survivors, given the salience of relational factors in many forms of traumatization as discussed throughout this chapter, and the potential of the therapeutic context to serve as a healing relational experience.

Psychological intervention with trauma frequently requires collaboration with clients' families, the people in their social circles, and other systems of care (APA, 2015a). This goes well beyond the people in the therapy room to consider the systems they are embedded within and to collaborate with professionals across disciplines to facilitate continuity and convergence of care (more on this in Chapter 6 in this volume). Considering the challenges within mental health care systems, this also includes addressing and reducing the risk of iatrogenic harm that many survivors experience. For example, lack of shared decision-making can compound traumatization, leaving families feeling silenced, misunderstood, or overpowered. High-risk clinical situations (e.g., suicidality, domestic violence) can particularly set the stage for this. Power dynamics around race, gender, and other therapist identity characteristics are also salient, as are the ways that families' perception of mental health professionals is influenced by their historical and current experiences of marginalization and oppression, including sometimes within health care. While developing these competencies is an ongoing endeavor, they offer valuable guideposts orienting practitioners toward greater clinical sophistication in how we approach, conceptualize, and work with couples and families who have experienced trauma . . . moving beyond "treatment by manual."

SUMMARY AND KEY TAKEAWAYS

This chapter has grappled with the interplay of trauma and the family system, orienting readers beyond objective events to the subjective experience of what is unfolding for each person and the dynamic interplay between family members. Relational and family contexts are implicated in whether one's subjective experience is marked by chaos and helplessness, overwhelming emotion, utter aloneness, and a breakdown in ability to think—or alternatively, if the sense of threat is made more bearable through companionship and working together to try to survive and get better. Systemically oriented practitioners understand family and kinship networks as dynamic systems that are adapting to—and at times frozen by—toxic stress. Putting together the puzzle pieces of family trauma necessitates considering each family member's experiences, the interplay between their subjectivities, and potential spillover effects across subsystems and generations, as well as how the family system as a whole moves through potentially traumatic situations. Stolorow (2007) aptly described such complexity in the parent–child relationship, in particular:

> Trauma is constituted in an intersubjective context in which severe emotional pain cannot find a relational home in which it can be held. In such a context, painful affect states become unendurable—that is, traumatic. . . . It is the absence of adequate attunement and responsiveness to the child's painful emotional reactions that renders them unendurable and thus a source of traumatic states and psychopathology. (p. 10)

How clinicians answer the question "What is trauma?" significantly informs how they approach, understand, and engage with individuals, couples, and families. Systemically oriented therapists consider potentially traumatic stressors experienced by each family member, as well as the transmission of traumatization via secondary stress or intergenerational processes. We consider, too, the system's cumulative trauma burden, track the energy expended just to survive, and seek to understand how each family member is experiencing, narrating, and coping with what has happened. Given the unspeakability and unformulated nature of trauma, we listen for what is said and what is not said. We listen to how clients talk about their experiences, particularly noting discrepancies between content and affect. We listen for and honor core schemas (e.g., I am bad, the world is unsafe) and stabilizing psychological defenses (e.g., denial, dissociation) that helped people survive horrific situations but get in the way of living and flourishing. We also listen for and reinforce the strengths embedded within the family that can help facilitate resilience and adaptation. We heed the story we are living out together in treatment, noting relational dynamics and transferences unfolding in the room. And we seek to cultivate a space within therapy where severe emotional pain can be held, approached, talked and felt about, and ultimately find a home.

In beginning to comprehend what trauma feels like subjectively, we are already well on our way to identifying potential intervention points to ameliorate these conditions. To put it simply, each of the four dimensions discussed in this chapter that coalesce in the experience of traumatization represent key areas to explore as part of resilience, healing, and growth. We summarize them here as a preview for the coming chapters:

- Where there is helplessness and lack of safety, clinicians can foster family members' sense of personal and collective agency, power (e.g., realistic sense of control and predictability), and physical, emotional, and existential safety, including through approaching them as collaborators—not victims—and maintaining a stance of curiosity and cultural humility.
- Noticing intense and unregulated affects, we can support family members in approaching, naming, experiencing, and processing difficult emotion (e.g., anger, shame, fear) in titrated ways through developing greater emotion regulation capacity (avoiding cutoff/dissociation and reactivity/flooding) and upregulating vitalizing affects (e.g., enjoyment, humor), including through modeling and facilitating coregulation.
- Where members of a couple or family are detached from or enmeshed with each other, therapeutic interventions can cultivate attunement to each other's needs for both attachment and differentiation, including tracking where members have felt shut out, shut down, or intruded on, and orchestrating relational interactions in which members can soften their defenses in order to be more deeply seen and known, thus strengthening the family attachment network.
- Recognizing the ways that trauma may be unspeakable in a family, we can help members talk about, symbolize, and metabolize traumatic experiences (e.g., through words, action, art, play), including through respecting the dignity and importance of each person's perspectives while working toward constructing healing narratives.

While such clinical work can be challenging and fraught with difficulty, it has the potential to change the trajectory of a family's life cycle and support the intergenerational transmission of strengths and resilience. To help bring these foundational concepts to life, the next chapter offers a primer of dyadic and family-based approaches to treating trauma.

3 DYADIC AND FAMILY-BASED APPROACHES FOR TREATING TRAUMA

Integrating Multiple Frameworks as Part of Evidence-Based Systemic Practice

We presume it is experience, not education, that changes families.

—D. V. KEITH & C. A. WHITAKER (1982, P. 43)

The referral note on Malik's psychiatric evaluation stated "complex symptom presentation, rule out psychosis." Malik, a 6-year-old Afro-Dominican boy, lived with his mother, Charise, at an undisclosed shelter system location. Malik's mother (known to the clinic due to her own chronic mental health challenges) kept bringing her son to the emergency room after he was reportedly "tripped by demons." In each case, the boy sustained minor abrasions due to falling and tearfully stated that the devil was making him do "bad things." Malik received speech therapy due to a significant impediment, but was otherwise functioning well in the classroom, per his teacher. He engaged well with his peers and was responsive to redirection, though school staff did note the presence of devils/demons in his art and stories.

The psychiatric resident working with Charise prescribed antipsychotics to address what was presumed to be schizophrenia, but concluded that

---

This chapter contains a composite case vignette drawn from multiple clients and fictitious aspects. Details have been substantively changed to protect confidentiality.

https://doi.org/10.1037/0000487-004
Systemic Treatment of Trauma-Impacted Families: A Clinician's Guide to Assessment, Formulation, and Intervention, by S. A. Riggs and L. E. Captari

psychotherapy was unlikely to be helpful, given the chronicity of her symptoms and her "lack of engagement in treatment." Upon meeting with Malik and Charise for the boy's intake, you notice how this mother seems to oscillate between affection that verged on intrusive (e.g., "Little angel . . . come give mommy a hug.") and punitive redirection in cases of fairly normative misbehavior, such as when he begins fidgeting (e.g., "You sit still, Malik . . . don't you be listening to the devil!"). The boy appears quite anxious, constantly monitoring his mother's mood and trying hard to be "good."

When you inquire about developmental and family history, Charise proudly declares that her son saved her life, recounting that when the boy's father put his hands on her "once again" when Malik was a toddler, "everything became clear, and I knew I had to get out." She chokes up, taking a deep breath to compose herself. "I wanna make a family better than what I had," Charise continues, describing being raised in a family marked by neglect and abuse. There was no mention in Charise's chart of this history of complex trauma, including losing her own mother when she was young and experiencing domestic violence. You wonder if anyone asked her about her relational history, or perhaps the label of schizophrenia foreclosed providers' case formulation, a tragically common phenomenon among clients who hold minoritized racial identities and have less social power (Jegarl et al., 2023).

Citing her religion as a source of guidance, Charise describes how they are part of a new family now. "Isn't that right, Malik? We follow the way of God. Jesus and his angels protect us." She continues on to complain about Malik's misbehavior, "But I'm at my wits end. Some days, he's such a good boy. But most of the time, he won't listen. He won't sit still. He won't get up in the morning. And when he walks, he shuffles his feet." With each critique, you watch Malik physically shrink. He slides down in his seat and onto the floor, crawling under the couch in your office. If all behavior is communication, Malik has just communicated so much. (Unfortunately, no classes covered what to do when a client crawls under the furniture!)

In a busy and underresourced public clinic, no trauma-focused assessment had been conducted to distinguish between this mother's symptoms arising from a trauma-related disorder versus those stemming from a psychotic disorder. Now, her son is being approached similarly. Thus, you question your vastly different formulation: You see a woman who seems to be contending with complex posttraumatic stress disorder (CPTSD) in combination with a psychotic process and ineffective parenting skills. You see a boy who is enmeshed with his mother's experience . . . and buckling under the pressure of "saving her life." Every action he takes seemed to have power to fuel hope about creating a different . . . better . . . perfect family, or power to shatter his mother's dreams. That is a lot of weight for a 6-year-old to carry!

The starting point for understanding symptoms can lead to very different interventions. If not considered within this family's worldview, Malik's "being tripped by demons" could easily be misunderstood as purely delusional and treated as such. Yet, this boy's attribution of losing his footing is consistent with his mother's language—and the family's spirituality—around angels and devils as metaphorically on his shoulder.

Such cases can provoke intense countertransference reactions of empathy, helplessness, and frustration, out of which practitioners may unconsciously compensate by focusing on fidelity to a particular treatment protocol. Whether through exposure in graduate school, independent reading, or attending workshops and trainings, most therapists are familiar with a handful of trauma treatments (Cook et al., 2017) that focus on individual symptoms with less attention to underlying relational patterns and contextual influences. Most family therapy approaches, in contrast, are oriented to dynamic processes of interpersonal interaction, but may not fully attend to the individual consequences of traumatization. In working with families like Charise and Malik, the blind spots of both individual trauma treatments and traditional family therapy can limit potential for healing (Figley & Kiser, 2013).

The current chapter interweaves trauma science and systemic paradigms to illuminate how drawing from both are critical in order to more fully meet the needs of families who have experienced trauma. Specifically, "the ability to move up and down the family system, to move back and forth between the two visions" enables clinicians to treat family dysfunction and also facilitate both individual and family recovery from trauma (Silvestre & Tarquinio, 2022, p. 5). How might this objective be actualized in clinical practice? Rather than getting caught up in allegiance to a particular therapy acronym, one important step is to gain clarity about what does—and does not—constitute evidence-based systemic practice for the treatment of trauma, including underlying common factors. Considering model-specific contributions to therapeutic change as well, we take readers on a tour of the broad array of dyadic and family approaches to address the sequelae of trauma. We also discuss ways to weave in a systemic focus when working with individual clients. Taken together, these pages aim to stoke your clinical imagination and bring into focus new possibilities for integrating multiple frameworks to enrich your practice.

WHAT CONSTITUTES "EFFECTIVE" TRAUMA TREATMENT?

The medical model that underlies most mental health care and training focuses on first-order change by reducing symptom distress, rather than aiming at second-order change by intervening "upstream" to address and alter relational dynamics and systemic patterns that activate or exacerbate distress (Axberg & Petitt, 2023; Wampler et al., 2020). An unfortunate consequence of this is evident in the limited scope of current clinical practice guidelines for the treatment of posttraumatic stress disorder (PTSD), which focus on individual treatment and are based mainly on research evidence with adults (American Psychological Association [APA], 2017a). This does not mean that dyadic and family approaches do not work, but rather, that research on these modalities to treat trauma is often sidelined and lags behind investigation of individual approaches due to multiple, interrelated factors. Yet, many practice guidelines obscure the growing research and theory about couple and family interventions for trauma and trauma-related disorders (for reviews, see Carr, 2018, 2025; Monson & Fredman, 2021; Suomi et al., 2019).

The available evidence for systems-oriented psychotherapy models is significantly shaped by—and some would argue, confounded by—funders' and researchers' priorities, research design constraints, and the types of studies perceived to constitute "evidence" (APA, 2024). Funders and researchers are often less interested in dyadic and family-level interventions, perhaps because these approaches tend to be oriented beyond a single identified patient/diagnosis and thus are less conforming to the traditional medical model. In addition, systems-oriented therapies are more difficult to manualize (as in-session responsiveness to processes and patterns in the family system is paramount to effectiveness), require additional training and supervision, and are more complex to study due to engaging multiple family members at various developmental stages. Despite this, it is encouraging to see increasing attention to family-centered care as part of cultural responsiveness (Jain et al., 2019; Kilmer et al., 2010).

Another barrier to couple and family intervention research has been bias toward certain types of evidence at the exclusion of others. While tightly controlled designs (e.g., randomized controlled trials [RCTs]) have high internal validity and are important to help establish efficacy, such studies have less external validity and generalizability to real-world clinical settings.[1] RCT findings of trauma treatment do not neatly translate into routine practice, where clients and families present with complex histories, comorbid diagnoses, and distinct cultural backgrounds, and therapists frequently draw from multiple treatment approaches as part of clinical responsiveness

[1] Internal validity tackles the question, "Is the effect real?" It captures the extent to which a study can show that changes in a client's PTSD symptoms, for example, are attributable to a particular treatment. By contrast, external validity takes up the question "Does it apply elsewhere (i.e., outside of a tightly controlled experimental setting)?" It assesses the extent to which study findings can be generalized to routine practice, including other types of clients, treatment settings, and so forth.

to families' needs (Fernández-Álvarez et al., 2016). Outcomes of interest to researchers also vary from those that matter to clients. For example, while most clinical research tracks symptom change, clients also care about more holistic outcomes—the ability to create healthy relationships, navigate difficult emotions more effectively, and build a meaningful life. Considering all this, the APA Presidential Task Force on Evidence-Based Practice (2006) emphasized the need for "multiple streams of research evidence" (p. 273), including practice-based research utilizing multiple methods to evaluate the practical effectiveness of dyadic and family therapies. This includes case studies, clinical observation, process-outcome research, single-case experimental designs, and qualitative and mixed-method designs. Such studies in naturalistic community settings are critical to understanding what is effective and for whom (Stratton, 2016).

Why does all this research-y stuff matter for systemically oriented clinicians? One central reason is that it informs the reference points we draw from in the provision of trauma-focused treatment and how we understand evidence-based practice (EBP), which ultimately shapes the care available to families. EBP is frequently misconstrued as fidelity to a particular model or protocol that has been empirically supported by multiple RCTs (La Roche & Christopher, 2009). But an empirically supported treatment (EST) is not the same as EBP. Many of us were taught that adhering to a particular treatment model is important . . . because it has been shown to work, right? Actually, "therapist adherence to an EST is often unrelated to patient outcome" and "perseverative adherence when facing disruptive clinical process can relate to worse outcomes" (Constantino et al., 2020, p. 405). As APA (2021) delineates, EBP is a broader framework that involves a three-legged stool, integrating (a) the best available research evidence; alongside (b) clinical competence and expertise; and (c) responsiveness to each family's culture, values, and preferences. Therapists who approach trauma treatment by uncritically applying a single model are relying on a one-legged stool, which is wobbly indeed! Attention to all three aforementioned areas is necessary in order to promote change at a systemic level, which is precisely what this book intends to facilitate through helping readers develop a metatheoretical systemic perspective of trauma healing rooted in the application of common factors.

WEAVING THE FABRIC OF SYSTEMIC CHANGE: UNDERLYING COMMON FACTORS

Noting how clinicians' attunement, responsiveness, and flexibility are central to therapeutic change, scholars have argued for "a new therapy for each patient" (Norcross & Wampold, 2018, p. 1889), and we extend this notion to argue for a new therapy for each family. In contrast with the medical model's individual focus, systemic interventions are "socially situated healing practice[s]" (Wampold & Imel, 2015, p. 37), comprising not only the therapist–client relationship but also interactions among family members. Systemically oriented psychotherapy involves drawing from one or more intervention models and creating therapeutic conditions for systemic change, based on the well-developed literature on common factors. Much of what accounts for psychotherapeutic change is not specific to one model; for example, building a strong alliance, repairing ruptures, instilling hope, facilitating interpersonal learning, and supporting clients in taking new actions (Cuijpers et al., 2019; Wampold & Imel, 2015). In addition, common factors recognize "the client as the main 'hero' of the therapy, rather than the model or therapist," given that client motivation, willingness to take risks, and "everything that happens in the client's life during treatment" are hugely impactful in facilitating change (Verbnik & Možina, 2021, p. 155). Zooming out to a systemic perspective, the couple or family is the main "hero"; thus, interventions are fundamentally focused on facilitating healing relational experiences within the family and one's broader relational life (S. D. Davis & Hsieh, 2019).

Within systemic treatment approaches, a number of unique common factors and mechanisms of change have been identified, which we summarize here as relevant to trauma treatment (for reviews, see D'Aniello & Fife, 2020; Lebow, 2014; López-Zerón & Blow, 2017; Sprenkle et al., 2013; Verbnik & Možina, 2021). Foremost among these, couple and family therapists intervene to create change in trauma-impacted families via fundamentally relational means, including through an expanded therapeutic alliance and expanded direct treatment system (D'Aniello & Fife, 2020). Relational common factors may be embodied in a variety of ways, including identifying and working to address how trauma is interwoven in clients' relational patterns and family processes; helping members identify their survival-oriented coping responses, while also acknowledging negative effects on couple and family interactions; and making implicit family rules, roles, and norms explicit in order to increase members' sense of awareness and freedom in relating to each other (Sprenkle et al., 2013). As part of activating change in particular areas of the family and its subsystems, clinicians often move between individual, couple, and family session formats (Lebow, 2014). One way these strategies catalyze change is through increasing family members' engagement in treatment, and with each other, thereby decreasing risk of dropout and facilitating access to healing relational interactions.

Considering the extreme, unbearable feelings inherent in traumatization, systemic intervention involves attention to—and transformation of—family members' emotions, including developing increased capacities for emotional awareness, adaptive expression, and both self-regulation and coregulation (D'Aniello & Fife, 2020; S. D. Davis & Hsieh, 2019). Emotion-related common factors include increasing family members' emotional awareness and ability to recognize trauma-related reactivity (e.g., fight, flight, freeze, fawn) in order to utilize coregulation more effectively when trauma triggers occur. This may include giving language to and processing trauma-related affects (e.g., shame, guilt, terror, rage, etc.) within safe relational contexts, as well as nonverbal forms of emotional experiencing and expression (Sprenkle et al., 2013). To promote the full range of emotional experience, systemic interventions likewise target the upregulation of positive emotion and reinforce families' inherent strengths, such as humor and creativity (Lebow, 2014; Walsh, 2012b).

Trauma-informed couple and family interventions also enact change through common factors focused on reshaping interaction patterns. This involves helping members move beyond rigid and reactive (often unconscious) ways of coping and relating that perpetuate trauma-related avoidance, denial, projection, detouring, and so forth, which stymy the family's ability to grow, change, and heal. Systemic therapists offer process-oriented feedback in order to interrupt these trauma-related patterns and provide guidance in new ways of relating (Anker et al., 2009; Verbnik & Možina, 2021). Barriers and roadblocks to connection are examined compassionately, with attention to developing more adaptive ways to express oneself and one's needs. Ultimately, an underlying goal is to support earned security and emotional bonding in the family attachment network (e.g., family relationships as a safe haven), as well as strengthening family norms and patterns that create a sense of predictability and order (Lebow, 2014). A related but distinct aim involves helping members learn to use the family system as a secure base, which can encourage exploration, personal agency, and differentiation of self (Mones & Schwartz, 2007).

Given how trauma can disrupt and potentially shatter a family's sense of coherence, systemic interventions also attend to members' ways of thinking about and understanding adversity and tragedy, integrating the family's cultural/spiritual resources as part of finding a way forward in a forever-altered world. Common factors around cognition and meaning include helping families gain new perspectives through reframing and expanding on implicit beliefs, facilitating new narratives around trauma, and developing increased ability to hold complexity, ambiguity, and multiple perspectives in relating to each other (D'Aniello & Fife, 2020). For example, systemic therapists "offer reframes, interpretations, practical information, explanations, or justifications" (Verbnik & Možina, 2021, p. 157), as well as facilitating the more emergent process of each family's meaning-making (Walsh, 2016; see also López-Zerón & Blow, 2017).

In addition to these areas, the person of the therapist (see Chapter 7 in this volume) plays a vital role in the effectiveness of systemic interventions, as captured in Blow et al.'s (2007) provocative question, "Is who delivers the treatment more important than the treatment itself?" (p. 298). In fact, therapist factors may be even more influential in facilitating change within systemic treatment, given that working with multiple family members necessitates greater directiveness, flexibility, collaboration, and assertiveness, to name a few areas (Blow & Karam, 2017). This aligns with the EBP framework, which emphasizes the importance of practitioners gaining clinical experience and developing expertise in the nuances of systemic intervention, not simply following a manual (Karam et al., 2015). To that end, we now offer a tour of the manifold ways that systemic treatment with trauma-impacted families might be embodied.

HOW TO USE THIS CHAPTER TO ENRICH YOUR PRACTICE

Treatment models "are the vehicle through which the common as well as specific factors operate" (Sprenkle & Blow, 2004, p. 151). Thus, we have crafted the coming sections to serve as an accessible reference you can return to often as you consider the specifics of a case and your treatment context. Because whole volumes already exist detailing the many available approaches, our focus here is on increasing readers' familiarity with the extensive options at your disposal so that you can weave together aspects of multiple approaches to meet the needs of each client, couple, and/or family. In line with cocreating a new therapy for each client and family, this chapter does not attempt to provide concrete specifics about how to intervene in the particularities of a case. Such an exposition would inevitably be surface-level and reductionistic, as each family holds unique complexity that only the therapist in the room (and possibly their supervisor) would fully understand. Rather, we aim to stoke your clinical imagination so that you can approach sessions from a metatheoretical systemic perspective, utilizing the contributions of multiple clinical frameworks to intervene creatively and flexibly in order to embody true EBP.

To capture the zeitgeist of this invitation, imagine visiting an art gallery and pausing to take in a particularly intricate, multilayered, and sizeable piece of art. Perhaps the canvas spans multiple floors, and each floor offers a unique angle to notice distinct aspects of the painting. Within this metaphor, each of the next three sections could be understood as its own floor of the gallery, offering unique vantage points that enrich trauma-informed systemic formulation and intervention. First, we discuss innovative models specifically developed to involve family members in the treatment of trauma. Next, we explore established couple/family treatment approaches that are well-suited to addressing trauma impacts. Finally, we explicate how established individual approaches for trauma can be enriched through a systemic formulation. We have included these particular therapeutic models based on an extensive review of the literature as well as consultation with other experts in the field. Given the constantly evolving research in these areas and space constraints here, we also refer readers to comprehensive databases such as the National Child Traumatic Stress Network (https://www.nctsn.org/interventions) and the Title IV-E Prevention Services Clearinghouse (https://preventionservices.acf.hhs.gov).

Working with trauma-impacted families can leave clinicians feeling lost—as if they can't see the forest for the trees! As human beings in relationship with our clients, our own nervous systems can get activated in ways that reinforce a sense of rigidity and reductionistic thinking. To counter this and hold space for greater complexity, it is vital to zoom out beyond questions like "What is the right treatment for this presenting concern?" and critically reflect from a broader systemic perspective. We bring the forest (i.e., the system!) into focus by instead considering: "What treatment approaches do the current evidence base suggest might meet the needs of this couple or family at this moment, given their history, relationships, cultural context, preferences, goals, and hopes?" How practitioners answer this question sometimes changes across time within a case, necessitating metatheoretical fluency and skill. Thus, this chapter may orient you to—and pique your interest in—specific areas for ongoing training and supervision.

SYSTEMICALLY FOCUSED TRAUMA TREATMENT MODELS

On the first floor of our gallery tour, we explore therapeutic approaches to treating trauma that utilize a systemic formulation and involve multiple family members in session. You may find the application of one or more of these approaches salient when a couple or family's presenting problems include reference to one or more traumatic experiences or there is evidence of a complex trauma history, and multiple members are willing to engage as part of treatment.

After working for many years with families of military veterans and those exposed to other traumatic events, Figley (1989) published *Helping Traumatized Families*. Arguing that families and supportive others can act as an "antidote" to PTSD and should be included in treatment, Figley developed a five-phase family empowerment model, which focuses on rebuilding safety and regulatory structure, developing new rules and communication skills, and enhancing within-family support. Updated in 2013 (Figley & Kiser, 2013), the five phases of this intervention include (a) joining the family, (b) understanding and framing the family's trauma response, (c) building effective coping, (d) sharing and healing (based in narrative therapy), and (e) moving forward. Many subsequently developed models for family trauma work build on these core principles.

More recently, Integrated Family and Systems Treatment (I-FAST; Grove et al., 2020) offers a meta-level framework that combines systemic principles with attention to strengths. In contrast with particular steps (e.g., exposure paradigms, constructing a trauma narrative), I-FAST prioritizes responsiveness to what members want to focus on. Trust in the family system is paramount, with attention to tracking and engaging "beliefs regarding why symptoms occur and what should be done to help" (Grove et al., 2020, p. 54). This empowers the family and makes use of implicit processing: "Even if trauma symptoms are not selected as a focus, they can still be resolved by resolving the problems the client is motivated to focus on" (Grove et al., 2020, p. 50). I-FAST orients clinicians to understanding how the trauma is "framed" by family members, including associated beliefs and meanings, such as how members view the identified client (e.g., as defiant, traumatized), the problem (e.g., as biology, behavior, or both), and possible solutions (e.g., punishment, communication). Where frames are constrictive and distress-inducing, therapists engage families in reframing and expanding narratives, seeing problems as coconstructed and members as capable of change. I-FAST also focuses on elucidating and disrupting interaction patterns that are not working, with therapists highlighting interactional exceptions to support awareness and ownership. I-FAST is designed to integrate "interventions from any treatment approach or ethnic healing practice" when relevant and helpful (Grove et al., 2020, p. 6). While originally developed for intensive in-home treatment, efficacy and effectiveness studies in outpatient settings have also shown its utility in addressing child mental health, family functioning, and intergenerational trauma (M. Y. Lee et al., 2009, 2013, 2016).

Attachment-based family therapy (ABFT; Diamond et al., 2021) specifically targets shortcomings in a family's ability to provide a safe haven and secure base, which may underly or exacerbate traumatic stress, depression, and suicidal ideation among children and youth. By uncovering attachment ruptures that trigger family conflict, ABFT supports families in restoring—or developing for the first time—relationships of trust, openness, and collaboration. Treatment is process-oriented and involves a combination of family, child/adolescent, and parent/caregiver sessions. In line with a systemic formulation, sessions with the caregiver or parental subsystem explore how intergenerational legacies of neglect, abuse, and misattunement inform their emotional bond and approach to parenting, with the goal of increasing emotional awareness and empathy. In tandem, individual sessions with children focus on identifying and articulating experiences of feeling ignored, shut down, and/or misunderstood by caregivers that make it difficult to turn to them for support. Subsequently, conjoint family sessions focus on "accessing, connecting to, differentiating between, and expressing adaptive and often vulnerable emotions" (Diamond et al., 2021, p. 288). Changing the family emotional climate through corrective attachment experiences can help establish a new foundation for family members in communicating about their needs, coregulating difficult emotions, effectively problem solving, and accessing emotional support. Multiple efficacy studies, as well as process and effectiveness research, support the use of ABFT to treat adolescent depression and suicidal ideation as well as to increase parent–child attachment security (Diamond et al., 2016, 2021).

Trust-based relational intervention (TBRI; Purvis et al., 2013) similarly draws from attachment and affective neuroscience, and is designed specifically to address the needs of children who have experienced developmental and complex trauma. This flexible framework is frequently used with foster and adopted children in individual, dyadic, and family modalities as well as broader systems (e.g., school, residential milieu). TBRI delineates three core principles of treatment. First, empowerment involves "creating an environment that fosters felt safety" (Purvis et al., 2013, p. 363), recognizing that being safe and feeling safe are not the same. Therapeutic attention is given to creating predictability, navigating transitions, considering sensory needs, and supporting nutrition, rest, and physical activity. Second, connecting focuses on increasing caregivers' observational awareness of children's nonverbal signs of stress and anxiety, monitoring their own emotional state, and engaging the child in attuned, responsive, and playful ways. TBRI implements aspects of Theraplay, an attachment-focused parent–child approach (Tucker & Smith-Adcock, 2017). The final principle of correcting emphasizes the cultivation of children's self-regulation and social competence, rather than merely compliance. In the face of challenging behaviors, caregivers are taught to respond immediately, directly, and in a measured manner, offer a behavioral alternative, and focus on the behavior, not the child. TBRI has been shown to be effective in improving family functioning and reducing both child symptomology and parent stress when incorporated in trauma-focused therapy (Howard et al., 2014; Nielsen, 2014) and other community settings (Misevičė et al., 2024; Stephenson & Yost, 2023).

The attachment, regulation, and competency (ARC) framework (Blaustein & Kinniburgh, 2018) focuses therapeutic intervention on three key components that are centrally impacted by chronic exposure to traumatizing developmental environments. Synthesizing research on normative child development with trauma psychology, ARC "identifies important childhood skills and competencies which are routinely shown to be negatively affected by traumatic stress and by attachment disruptions, and which—when addressed—predict resilient outcome" (Attachment, Regulation and Competency, 2024, n.p.). First and foundationally, attachment interventions address the child's caregiving system, broadly defined, in order to support the development of earned security. Thus, treatment may involve the biological and/or adoptive parents, extended family, and residential or school personnel. Key targets in this domain include helping caregivers recognize and regulate their own emotional experience, attune to the child's emotional needs, and respond in a consistent and appropriate manner. Building on this, the second domain supports children and youth in developing self-regulation, including identifying, modulating, and expressing emotion effectively. Third, ARC focuses on reactivating stalled developmental processes to foster competency. Children in "survival mode" have not had the luxury of learning skills that are part of normative development, including areas like effective problem solving and related executive functions, as well as cultivating identity and self-coherence. ARC's three domains work in tandem to address upstream factors that fuel posttraumatic outcomes. Growing evidence suggests ARC is effective for diverse symptom presentations and can be applied in working with children, parents, and caregivers as well as broader systems-level settings (e.g., therapeutic milieus, teachers; Bailey et al., 2024; Bartlett et al., 2018; Fehrenbach et al., 2022).

The neurosequential model of therapeutics (NMT; Perry, 2019) offers an assessment and treatment planning approach that draws from neuroscience and developmental psychology to explicate the brain-level impacts of pervasive and chronic trauma. Assessment data is used to create a heuristic "brain map" for the client, tracing brain areas/networks that are likely underdeveloped, which offers invaluable information about where to intervene first in order to support the normal sequence of neurological development (Perry, 2019). Foundationally, movement and somatic approaches are used to support sensory integration functions of the brainstem. Then, interventions targeting limbic involvement are implemented, including engaging parents/caregivers in providing a sense of safety and security and facilitating emotion coregulation. Building on this, relational strategies that support social and emotional skills are appropriate, and finally, insight/cognitive talk therapies that necessitate cortical activation. NMT prioritizes the "therapeutic web" of caregivers, adults, and peers, noting that "the quality and permanence of this relational milieu is one of the most vital elements to successful treatment outcomes" (Perry, 2019, p. 147). Exploring caregivers' internal and external resources and demands offers critical information about where to start, particularly in situations of intergenerational trauma. Rather than framing families as "resistant," NMT orients clinicians to what might be happening at a brain level, aligning therapy with the need for sequential mastery of functions. Distinct from treatment approaches that focus on insight, this often begins with "rhythmic, repetitive, and somatosensory" interventions (Perry, 2019, p. 144) like play, sand tray, art, and body-based practices (e.g., massage, yoga). Most cultures and religious groups have embedded healing activities involving music, rhythm, movement, and touch, so these are valuable options in treatment planning. Practitioners can apply NMT concepts by listening for, asking about, and reinforcing such practices within a family culture, as well as attending to neurodevelopment when selecting interventions. NMT is a promising clinical innovation with a growing empirical base (Evans et al., 2024; Johannessen et al., 2024; K. White et al., 2023).

Trauma systems therapy (TST; Saxe et al., 2015) offers a roadmap for comprehensive and intensive intervention with traumatized children and families, recognizing the severe and chronic problems embedded in their environments. Inspired by Bronfenbrenner's (1979) ecological systems theory, TST is designed to treat the trauma system, including both traumatized individuals whose symptomology represents their best attempt to cope and survive, and the environmental context (e.g., family, neighborhood, school, systems of care) that is struggling to help the child regulate their emotions and behavior (Saxe et al., 2015). TST addresses the painful reality that many families fall through the cracks of the systems intended to support them. "The organization of services . . . is the linchpin of effective treatment . . . it is not just services in isolation but the delivery system as a whole, that dictates the outcome of treatment" (U.S. Department of Health and Human Services, 1999). Thus, this therapeutic model directly addresses social ecology, including meeting with a client individually and as a family, as well as working with parents or other caregivers, and the school. TST also attends to the lack of continuity and "splintering" of care that frequently occurs in complex cases, where families may be receiving many different services in the absence of a systemic understanding. TST argues for the necessity of a multidisciplinary treatment team, as well as careful consideration of larger organizational dynamics and the overarching service system. Treatment is phase-based, focusing on establishing safety, then regulation, and finally building on a family's strengths and dreams. The developers employed the mantra "whatever it is and whatever it takes" to capture their flexible framing of treatment.

TST has been shown to be effective in reducing children's hospitalization rates and the need for crisis stabilization services across time through working upstream to stabilize family and community social environments (Ellis et al., 2012; Saxe et al., 2005) and has recently been applied to working with refugee families (Kaplin et al., 2019).

Family centered treatment (FCT; Painter & Smith, 2020) is a home-based intervention framework aimed at reducing out-of-home placements for youth involved in the juvenile justice system. FCT is rooted in eco-structural family therapy (Aponte, 1994; Lindblad-Goldberg et al., 1998; Minuchin & Fishman, 1981), orienting clinicians to the functions of behaviors, with the goal of addressing and restructuring systems-level patterns. This approach also draws heavily from emotionally focused couple therapy with trauma survivors (S. M. Johnson, 2002), emphasizing family members' emotional awareness, adaptive expressiveness, and regulation in support of strengthening attachment bonds. FCT moves beyond a focus on symptom reduction to assess and address unhealthy family interaction patterns that may contribute to individual symptoms and family dysfunction (National Child Traumatic Stress Network, 2019). The model outlines four phases. As part of joining and assessment, FCT prioritizes timely referral response (within a matter of days) to build rapport and instill hope. The therapist collaborates with the family to evaluate the sequelae of trauma and its impact on family functioning. Then, the restructuring phase helps the family recognize repetitive patterns of relating, often through enactments. Building on this, the valuing change phase supports the family in noticing and appreciating new behaviors and cultivating pride and mastery. Amid crisis, families are often willing to "do anything to make it better," so this stage helps support motivation and second-order change as the family moves out of crisis mode. Finally, generalization focuses on reinforcing family-level changes and internalizing gains made. The FCT model has been implemented in many states as part of juvenile court diversion programs, with evidence of improved child mental health and family functioning and decreased legal involvement (Bright et al., 2018; Sullivan & Bennear, 2021; Sullivan et al., 2012).

Developed specifically for multitraumatized and socially marginalized youth, integrative treatment of complex trauma (ITCT; Briere & Lanktree, 2013) offers a multicomponent approach that draws from attachment science, play therapy, skill development (e.g., mindfulness, distress tolerance, affect regulation), titrated exposure principles, and cognitive processing. Treatment formulation and modification are informed by a detailed assessment every few months. The model emphasizes the importance of catalyzing positive processes, such as identity formation, relational self-efficacy, and adaptive family interactions. ITCT includes both a child and adolescent format that outlines individual, family, and group intervention points applicable to diverse treatment settings, ranging from outpatient and in-home to inpatient and residential. While acknowledging that many within this population are separated from families of origin, ITCT includes caregivers whenever possible in order to provide psychoeducation and support about key factors underpinning difficult behaviors and to increase adaptive parenting skills. This may include foster parents, extended family, and other caregivers. Furthermore, ITCT recognizes that caregivers' untreated mental health problems have a spillover effect that can negatively impact children's developmental trajectories; as such, therapy intervenes with the caregiver subsystem where there are psychological vulnerabilities and also addresses relational dynamics rooted in traumatization. Research suggests that ITCT is suitable for diverse diagnoses, ranging from depression to PTSD, as well as other trauma-related symptoms like dissociation, self-injury, and problematic substance use (Lanktree et al., 2012).

Our discussion would be incomplete without also considering proactive efforts to promote posttraumatic adaptation. The child and family traumatic stress intervention (Berkowitz et al., 2011) is one such example of a prevention-focused paradigm, offering brief support following a potentially traumatic event for a child or recent disclosure of abuse. This approach rotates between family sessions and individual sessions with the child(ren) and caregiver(s). The child and family traumatic stress intervention targets two key risk factors for PTSD: (a) lack of support and (b) ineffective coping, and has been shown to decrease traumatic stress symptoms among children and parents (H. Hahn et al., 2019; Stover et al., 2022). Risk reduction through family therapy (RRFT; Danielson et al., 2019) is a similar approach, concurrently addressing mental health and substance use risks among trauma-exposed adolescents. RRFT integrates the contributions of several individual treatments (trauma-focused cognitive behavioral therapy [TF-CBT], dialectical behavior therapy, motivational interviewing, contingency management) within the larger focus of multisystemic therapy (Henggeler et al., 2009), engaging youth and their caregivers in proactively addressing risk factors and promoting resiliency following trauma exposure. Research has shown RRFT to be effective in supporting adolescents who have experienced interpersonal violence (e.g., physical abuse, witnessing violence; Danielson et al., 2012, 2020; A. M. Hahn et al., 2020).

COUPLE AND FAMILY APPROACHES ADAPTED FOR TRAUMA TREATMENT

Moving to the next floor of the gallery, we now turn our attention to therapeutic approaches developed for working with dyads (e.g., couple, parent–child) or entire families that have been adapted for addressing the broad ramifications of trauma. This is especially fortunate because some families, like some individuals, may not disclose histories of trauma until later in treatment when trust and safety are well-established. When trauma histories are embedded in a family's relational and intergenerational milieu, systemically oriented practitioners may find it helpful to incorporate one or more such frameworks into treatment.

Child–parent psychotherapy (CPP; Lieberman et al., 2020) is a relationship-based dyadic approach for infants, toddlers, and very young children (ages 0 to 6) who are struggling with attachment or behavioral problems, have been exposed to early life trauma (e.g., domestic violence, death of a parent), or whose mothers are experiencing perinatal mental health challenges. CPP integrates psychodynamic, developmental, social learning, and cognitive behavioral frameworks, and builds on Fraiberg et al.'s (1975) work to address intergenerational trauma by exploring "ghosts in the nursery." CPP also attends to "angels in the nursery" (Lieberman et al., 2005) by helping parents access internal relational resources through reflecting on benevolent relational experiences in their own development. In CPP, strengthening attachment security is the primary mutative mechanism—"the vehicle for improving the child's emotional, cognitive, and social functioning" (Lieberman et al., 2006, p. 914). Using a systemic formulation, considerable attention is paid to the mother's own mental health and developmental history, including individual sessions to allow for deeper work. Key components include establishing safety and playfulness; increasing mothers' attunement, responsiveness, and mentalization; supporting the child's sensorimotor systems and biological rhythms; regulating trauma-related affects in the dyad; expanding on maladaptive interaction patterns; and constructing an age-appropriate trauma narrative. CPP offers the opportunity to intervene preventatively (Cicchetti et al., 2006; Toth et al., 2015), rather than waiting for child symptomology to develop. Research has supported the effectiveness of CPP, even in situations of multiple, overlapping traumas (Ghosh Ippen et al., 2011). In addition to initial changes in attachment and symptom reduction, there is evidence of positive spillover effects beyond the dyad, including stronger peer relationships among children and greater couple satisfaction among mothers (Guild et al., 2017; Peltz et al., 2015).

Parent–child interaction therapy (PCIT; Eyberg, 1988; Funderburk & Eyberg, 2011) is a dyadic approach for young children (ages 2 to 7) that addresses diverse emotional and behavioral issues through strengthening the attachment bond and supporting authoritative parenting qualities, such as warmth and setting clear limits. One hallmark of this intervention is the use of real-time parental coaching by the therapist (through a "bug in the ear" in the room or via telehealth) to reinforce, shape, and prompt new ways of relating. PCIT was originally developed with two phases: child-directed and parent-directed interaction. In the child-directed phase, the parent is encouraged to be present and follow their child's lead in play, embodying the PRIDE skills (praise, reflect, imitate, describe, enjoy). These areas are particularly salient for parents who experienced maltreatment, abuse, or neglect in their own childhood, and thus have few reference points for parental warmth or attunement. A recent trauma-focused adaptation (Gurwitch & Warner-Metzger, 2022) attends to these areas through a trauma-directed interaction phase. This involves providing the parent with psychoeducation about trauma impacts, helping them differentiate between emotional upset and trauma reactions, and teaching and coaching SAFE (state the feeling, address safety, find a coping skill, and reengage PRIDE) skills. Finally, the parent-directed phase implements behavioral management skills. PCIT has been found to be efficacious in reducing parenting stress and risk of abuse and neglect, as well as in supporting both parent and child mental health (Messer et al., 2024; Warren et al., 2022). Child adult relationship enhancement makes these skills accessible outside of therapy alone (Messer et al., 2018), such as in schools that want to become more trauma-informed.

Albeit its similar name, child–parent relationship psychotherapy (CPRT; Landreth & Bratton, 2019) differs somewhat in that it is a short-term, play-based approach for parents (with children ages 2 to 10) that prioritizes "the inner person of the child, what the child is capable of becoming" (p. 7). CPRT makes use of interpersonal learning through its group format. Each session involves the therapist describing and demonstrating child-centered play therapy techniques, which parents then role-play. Between sessions, parents conduct a play time with their child, and record this for review and feedback. In subsequent sessions, parents take turns sharing their videos in CPRT sessions and receiving feedback. Foundational to CPRT is the idea that "a relatively small amount of affection, attention, interest, and so on, from the parent can be expected to be more therapeutic than a larger amount from a therapist" (Guerney, 1964, p. 309). Multiple parts of the family system are targeted, such as increasing children's sense of responsibility and self-esteem, while also developing parents' ability to respond effectively to their child's needs. CPRT has been shown to be effective in reducing children's externalizing and internalizing problems, strengthening the parent–child relationship, decreasing parental stress, and shifting family dynamics, such as increasing flexibility, cohesion, and communication (Cornett & Bratton, 2014; Landreth & Bratton, 2019; Narimani & Taghizadeh Hir, 2021).

Emotionally focused therapy (EFT; Greenberg & Johnson, 1988; S. M. Johnson, 1996/2019b), distinct from the individual modality of emotion-focused therapy (Greenberg, 2011), is a couples intervention rooted in attachment theory, emotion science, and experiential and structural family therapy. EFT capitalizes on the healing power of emotions and connection through three iterative treatment phases. First, assessment and de-escalation focuses on alliance-building, tracking negative interaction cycles underlying conflicts, and accessing unacknowledged needs and feelings that can be used to reframe problems. Second, in the reengagement/softening phase, the therapist supports the couple or family in becoming aware of disowned self-aspects, wants, and needs, while cultivating a safe haven for the partner's (or other family members') experience and vulnerabilities. Finally, consolidation reinforces new ways of relating that foster security, connectedness, and intimacy, and using the relationship as a secure base. EFT has been adapted for families (EFFT; Furrow et al., 2019; S. M. Johnson & Lee, 2005) and trauma survivors (S. M. Johnson, 2002; Paivio & Pascual-Leone, 2023). Paivio and Pascual-Leone (2023) developed emotionally focused therapy for complex trauma (EFTT), with affect regulation, social support/attachment, and narrative processing targeted as primary mechanisms of change. EFTT attends to the complexities of alliance-building with survivors; emphasizes the need to titrate emotional experiencing; intervenes to transform shame, guilt, and self-blame; taps into the power of adaptive anger; incorporates imaginal exposure (e.g., confronting one's abuser); and promotes integration of trauma memories. EFT has been found to be effective in treating couples with and without trauma histories (Beasley & Ager, 2019; Dalton et al., 2013; Spengler et al., 2024), and recent work has combined EFT with eye movement desensitization and reprocessing (EMDR) to address traumatization from infidelity (Negash et al., 2018).

Cognitive behavioral conjoint therapy for PTSD (CBCT; Monson & Fredman, 2012) is designed for couples in which one or both partners suffer from PTSD. This approach is rooted in the cognitive behavioral interpersonal theory of PTSD (Monson et al., 2010), which postulates a bidirectional relationship between symptom distress and relationship difficulties. Specifically, partner PTSD symptoms can contribute to relationship problems (e.g., anger, conflict, sexual dissatisfaction), whereas the couple's relational patterns (e.g., avoidant or demand–withdraw tendencies) can trigger or exacerbate PTSD. CBCT outlines three phases. The rationale and psychoeducation phase focuses on building alliance and establishing safety. Building on this, treatment focuses on enhancing relational satisfaction and challenging avoidance by sharing thoughts and feelings and beginning to master trauma triggers. The final phase facilitates joint meaning-making, including working through self-blame and developing acceptance and trust. CBCT research has primarily been conducted with veterans (Liebman, Whitfield, et al., 2020; Pukay-Martin et al., 2022), with recent innovations including the integration of mindfulness and delivering CBCT in multi-couple groups and weekend retreat formats (L. W. Davis et al., 2021).

Multisystemic therapy (MST; Henggeler et al., 2009) is an intensive in-home and community-based treatment originally developed for adolescents exhibiting antisocial behavior (e.g., substance abuse, criminal activity). The model includes a multidisciplinary team involving therapists, a crisis caseworker, and a psychiatrist. Synthesizing Bronfenbrenner's (1979) social ecological model with family systems, behavioral theories, and cognitive theories, MST orients clinicians to the reciprocal nature of interactions and explores the multi-determined, functional nature of adolescents' problematic behaviors. MST harnesses family strengths (e.g., parental love) and addresses vulnerabilities (e.g., parental stress or hopelessness about change) to increase parental involvement and support. MST also intervenes to address "the interplay of risk factors associated with the multiple systems in which youth are embedded," such as peers, neighborhood, and school (Henggeler et al., 2009, p. 4), with the goal of surrounding the adolescent with contexts that reinforce prosocial behavior. Adapted for trauma-specific contexts, MST–Child Abuse and Neglect (MST–CAN; Swenson & Schaeffer, 2018) incorporates a multisystemic focus with families referred to child protective services. Such families are often mistrustful and guarded, and MST–CAN offers a holistic framework to engage families collaboratively. Therapists help families identify specific risk factors, such as inconsistent/reactive discipline, domestic violence, caregiver PTSD, or problematic substance use in the home. MST also attends to larger systemic influences, like poverty, racism, and community violence. Interventions are tailored to address these areas in support of family stability and to prevent further abuse and neglect. There is evidence for MST–CAN's effectiveness in changing family environments, including decreasing parental stress and supporting both parent and child mental health (Bauch et al., 2022; Buderer et al., 2020).

Under the broad umbrella of family therapy approaches, several are worth noting that have substantial empirical evidence and are well-suited to addressing underlying family structures and interaction patterns constrained by intergenerational trauma. These include strategic-structural approaches like brief strategic family therapy (Szapocznik & Hervis, 2020), multidimensional family therapy (Liddle, 2009), and the more cognitive behavioral leaning functional family therapy (Sexton, 2011). Concepts and techniques from ecosystemic structural family therapy (Lindblad-Goldberg & Northey, 2013) may also be extremely useful with traumatized families. In many cases where trauma "lives" in the family system, there is no single traumatic event to identify and process, but rather a backdrop of chronic, toxic stress. The family may not be coming into treatment because of an explicitly stated trauma, yet the attuned clinician observes survival-oriented interaction patterns rooted in dysregulated and traumatized nervous systems. This may be exhibited, for example, by members' tendencies toward fight, flight, freeze, or fawn, as well as system-wide patterns of avoidance or denial. Supporting the development of coregulation and healing interaction patterns helps break the oft-covert process by which trauma is passed down intergenerationally. Finally, considering the angle of prevention, family focused grief therapy (Kissane & Bloch, 2002) offers one example of family-centered palliative care that works upstream of potential traumatization (Kissane et al., 2006; Masterson et al., 2013).

INDIVIDUAL TRAUMA TREATMENT ENRICHED BY A SYSTEMIC FORMULATION

Our final stop on the gallery tour of treatment possibilities involves considering how to integrate a systemic perspective into individual approaches that are focused on a single family member's psychological and emotional experience; for example, seeking to reduce trauma-related physiological arousal, avoidance, and alterations in mood. However, such trauma therapies often fail to intervene on traumatic processes within the family environment that have either initiated or exacerbate individual distress. Thus, you may find it useful to integrate one or more individual models with some of the frameworks explored above. This could take many forms; for example, in working with an individual client, you might invite them to bring in a family member to gather additional information relevant to a systemic understanding of change (e.g., as part of assessment, treatment planning, psychoeducation). In another context, you may take a multimodal approach, meeting with some family members individually—as well as family subsystems and the family as a whole—across different phases of treatment. Or, if your role is primarily providing couple or family therapy, you can incorporate the ethos and core principles of these well-established trauma interventions, and might refer a member with heightened trauma symptoms to a colleague for targeted individual intervention. Even if it is not possible—or advisable—within a particular individual case to include additional family members in session, application of systemic principles can deepen treatment by bringing into focus family and relational factors.

Importantly, systemically focused therapeutic work can facilitate second-order changes in clients' family systems and relationships, regardless of who is physically present in the room. Formulating a client's symptomology in light of the relationships and larger systems they are embedded within brings into focus contextual strengths and vulnerabilities that can be incredibly influential in therapeutic improvement. This does not stop with the family unit, and group modalities can also help clients gain insight into how trauma impacts play out in their relational lives, while benefiting from group therapeutic factors (Yalom & Leszcz, 2005). Furthermore, group work can enable clients to gain access to a healing relational milieu when their family is not available and/or willing to be part of treatment. In line with Bronfenbrenner's (1977) work, clinicians should always consider the roles of family dynamics, spillover influences (e.g., parents' work-related trauma exposure), school and peer relationships, neighborhood and community conditions, and larger cultural forces. Systemic formulation (see Chapter 5 in this volume) is a key aspect of culturally responsive treatment, particularly when working with clients whose distress is fueled by threatening conditions, instability, and/or community violence.

Among the broad family of cognitive behavioral therapies, trauma-focused CBT (TF–CBT; J. A. Cohen et al., 2016) was originally developed to address sexual abuse but has utility following diverse traumatic experiences for children ages 3 to 18 years old. TF–CBT intervenes to address key areas that set the stage for and maintain PTSD, including physiological dysregulation, avoidance stemming from overgeneralized fear, and trauma-related cognitions. While treatment centers primarily on the child, nonoffending parents/caregivers are involved in parallel and sometimes conjoint sessions, particularly with younger children.[2] TF–CBT presumes that "caregivers can positively influence traumatic impact through providing support, believing their children related to their traumatic experiences, modeling positive coping strategies, and providing effective parenting practices" (E. J. Brown et al., 2020, p. 41). Two adaptations have a substantial systemic component, focused on changing coercive and high-control parenting. Alternatives for families CBT (Kolko et al., 2014; Kolko & Swenson,

[2] When a caregiver has been or is currently abusive, additional ethical considerations and clinical assessment are necessary to determine their level of involvement (if any) in a child's treatment. These details are discussed further in Chapters 1 and 5 in this volume.

2002) recognizes individual and systemic factors associated with conflict or coercion among family members, and is well-suited for parents who have been emotionally, verbally, and/or physically abusive. Combined parent–child CBT (Runyon & Deblinger, 2013) was similarly developed for parents who are at risk for or have engaged in physical abuse. Both frameworks involve parallel individual sessions with the offending parent and child, as well as joint sessions that provide real-time opportunities for practicing positive parenting skills.

Cognitive processing therapy (Resnick et al., 2016) for adults and its adolescent version, developmentally adapted cognitive processing therapy (Matulis et al., 2014) focus on how traumatic experiences impact schemas around safety, power/control, trust, esteem, and intimacy, and how overgeneralized narratives (e.g., "I can't trust anyone") fuel emotional distress and avoidance. Prolonged exposure (Foa et al., 2007) for adults and its adaptation for adolescents (Foa et al., 2009) involve disrupting patterns of avoidance and building mastery in approaching trauma-related feelings, memories, and situations. Clients are taught coping skills to manage physiological reactivity, and then utilize this to ground themselves in order to talk about the details of their trauma. They are asked to record and listen to their trauma narrative repeatedly as a way to confront what happened and consolidate memories. Although identifying a single "index" trauma to process is somewhat at odds with a systemic formulation of the overlapping, cumulative, and intergenerational impacts of trauma, these treatments could be enhanced by considering the family, contextual, and cultural narratives that contribute to schemas around suffering and healing, as well as through exploring communal and holistic means of emotional processing. There is significant variation in how meaning is made from trauma, and in many cultures, processing is not mediated by language (Duran, 2019; Ringland, 2019), so exploring the client's cultural and religious beliefs may offer valuable alternatives.

Narrative exposure therapy (Schauer et al., 2011) and the associated children's version (Schauer et al., 2017) lean into this complexity by considering impactful life events holistically and integrating creative elements (e.g., play, creative media, theatre). Treatment is organized around creating a chronological narrative—a "lifeline"—by placing flowers (representing positive events) and stones (negative/traumatic events) along a rope. Sessions facilitate storytelling to help "transform the generally fragmented reports of the traumatic experiences into a coherent narrative," weaving together salient "emotions, cognitions, sensory information and physiological reactions" (Schauer et al., 2017, p. 227). The therapist creates a written biography of these narratives for the client; for children, this could be replaced by a picture book. This approach is well-suited to treating chronic, complex trauma, and has been extensively used with those who have experienced forced migration (Samarah, 2024; Wright et al., 2020). In line with a collectivist ethos, this treatment is often conducted in groups, and thus easily translates to use with a couple, dyad, or entire family. One benefit of doing so includes facilitating deeper connection through bearing witness to each other's suffering, challenging family patterns of minimization and denial. However, clinical assessment is needed to determine if a family is ready to enter this sort of emotionally vulnerable terrain together.

Given individual and cultural differences around disclosure as well as the reality that language sometimes fails to capture felt experience, EMDR (Shapiro, 1989, 2017) taps into nonverbal trauma processing through dual attention bilateral stimulation. Originally developed for adults, it has also been adapted for and found to be effective with children (Adler-Tapia & Settle, 2023; Gomez, 2012). EMDR involves eight phases, beginning with assessment and preparation/resourcing to help cope with trauma-related affects. Then, treatment focuses on activating a client's information processing system (e.g., by bringing to mind images, sensations, beliefs, and feelings related to a traumatic experience) while also staying anchored in the present moment. This dual attention helps integrate split-off aspects of memory and support the emergence of new perspectives. EMDR has been incorporated in systemic treatment via multiple means (Doğan et al., 2021; Shapiro et al., 2007; Wesselmann, 2025; Wesselmann et al., 2018). Silvestre and Tarquinio (2022) utilized a multimodal therapeutic frame, arguing that "the relational work with a wounded family is a prerequisite to the individual work with a wounded child" (p. 5). They suggest a two-phase approach that begins by "zooming out" and working at a family level, including addressing relational dynamics fueling symptomology; increasing family cohesion, closeness, and trust; and bolstering coregulation. Individual EMDR sessions with a particularly traumatized family member can then "zoom in" on trauma processing and memory integration. Others have adapted EMDR for use with couples and multiple family members in the room concurrently, noting that a parent or partner's quiet presence can be a grounding resource during processing for some clients (Doğan et al., 2021; Shapiro et al., 2007).

Consistent with growing recognition of complex PTSD, trauma processing is not the "be-all and end-all" to trauma treatment. Survivors often need support in activating stalled developmental processes around emotional awareness and regulation, as well as navigating interpersonal relationships, to name a few areas. In line with safety and stabilization as prerequisites for trauma processing (Herman, 1992/2015), skills training for affective and interpersonal regulation narrative therapy (Cloitre et al., 2020) begins with a focus on building emotional and social resources. This includes cultivating hope, increasing awareness of how trauma lives in the body, capacity-building to tolerate emotional distress, and changing relationship patterns. Only after this groundwork is in place does treatment deepen into creating narratives, with particular attention to working with shame, loss, and fear. Cultivating adaptive strategies to manage trauma-related affect is also central to dialectical behavior therapy (Linehan, 2014) and compassion focused therapy (Gilbert & Simos, 2022).

Trauma affect regulation: guide for education and therapy (TARGET; Ford, 2020) is another developmentally focused and neurobiologically informed metamodel focusing on two mechanisms of change: trauma processing and affect regulation. TARGET uses accessible language to educate survivors and key stakeholders in their care about how trauma impacts the brain; for example, delineating between the "learning brain" (e.g., executive functioning, emotion regulation, self-reflection) and the "survival brain" (e.g., PTSD/complex PTSD symptoms as the mind's best attempt at coping with unbearable situations). As a metamodel that can be integrated in couple and family modalities or serve as a primary phase of treatment, TARGET supports clients in using SOS skills (slow down, orient yourself, self-check) to notice and reset their "survival brain." More broadly, treatment focuses on cultivating FREEDOM skills (focus, recognize triggers, emotion self-check, evaluate thoughts, define goals, options, make a contribution) in order to cultivate agency and mastery. TARGET's effectiveness in juvenile and child welfare systems (Ford et al., 2011, 2012; Marrow et al., 2014) speaks to its flexibility as part of individual, group, and family modalities. This framework could be folded into family sessions when psychoeducation about trauma and skill development are clinically indicated.

Trauma-focused psychodynamic and psychoanalytic therapies (Busch et al., 2021; Summers et al., 2024), which have substantial empirical support, are particularly well-suited for clients who do not respond to brief, symptom-focused therapies. Central to such approaches is the idea that what we cannot remember, we are bound to repeat. Psychodynamic and systemic perspectives share attention to creating second-order changes. When families repress the memory and pain of past trauma, members tend to re-create similar dynamics in current relationships in an attempt at trauma mastery. Furthermore, defenses like dissociation and denial, while adaptive in the context of acute or ongoing trauma, often impede family members' ability to engage fully with life. These frameworks attend to how unprocessed trauma stored as procedural memory spills over into present experience (i.e., transference; Freud, 1914/1958; Reis, 2019). The therapeutic relationship offers a space to understand and address these aspects, integrating links between somatosensory states and visceral narratives (Piccolo, 2019). When working with multiple family members, clinicians have the opportunity to address the unique transferences alive in each relationship.

In particular, trauma-focused mentalization-based therapy (Bateman et al., 2023) targets three core areas disrupted by complex trauma: attachment, mentalization, and epistemic trust. When early relationships are rife with abuse and neglect, a child's "understand[ing] of self and others in terms of intentional mental states" (Smits et al., 2022, p. 12) is severely constrained. This can lead to persistent confusion about one's own and others' minds, as well as lack of trust in and vigilance about one's environment. Mentalization-based therapy is well-suited to address the intergenerational transmission of trauma and has been found effective in individual, family, and group modalities (Malda-Castillo et al., 2019; Volkert et al., 2022). From a systems vantage point, working with parents to help them understand their child(ren)'s and their own minds can deepen earned security and shift the developmental trajectory of the next generation (Malberg et al., 2023).

Internal family systems (IFS) therapy (Schwartz & Sweezy, 2020) represents a novel synthesis of psychodynamic and systemic approaches, explicating how psychological distress can be fueled by conflict and lack of integration between self-aspects that are framed as one's internal "family members" with distinct perspectives, emotions, and roles. In addition to one's core self, IFS distinguishes between exiles, managers, and firefighters. Exiles are wounded, vulnerable self-aspects banished from awareness because the associated trauma-related affects (e.g., shame, fear) are overwhelming. Managers represent parts that prevent exiles' pain from being triggered through perfectionistic or overly responsible behaviors. Finally, firefighters react to extinguish exiles' emotional pain through self-destructive behaviors (e.g., substance use, bingeing) that have a protective function. IFS concepts can be flexibly integrated as part of couple and family trauma treatment (Herbine-Blank & Sweezy, 2021; Spiegel, 2017).

Growing attention to how trauma affects the nervous system (Porges, 2011; van der Kolk, 2014) has led to the development of somatic interventions, which consider "the body as an integral source of information [that] can guide resourcing and the accessing and processing of challenging, traumatic, and developmental experience" (Sensorimotor Psychotherapy Institute, 2024, n.p.). Two common models are somatic experiencing (P. A. Levine, 2010) and sensorimotor psychotherapy (Ogden & Fisher, 2015); research suggests their effectiveness as experiential pathways to healing through addressing chronic dysregulation of the nervous system (Brom et al., 2017; Kuhfuß et al., 2021). The recent explosion of interest in this area is perhaps a counterbalance to the field's historic emphasis on the mind, and somatic interventions are now being integrated in couple and family modalities (Fox, 2024; Kailanko et al., 2022; Lohrasbe & Ogden, 2017). Within a broader systemic treatment focus, attending to somatic vulnerabilities and resources within the family can orient therapists to how members' nervous systems interact with and influence each other in order to support greater coregulation.

Finally, approaches have also been developed specifically to address traumatic loss and prolonged grief disorder. For example, trauma and grief component therapy (TGCT; Layne et al., 2001; Saltzman et al., 2017) synthesizes contributions from multidimensional grief theory, positive psychology, developmental psychopathology, and CBT. As far as systemic integration, TGCT includes a family/parent-focused component, and research has begun to examine its effects on parenting style, family conflict, and recovery after the death of a parent (Howell et al., 2014, 2016; Kaplow et al., 2013). Given the ripple effect of grief across family systems, TGCT could be hugely beneficial in working with multiple members to explore and understand how each member has been impacted, including separation distress, existential/identity distress, and distress related to circumstances surrounding the loss.

SUMMARY AND KEY TAKEAWAYS

Entire volumes have been written about trauma treatment, and there is no shortage of advanced trainings and certifications you might seek out, including many of the models reviewed here. The proliferation of approaches to treat trauma can feel overwhelming. Some practitioners manage this by identifying with and privileging a single approach; for example, "I provide TF–CBT" or "I am trained in EMDR." Going beyond this, observant readers can readily identify how each framework we have overviewed herein offers a distinct vehicle for common mechanisms of therapeutic action and change, such as (a) strengthening the caregiver–child attachment bond (and other relationships, e.g., spouses/partners, parents, siblings, peers) and repairing relational ruptures, while supporting healthy differentiation; (b) facilitating emotional awareness, regulation, and processing to downregulate trauma affects and upregulate healing affects; (c) cultivating agency, competence, and pride through supporting the family in creating positive changes in rules, roles, and hierarchy; and (d) revising distress-inducing family narratives, and increasing mentalization, communication, and problem solving. This is the heart of EBP: not merely "plugging and playing" a treatment protocol, but embodying an integrative, critically reflective, and personalized approach, including working flexibly with one or more family members and across multiple subsystems toward overarching treatment goals.

Given the multifaceted and diverse sequelae of traumatization, a transdiagnostic and metatheoretical clinical approach enables greater sophistication and flexibility in order to effectively assess, formulate, and intervene with the complexity and uniqueness of families' lived experiences and needs. While some models reviewed here prescribe specific therapeutic strategies, others operate at a meta-level to shape assessment, treatment planning, and coordination of care. Many delineate iterative phases or stages, highlighting how appropriate timing of various intervention elements is imperative. Multiple perspectives are helpful in enriching our practice. Systemically oriented practitioners do not fixate on a particular diagnosis or index trauma; instead, we work with the complexity of family members' responses to trauma by addressing underlying patterns and impairments (e.g., compromised development) that fuel suffering. As ongoing research examines treatment "fit," cultivating metatheoretical fluency and integration help us meet families where they are at and transcend the "psychotherapy wars" that so often fuel dogma and splitting in the field.

Taken together, systemically oriented therapists are far from scientists injecting a treatment into a family system like a vaccine. Instead, we are more like gardeners working to create conditions for growth and healing by infusing the system with nutrients and fertilizer. Circling back to the four domains of trauma's impact discussed in Chapter 2 in this volume, several meta-level questions are worth holding in mind as you consider each of your cases: Who in the family system holds the power (and who is powerless)? Where does intense affect reside within the family system (and where is it strikingly absent)? What relational patterns create or maintain disconnection and/or misattunement? And what is unspeakable and not able to be acknowledged?

Such clinical work is dynamic, messy, and complicated, requiring creativity, innovation, and patience. This is where art and science meet: in cocreating a new treatment for each family; drawing from the best available research evidence; our developing clinical expertise; and each family's culture, values, and preferences. Building on this, we turn our attention in the next chapter to skillful assessment concerning what is (and is not) happening in the family system. Metatheoretical questions such as what to do, when, and why are fundamentally informed by ongoing systemic observation, as well as conversation about family members' goals and hopes for treatment.

4 SYSTEMIC ASSESSMENT OF FAMILY TRAUMA

Uncovering Underlying Patterns and Processes

For every complex problem there is an answer that is clear, simple, and wrong.
—PARAPHRASED FROM H. L. MENCKEN (1917)

Anthony puts off vibes of a disaffected 15-year-old, pulling out his phone frequently to play a game. He shrugs his shoulders or responds with single-word answers to most of your questions during the intensive in-home therapy intake.

When his dad, Ben, attempts to take the phone away, Anthony erupts. "You know what? This whole situation is f—king stupid! I'm not the problem here." He glares at his dad, who you learn has recently returned from deployment as a Marine.

"Shut up, Anthony!" Ben slams his fist down on the arm of the couch and turns to you in consternation. "Ever since I got back, he's been like this … disrespectful and rebellious. I can't stand it. In the Marines, if one of my soldiers acted this way, they'd be discharged."

This chapter contains composite case vignettes drawn from multiple clients and fictitious aspects. Details have been substantively changed to protect confidentiality.

https://doi.org/10.1037/0000487-005
Systemic Treatment of Trauma-Impacted Families: A Clinician's Guide to Assessment, Formulation, and Intervention, by S. A. Riggs and L. E. Captari

"Yeah, and I told you, I'm NOT a Marine. Who are you to talk anyway . . . like you've got your sh—t together?" Anthony mocks. The quickly escalating conflict between these two is evident, raising questions for you about what is happening at home and how Anthony's behavior might be linked to dynamics around Ben's reintegration into the family.

"Anthony, chill out," his mother, Janela, interjects. "We don't talk that way in this house. Your dad has been stressed, that's all."

The referral from the school counselor stated that Anthony regularly mouths off at teachers, has been skipping classes, often smells like marijuana, and is currently suspended for an altercation with another student.

You decide to take a walk and shoot some hoops with Anthony to help him blow off steam and build rapport. You want to understand the bigger picture of what is happening for this family in transition, especially given that Anthony's sister, Adelya, recently left for college.

Anthony may be reticent to talk about himself, but he has lots to say about his parents. "They're such hypocrites! Getting on my case when they're the ones always fighting. Ever since dad got back, they can't seem to agree about anything. He drinks all the time, and then goes on these rages about how none of us would last a day in the Marines.

"And then if I say anything about it, they ground me and try to take away my phone. They're even threatening to pull me off the basketball team. Like, wtf? That's one thing I'm good at."

When you meet with Anthony's parents, you hear a very different story: They are worried about his slipping grades and a couple of his friends were recently caught selling drugs at school. "He's always been a bit shy and anxious, so he goes along," Janela reflects. "In second grade, an older kid touched him inappropriately and he was pretty withdrawn after that for a while. Pretty sure he got bullied a lot too. Kids can be brutal sometimes, especially when your parents are different races and you're stationed in the South."

"Sure, kids can be mean, but Anthony needs to be stronger," Ben interjects. "We've dealt with racial crap before and sometimes bullies need to be put in their place. I think it's the losers he's hanging out with."

"And what about you two?" you inquire. "You're bringing different perspectives to the table here. After a deployment, it can be a big adjustment reintegrating as a couple and as parents."

The awkward silence is telling. "Well, you know . . . we're figuring it out," Janela responds finally. "It's so good to have Ben back, but I think, honey, you can be a bit harsh with Anthony sometimes."

"Phhh, and you're too easy with him!" Ben shoots back. "He got away with soooo much stuff while I was gone. I'm just trying to bring some order to this household. The chaos is driving me crazy!"

You're beginning to wonder if Anthony's marijuana use and his father's drinking are serving self-regulatory functions in this family environment. With your clinical night vision goggles (equipped with thermal imaging, mind you!), multiple systemic hypotheses about the referral question run through your mind. Anthony's short fuse and fights at school may reflect attachment-related anger at his father's extended absence with some resentment at his return, or triangulated tension between his parents, and/or possibly a misguided effort to prove he is "strong" for his father. "Not caring" at home could be a way to try to differentiate himself from the chaos and claim some sense of agency, perhaps envying his sister's ability to escape to college. With a reported history of being bullied and sexually molested, much remains unknown about how Anthony made sense of these experiences, particularly given family norms around being tough and pushing through.

Going deeper, where might these family norms have come from? Could they represent Ben and Janela's ways of coping with military culture, intergenerational patterns, or ongoing discrimination as a biracial couple? What life experiences have each of them endured that could represent a traumatic backdrop to their current conflicts? Questions also emerge about what Ben encountered on his military tour and whether he is experiencing posttraumatic symptoms that could be contributing the situation. It is also unclear how intense the conflicts get at home, and if there is a risk for physical violence.

An individual therapist working with Anthony would likely focus an assessment on clarifying individual symptoms, such as anger, depression, and potential suicidality, and possibly examine peer relationships and school performance. A systemically oriented approach to assessment considers all of the above but also holds the entire family in mind as part of the assessment, including measures that evaluate multiple levels of the family system (e.g., couple, parent, child). Given this level of complexity, what do we assess for and where do we begin clinically? In addition to evaluating each person's symptomology, holistic assessment in the above case might attend to Ben and Janela's couple and coparenting dynamics, the relationships between Anthony and his parents and sister, the dynamics of the larger family system (including how Ben's return and Adelya's recent departure affected the family), and contributing external factors (e.g., social relationships, school context, military cultural milieu).

Before jumping into treatment, it is important to gather information and begin to formulate what might be fueling various family members' distress—particularly the role of trauma impacts, the potential functions of maladaptive behaviors, and the family's strengths and adaptability that can be capitalized on.

Getting a clear sense of systemic functioning beyond the individual "identified patient" alone is a key part of evidence-based practice in order to personalize treatment to each family's distinct context, culture, and needs.

This chapter examines clinical assessment with families impacted by trauma, discussing screening and assessment possibilities, distinctions between individual and systemic assessment, and practical decisions regarding who to include, factors to assess, and what measurement methods to incorporate. We then introduce the case of the Garcia family, who present for therapy following traumatic loss, as one example of what comprehensive systemic assessment could look like. In routine practice, systemic assessment may take many forms, depending on your treatment setting, available time, and family members' openness to involvement (or not). Even if you are limited to brief screening measures and a clinical interview, applying a systemic lens can meaningfully inform your understanding of what is happening both within and between members that may be contributing to the presenting problem.

HOW TO APPLY THIS CHAPTER IN YOUR PRACTICE SETTING

Assessment is a profession-wide competency in a number of mental health disciplines, including social work (Council on Social Work Education, 2022), counseling (Council for Accreditation of Counseling and Related Educational Programs, 2024), marriage and family therapy (Commission on Accreditation for Marriage and Family Education, 2021), psychology (American Psychological Association [APA], 2018; Hatcher et al., 2013; Health Service Psychology Education Collaborative, 2013), and psychiatry (Accreditation Council for Graduate Medical Education, 2023). Thus, students graduating from accredited programs in these fields must receive training and demonstrate competency in this domain. The exact meaning and operationalization of assessment, however, can vary somewhat by discipline and level of education. Each discipline's identified competencies guide both training and ethical practice, so it is essential that therapists carefully consider their own training and scope of competence before embarking on the assessment procedures described in this chapter.

We acknowledge that there are a variety of approaches to the assessment of trauma and families, ranging from a single clinical interview to a comprehensive process involving the administration of multiple instruments with two or more people. Decisions regarding how to conduct an assessment will hinge not only on a therapist's training but also the availability of resources (e.g., instruments, time), the client and family members' willingness to participate, and limits on insurance billing (e.g., if the client is a child, can you administer a questionnaire to a parent?). For the purposes of this book, we focus on procedures and considerations for conducting a formal comprehensive family assessment; such level of detail may be especially helpful when there is a complex clinical presentation, multiple family members with trauma histories, and/or when previous treatments have proven ineffective.

We invite you as the reader to adapt these procedures to your own practice setting and the populations you serve, taking into consideration each family's clinical presentation, goals, preferences, needs, and bandwidth. For example, the assessment process may be quite brief in inpatient, primary care, and low-resource community settings, particularly when families are presenting in crisis. However, as with the last chapter, we encourage you to engage with these pages like taking a tour of the multifaceted dimensions and methods that can be part of systemically oriented assessment. In line with the ethos of evidence-based practice, we do not outline a particular assessment protocol, but rather aim to increase your clinical frame of reference at the intersection of systems thinking and trauma science, so that you can integrate this foundational knowledge with your own clinical wisdom as well as the preferences and needs of the clients and families you serve in order to select the appropriate assessment methods for each case.

TRAUMA-FOCUSED SYSTEMIC ASSESSMENT

In recent years, there has been a push for universal trauma screening of children in primary care and school settings. Screening refers to a very brief, focused evaluation, typically consisting of one or two short instruments, often administered by frontline employees or other direct service staff during the intake process (Kisiel et al., 2021). Trauma screening is designed to determine whether individuals have experienced potentially traumatic events and to identify any ensuing symptoms of distress. Commonly used self-report screeners include the Adverse Childhood Experiences Questionnaire (Felitti et al., 1998) and recent adaptations that include items assessing community violence and racism (Cronholm et al., 2015). There are also many versions of Life Events Checklists (Charney & Keane, 1990; J. H. Johnson & McCutcheon, 1980), including the Life Events Checklist for *Diagnostic and Statistical Manual of Mental Disorders,* fifth edition (*DSM-5*; Weathers et al., 2013b). Brief symptom measures for adults include the Posttraumatic Stress Disorder (PTSD) Checklist for *DSM-5* (Weathers, Litz, et al., 2013) or the Primary Care PTSD

Screen (Prins et al., 2015). For children and youth, instruments that assess both life history of trauma and associated posttraumatic symptoms include the Child and Adolescent Trauma Screen (CATS; Sachser et al., 2017) and the Trauma Symptom Checklist for Children (Briere, 1996). If screening is positive, further assessment should explore the nature and severity of the traumatic events, what happened after those events, and supportive relationships, and include a more thorough examination of current symptoms.

By contrast, a comprehensive psychological assessment is a more in-depth examination that generally includes a clinical interview, standardized self-report instruments, and other tools measuring constructs of interest that are administered by credentialed mental health providers with advanced training in the administration, scoring, and interpretation of assessment measures (Kisiel et al., 2021; Substance Abuse and Mental Health Services Administration, 2014). In psychology, the Guidelines for Psychological Assessment and Evaluation (APA Task Force on Psychological Assessment and Evaluation Guidelines, 2020) describes the assessment process as

> a complex activity integrating knowledge, clinical judgment, reliable collateral information (e.g., observation, semi-structured or structured interviews, third-party report), and psychometric constructs with expertise in an area of professional practice or application. Psychological assessment is a problem-solving process of identifying and using relevant information about individuals, groups, or institutions for the purpose of decision-making and recommendations (APA, 2001). This includes sensitivity toward the inclusion of diverse and underserved populations. (p. 5)

Assessment in the mental health field is traditionally viewed as a single-session activity that is conducted and completed at the onset of treatment, possibly with routine outcome monitoring to track symptom change. However, both trauma-informed and systemic assessment often entail multiple test sessions at the outset and continue as an ongoing process throughout treatment (Kisiel et al., 2014; Snyder et al., 2019). Follow-up assessment is common, sometimes after several weeks or months of treatment (Kisiel et al., 2021), or even routinely at the end of each session as part of "think[ing] assessment all the time" (L. Williams et al., 2011, p. 11). In some settings where a full assessment of every client is not possible at the outset of treatment, clinicians may only conduct a comprehensive assessment when the complexity of the case brings treatment to a stand-still and further consultation and assessment is needed to better understand the case before proceeding. Taken together, trauma-informed systemic assessment is not just a battery of measures, but rather a broader practice and skill set that is interwoven with treatment.

Assessment guidelines (APA Task Force on Psychological Assessment and Evaluation Guidelines, 2020) recognize that specialized areas of practice require additional knowledge and assessment skills to effectively evaluate particular populations and situations. Couple and family assessment and trauma assessment represent two such specializations. The trauma field is concerned with accurate, thorough, clinically attuned, and responsive assessment. APA's (2015a) Guidelines on Trauma Competencies for Education and Training outlined the importance of understanding how developmental stage and relational context shape clients' subjective experience of a traumatic stressor, delineating between short- and long-term trauma impacts, and considering relevant person–environment interactions. Best practices for trauma assessment in psychology (APA, 2015a) incorporate

- routinely asking about trauma experiences in intakes, avoiding assumptions based on clients' background or mental status;
- utilizing comprehensive measures of trauma exposure and impacts;
- choosing assessment instruments according to client characteristics and test interpretation issues (e.g., validity scales, motivation);
- adjusting assessment procedures to align with clients' present mental state (e.g., dissociation, avoidance);
- attending to strengths and resilience (pre- and posttrauma), as well as the influence of cultural factors (e.g., on coping, meaning-making, and openness to treatment); and
- exercising prudence about the consequences clients may experience from particular diagnoses in some contexts (e.g., military, forensic).

When working with children and adolescents, additional guidelines for comprehensive trauma assessment include creating a safe environment for assessment, collecting information from multiple sources using a variety of assessment methods, assessment of both child and caregiver trauma responses over time, and collaboration with the family and other service providers to understand the assessment results and plan treatment (Kisiel et al., 2014).

Systemically oriented assessment also necessitates the development of specific competencies (Celano, 2019). The couple and family psychology specialty regards assessment as part of the broader, overarching functional competency of case conceptualization, which provides the framework for systemic practice (Celano, 2019; Stanton & Welsh, 2011). Adapting the work of Sperry (2005), Stanton and Welsh (2011) described three distinct phases of systemic conceptualization for couple and family practitioners. Problem formulation is descriptive and includes setting the therapeutic frame (e.g., establishing rapport, informed consent process, etc.), interviewing the couple/family about the presenting problem, generating testable hypotheses, conducting a comprehensive assessment, and diagnosing or describing the problem. Case formulation is explanatory and involves organizing all the information obtained in the problem formulation stage, providing a systems theory-based explanation that makes sense of the assessment data, and identifying and prioritizing targets for therapeutic change. The final conceptualization phase is treatment formulation, which is prescriptive and includes assessment feedback to the couple/family, collaborative goal-setting, identification of target interventions and delivery format, and a monitoring plan.

This chapter focuses primarily on systemic problem formulation surrounding the broad sequelae of trauma, including information gathering, preliminary hypothesizing, and assessment/diagnostic processes, while the next chapter will address case and treatment formulation. In all three phases, systemically oriented practitioners attend to individual, interpersonal, and contextual factors related to presenting problems. Assessment competencies in couple and family psychology (Celano, 2019), include

- an understanding of the nature and scope of couple and family assessment methods, as well as the measurement and psychometrics of assessment instruments;
- competent use of multimodal assessment methods and application to case conceptualization;
- an understanding of systemic case conceptualization in service delivery;
- a client-centered perspective in assessment and conceptualization; and
- the ability to develop a systemic case conceptualization, including problem identification, case formulation, and treatment recommendations.

Drawing from these two literatures regarding the assessment of trauma and family functioning, we describe how practitioners can apply systems theory and skills to assessment when traumatic events have been experienced by one or more family members, either in the distant or recent past. Even when a client's or family's presenting concern is not explicitly related to trauma (as in the vignette beginning this chapter), the effects of trauma can be far-reaching across time and the family system. While there are a variety of approaches to assessment associated with specific treatment models, our focus here is to elucidate cross-cutting knowledge and skills, so that therapists utilizing different intervention approaches can effectively incorporate systemic assessment.

WHAT DOES A SYSTEMIC LENS ADD TO ASSESSMENT OF TRAUMA-IMPACTED CLIENTS?

Early family theorists and practitioners viewed the linear, individual focus of traditional assessment and diagnosis as incompatible with systems theory, citing concepts such as wholism, circular causality, and recursive and reciprocal influences over time (Stanton & Welsh, 2011). In contrast with the medical model's focus on the individual, which typifies most approaches to trauma assessment and treatment, a systemic perspective treats the couple or family system as the client, rather than any single "identified patient" the family has labeled as the problem. In many first-generation family therapy theories, individual symptoms were conceptualized as systemic indicators of family dysfunction that emerged to maintain homeostasis and/or signal the need for recalibration of the status quo in the family system. Although the fifth edition of the *Diagnostic and Statistical Manual of Mental Disorders* (*DSM-5-TR*) takes an ecological stance that recognizes the importance of relationships in mental health, it still maintains that mental disorders exist within individuals (Heyman & Slep, 2019). Systemically oriented assessment lives at the intersection of these perspectives, recognizing the complex interplay of both individual and systemic factors that contribute to each family member's functioning.

Systems theory can accommodate individual trauma-related distress in context and also recognizes relational disorders and syndromes that can exist within a relationship with or without the presence of an individual disorder (Lawrence et al., 2009). Contemporary couple and family practitioners view systemic assessment as the application of diverse methods for identifying the strengths and vulnerabilities of individuals, couples, and families in order to pinpoint problems, plan treatment, and answer focused questions (Stanton & Welsh, 2011). Conceptually, with some exceptions for biologically/neurologically based disorders (e.g., autism, attention-deficit/hyperactivity disorder [ADHD]), individual diagnosis is thought to reflect the emotions and behaviors adopted by family members to balance the relationship network (Gehart, 2018), and family interactions and processes can function as homeostatic mechanisms that help maintain problematic individual behaviors (Carlson, 1995).

A distinctive feature of systemic assessment is the evaluation of multiple family system levels.[1] When a comprehensive assessment is possible, systemic evaluators try to include multiple informants and use a variety of assessment

[1] See Chapter 1 in this volume for a detailed explanation of family system levels, which generally include the couple subsystem, parental subsystem, sibling/child subsystem, and parent–child dyads, but are unique within each family.

modalities that are developmentally appropriate for family members. This practice aligns well with trauma assessment guidelines for children and adolescents (Kisiel et al., 2014). While traditional psychological assessment examines biopsychosocial factors affecting individuals and considers multiple sources of behavioral, cognitive, affective, and interpersonal functioning, systemic assessment goes further by utilizing a wider range of methods and collecting data across individual, dyadic, family, and macrosystem levels (Celano, 2019; Stanton & Welsh, 2011). In addition to individual functioning, systemic assessment evaluates relationship functioning in dyads and subsystems, whole family interaction processes, and the relevance of external systems to individual, couple, and family functioning. As discussed in Chapter 1 in this volume, familiarity with child and family development, parenting, healthy/unhealthy interaction patterns, and other important systems theory concepts is vital in order to conduct a systemic assessment (Stanton & Welsh, 2011). All this informs the clinician's observations and interpretations of family patterns and behaviors as part of pretreatment and ongoing assessment.

Although individual assessment can be conducted using a systems theory framework, a comprehensive systemic assessment generally involves multiple people and subsystems, capturing various perspectives and subjective realities of family members about the presenting concern. This naturally increases the level of complexity, given the extensive amount of information collected, which must then be synthesized in a cohesive interpretation that can guide treatment planning. Family members commonly hold divergent perceptions and may have conflicting goals for treatment. Fortunately, the systemic conceptualization process helps with this task, lending itself to explaining these interconnections as part of individual, dyadic, and family processes. For example, as noted in Anthony's family described in the vignette, assessment results might reveal how adolescents view a situation very differently from their parents. Family members' varying views can often be just as—if not more—informative as similarities when viewed from a developmental systems perspective. We might hypothesize that Anthony's defiance and behavioral problems symbolize engagement with the developmental tasks of identity formation and renegotiating autonomy/connection with his parents. His father's recent return from military duty and reintegration into the parental subsystem, and his sister's departure to college, likely further disrupted the family homeostasis and suggest that previously established roles and boundaries may no longer be workable for this family. Significant differences between parents and children on measures of family independence, cohesion, conflict, and organization would be consistent with this hypothesis.

As part of cultural responsiveness, it is also important to consider differences in family relationships and functioning where collectivism is the norm and/or perceptions of what experiences are traumatic differ. While hypotheses about adolescent identity formation and autonomy may be applicable to the problem behaviors of a teenager in a middle-class American family like Anthony's, this conceptualization may not be sufficient for families who identify with more collectivist cultures. Parents who are first-generation immigrants, for example, may complain about adolescent defiance and oppose the increasing acculturation of their teenagers who are learning "Americanized" behaviors from school classmates and social media, which can create dissension and conflict between parents and children. Despite different conceptualizations of the problem, however, in each case, one goal of intervention could be to increase the family's awareness of sociocultural expectations for adolescent behavior (including pertinent differences between country of origin and country of residence), facilitate communication and mutual understanding between parents and children across differences, and help the family renegotiate boundaries and rules to achieve balance between closeness and autonomy without compromising their fundamental values and beliefs. Next, we turn to assessment of different system levels, including individual trauma symptoms and dyadic or family-wide dynamics.

Assessing Individual Trauma Symptoms

The individual member is the smallest and most basic unit of the family, functioning as an organismic subsystem nested within the larger family system. As such, individual family members are essential constituents of systemic assessment, particularly when individual symptoms affect or are affected by the family's functioning. Theory and research supporting the phenomena of vicarious trauma and secondary traumatic stress (e.g., Galovski & Lyons, 2004; Perilloux et al., 2012) make this especially clear in cases where one family member has experienced a traumatic event and both the affected individual and other family members are struggling with the aftermath. While screening measures can identify highly stressful experiences that could be traumatic, sometimes they do not fully capture the intersubjective nature of traumatization as discussed in Chapter 2 in this volume. More covert and chronic experiences of traumatization (e.g., childhood emotional abuse, racial trauma) should also be explored. Taking care to avoid reducing trauma to particular events, it is best practice to listen for and inquire about developmental circumstances at the nexus of a traumatized client's feelings of helplessness in the face of perceived threat, relentless invasion of personal boundaries and/or its opposite in the form of profound aloneness, as well as intense emotions and a sense of incomprehensibility.

When a trauma history is endorsed by one or more family members, clinicians should strive to follow procedures for trauma assessment outlined by experts in the field (see Cook et al., 2014; Kisiel et al., 2021; Substance Abuse and Mental Health Services Administration, 2014). In systemic assessments with trauma-impacted families, self-report measures of symptoms can be included in the assessment battery for all involved family members, given that they may be indirectly affected by the traumatic event. This also serves the purpose of expanding the presenting concerns and making it less likely that one member is considered "the problem." In addition to the brief symptom measures mentioned previously, the Trauma Symptom Inventory–2 (Briere, 2011) assesses a broader set of psychological outcomes, including symptoms of PTSD as well as impaired self-reference, insecure attachment, depression, anger, sexual disturbance, somatic preoccupation, and tension reduction behavior. Where complex PTSD is suspected, recently developed measures such as the Complex Trauma Inventory (Litvin et al., 2017) or its briefer Complex Trauma Screener (Litvin et al., 2024) can be administered.

Beyond self-report measures that track symptoms, the Clinician-Administered PTSD Scale for *DSM-5* (Weathers et al., 2013a) is a well-established structured interview for adults, often considered the "gold standard" for PTSD diagnosis. For children, the UCLA PTSD Reaction Index for *DSM-5* (Roulon-Arroyo et al., 2019) is a semi-structured interview that assesses trauma types, PTSD symptoms, and impairment. In addition to PTSD-related instruments, measures of other mental health problems linked to trauma history (e.g., anxiety, depression, suicidal ideation, problematic substance use, disordered eating) may be added to the battery as needed. One benefit of family-wide assessment is the ability to consider how members' traumatic experiences may be both distinct and interconnected. For example, clinicians can explore more covert aspects of the relational "fallout" of trauma within clinical interviews, such as patterns of fight, flight, freeze, and/or fawn that compromise family members' ability to cultivate meaningful, authentic relationships both inside (e.g., attachment bonds) and outside (e.g., friendships) of the family.

Assessing Underlying Family Characteristics and Dynamics

In addition to individual symptoms, a trauma-focused systemic assessment examines dyadic and family-wide characteristics, within which the intergenerational imprints of trauma often live. Aspects of the family typically assessed are described below, including structure and composition (i.e., who is a member of the family, including chosen family members), process (e.g., communication, problem solving, coping, conflict, cohesion, autonomy, adaptability), relationship patterns and sequences (e.g., attachment quality, parent–child interactions), affect (e.g., emotional regulation and expression), organization (e.g., roles, boundaries, leadership/hierarchy), and diversity as described in Chapter 1 in this volume (Bray, 2013; National Child Traumatic Stress Network, Family Systems Collaborative Group, 2011). Other factors to keep in mind include the stages of individual development and the family life cycle; family history of mental and physical illness, problematic substance use, domestic violence, and exposure to traumatic events; intergenerational patterns; and external sources of stress and support.

The structure and composition of the family affects the nature of assessment. Every family is unique and typically consists of several subsystems; however, those subsystems may vary significantly based on cultural values and expectations, family dissolution or blending, and other factors. For example, in single-parent families, an assessment of the couple subsystem is unnecessary if there is not a romantic partner who is regularly involved in the children's lives. It is quite possible, however, that the parental subsystem in single-parent families may include the other biological coparent, cohabitating romantic partners, grandparents, or even older children who consistently carry out parenting tasks. In more collectivistic cultures, it is common for the parental subsystem (even in two-parent households) to include extended family members who play critical roles in child-rearing. Depending on a family's unique situation, all of these people may be appropriate to involve in the assessment process, if they are available and willing to participate.

As opposed to what the family says and reports, family process refers to how family members interact at dyadic, subsystem, and whole family levels, which may not be consciously recognized or described by the family. This might include assessment of problem solving or coping strategies, communication patterns, and conflict styles. For example, the process model of family functioning (Skinner et al., 2000; Steinhauer et al., 1984) assesses seven key areas within the empirically supported Family Assessment Measure–III (FAM–III; Skinner et al., 1995): task accomplishment, communication, role performance, affective expression, control, values and norms, and involvement. Consistent with systemic inclusion of multiple perspectives, the FAM–III offers three different forms: (a) the Self-rating Scale assesses members' perceptions of their own functioning, (b) the Dyadic Relationships Scale measures functioning in specific pair relationships, and (c) the General Scale assesses overall family health. Other family assessment instruments include additional scales measuring processes related to conflict, organization, cohesion, flexibility/adaptability, problem solving, and leadership (see Table 4.1).

TABLE 4.1. Examples of Questionnaires for the Family System and Subsystems

Measure	Key information	Scale/subscale	Informant
		Couple/marital subsystem	
Marital Satisfaction Inventory–Revised (Snyder & Aikman, 1999)	150-item standardized measure assessing nature and extent of conflict within couple relationships; reliable and valid; includes one validity scale (Inconsistency)	Global Distress Scale and 10 subscales: Affective Communication, Role Orientation, Problem Solving, Aggression, Family History of Distress, Time Together, Dissatisfaction with Children, Financial Disagreement, Conflict over Child-Rearing, Sexual Dissatisfaction	Self-report by spouses/ partners
Dyadic Adjustment Scale (DAS; Spanier, 1976) Also available: Revised DAS (Busby et al., 1995) and DAS7 (Sharpley & Rogers, 1984)	Widely used 32-item measure of couple relationship quality; reliable and valid across gender and culture/nationality	Total Dyadic Adjustment Scale and four subscales: Dyadic Consensus, Dyadic Cohesion, Dyadic Satisfaction, Affectional Expression	Self-report by spouses/ partners
Conflict Tactics Scale-2 (Straus et al., 1996) 20-item short form also available (Straus & Douglas, 2004)	Widely used measure of engagement in (39 items) or victimization by (39 items) physical or psychological violence with an intimate partner. Strong psychometric properties and cross-nation validation	Five scales: Negotiation, Psychological Aggression, Physical Assault, Sexual Coercion, Injury	Self-report by spouses/ partners
		Parenting subsystem	
Parenting Stress Index (PSI; Abidin, 1995) Also available: Stress Index for Parents of Adolescents (SIPA; Sheras et al., 1998)	Widely used 120-item standardized measure of parental stress. Cross-culturally validated; normed with a variety of clinical groups; contains an internal validity check for defensive responding	Global Stress Scale Child Domain: Mood, Adaptability, Distractibility/Hyperactivity, Demandingness, Acceptability, Reinforces Parent	PSI–Parents of children 12 years or younger SIPA–Parents of youth 11 to 19 years

		Parent Domain: Competence, Isolation, Health, Role Restriction, Attachment to Child, Depression, Parenting Partner Relationship	
Conflict Tactics Scales–Parent-Child (Straus et al., 1998)	35 items measuring how often parents use specific disciplinary acts (both violent and nonviolent)	Six scales: Nonviolent Discipline, Psychological Aggression, Minor Physical Assault, Severe Physical Assault, Very Severe Physical Assault, Neglect	Parent self-report on their own parental behaviors with child
Parent Perception Inventory (Hazzard et al., 1983) Available in 34-item child and parent forms (Bruce et al., 2006; Cole et al., 2018)	Orally administered questionnaire measuring child's perception of parental behavior; 18 items per parent; acceptable internal consistency	Two scales: Positive Parenting (warm, supportive) and Negative Parenting behaviors (harsh, critical)	Children 5 to 12 years on parents
Children's Perception of Interparental Conflict (Grych et al., 1992) Shorter version available for children 6 to 9 years (McDonald & Grych, 2006)	48 items assessing children's views of parental conflict and child adjustment; demonstrated internal consistency and test-retest reliability	Broad Factors: Conflict, Threat, Self-blame; nine subscales: Frequency, Intensity, Resolution, Content, Perceived Threat, Coping Efficacy, Self-Blame, Triangulation, Stability	Children 9 to 17 years on interparental interactions
	Child subsystem		
Achenbach System (Achenbach & Rescorla, 2001): Child Behavior Checklist (two versions by age) Teacher Report Form Youth Behavior Checklist	Widely used system of standardized measures (99–114 items each) assessing emotional and behavioral symptoms in children and youth; cross-cultural validation; offers child self-report, parent observer report, and teacher observer report	Composite scales for Total Problems, Internalizing Problems, and Externalizing Problems. Subscales vary by form; examples include: Anxious/Depressed, Withdrawn, Sleep Problems, Somatic Complaints, Attention Problems, Hyperactivity, Aggressive Behavior. Also	Parents on children 1.5–5 years and 6–18 years Teachers on students 5–17 years Youth 11–18 years self-report

(*continues*)

TABLE 4.1. Examples of Questionnaires for the Family System and Subsystems (*Continued*)

Measure	Key information	Scale/subscale	Informant
		includes *DSM*-Oriented Scales: Affective Problems, Somatic Problems, Attention-Deficit/Hyperactivity Disorder Problems, Oppositional Defiant Problems, Conduct Problems	
Behavior Assessment System for Children (Reynolds & Kamphaus, 1992): Parent Rating Scales (two versions by age) Teacher Rating Scales (three versions by age) Child Self-report of Personality (two versions by age)	Widely used system of standardized measures (100–165 items each) assessing emotional and behavioral symptoms in children and youth; includes adaptability scales assessing strengths; offers child self-report, parent observer report, and teacher observer report	Composite scales include Behavioral Symptoms Index, Internalizing Problems, Externalizing Problems, School Problems, Adaptive Skills. Subscales vary by form. Symptom scale examples include: Anxiety, Depression, Withdrawal, Somatization, Attention Problems, Hyperactivity, Aggression, Atypicality, Learning Problems, Anger Control, Negative Emotionality, Bullying. Adaptive scales include: Adaptability, Social Skills, Functional Communication, Leadership, Study Skills	Parents on children 6–11 years and 12–21 years Teachers on children 3–5, 6–11, or 12–21 years Child/youth 8–18 years self-report
	Family system as a whole		
Family Assessment Device (Epstein et al., 1983)	60-item widely used, well-established measure with good psychometric properties; community family norms; cross-cultural validation; excellent internal consistency	General Functioning Scale, six subscales: Problem Solving, Communication, Roles, Affective Responsivity, Affective Involvement, Behavior Control	Family members aged 12 and older
Family Assessment Measure–III (Skinner et al., 2000)	Well-established measure with good psychometric properties; offers three forms: the General Scale (50 items) assesses overall	Seven scales: Task Accomplishment, Role Performance, Communication, Affective	Family members aged 10 and older

	family functioning; Dyadic Relationship Scale (42 items) assesses functioning in any dyadic pair; Self-rating Scale (42 items) is a self-report of own functioning in family	Expression, Involvement, Control, Values and Norms	
Family Adaptability and Cohesion Evaluation Scales (Olson et al., 2011)	42-item instrument widely used in clinical settings with diverse populations; demonstrates good psychometric properties	Three broad domains: Cohesion, Flexibility, Communication. Taps healthy and unhealthy levels of these domains with six scales (Balanced Cohesion, Balanced Flexibility, Disengaged, Enmeshed, Rigid, Chaotic) that yield family profiles	Family members aged 12 and older
Self-report Family Inventory (Beavers & Hampson, 1990)	36-item screening measure of family functioning; norms provided in manual; approaching well-established with acceptable reliability overall, although there are discrepant findings for test-retest reliability and factor structure	Five scales: Health/Competence, Conflict, Cohesion, Leadership, Emotional Expressiveness	Family members aged 10 and older
Systemic Clinical Outcome and Routine Evaluation (Stratton et al., 2010)	Brief screening tool with 15- and 28-item versions; good psychometric properties with stable factor structure	Total Family Problems Scale and three subscales: Family Strengths, Family Difficulties, Family Communication	Family members aged 12 and older
Family Environment Scale (Moos & Moos, 2002) Also available 30-item Child-Version FES (Pino et al., 1984)	90-item forced choice questionnaire assessing family environment; approaching well-established although some research suggests alternate factor structures; true/false format weakens internal consistency estimates; norms provided for diverse family groups, including distressed and nondistressed adults and adolescents	Nine scales: Cohesion, Expressiveness, Conflict, Independence, Achievement Orientation, Intellectual-Cultural Orientation, Moral-Religious Emphasis, Organization, Control	Family members aged 11 and older

Relationship patterns in the family are behavioral sequences that develop over time and often operate outside of conscious awareness (Bray, 2013). There is ample empirical evidence of individual and relational outcomes related to attachment patterns in parent–child and couple dyads, as well as the demand–withdraw (i.e., pursuer–distancer) cycle and other processes related to couple functioning and satisfaction (e.g., Demby et al., 2017; Gottman, 1993; Riggs et al., 2020). In families with trauma exposure, attachment dynamics are especially important to explore. The development of secure attachment in parent–child relationships can be jeopardized by traumatic experiences in early life. A large literature supports the negative effects of child maltreatment on children, including disorganized attachment, neurobiological changes, and deficits in social skills (for reviews, see DeKlyen & Greenberg, 2018; Lyons-Ruth & Jacobvitz, 2018). Similarly, some evidence suggests that traumatic events in adulthood can alter the attachment system through a "reciprocal, recursive, amplifying cycle of reactivation of the trauma and attachment insecurities" (Mikulincer & Shaver, 2016, p. 423). Theories of intimate partner violence propose that partners with negative self-models associated with preoccupied and fearful adult attachment are chronically anxious about abandonment and can respond with anger, jealousy, and abusive behavior (Dutton et al., 1994). Systemic assessment that attends to the interplay of trauma and attachment can identify important relational processes and emotions that help clinicians better understand and target maladaptive patterns contributing to family difficulties.

As explored in Chapter 2 in this volume, overwhelming affect is a key aspect of traumatization; thus, this area is particularly important to explore at a family level, beyond individual symptoms. Family affect refers to patterns of emotional expression or regulation in the system, which can be operationalized in different ways, making it essential for clinicians to carefully check instrument manuals to gain clarity on what exactly is being evaluated. For example, the FAM–III Affective Expression scale refers to the content, intensity, and timing of emotions expressed in the family, as well as the range and situational appropriateness of emotions expressed (Skinner et al., 1995), whereas the Expressiveness Scale on the Family Environment Scale (FES) measures "the extent to which family members are encouraged to express their feelings directly" (Moos & Moos, 2002, p. 1). Similarly, depending on the instrument selected, family organization may be measured in various ways and is sometimes separated into different components, such as control or power (e.g., parental hierarchy), implicit or explicit family rules and roles, and system and subsystem boundaries.

It is also crucial to consider diversity in all systemic assessments, because these differences can contribute to variations in the family characteristics and processes mentioned above (Bray, 2015). Diversity factors, including a family's social location, experiences of prejudice and discrimination, and cultural and religious context, may be relevant to individual, family, and ecological levels of a family system. For example, individual family members may differ in their acculturation, sexual identity, and religious/spiritual beliefs, which may impact the level of family cohesion, expected roles, and even who is considered "family." A household's functioning is also influenced by embeddedness in neighborhood, school, work, and other community ecologies (McIntosh et al., 2008). These cultural frames of reference are critical to hold in mind at every stage of assessment, including collaborating with the family to identify key questions, selecting and administering measures, synthesizing findings, providing feedback, and planning treatment.

Based on your workplace situation and the presenting concerns for each case, you may choose to focus on assessing a few of the most salient symptom areas and family processes, or take a more comprehensive approach. Clinical decision making should always be guided by the specific question(s) that the assessment for a particular individual and/or family seeks to answer. The more comprehensive your battery, the greater the time investment for both family members and yourself, so attention to feasibility is important. Systemic assessment can result in large amounts of information, which then needs to be integrated and interpreted; when families have been impacted by trauma, the complexity often rises another notch. To clarify this process and assist with decision making, the next section addresses practical considerations in deciding what to assess, who to ask, and how to go about measuring each area that you are trying to gather information about.

GETTING PRACTICAL: WHO, WHAT, AND HOW TO ASSESS

Systemic evaluation generally begins with an intake interview and sometimes brief screening measures, the results of which guide decisions about assessment measures and methods, which might include questionnaires, interviews, diagrammatic and drawing tools, and formal or informal observations. This includes considering who and what to assess as well as how to elucidate relevant information (Snyder et al., 2019). Because traumatic events, whether experienced by one member or the entire family, can affect family members and subsystems in various ways, it is important to assess the functioning of interparental relations, parent–child interactions, and sibling exchanges (NCTSN, 2011), as well as the functioning of the whole family system and its interface with extended family and other external systems. The particularities of the presenting problem and assessment goals should always guide selection of measures and methods.

Throughout this chapter and in Table 4.1, we offer examples of commonly used measures but do not exhaustively examine the vast array of available assessments. We refer readers to in-depth volumes on trauma-related (Kisiel et al., 2021; J. P. Wilson & Keane, 2004; Wycoff & Franzese, 2019) and systemic (Wampler et al., 2020; L. Williams et al., 2011) assessment, and advise examination of the latest empirical support for the assessment measures that you plan to use. Given the constant development and validation of new (and more culturally informed) measures, helpful resources also include online repositories, such as the International Society for Traumatic Stress Studies (www.istss.org/clinical-resources/), the National Center for PTSD (www.ptsd.va.gov/professional/assessment/), and the National Child Traumatic Stress Network (www.nctsn.org/).

In addition to gathering data from multiple informants, a systemically oriented assessment generally utilizes multiple methods. Here, we outline foundational considerations in test selection, and then discuss four key methods of gathering information that can be incorporated in various combinations most suitable to the presenting family and trauma characteristics: clinical interviews, questionnaires/checklists (including self- and other-reports), diagrammatic/drawing tools, and direct observation (including structured and unstructured play). To bring these concepts to life, we then describe the Garcia family's assessment process, an amalgamated case of traumatic loss used for illustration that will be expanded on in Chapters 5 (treatment) and 6 (consultation/advocacy) in this volume.

Foundational Considerations

Important factors to consider when selecting instruments include cost, clinical utility, ease of administration and scoring, assessment burden on family and clinician, and established research support. As noted earlier, the constraints and focus of your work setting will also shape clinical decision making here. Systemic assessment can be embodied in a variety of ways. On the one end, a "bento box" version—suited to treatment sites where you only have 1 hour allotted for intake (and where parents are less open to filling out measures about themselves)—could include a clinical interview, informal observation of parent–child interactions, and brief screening measures of the child's symptoms/functioning. On the other end, your situation may lend itself to a "buffet" approach—engaging multiple family members in a multi-hour assessment process distinct from the initial intake, as described in the Garcia family's case. And there are many possibilities on the spectrum in between! Regardless, we as clinicians must always take care to avoid an assessment process so lengthy that it unduly strains traumatized families, who often are burdened by symptoms and have limited mental and emotional resources ... in addition to time! This is not trauma responsive and could contribute to lack of treatment engagement and early dropout. Our task, then, is to strategically pull from the many available measurement options to elucidate key information needed for case formulation. We must always consider the clinical utility of each measure relative to the burden it places on an already-stressed family.

Established models of family assessment include the McMasters model (Epstein et al., 1983; I. W. Miller et al., 2000), the circumplex model (Olson, 1993, 2000), and the process model of family functioning (Skinner et al., 2000; Steinhauer et al., 1984). Each includes multi-method assessments measuring constructs tied to a particular view of optimal family functioning. These standardized assessment systems can be helpful to draw from, rather than creating test batteries "from scratch," but may be less accessible in some settings, such as primary care and low-resource social service agencies, due to the associated time and expense.

Best practice recommendations include using reliable and valid instruments that are empirically supported and normed on the population to which the client/family belongs. Many self-report questionnaires are only valid with older children (e.g., 8+ or 12+ years) or have not been normed for certain racial/ethnic populations and family structures. Drawing and play-based tasks, as well as parent–child observation, may rely more on clinical judgement than research evidence but are considered fundamental to child assessment and play a key role in capturing children's perceptions, particularly in child protection matters, when it does not jeopardize child safety or violate court orders barring parent–child contact (APA, 2013b; McConaughy, 2005; Sattler, 2001).[2] This can be supplemented by parent and teacher reports that have more rigorous research support. While standardized instruments can be administered to families who match some, but not all, characteristics of the normative sample, clinicians might also opt to gather information from

[2] As detailed in Chapters 1 and 5 in this volume, when caregivers have been abusive, additional ethical and legal issues must be considered to determine their level of involvement. This book does not address forensic and child custody assessment, which are distinct specialties, and we refer readers to existing resources in this area (Drozd & Flens, 2014; Giardino et al., 2018).

such families through a more loosely structured interview as part of culturally responsive assessment (Stanton & Welsh, 2011).

Clinical Interviews

The clinical interview serves the dual purpose of gathering information about the presenting problem with respectful curiosity, while also beginning to build rapport and trust with family members (Allen & Becker, 2019; Sommers-Flanagan & Sommers-Flanagan, 2016). Traumatized families are understandably anxious and distrustful, so utilizing a collaborative approach to assessment is a critical part of alliance-building. Family members' self-disclosure about sensitive topics hinges on establishing a certain level of safety and comfort that allows the examiner/therapist to temporarily "join" the family system. First steps in assessment involve partnering with the family as their ally, evaluating safety concerns, and orienting the family to the evaluation process. In situations of current or past family violence, members may not openly share information and the assessor must determine whether proceeding with a family-based assessment could potentially increase the risk for violence (Bograd & Mederos, 1999; Cooper & Vetere, 2005). Risk factors contraindicative of family or perpetrator involvement are discussed in Chapters 1 and 5 in this volume, but even if risk of violence is reasonably low, a safety plan can be developed and agreed upon by the family members before proceeding. Safety plans can take a number of different forms that might involve only the abused family member(s), but may also include the perpetrator of violence, depending on the outcome of risk assessment (Cooper & Vetere, 2006). Typically, the development of safety plans comprises a collaborative discussion between therapists and the adults in treatment in order to identify current threats and develop a detailed, step-by-step strategy for leaving a potentially dangerous situation and getting to a safer environment, such as a friend's or relative's home (Briere & Scott, 2025; Figley & Kiser, 2013; Sells & Souder, 2018).

A systemically oriented clinical interview seeks multiple viewpoints on the same issues. The therapist attempts to connect with all family members, often through circular questions that get at points of connection as well as differences. This takes considerable time and patience, such that clinical interviews often last 90 minutes. The full assessment process can span multiple sessions, including individual and family meetings, and should be described to families and negotiated with them. In addition to obtaining problem- and trauma-related information, clinicians should inquire about individual and family strengths, which can instill hope, convey the therapist's positive view of the family, and elucidate culturally embedded practices that can be integrated as part of trauma healing (L. Williams et al., 2011).

Unstructured or semi-structured interviews are the norm when working with couples and families. For example, the Relationship Quality Interview (Lawrence et al., 2011) is a semi-structured individual interview designed to assess dyadic relationship qualities using behavioral anchors that has demonstrated strong reliability, convergent validity, and divergent validity. Although less common in routine practice, structured clinical interviews with behaviorally anchored definitions have been field tested, for example, to assess marital distress and partner aggression (Heyman et al., 2001) and family maltreatment (Heyman & Slep, 2006). Given a lack of research attention to empirically supported interviews in couple and family assessment, practitioners often rely on clinical judgement through conducting unstructured interviews and balance this with well-validated self-report instruments to assess salient family constructs.

Questionnaires and Checklists

Standardized self-reports are the most common measurement tool in couple and family assessment. In cases of reported or suspected trauma, such measures are often less threatening than a clinical interview and may encourage family members' honest self-disclosure (Substance Abuse and Mental Health Services Administration, 2014). Depending on the presenting problem, a family assessment might include measures of individual psychological and interpersonal functioning, parenting practices, parental stress, dyadic relationships (e.g., spouses/partners, parents, parent–child, siblings), family functioning along multiple dimensions, and external supports and stressors.

In addition to psychometric properties and appropriateness of the normative group, selection of standardized instruments is in large part guided by the match between the clinical questions or goals of the assessment and the specific constructs (subscales) produced by the instrument. One approach to instrument selection for systemic assessment involves identifying the family's relevant subsystems and choosing measures that assess each of these from different perspectives (e.g., perceptions of family conflict by mother and/or father, child, and sibling). Table 4.1, which is organized by subsystem level, presents just a few examples of commonly used self-report measures of the couple relationship (e.g., relational satisfaction and adjustment, sexual functioning), parenting (e.g., parenting practices, warmth, discipline, parent–child relationships, parenting stress, risk for maltreatment), child functioning (e.g., internalizing and externalizing behaviors, symptomology, social connectedness), and the family system as a whole (e.g., communication, problem solving, organization, control, affective expression and/or involvement, cohesion, conflict).

Informant (or "other-") report measures are customarily utilized in assessments involving children and adolescents to capture multiple perspectives from adults familiar with the child. These might include behavior checklists completed by parents, relatives, teachers, coaches, or other adults closely involved in a child's life, each of which offers a distinct perspective on the child's functioning. Informant report measures can also capture intersubjective perspectives, such as a child's observations of the parental subsystem, a parent and child's experience of their attachment bond, siblings' perceptions of their dynamic, or romantic partners' satisfaction with or opinions about their functioning as a couple.

Diagrammatic and Drawing Tools

Diagrammatic (e.g., genogram, ecomap) and drawing (e.g., house–tree–person) tools tend to be informal to the extent that there may limited empirical support, and administration/scoring procedures may not be a standardized. As such, consistent with Coupland et al.'s (1995) assertion regarding the genogram, we consider these tools to be heuristic devices rather than assessment instruments, per se. That is, they assist in organizing large amounts of information obtained during a systemic assessment and making sense of the data in order to conceptualize the larger family system and its functioning. These methods have a long-standing and prominent role in the field of family therapy, and are also applicable to working with individual clients through a systemic lens. A further advantage is that children often enjoy the drawing activities and colors that can be creatively incorporated into the administration of the genogram and ecomap (e.g., colored markers, a white board or large easel pad). The purposeful dialogue and collaborative work toward a common goal on these group tasks can facilitate a sense of teamwork and the development of a strong working alliance. The pictorial products of these heuristic exercises also can be helpful for clients in developing an understanding of intergenerational family dynamics and history, which may include other traumatic events. As discussed in Chapter 2 in this volume, systemic visual mapping of trauma is one way to gain a deeper understanding of the system's cumulative trauma burden. Developmental considerations are important when using visual mapping of trauma; for example, this tool may be more appropriate to complete with adults and older adolescents present. Examples of the genogram, ecomap, and visual map of trauma are provided as part of the Garcia family case study at the end of the chapter; here, we discuss each in further detail.

Genograms are family trees that depict basic family history (e.g., marriage/divorce, birth order, age, deaths, etc.) and visually map out family relationships and characteristics, including intergenerational patterns that can represent strengths and vulnerabilities, such as closeness/distance, occupations, and physical/mental health. Genograms are extremely useful in revealing intergenerational patterns of violence and abuse that may be pertinent to treatment. Originally developed for use in Bowenian family therapy, which emphasizes psychodynamic and intergenerational processes, McGoldrick et al. (2008; McGoldrick & Gerson, 1985) elaborated on the genogram, outlining general interview content and standard symbols. Genograms are most often used informally to gather information and get to know the family, but if more empirical rigor is desired, the Family Genogram Interview (Platt & Skowron, 2013) is a standardized interview protocol that has demonstrated good inter-interviewer reliability, internal consistency, and construct validity. Thematic variations include cultural genograms (Shellenberger et al., 2007), community genograms (Ivey et al., 2017), and trauma-focused genograms (James & MacKinnon, 2012; Jordan, 2004). As one example, the Transgenerational Trauma and Resilience Genogram (Goodman, 2013) provides a framework for tracing trauma across generations and considers ecosystemic issues, client strength and resilience, and sociopolitical factors that may impact trauma and recovery.

Structural family maps and family ecomaps are also often used by systemically oriented practitioners. Emerging from structural family theory and therapy, the structural family map provides a graphic tool to represent clinical hypotheses, therapeutic progress, and goals regarding family structure, relationships, and boundaries, regardless of theoretical approach (see Box 4.1). Given that assessment is an ongoing process in structural family therapy, Minuchin (1974) recommended that clinicians map their systemic hypotheses after each session to track new developments, confirm or disconfirm earlier hypotheses based on new session data, and identify changes or continuing "stuckness" in the family structure. Family ecomaps (Hartman, 1978), by contrast, focus on the larger ecological system to depict the strength, impact, and quality of contacts with people outside of the family, organized activities in the community, and institutions. By exploring broader connections to neighbors, friends, communities, schools, extracurricular activities, and cultural/religious bonds, ecomaps provide clinically relevant information about how a family views their surrounding environment and identify both external resources and strains that could affect the family and/or individual members.

BOX 4.1

MINUCHIN'S SYMBOLS FOR STRUCTURAL FAMILY MAPS

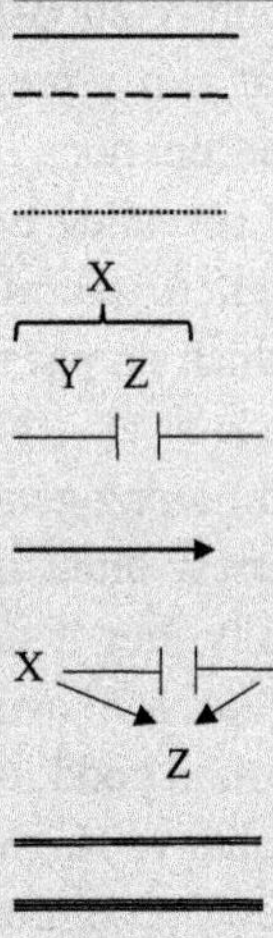

Rigid Boundary	Potential disengagement
Clear Boundary	Balanced closeness-autonomy
Diffuse Boundary	Potential enmeshment
Coalition	2+ members (Y, Z) team up against 1+ (X) members
Conflict	2 members in frequent conflict
Focused on	1+ member focused on another member
Detouring	2 members (X, Y) focus on another member (Z) to avoid own conflict
Affiliation/involvement	Close relationship
Overinvolvement	Enmeshed relationship

Note. Similar symbols on the genogram may mean something different, for example, Minuchin's symbol for "conflict" means "cutoff" on the genogram. Because students learning genograms, ecomaps, and structural maps can easily confuse symbols, my rule of thumb as an instructor has always been to allow some logical crossover in symbolization *as long as a correct key is provided for each figure.*

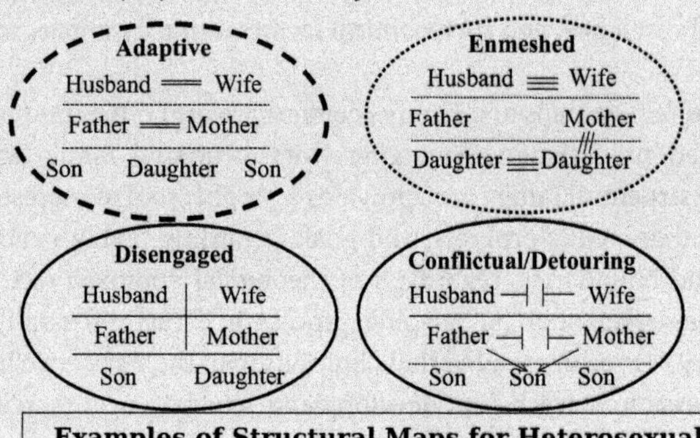

Examples of Structural Maps for Heterosexual Two-parent Families

Family and individual timelines depict a chronological sequence of significant life events and life cycle transitions, and may include both negative/traumatic and positive/memorable events as part of a holistic approach (Schauer et al., 2017). As described in Chapter 1 in this volume, normative transitions include predictable events common to most people, such as starting school, leaving home, marriage, childbirth, and so forth. Nonnormative transitions, on the other hand, are unplanned shifts or traumas in the family, such as illness, job loss, divorce, immigration, accidental injury or death, natural disasters, etc. Timelines can assist clinicians in understanding the timing of treatment-seeking, how a family coped with previous challenges, and the significance of earlier life events to current individual and family experiences and emerging symptoms (L. Williams et al., 2011). In trauma intervention, timelines are used to depict the chronological order of specific traumatic experiences that can be targeted as part of treatment. Trauma timelines may be especially helpful as part of intervening with complex PTSD, bringing some sense of coherence to a history rife with trauma. Timelines also prove useful when tracking pre- and posttrauma functioning of family members and systemic processes, particularly in cases of one-time catastrophes that altered previously workable interaction patterns.

Projective tests, while not a standard part of family assessments, can be helpful with children too young for standardized self-report instruments. Relevant examples include the Children's Apperception Test (Bellak & Abrams, 1993; Bellack & Bellak, 1949), House–Tree–Person (Buck, 1966), and Kinetic Family Drawing (Burns & Kaufman, 1987). Although often lacking the psychometric evidence of standardized instruments, projective tests can nevertheless shed light on the child's experience in the family, and serve as a springboard for conversation. From a practical standpoint, when parents and caregivers are participating in individual interviews or completing other assessment instruments, it is prudent to keep children busy with their own assessment activities that can supplement other data. An added benefit is that children seem to enjoy these projective activities, which ask them to tell stories or draw pictures.

Observational Methods

In the general practice of assessment, observations of test behavior (e.g., loss of focus, fatigue, giving up, or not trying) inform the examiner's evaluation of the validity of test results. Within couple and family assessment, observation takes on a more prominent role, offering a rich source of information about parent–child and family interaction patterns that may be outside of the clients' conscious awareness. This is especially the case when there are young children in the family, given growing attention to dyadic observation as part of supporting infant–parent mental health (Brandt et al., 2013; Tryphonopoulos et al., 2014; Zeanah, 2018). Direct observation helps counter the limitations of self-report questionnaires, with evidence suggesting that formal observations by trained professionals provide less biased information than parent and teacher reports (Aspland & Gardner, 2003; Eddy et al., 1998; G. R. Patterson & Forgatch, 1995; Prescott et al., 2000). Professional standards and guidelines for psychiatric, forensic (e.g., child protection, custody), and trauma assessment often recommend direct observations of children, both alone and in the company of each (nonoffender) parent, as well as during a family meeting (American Academy of Child and Adolescent Psychiatry, 1997, 2007; APA, 2013a, 2013b, 2022; Association of Family and Conciliation Courts, 2006; National Child Traumatic Stress Network, Family Systems Collaborative Group, 2011).

Behavioral observation procedures can be informal or formal. Formal procedures for systematic observation of family behavior provide a structured format for assessing specific behaviors or defined constructs. Examples include clinician rating scales and behavioral coding systems, the latter of which are more commonly used in research due to the extensive time and expense of training, administration, and coding (for reviews of formal coding systems, see Alderfer et al., 2008; Aspland & Gardner, 2003; Hampson & Beavers, 2004; Kerig & Lindahl, 2001; Zumbach et al., 2022). Clinician rating scales are used to code behavioral observations, typically during a structured or semi-structured interview. While still requiring training, some clinical rating scales offer a practical alternative for clinicians to learn how to administer and score instruments fairly quickly and easily. Several clinician rating scales assessing family functioning have been deemed "well-established," including the Circumplex Clinical Rating Scale and the McMaster Clinical Rating Scale (Alderfer et al., 2008). Notable examples of trauma-specific clinician rating scales for children and families include the trauma versions of the Child and Adolescent Needs and Strengths (Kisiel et al., 2013; Lyons et al., 2000) and the Family Assessment of Needs and Strengths (Kiser et al., 2009).

Informal clinical observations tend to be loosely structured and take place during the clinical interview, testing procedures, and subsequent therapy sessions. Early family therapy models rarely involved a separate, initial assessment phase and instead relied on observations of family interactions throughout treatment, whether naturally occurring or set up by the therapist, to develop conceptual hypotheses regarding family structure and functioning (e.g., boundaries, parental hierarchy, organization, subsystems, coalitions, alliances) and guide interventions. Stanton and Welsh (2011) noted, "Regardless of type of assessment methodology used, structural/strategic observational assessment (e.g., structural family maps), because of its foundational link to evaluating family systems, is considered an important element of demonstrating competency in couple and family psychology assessment" (p. 73).

Clinical inferences made from informal observations of behaviors and interactions are derived from systems theories and the research literature regarding individual development and mental health, the family life cycle, parenting practices, attachment relationships, family functioning, and sociocultural factors, as well as from the trauma literature when relevant. Depending on the nature and purpose of the assessment, clinicians may choose to observe a wide range of behaviors. Acklin and Cho-Stutler (2006) recommended that examiners focus on observable behaviors germane to other data sources in order to triangulate data points and arrive at reasonable conclusions. Standardized self- and other-report measures may yield scales or subscales that pertain to behavior observed during natural and task-related family interactions. Observing what happens in the room can help support or disconfirm interpretation of other testing measures and resulting hypotheses.

CASE STUDY
The Garcia Family

Given the challenges of systemic trauma assessment, with its many diverse and complex considerations, we now apply these concepts and assessment procedures to an amalgamated case that will be elaborated across the next few chapters. Here, we demonstrate how to select appropriate test instruments and integrate findings as part of a comprehensive systemic assessment. Subsequent chapters will further elaborate systemically oriented case conceptualization, treatment planning, and intervention for this family.

Mrs. Jessica Garcia and her two children, Luke (9 years old) and Amelia (14 months old), presented at the community mental health clinic for an initial intake interview 6 months after her husband's death by suicide. After informed consent was obtained, a release of information was requested for the therapist to conduct a phone interview with Luke's elementary school counselor, who referred them for treatment. As explained in the intake report (see Box 4.2), Mrs. Garcia noted that she was still struggling but mostly was worried about Luke, who was exhibiting problematic behavior at school and home that left Mrs. Garcia at her wit's end. Mrs. Garcia explained that she didn't know how to (or if she should) talk to her children about their father's death and was worried about upsetting them further.

BOX 4.2

INTAKE: GARCIA FAMILY

REASON FOR REFERRAL

Mrs. Jessica Garcia is a 27-year-old White, heterosexual woman who was referred to the mental health clinic by her son's elementary school counselor. Following the sudden traumatic loss of her husband, who committed suicide approximately 6 months ago, Mrs. Garcia reported an increase in her son's "acting out" behaviors, both at home and school. In addition, she acknowledged feelings of anger and guilt regarding her husband's death and the loss it represents to her son and daughter. Mrs. Garcia is seeking assistance for her son and wants to learn how to help her family cope with the traumatic loss.

BACKGROUND INFORMATION

Data provided by Mrs. Garcia in intake paperwork and 50-minute intake interview

The Garcia family is a middle-class, multiracial family living in El Paso, Texas. Mrs. Garcia was born and raised in the area with her parents and older sister. She described a good relationship with her mother, who is a recently retired legal secretary, and a "so-so" relationship with her father, who worked in civil service until his retirement. Mrs. Garcia is currently employed full-time and frequently works overtime as a paralegal at a law firm. During her senior year in high school, Mrs. Garcia became pregnant with Luke, her 9-year-old White son. Mrs. Garcia stated that Luke's biological father "wanted nothing to do with his son," so she and Luke continued to live with her parents for social and financial support for approximately 5 years.

When Luke was 3 years old, Mrs. Garcia reported that she met and fell in love with Daniel Garcia, a Mexican American man who worked as an electrician and grew up in a small town several hours east of El Paso. She married Daniel 18 months later and moved to their new home about 20 miles from her parents' house. She reported being very happy in her marriage, despite Mr. Garcia's periodic depression that she attributed to "drama" in his extended family. Mr. and Mrs. Garcia also had a biological daughter, Amelia, who is now 14 months old. She indicated that everyone in her family "got along great," but admitted increasing marital stress in the last few years, mostly related to finances and his extended family's "rude" treatment of their family.

While her husband was not close to his family of origin, Mrs. Garcia reported those relationships became even more strained after Amelia was born.

Specifically, she indicated that Daniel's parents wanted him to visit more with the baby, but after several unpleasant visits that left him depressed, he refused the invitations, which brought anger and criticism from other relatives.

Mrs. Garcia moved into her parents' home after her husband's death as she adjusted to the heightened demands of being a single, working parent. Since the move, Mrs. Garcia described increasing disagreements with her parents, stating that her parents undermine her parental authority with her son while her father seems to ignore the baby. Mrs. Garcia stated she hopes to move back into their own home but admitted uncertainty about when that might happen or if she can afford it.

Mrs. Garcia reported that Luke has become more disruptive, both at home and at school, since his stepfather's death. Luke was diagnosed with ADHD Inattentive type when he was 6 years old and is currently receiving additional accommodations and guidance in school. Mrs. Garcia said Luke was fairly well-behaved despite being distractible and forgetful, so instead of medication, she attended a class on how to parent children with ADHD. However, she described increasing difficulty in effectively managing Luke's behavior at home, which she attributed to inconsistent parenting strategies by her parents. Mrs. Garcia also acknowledged that her husband's suicide has adversely affected Luke, but she felt uncertain about how to help him during this time of loss and transition. Mrs. Garcia described her daughter as sweet, with good sleep and eating habits, denying significant behavioral concerns. During the weekends, the family finds enjoyment by spending time together at a local park and watching Disney movies.

IMPRESSION

Mrs. Garcia arrived on time for therapy, well-groomed and dressed professionally, having come directly from work. She was calm and self-disclosing for the most part, although reference to her husband's death caused obvious distress and she quickly moved past the topic. She was oriented to person, place, and time, and seemed cooperative and eager for help. Mrs. Garcia agreed to an assessment in order to better understand her family's current need for services. She also signed a release of information to allow a phone interview with the school counselor.

INITIAL RECOMMENDATIONS

1. Family and individual assessment to identify difficulties and determine goals for intervention.
2. Depending on results of assessment, family may be referred for individual and/or family therapy, as well as other community resources.

Based on the information provided by the school counselor and Mrs. Garcia in the initial intake interview, the therapist recommended a systemic treatment approach, beginning with a comprehensive family assessment. The therapist revisited informed consent, covering additional ethical and legal issues related to family therapy, with the system as the identified patient. Mrs. Garcia expressed relief that she wouldn't have to juggle multiple intakes and coordination with therapists for both herself and her son. She consented for herself and her children to participate in a family assessment to inform treatment planning. Of note, Mrs. Garcia and her children had moved in with her parents following the suicide. Despite encouragement and an explanation about the importance of including all household members, Mrs. Garcia declined to allow her parents to attend the assessment sessions, stating that she planned to move back to her own home with the children soon. She did, however, sign a release of information allowing the clinician to mail her mother and Luke's teacher assessment questionnaires about her son. The following sections describe the clinician's process of selecting appropriate methods and measures to assess the family, administering the assessment instruments in a trauma-informed manner, and reporting findings as part of collaborative treatment planning.

Selection of Assessment Methods and Measures

Systemic family assessment gathers information at individual, subsystem, and system-wide levels, so one of the first tasks is to identify household members, the family system levels, and potential informants that are relevant to the specific family you are seeing. Table 4.2 presents one approach to instrument selection used with the Garcia family, which specifies each family system level that needs to be measured, the selected instrument and its description, along with the informant for each measure. Under ideal circumstances, the grandparents in the Garcia family, who likely are actively involved in parenting tasks, would participate in both assessment and therapy. If a reasoned explanation of the importance of including the whole family does not convince the client, however, it is best to prioritize building trust in the therapeutic relationship and honoring client agency, keeping in mind that Mrs. Garcia could change her mind as treatment progresses. In working with the Garcia family, the therapist assessed individual functioning, the parenting and child subsystems, dyadic parent–child relationships, family-wide processes, and other external systems, such as extended family, school, and social or community activities/engagement. If the grandparents participated in the assessment, it would be particularly important to assess their parental roles and practices in addition to their observations of child behavior and family interactions. Given that Mrs. Garcia is

TABLE 4.2. Systemic Approach to Selection of Instruments: The Garcia Family

System level	Measure	Description	Informant
		Individual functioning	
Parents	Brief Symptom Inventory	Self-report of psychological symptoms	Mrs. Garcia
	PTSD Checklist	Self-report of trauma symptoms	Mrs. Garcia
	Experiences in Close Relationships	Self-report of adult attachment style	Mrs. Garcia
Child	BASC-Parent Rating Scales	Parent report of child behavior	Mrs. Garcia, Grandmother
	BASC-Teacher Rating Scales	Teacher report of child behavior	Teacher
	BASC-Self-Report of Personality	Child self-report of behavior and personality	Luke
	Child and Adolescent Trauma Screen	Brief self-report of trauma symptoms for children/adolescents	Luke
		Dyadic functioning	
Couple/marital	Not applicable		
Coparenting	Not applicable		
Parent–child	Parent Perception Inventory	Child self-report of parents' behavior toward child	Luke
	People in My Life	Child self-report of relationship to parents	Luke
	Parenting Stress Index	Parent self-report of stress re: child behavior, parenting	Mrs. Garcia

(*continues*)

TABLE 4.2. Systemic Approach to Selection of Instruments: The Garcia Family (*Continued*)

System level	Measure	Description	Informant
		Family functioning	
Family system	Clinical Interviews	Individual and family interviews to gather data relevant to concern	Family members, mostly mother
	Observation and Family Mapping	Observation of family interactions in assessment and therapy inform systemic hypotheses and family maps	Therapist
	Family Environment Scale	Self-report of family organization and functioning	Mrs. Garcia, Luke
	Genogram	Three-generation family diagram	Mrs. Garcia, Luke
		Contextual influences	
Family Ecosystem	Ecomap	Diagram of external factors interacting with family and its members	Mrs. Garcia, Luke
	People in My Life	Child self-report of relationship to peers and school	Luke
	Phone Interview	Information from referral source	School Counselor
	BASC-Teacher Rating Scales	Teacher report of child school problems	Teacher
	BASC-Self-Report of Personality	Child self-report of attitudes toward school	Luke

Note. PTSD = posttraumatic stress disorder; BASC = Behavior Assessment System for Children.

now single, the marital/couple subsystem is less relevant; however, the history of her and her husband's relational dynamics could inform her experience of his death and thus be pertinent to case formulation.

It is also important to determine the utility of including outside informants in the assessment (De Los Reyes & Makol, 2022)—that is, are there persons and specific informant measures that could improve clinical understanding and treatment planning? Best practices in the assessment of children and adolescents have long included a multi-method, multi-informant approach (Hunsley & Mash, 2007), and this is also true in family assessment. In the Garcia's case, the therapist decided that Luke's teacher and grandmother had important perspectives on Luke's behavior and should be asked to complete a behavior checklist if possible. Finally, when selecting specific instruments, it is important to consider Luke and Amelia's ages as well as ease of administration, given the family context of acute stress related to traumatic loss. Table 4.2 details the full battery of measures utilized, and the rationale for each is described here.

Trauma exposure can have a wide range of effects, so at the individual level, the clinician elected to administer self-report inventories to assess Mrs. Garcia's psychological functioning and potential traumatic stress, including the Brief Symptom Inventory (BSI; Derogatis, 1993) and the PTSD Checklist for *DSM-5* (PCL–5; Weathers, Litz, et al., 2013). Also, the Experiences in Close Relationships scale (Brennan et al., 1998) was administered to gain an understanding of her attachment dynamics and relational strategies. As a key presenting concern, the assessment of Luke's behavior in multiple settings is a clear priority in this evaluation. The Behavior Assessment System for Children (BASC; Reynolds & Kamphaus, 1992) was utilized to capture multiple perspectives on his functioning: Mrs. Garcia and her mother independently completed the BASC–Parent Rating Scales about Luke, Luke completed the BASC–Self-Report of Personality, and his teacher completed the BASC–Teacher Rating Scales (TRS) on his behavior at school. Luke also completed the Child and Adolescent Trauma Screen (CATS; Sachser et al., 2017) to identify history of trauma exposure and related symptoms. Given Amelia's young age, informal observational and play-based strategies provided opportunities to learn more about her socioemotional development, the sibling relational dynamic, and parent–child attachment.

Moving from the individual to the dyadic and/or subsystem level, intake information suggested that the grandparents provide instrumental parenting support currently and perhaps serve as secondary attachment figures to the children. As a result, the clinician hypothesized that the current parental subsystem consisted of Mrs. Garcia and the grandparents, but there was limited access to the grandparents' perspectives except for the grandmother's report on Luke's behavior. Thus, instead of the parental subsystem per se, the therapist evaluated the parent–child subsystem from both Luke's and Mrs. Garcia's perspectives. The Parenting Stress Index (PSI; Abidin, 1990) evaluated Mrs. Garcia's perception of parenting Luke, including her sense of their attachment bond, his behaviors that contribute to her stress, and overall life stress. To capture Luke's perceptions, two measures were used: the People in My Life questionnaire (PIML; Ridenour et al., 2006), which tracks attachment dimensions, and the Parent Perception Inventory (Cole et al., 2018; Hazzard et al., 1983), which yields information on two parenting dimensions: warmth/supportiveness and the tendency to be harsh/critical. Given the recency of the loss, Luke completed these instruments for both his mother and deceased stepfather.

At the family-wide system level, clinicians might select a multi-rater family assessment instrument that is validated for the appropriate ages and yields pertinent systemic information. In this case, the therapist utilized the Family Environment Scale (FES), which has adult (Moos & Moos, 2002) and child (Pino et al., 1984) self-report versions, allowing both Mrs. Garcia and Luke to report their sense of current family functioning. The FES includes scales assessing family relationships (cohesion, expressiveness, conflict), system maintenance (organization, control), and a personal growth dimension that identifies family strengths (independence, achievement orientation, intellectual–cultural orientation, moral–religious emphasis).

Systemic assessment also considers environmental contexts affecting the family and its members. To obtain additional information in this domain, the clinician administered an intergenerational family genogram (Box 4.3) and a family ecomap (Box 4.4). Considering the school context, several already included measures (i.e., PIML, BASC–SRP, and BASC–TRS) helped elucidate Luke's behavior, peer relationships, and interactions with teachers.

Administration

When the intake and any initial screening suggest a full assessment and the clinician has identified which instruments to include, the systemic assessment process generally begins with a family interview to meet/connect with each member, gather more background information and details regarding the presenting concern, and observe family behavior and interactions. If trauma exposure is likely, additional information about trauma history is needed.

Before proceeding with information gathering, however, the clinician and family must consider issues affecting appropriateness of member participation in a trauma-focused clinical interview and genogram. In this case, Mrs. Garcia agreed to have her children present for the first assessment session but requested that details about her husband's suicide be discussed in a private interview. This represented a strength in family differentiation (i.e., clear boundaries between the parent and child subsystems) and was reinforced by the clinician. In cases where parents begin "spilling" trauma-related details in the presence of children, therapists may need to intervene to provide containment and protect children from further traumatization. Age and developmental level of family members, type and severity of trauma, and a traumatized member's readiness for family discussion can guide the clinician's decision about exploring traumatic events with individual members alone, specific subsystems, or the whole family (Jordan, 2004).

When appropriate with the whole family present, the clinician can complete the clinical interview, genogram, ecomap, and/or potentially more formal coded or clinician-rated interaction tasks. In cases where multiple traumatic events are suspected, it may also be useful to include a trauma timeline or trauma-focused genogram (Goodman, 2013; Jordan, 2004). With the Garcia family, the clinician took time to connect with both Luke and Amelia, inviting all three members to draw their family as part of gathering information to complete the genogram and ecomap, using a whiteboard and colorful dry erase markers (don't forget to take a photo for later use!). The resulting genogram (Box 4.3) and ecomap (Box 4.4) began to organize information for the clinician, cultivated a sense of family teamwork and togetherness, and offered a measure of coherence amid disorientation and stress. Clinical observations during these family tasks are essential and can contribute to systemic hypotheses—for example, who takes the lead, who follows, who asks questions/instructs, who participates/cooperates, and who does not. In this case, Mrs. Garcia responded first to most interview questions, whereas Luke was fairly quiet and appeared reluctant to participate in the family interview despite his mother's encouragement, although he became much more friendly and animated when alone with the examiner. This disparate behavior by Luke might inform several systemic hypotheses that could be explored later in treatment. For example, it could suggest that Mrs. Garcia provides strong leadership in the family, and it could also mean that Luke is afraid to share his thoughts with his mother or does not want to cooperate with her.

BOX 4.3

GARCIA FAMILY GENOGRAM

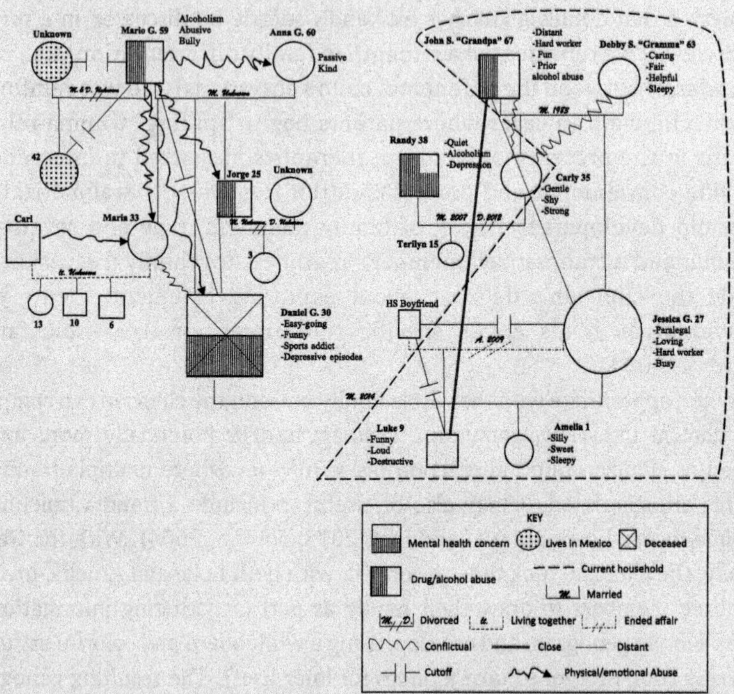

Mrs. Garcia reported growing up in a "typical middle-class family with two kids and a dog." She described her mother as caring and helpful, while she reported that her father worked a lot and is the "strong, silent type," so he seemed somewhat distant when she was growing up. She added that her father stopped drinking about 20 years ago and joked that her father is "making up for it" with Luke, who is very close to his grandfather. Luke added that his grandfather was fun and his grandmother and sister were sleepy a lot. Mrs. Garcia reported that her parents, who have been married for almost 37 years, raised her and her sister, who is 7 years older and was described as gentle and shy, but strong. Her sister has one teenage daughter and divorced her husband some years ago. Although she and her sister are friendly, their parents have had conflictual relations with her sister for many years. As a result, they do not have much contact except on holidays, when the family celebrates with maternal relatives. Mrs. Garcia reported she has always been close to her cousins and aunt, who is from Brazil. Mrs. Garcia indicated that she has enjoyed a consistently good relationship with her parents, who helped her raise Luke while she was earning her associate's degree. Prior to her husband's death, Mrs. Garcia recalled that they frequently enjoyed family dinners and other activities with her parents, who often helped with childcare and attended most of Luke's sporting events.

Mrs. Garcia described her husband, Daniel, as fairly easy-going, good with tools, and social, but quiet/withdrawn when upset and not a "serious talker." Luke added that he was funny and a "sports addict," with which Mrs. Garcia laughed and agreed. She then shared what Daniel had told her about his family of origin. She reported that Daniel's father left his first wife and oldest child in Mexico when he moved to the United States, so Daniel never met his half-sister. Daniel was born in a small rural town, the middle of three children with his father's second wife. The family was poor and moved around a lot to follow his father's construction jobs. Mrs. Garcia described her husband's father as an angry alcoholic who had been verbally and physically abusive to his wife and children for years, whereas Daniel's mother did not work and was perceived as kind but passive. According to Mrs. Garcia, as long as she had known him, her husband was not close to his family, so they visited only a couple times a year. After one drunken episode with his father and brother when they bullied her and her son, Mrs. Garcia began to stay home with Luke when Daniel visited his family. When Amelia was born, however, Daniel's parents wanted to see their granddaughter, so she began to accompany her husband and children on more frequent trips to the grandparents' home in a small town approximately 2 hours away. These family trips ended abruptly 9 months ago after an intense argument ensued when Daniel told his father to stop insulting his wife and stepson. After backlash from other extended family members, Daniel's brother mostly stopped talking to him. Mrs. Garcia and her children have had no contact with her husband's family since the funeral.

BOX 4.4

GARCIA FAMILY ECOMAP

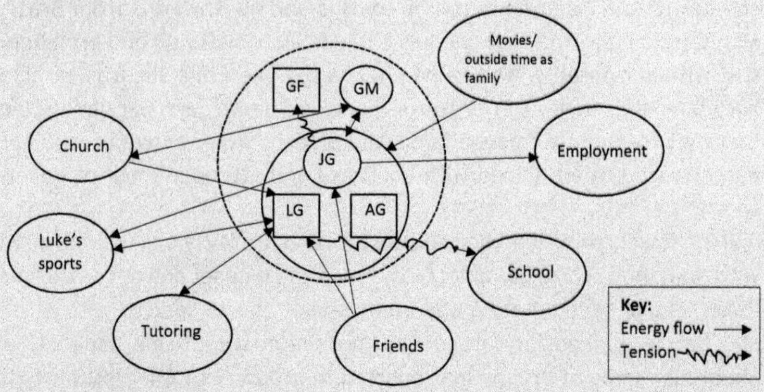

Note. GF = grandfather, GM = grandmother, JG = Jessica Garcia, LG = Luke Garcia, AG = Amelia Garcia.

During the construction of the ecomap, several areas of family strain and strength were identified. Mrs. Garcia and Luke described their family activities, such as going to the movie theater and playing at neighborhood parks, as areas from which the whole family draws strength. Depending on the season, Luke is involved in baseball and soccer after school, which Mrs. Garcia stated is helpful for her son but also means a busy week for both of them with minimal free time. Luke added that he and his grandmother often go to church, and he enjoys Sunday school class, but he wishes the rest of the family would go too. Mrs. Garcia responded that she is too tired and needs "downtime" from work, noting that her mother always seems to be doing something for the church. Mother and son also agreed that they enjoyed visiting with a few close friends. Although Mrs. Garcia is friendly with people at work, she does not consider them friends and has lost touch with many of her old friends.

Mrs. Garcia described a number of activities that were draining for her, including her job and taking Luke to his after-school activities, which Daniel used to do and her father is now helping with. Luke indicated that he disliked his teacher and school in general, with Mrs. Garcia confirming that school is a strain and sometimes creates conflict for Luke. She did, however, express that Luke's individual tutoring is an area of strength for him, providing individualized attention that Luke often needs to manage his ADHD symptoms while learning. Mrs. Garcia reported that Amelia enjoys positive relationships with her brother and grandmother, who currently takes care of Amelia during the day. While Mrs. Garcia acknowledged the instrumental support she receives from her parents in helping with parental responsibilities, she also described living in their home as a current area of strain due to cramped space, disagreements about parenting her children, and increasing conflict with her father.

Depending on the family size and assessment battery, the clinician may decide to either conduct the evaluation over several sessions or extend a single assessment session to 2+ hours and allow some self-administered questionnaires to be completed outside of session, if test guidelines allow. For example, in the Garcia family's test battery, the BASC–3 parent and teacher forms could be self-administered. Thus, the BASC–3 parent form was given to Mrs. Garcia for completion at home, and after obtaining a release of information, the clinician mailed the BASC–3 measures to Luke's grandmother and teacher, along with an explanatory letter and a stamped self-addressed envelope for return mail to the clinic. Some instruments also have online administration options and/or cross-informant interpretive reports available, which many clinicians may find useful. In our experience with in-person administration, questionnaires often can be administered in a standardized manner to two or more adults in the same assessment room with an examiner, whereas test administration for children is more effective one-on-one in a separate room to allow oral administration, improve child focus, and possibly increase candid responses to test items. The Garcia's assessment included a family interview ending with the genogram and ecomap, separate testing and clinical interviews for Mrs. Garcia and Luke, and play-based observation with the family. The full assessment process lasted approximately 2.5–3 hours, but the time would be extended (and potentially broken into two meetings) if some instruments had not been provided/mailed for self-administration and two examiners had not been available for the separate testing and interviews with the children and Mrs. Garcia. The clinician completed visual mapping of the family's trauma burden (see Box 4.5) independently, using information gathered throughout the assessment.

BOX 4.5

SYSTEMIC VISUAL MAP OF FAMILY STRESS AND TRAUMA: THE GARCIA FAMILY

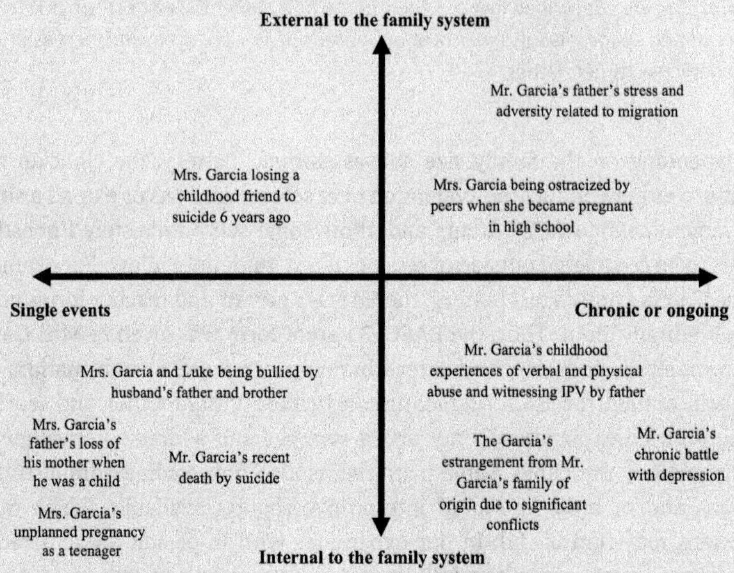

Note. IPV = intimate partner violence.

Central to the Garcia family's cumulative burden of stress and trauma are the intergenerational impacts of Mr. Garcia's complex childhood trauma, which significantly fueled his chronic battle with depression that ultimately ended in suicide. Mr. Garcia's childhood included chronic verbal and physical abuse and witnessing violence between his parents. The perpetrator of this abuse, Mr. Garcia's father, was reportedly an "angry alcoholic" and may have used alcohol to cope with both premigration and postmigration stressors as well as other traumatic incidents in his life. Relatedly, there is unclear context for the circumstances leading to his father's cutoff from his first wife and child. All of this may have complicated Mr. Garcia's ability to be emotionally present and responsive as a partner and parent. With regard to the ongoing spillover effects of trauma-related dynamics from Mr. Garcia's family of origin, Mrs. Garcia and Luke were both bullied by his father and brother. This ultimately escalated into an intense argument that resulted in estrangement from his family.

With regard to Mrs. Garcia's family of origin, it is unclear the extent to which her father's problematic alcohol use may have functioned as a means of coping with unresolved trauma in his own life, for example, the death of his mother when he was a young child. Possible developmental impacts of his lack of emotional presence throughout Mrs. Garcia's childhood are worth exploring, particularly as this may have been exacerbated by other relational situations where she has felt utterly alone. Beyond the family system, Mrs. Garcia was ostracized by peers and lost some of her closest friends during the stressful experience of navigating an unplanned pregnancy in high school. Furthermore, she reported losing a childhood friend to suicide 6 years ago, making this her second significant loss by suicide. All of this holds import for Mrs. Garcia's capacities to attune to and support her children in navigating the traumatic loss of their father, as she herself struggles to make meaning of "being left" by her spouse.

Results

Box 4.6 presents a sample write-up summarizing the Garcia family's assessment findings. Although Box 4.6 includes only the results section for space reasons, reporting systemic assessment findings includes the usual sections for referral reason/presenting concern, tests administered, background, behavioral observations, test results and clinical impressions, diagnosis, and recommendations. There is no specific format for systemic assessment reports, but several additional subsections in the results are generally included. In our own practice and supervision, we begin the results with a discussion of contextual considerations to set the stage, so to speak, for understanding the family where they "live." This includes the results of the genogram and the ecomap, as well as any other data relevant to the family's context. Next, a subsection on individual functioning separately summarizes test findings for individual family members, such as symptoms and attachment profile. Expanding to the family system level, another major subheading for family functioning presents data related to the family environment, parenting, parent–child dyads, couple dyad, and/or other important family subsystems and characteristics, all of which may warrant separate subheadings. Synthesizing this information in a concise manner elucidated important details to inform case conceptualization and treatment planning for the Garcia family.

BOX 4.6

GARCIA FAMILY ASSESSMENT RESULTS

See Table 4.2 for sources of information (e.g., clinical interview, self- and other-report measures).

BEHAVIORAL OBSERVATIONS

Mrs. Garcia, Luke, and Amelia arrived 10 minutes late to the testing session and were dressed in seasonally appropriate casual attire. In the scheduling phone call, Mrs. Garcia insisted that her parents not attend but after some discussion in session she signed release of information forms allowing the examiner to ask her mother and Luke's primary teacher to complete assessment instruments outside of session.

During the family interview, genogram, and ecomap, Mrs. Garcia took primary responsibility for question responses. Luke sat quietly on one end of the couch with his mother on the other end, while Amelia toddled around the room, often interrupting her mother and brother to show them toys. Luke appeared small for his age and somewhat shy initially, showing some reluctance to answer questions or engage with the interviewer. Mrs. Garcia provided multiple encouragers to Luke throughout the interview, explaining to him that the purpose of the assessment was to help their family and they did not need to have any "secrets" during this process. Luke seemed more interested in playing with his little sister and the toys, eliciting reminders from his mother to come sit back down and pay attention. He appeared to enjoy the genogram, however, adding adjectives to describe his mother, stepfather, sister, and grandparents. Subsequent to the family interview, Mrs. Garcia remained with the primary examiner/therapist for further testing, Amelia was taken to a supervised playroom in the clinic, and Luke went to a different test room to complete individual child assessment measures. After relocating, Luke appeared friendlier and engaged more with the second examiner, even telling a few jokes. Although some distractibility was noted, Luke responded easily to redirection, completing all testing without complaint. Mrs. Garcia was forthcoming in the individual clinical interview and became tearful when discussing her husband's death.

TEST RESULTS AND CLINICAL IMPRESSIONS

Mrs. Garcia and Luke were alert and cooperative with testing procedures. Although Luke seldom spoke when with his mother, he became more talkative in individual testing. Despite Amelia's interruptions, both family members appeared able to focus and put forth their best effort in testing. Furthermore, test validity indices, when available were within normal limits, suggesting that respondents answered questions honestly and openly. As a result, current findings are considered a valid estimate of individual and family functioning.

Contextual Considerations

Family Genogram

See Box 4.3.

Family Ecomap

See Box 4.4.

School, Peers, and Neighborhood

Luke completed the People in My Life (PIML) questionnaire to assess his perceptions of relationships with his parents, friends, and teachers, as well as his perceptions of his school and neighborhood. Luke indicated average levels of trust, communication, and satisfaction with his peers. He also reported average affiliation and bonding with his school environment, but low affiliation and high dissatisfaction with his teacher. Overall, PIML results suggest Luke perceives his school and neighborhood as generally positive, safe environments for him, but he feels alienated and unhappy with his teacher.

Consistent with ecomap and PIML results, moderately high elevations on Behavior Assessment System for Children (BASC) scales indicated that Luke dislikes school and often wishes to be elsewhere. He reported viewing his teachers as unfair or uncaring. Relatedly, on the BASC-Teacher Rating Scale (TRS), Luke's fourth-grade teacher reported clinically significant concerns about Luke's behavior in the school setting, indicating that Luke's study skills and ability to complete academic work are significantly weaker than other children in the ADHD norm group. A phone interview with the school counselor, who referred the family for therapy, suggested that Luke gets along well with his peers but has been having increasing disciplinary problems with teachers.

Individual Functioning

Mrs. Garcia

An individual clinical interview, the Brief Symptom Inventory (BSI), and PTSD Checklist (PCL-5) were administered to assess Mrs. Garcia' psychological functioning. In her clinical interview, Mrs. Garcia elaborated on the circumstances of her husband's death. She reported strained relationships with her husband's family, which had worsened after Amelia was born. According to Mrs. Garcia, her husband's sister and maternal aunt frequently called to berate him for not visiting his parents, blaming the problem on Mrs. Garcia.

(*continues*)

BOX 4.6

GARCIA FAMILY ASSESSMENT RESULTS (*Continued*)

After one evening phone call from his sister, Mr. Garcia appeared pale and shaking and said he was going to lie down. With both children already asleep, Mrs. Garcia was cleaning in the kitchen when she heard a gunshot and ran to find her husband's body in their bathroom, which was covered in blood. While Amelia remained sleeping, Luke was woken by the gunshot and his mother's cries. Although she managed to close the door before Luke saw the body, he stared at her in horror as she came forward to hug him, then ran to his room. At that point, she called 911 and then her parents, Mr. and Mrs. Smitt, who came over immediately. Her mother took the children to the grandparents' home while her father stayed with her until the police departed and the body was removed, then took her to join her children at the grandparents' home.

Based on nonpatient norms, Mrs. Garcia's BSI responses suggest she is experiencing clinically significant levels of emotional distress, including a focus on health-related concerns, symptoms related to intrusive and unrelenting thoughts or impulses, and feelings of personal inadequacy and self-doubt. Results also indicated moderate levels of persistent fear responses and feelings of apprehension and dread. Mrs. Garcia expressed frustration and confusion about her current emotional reactions while crying in the individual interview, asserting that she is usually strong and able to "take care of her own business" without crying or much emotional distress.

With a total PCL-5 score of 36, exceeding the clinical cutoff for probable PTSD, Mrs. Garcia endorsed posttraumatic symptoms that included active efforts to avoid thinking about the suicide, frequent sleep disturbance and nightmares, self-blame, irritability, watchfulness, and detachment from others. In the clinical interview, she explained that on the few occasions when she returned to the home she shared with her husband to pick up needed items, she would relive the experience of finding her husband dead and it would take her days to stop obsessing about it again. Mrs. Garcia also described avoiding images of "anything bloody" (e.g., movies, news reports, roadkill), frequently waking up in a cold sweat after nightmares, and having a strong fear response to loud noises that remind her of gunshots.

The Experiences in Close Relationships (ECR) scale was also used to assess Mrs. Garcia's adult attachment style. Mrs. Garcia endorsed a fearful attachment style characterized by fears of abandonment and distrust of others, resulting in paradoxical approach-avoidance behaviors. She may desire close relationships but experiences high levels of distress or discomfort when relying on those she is closest with. While this may represent an enduring relational style, it is also possible that her current attachment functioning reflects disorganization related to recent traumatic loss.

Luke

Luke was administered the Child and Adolescent Trauma Screen (CATS). Results were not clinically elevated. However, Luke endorsed experiencing negative emotions (e.g., fear, guilt, anger, shame) "almost always," as well as frequent experiences of self-blame, angry outbursts, upsetting reminders, and trying not to think or talk about his stepfather's death. Luke also reported problems paying attention, which may be due to ADHD or may have been exacerbated by the stressful events of the past 6 months.

Luke, his mother, grandmother, and 4th grade teacher completed a version of the BASC, which assesses children's behavior and personality. Mrs. Garcia also completed the Parenting Stress Index-2 (PSI-2), which assesses six areas of child behavior that may make parenting more difficult. Luke's self-ratings on the BASC Self-report of Personality (SRP) yielded an overall Emotional Symptom Index in the at-risk range relative to the ADHD norm group. Luke may worry excessively and lack confidence in his ability to solve problems or make decisions independently. He also endorsed clinically significant difficulties with inattention and feelings of being unsuccessful or inadequate, which may be related to his recent school performance. Notably, Luke's responses suggest that he enjoys positive relationships with parents and peers. All other BASC scales were within normal limits.

Mrs. Garcia and her mother, Mrs. Smitt, completed the parent version of the BASC (Parent Rating Scale [PRS]). Using the ADHD normative group,[3] Mrs. Garcia's ratings of Luke's behavior fell in the clinical range for inattention and in the at-risk range for depressive symptoms, hyperactivity, and emotional self-control. Mrs. Smitt's ratings also indicated at-risk levels of inattention and sadness, but otherwise noted no other behavioral difficulties. Similarly, Mrs. Garcia reported on the PSI that Luke exhibits clinically significant symptoms related to ADHD, mood problems, and difficulty adjusting to changes in his social environment. PSI results also suggest Mrs. Garcia perceives her son to be fairly needy and demanding compared to other children his age. Despite these concerns, BASC results for both women suggest that Luke's overall adaptive skills (activities of daily living, adaptability, functional communication, leadership, social skills) are typical relative to same-age peers with ADHD.

(*continues*)

[3] Compared to the general norms for Luke's age, all of Mrs. Garcia's ratings on the BASC-PRS clinical scales fell in the at-risk or clinically significant range, whereas Mrs. Smitt's ratings were clinically elevated in anxiety, depression, and attention problems. When using ADHD norms, however, the two women's ratings fell within normal limits for boys his age with ADHD, with the exceptions noted in the report. This difference underscores the importance of using appropriate norm groups for interpretation.

BOX 4.6

GARCIA FAMILY ASSESSMENT RESULTS (*Continued*)

Luke's fourth-grade teacher, Ms. Barnes, completed the BASC-TRS. In line with Luke's self-report, Ms. Barnes endorsed clinically significant concerns about Luke's behavior in the school setting. Clinical elevations also emerged for attention problems and hyperactivity. Findings indicated that Luke's ability to adjust to changes is in the at-risk range, which is consistent with his mother's PSI report. Additional at-risk areas that should be monitored in the future include regulation of emotions and anger, as well as the tendency to react to changes in an overly negative way.

Across informants, test results support the presence of inattention associated with Luke's prior diagnosis of ADHD Inattentive type. In addition, his teacher and mother reported clinical or at-risk hyperactive behaviors, respectively, which is in line with the school counselor's report of disciplinary problems at school, but historically uncharacteristic of Luke according to Mrs. Garcia. All informants noted that Luke exhibits some emotional dysregulation, including moderate depression or anxiety, negative emotionality, poor anger control, and difficulty adjusting to change. Taken together, the change in Luke's behavior and symptom profile over the past 6 months suggests that Luke is experiencing traumatic bereavement and would benefit from family intervention.

FAMILY FUNCTIONING

Family Environment

Mrs. Garcia completed the Family Environment Scale (FES) and Luke completed the Child Version of the FES to assess their perceptions of the family environment. The incongruence score was in the average range compared to other families, suggesting a level of disagreement in the family that is typical for other families in both the clinical and nonclinical norm groups. Mother and son agreed that their family was high average with respect to active and recreational activities, as well as organization and planning, and low average in encouragement to express emotions. Mrs. Garcia reported average levels of ethical and religious values, whereas Luke reported a high family emphasis in this area, which is consistent with his ecomap report of enjoying church with his grandmother. Mrs. Garcia endorsed high levels of family conflict, emphasis on achievement, and rules that help govern the family environment, whereas Luke reported that the family was average in the first two areas and low average in rules. Luke also reported average cohesion (i.e., help and support from family members), independence, and intellectual-cultural orientation, with Mrs. Garcia perceiving very low levels of these family dimensions. Notably, Mrs. Garcia's perception that family members demonstrate very low levels of self-sufficiency and independent decision-making is consistent with having an infant and also corresponds with PSI and BASC findings, suggesting that Luke may currently experience difficulties with self-reliance. In the clinical interview, Mrs. Garcia described a great deal of conflict in their home. In addition to conflict with Luke when he "pouts and throws tantrums," she reported growing discord with her parents, stating that they undermine her parental authority with Luke and her father seems to ignore the baby. Although she initially overlooked these things and withdrew to her room, she acknowledged building resentment culminating in several "blow-up" arguments with her parents regarding rules and discipline for Luke in the last couple months. Mrs. Garcia stated she would like to move back into her own home soon but has serious concerns about that possibility. In addition to another change of school for Luke, her extended hours on the job make it difficult to transport Luke to his activities without her parents' assistance. Her mother is also currently caring for Amelia during the day, so she needs to consider the cost of daycare.

Parenting and Parent-Child Relationships

PSI results indicate that Mrs. Garcia is experiencing clinically significant overall stress in her role as a parent to Luke. Mrs. Garcia's responses indicate clinically significant levels of stress associated with isolation in her parenting role and a struggle to understand and develop emotional closeness (i.e., attachment) to her oldest child. Results also suggest a deterioration in her health and moderately elevated depression symptoms that contribute to or are caused by her parenting stress.

Luke completed the Parental Perception Inventory to assess his parents' behaviors toward him. Luke completed this measure for both Mrs. Garcia and his deceased stepfather. Overall, his responses suggest that both parents used more positive than negative behavioral parenting strategies with him, with his stepfather using fewer negative parenting behaviors compared to his mother. In addition to peers and school, the PIML questionnaire assesses perceptions of trust, communication, and alienation in his parents. Luke's responses indicate positive perceptions of his level of trust and communication with both parents and low levels of alienation, which are generally indicative of a secure attachment relationship.

(*continues*)

BOX 4.6

GARCIA FAMILY ASSESSMENT RESULTS (*Continued*)

***DSM*-5 Diagnostic Impressions**

- **Mrs. Garcia:** Posttraumatic stress disorder
  Bereavement
- **Luke:** Attention-deficit/hyperactivity disorder, inattentive subtype (per history)
  Bereavement
- **Amelia:** Bereavement

SUMMARY AND KEY TAKEAWAYS

Trauma has diverse sequelae, extending well beyond trauma and stress-related disorders; thus, assessment must necessarily broaden its scope to uncover the ripple effects of trauma across multifaceted aspects of family members' functioning. Trauma-focused systemic assessment differs substantially from individual assessment and requires specialized competencies in scientific knowledge and measurement methods. In particular, this undertaking is guided by family systems theory and uniquely incorporates more varied methods, placing greater emphasis on observation and utilizing distinctive graphic tools like the genogram, ecomap, and structural maps. Furthermore, data collection attends to multiple family system levels and spotlights relationship functioning and family interaction patterns; these areas are inextricably interconnected with how trauma impacts are instantiated in members' ways of being, which often limit possibilities for healing and growth. Throughout the assessment process, a trauma-informed and -responsive approach necessitates nuanced attunement to members' emotional and behavioral reactions, taking care to build a sense of safety and collaboration, respecting clients' agency, providing coregulation when exploring difficult topics to help members stay within their window of tolerance, and adapting assessment procedures if anyone becomes emotionally flooded, dissociated, or otherwise dysregulated.

Given that a majority of graduate training is individually focused, the prospect of gathering data and synthesizing findings from multiple family members' perspectives—utilizing multiple methods—might seem to be a heavy lift! Yet, clinicians who think systemically are often quite energized to learn of the diverse and well-established measures they can draw from that shed light on common issues (and some are free!), such as trauma history, attachment bonds, relational and sexual functioning, parenting styles and stresses, coparenting processes and family affective expression, conflict, and cohesion. The sheer amount of data and potential disagreement between informants can be daunting, but the information gained from pretreatment assessment undoubtedly saves substantial time in therapy and underscores the belief that "clinical judgment alone [may be] insufficient as a means of assessing couples and families" (Snyder et al., 2019, p. 37). Assessment tools can help clinicians develop a more complete picture of the couple and family in a relatively short time, offer an efficient way to gather extensive information from multiple individuals (T. Patterson, 2013), and impart valuable clinical insight into the family's experience with trauma. Thus, the effort and time invested up front by both the family and clinician can bring focus and momentum to treatment.

Your particular way of integrating systemic assessment will look unique. The assessment process can be quite flexible and adapted to the setting in which you practice, as well as the couples or families you work with . . . ranging from a "bento box" to a "buffet" approach. In many settings (e.g., primary care, inpatient, low-resource community clinic), a comprehensive assessment battery such as described in the case of the Garcia family would not be feasible. However, even if your work environment limits assessment procedures to the initial intake session, you can readily incorporate a systemically focused clinical interview, informal behavioral observations, and several self- and other-report measures of key constructs to better understand family functioning as related to systemic impacts of trauma. Building on this, the next chapter addresses how trauma-focused case conceptualization and treatment planning can be informed by a systems theory framework and assessment findings, and provides an overview of common therapeutic techniques utilized in couple and family therapy that can be implemented in the treatment of trauma-impacted families.

5 SYSTEMIC FORMULATION, TREATMENT PLANNING, AND INTERVENTION

Facilitating Second-Order Changes as Part of Trauma Healing

The overall goal is to help family members become "systems experts" who could know [their] family system so well that the family could readjust itself without the aid of an outside expert, if and when the family became stressed again.

—MURRAY BOWEN (1978, P. 157)

Vanessa's disclosure at school of sexual abuse by an older cousin was investigated and substantiated by Child Protective Services, leading to a referral for family support. Reportedly, the family immigrated to the United States from El Salvador 7 years ago, with Vanessa's father, Fernando, and his brothers coming first, and their families arriving 2 years later. As one of the Spanish-speakers in the community-based clinic, you were assigned the case.

Vanessa's paternal grandmother, Luisa, brings her to the intake. A spunky yet shy 10-year-old, Vanessa fidgets a lot and avoids eye contact. In getting to know this family, you learn that Fernando works long hours at a local factory and Vanessa's mother, Maria, has been incarcerated for the past 2 years following an incident where she stabbed Fernando for suspected infidelity. Thus, Vanessa's

This chapter contains composite case vignettes drawn from multiple clients and fictitious aspects. Details have been substantively changed to protect confidentiality.

https://doi.org/10.1037/0000487-006
Systemic Treatment of Trauma-Impacted Families: A Clinician's Guide to Assessment, Formulation, and Intervention, by S. A. Riggs and L. E. Captari

recent abuse is layered on top of a traumatic family context and Luisa currently plays a primary parenting role for Vanessa and her siblings.

In line with best practice for trauma assessment, you meet with Luisa and Vanessa together and individually. Luisa also reveals a pattern of intergenerational trauma, reporting extensive childhood sexual abuse herself. She blames American culture for "sexualizando" children and points to Vanessa's clothing, which she believes is inappropriate for a child. Since the disclosure, Luisa notes that Vanessa has been more irritable, spent more time in the room she shares with her younger sister, and frequently skipped meals.

When you mention potentially looping Fernando in on the intake process, Luisa shakes her head: "You probably won't get much from him . . . he was so angry when CPS was called and blamed Vanessa for lying like her mom." This sparks curiosity for you about the nature of Vanessa's relationship with her dad and his behavior at home.

For her part, Vanessa is reticent to talk but seems to relax more when you bring out art supplies. You learn about her two best friends in school and the music she enjoys listening to. Vanessa struggles to describe how she is feeling, but seems happy to chat while drawing.

When asked about her cousin, she looks down and says, "He was nice to me. We used to have fun together until . . . it's so unfair." Though you hear possible grooming behavior in this, it also suggests complex feelings Vanessa may be experiencing, including grieving the loss of this friendship and second-guessing herself about having spoken up.

Where might treatment focus? Considering the three-legged stool of evidence-based practice, what is likely to be most helpful to support Vanessa? What part might her family and other close relationships have to play in that? While an individual therapist would likely focus mainly on distress stemming from the index trauma (i.e., sexual abuse), you are also tracking multiple traumatic disruptions in the family (e.g., immigration family violence, separation from mom, and mom's incarceration). Luisa's own abuse history could facilitate greater attunement and emotional support, or might set the stage for hypervigilance and intrusiveness in her parental role. The victim-blaming narrative of Vanessa's father is problematic and likely further traumatizing to her. At a systemic level, could an unresolved history of violence and ongoing conflict between Maria and Fernando be detoured onto Vanessa as the "problem"?

Clinical attunement to these sorts of relational patterns and family dynamics changes the way we listen, how we formulate presenting concerns, and the intervention techniques we might draw from to facilitate second-order changes wherever possible, rather than treating an individual in isolation. This can catalyze a deeper level of trauma healing by working upstream of symptom distress to help the family system change, grow, and adapt.

To that end, this chapter dives into the details of case formulation, treatment planning, and intervention with trauma-impacted couples and families. We describe common therapeutic techniques in systemically oriented treatment, with specific attention to how these might be applied in working with traumatized populations. Importantly, holding the family in mind and intervening at the level of various subsystems can be integrated within diverse therapeutic approaches and modalities (see Chapter 3 in this volume). Our focus is on supporting the development of practitioners' ability to integrate a systemic framework into their clinical practice with individuals, dyads, or families. To practically illustrate the application of systemic principles in trauma work, we also continue to follow the Garcia family's case introduced in Chapter 4 in this volume.

CASE FORMULATION: WHAT TO DO WITH ALL THAT DATA!

Case formulation provides a systems-based theoretical explanation for the client's concerns identified during problem formulation and assessment. As we have discussed throughout, these concerns may extend well beyond trauma and stressor-related disorders to include the wide-ranging sequelae of trauma impacts on psychological, emotional, and relational functioning. The therapist's tasks in this phase include organizing assessment data, interpreting the results to explain the presenting problem using systemic principles, and then identifying and prioritizing target areas for intervention (Stanton & Welsh, 2011). As a reminder, in systemic formulations, the family system is often understood to be the "client." Based on the Garcias' assessment introduced in the last chapter, Box 5.1 walks through one example of what a systemic formulation process could look like. We recognize that therapists may embody systemic assessment in a variety of ways, including utilizing a much more concise approach in some treatment contexts and/or in response to families' preferences and bandwidth. However, for learning and reference purposes, we offer a comprehensive case formulation in this chapter, drawing from the Garcia family's assessment findings, and encourage you to adapt this ethos to your clinical context, based on the available information and resources.

The more comprehensive the systemic assessment process, the more data that clinicians must synthesize and interpret, so an organizing framework that can accommodate all the data points across multiple measures and informants is essential. One commonly used transtheoretical approach is the biopsychosocial framework, which considers four key components, the "four Ps," applied to each of the biological, psychological, and social domains: predisposing factors, precipitating factors, perpetuating factors, and protective factors (Barker, 1995; Weerasekera, 1996). Note that the social domain encompasses all ecological levels, from microsystemic through macrosystemic (Bronfenbrenner, 1979). Thus, systemic formulations consider a broad array of social, historical, and environmental factors, including interactions with peers and friends, couple relationships, family functioning in current and previous generations, cultural context, socioeconomic conditions, and interactions in neighborhoods, school, work, and/or religious communities, as well as with medical, law enforcement, and other organizations.

Regardless of the organizing framework used for case formulation, the process integrally involves revisiting the presenting concern and applying newly gathered assessment data to inform diagnosis and clarify the problem through the lens of systems theory (Stanton & Welsh, 2011). Applying the four Ps to systemic formulation of trauma-impacted families, predisposing factors include all the individual, interpersonal, and systemic elements that place the client at risk for dysfunction as a result of trauma, whereas protective factors are the individual and systemic strengths that promote resilience, adaptive functioning, and trauma healing. Precipitating factors are the stressors or "triggers" that activate the client's pattern of functioning, and perpetuating factors act to reinforce the client's dysfunctional pattern (Sperry, 2005). When working with families, perpetuating factors often include system-maintaining processes that prevent families from solving problems and adjusting to normative or nonnormative transitions or stressors, leaving them "stuck" in old interaction patterns and unable to adapt to change. As discussed throughout, such patterns are a significant—but often overlooked—means by which trauma impacts spread throughout the family system and are instantiated across generations. Two central questions asked by systemic practitioners during case formulation are what is the meaning or function of the maladaptive behavior or symptoms in the family unit? And what systemic processes or interactions might be contributing to and/or sustaining those symptoms?

For example, one common presenting concern among trauma-impacted families is child behavioral problems, as with the Garcia family. Parents often believe this is a "child problem," without realizing that their child may be trying to communicate something important to them, and the family might somehow be fostering or reinforcing that behavior. In the Garcia case, for example, perhaps Luke is insecure, with disengaged parental figures, and needs more attention from caregivers that he obtains by acting out (albeit negative attention, it still means he matters). Perhaps he is angry about losing someone he loves but is silenced by the family's grief and is somehow reassured when his mother becomes angry too (albeit at him, but he now shares the same emotion as his mother). Perhaps the misbehavior only occurs when his mother and grandparents are fighting loudly and thus successfully interrupts the argument, detouring that hostility onto himself and thus preserving the security of the parental subsystem. All of these are valid hypotheses that can be explored and revised when additional information comes to light as treatment progresses.

After organizing assessment results using the selected framework, our next task is to examine the data for meaningful patterns and begin to develop theoretical hypotheses regarding connections between the findings and the presenting problem. This is an invaluable aspect of approaching trauma through systems theory, which provides a strong foundation for linking the converging, and quite possibly disparate, data points across the multiple measures and informants involved in family assessment. Stanton and Welsh (2011) noted that not all assessment data is meaningful, so this requires the clinician to decide what (and what not) to include in the formulation based on whether the information contributes to a better understanding of the presenting concern. To assist in this, systemic hypothesizing generates multiple possible, perhaps sometimes contradictory, explanations for the problem that consider family system processes as related to trauma impacts, such as recurring behaviors and interaction patterns, reciprocal influences among members, communication, intergenerational influences, the family life cycle stage, and extrafamilial influences. As opposed to the scientific sense of "hypothesis" as something to be proven, systemic hypotheses are viewed as neither true nor false, but rather more or less useful in providing a way to organize information and guide further exploration (Selvini Palazzoli et al., 1978). Based on the information available at any point before or during treatment, systemic hypotheses about patterns of relationships and beliefs in the family and how they influence the problem guide the identification of target areas for intervention.

Evidence-based case formulation and treatment with couples and families affected by trauma interweaves such clinical expertise with applying the latest research regarding trauma, as well as scientific evidence and contemporary theory about individual and family functioning after traumatic experiences (see Chapter 2 in this volume). Systemic conceptualization of trauma considers how traumatic events can affect individual and family functioning and how their trauma reactions might influence one another, attending to patterns of physiological dysregulation, emotional reactivity, and/or social withdrawal across the family. In addition to addressing individual stress reactions and differential expressions among family members, systemically oriented therapists consider how current individual and family functioning differ from pretrauma functioning, particularly with respect to the posttraumatic reorganization of the family system.

In order to prioritize target areas for intervention, it is important to understand that the source(s) and type(s) of trauma, as well as family members' developmental stages, will heavily influence these decisions. Trauma reactions in families often differ according to whether the traumatic event occurred outside or inside the family system; whether it directly happened to one person, several members, or the entire family; and whether it was a one-time crisis event or multiple events across time that ultimately overwhelm the family's ability to cope. Figley and Kiser (2013) delineated four ways family members can be traumatized: simultaneous effects of a sudden crisis directly impacting the entire family (e.g., natural disaster, home fire, traumatic death of family member), vicarious effects when a tragedy strikes a member who cannot be contacted immediately (e.g., hostage, war, school shooting), transmission effects whereby traumatic stress in one member spreads to other family members (e.g., secondary traumatic stress), and intrafamilial trauma via direct or witnessed violence (e.g., incest, intimate partner violence [IPV]). Familiarity with this literature is essential in determining goals for interventions that are well-suited to each family you work with. Box 5.1 demonstrates the process of systemic formulation with the Garcia family, synthesizing the contributions of research, clinical expertise, and the Garcias' preferences and needs in order to embody evidence-based practice.

BOX 5.1

CASE FORMULATION PROCESS: APPLICATION TO THE GARCIA FAMILY

In addition to assessment findings, systemic case formulation utilizes family systems theory and the scientific literature to organize and make sense of the data in order to inform treatment planning. A number of research fields can help us understand the Garcia family, including the literatures on traumatic bereavement/grief and suicide, attention-deficit/hyperactivity disorder (ADHD), posttraumatic stress disorder (PTSD), parents with mental illness/PTSD, attachment relationships, grandparenting, and others. For example, clinicians want to be alert to common grief responses among adults and children, the additional guilt and anger that often accompany a family member's suicide, and possible differences in the grieving and mourning process among family members that can lead to misunderstandings and resentment. In addition, we know that parenting becomes more difficult when children or parents experience psychological difficulties, such as child ADHD and parental PTSD in the current case.

Strong evidence suggests that the symptoms of ADHD in children can be distressing and difficult for parents to manage with patience and consistency. On the flip side, parents with mental illness may struggle to be available and responsive to their children when they are desperately trying to manage their own symptoms.

Applying the four Ps of case conceptualization across biopsychosocial domains, predisposing factors in this family include Luke's prior diagnosis of ADHD, his stepfather's depression and family of origin issues, and Mrs. Garcia's apparent avoidant tendencies, which seem to extend to the family system based on ratings of low family expressiveness. The primary precipitating factor is the suicide death of Daniel Garcia, which was witnessed by his wife and indirectly by his stepson. The loss of husband and father also led to major transitions in living situation and school setting. Information regarding perpetuating factors is currently limited but might include Mrs. Garcia's trauma-related avoidance, inconsistent parenting between Mrs. Garcia and her parents, and the family's silence or possibly even injunction against talking about the suicide. More information will be sought in session regarding specific family patterns that may perpetuate Luke's misbehavior and Mrs. Garcia's psychological distress. Protective factors in the Garcia family include relatively good health, stable pretrauma psychological functioning, a small network of friends, and supportive grandparents who offer a secure home base, instrumental assistance with parenting tasks, and a faith community. All of these factors are germane to the more in-depth analysis of system patterns below.

INDIVIDUAL FUNCTIONING

Assessment findings indicated that Mrs. Garcia's distress is more than uncomplicated bereavement, which is a normal response to the loss of a loved one. Specifically, Mrs. Garcia experienced the traumatic loss of her husband and was exposed to the bloody aftermath of his suicide in the bathroom of their home. Results of testing indicated that Mrs. Garcia meets criteria for PTSD. Given her difficulty in regulating emotions, referral for individual treatment is warranted, followed by family treatment to address problems at home after symptom reduction. Consultation with her individual therapist will guide the timing of family therapy, with a tentative benchmark represented by adequate emotional regulation while discussing the death of her husband.

Test results indicated that Luke continues to experience ADHD symptoms of inattention and suggested that his behavior and symptom profile changed since his stepfather's death. After ruling out PTSD and adjustment disorder, a diagnosis of uncomplicated bereavement seemed to best account for Luke's

(*continues*)

BOX 5.1

CASE FORMULATION PROCESS: APPLICATION TO THE GARCIA FAMILY (*Continued*)

symptoms of behavioral disorganization and emotional dysregulation emerging in the past 6 months. Importantly, his symptoms seem to represent normative child responses to traumatic loss in the context of additional ensuing stressors and family transitions (e.g., move to different school, transition to multigenerational household, maternal distress/unavailability, disliking current teacher). At this time, although he continues to meet with his school counselor for support every week, Luke appears to be reluctant to talk about feelings, so he would benefit from family therapy to help him process grief, learn emotional regulation skills, and adjust to the changes of home and school.

It is important to consider family members' behavior before and after the traumatic event in order to ascertain what, if any, changes have occurred and may be tied more directly to the trauma exposure. In this case, Mrs. Garcia's PTSD symptoms began soon after the traumatic event of suicide and are directly related to finding her husband's body. On the other hand, ADHD is a pre-existing condition for Luke, and his mother reported an escalation in "acting-out" behaviors that have become more difficult for her to manage. While it is possible that this represents an exacerbation of ADHD symptoms in response to stress, the pre-existing diagnosis specified Inattentive-type and Mrs. Garcia reported that Luke's reactive behaviors and angry outbursts only began a few months ago. In addition, his grandmother did not report behavior problems but did note that Luke appeared sad sometimes. Luke's disruptive behavior and anger at home and school seem directed at his mother and school authorities. In addition, multiple sources suggested that Luke is having difficulty adjusting to the traumatic loss of his stepfather and managing his emotions (e.g., anger, worry, sadness). Luke's self-report indicates that he is aware of his negative emotions and feels he is to blame for his stepfather's death and mother's pain, a false attribution with magical thinking that is not uncommon among children his age.

PARENT-CHILD RELATIONSHIP AND THE PARENTAL SUBSYSTEM

As might be expected after the tragic loss of her husband, Mrs. Garcia appears to be struggling with the transition to single parenthood, reporting a sense of isolation, deterioration in her health, and moderate depression related to the stress of parenting Luke. Assessment findings suggested that Luke perceives his mother and deceased stepfather favorably and feels relatively secure with them, but Mrs. Garcia acknowledged current difficulty in understanding and bonding with her son. This suggests potential weakening of the parent-child attachment bond or other disruption in the parent-child relationship. This might be further exacerbated by Luke's adjustment process to having a younger sibling. Another consideration regarding the parental subsystem in this family is the presence of maternal grandparents, who currently provide parenting support and housing.

The attachment literature may be helpful in this case and appears relevant in several ways. First, attachment theory and research in relation to loss and trauma suggest that the loss of an attachment figure represents an attachment crisis that calls for internal reorganization of the self. At the time of his death, Mr. Garcia served as his wife's primary attachment figure, and also likely held significant attachment relationships with his stepson and daughter. According to Mrs. Garcia, her husband treated Luke as a true son and spent a lot of time with Luke in sports and other activities. With the absence of his biological father, Mr. Garcia's parental role may have taken on additional significance such that his sudden death is highly disorganizing for Luke. During the assessment process, Mrs. Garcia reported attitudinal and coping strategies associated with dismissing-avoidant attachment style (e.g., discomfort with emotions, preference for coping independently, etc.), but results of the Experiences in Close Relationships Scale suggested a fearful-avoidant attachment style. Drawing on Simpson and Rholes's (2002) characterization of fearful-avoidant style in relation to trauma history, the therapist hypothesized that Mrs. Garcia may more typically demonstrate a dismissive-avoidant style, but the recent traumatic loss shocked the attachment system and led to internal disorganization to the extent that her characteristic dismissing-avoidant coping strategies are no longer working and have deteriorated into the fearful-avoidant style.

Furthermore, the grandparents are lifelong attachment figures for Mrs. Garcia, so the attachment history with her parents could be influential in her current functioning and recovery. While Mrs. Garcia appears to share a positive relationship with her mother, she described historical distance and recent resentment toward her father. The grandparents also serve as important secondary attachment figures for Luke, who lived with them for the first 5 years of his life and has remained in consistent and frequent contact with them. Amelia has lived with her grandparents for the past 6 months along with her brother and mother, so she may also now look to her grandparents for comfort and reassurance when her mother is absent or unavailable.

The parental subsystem in this multigenerational family has a complicated history. With an unplanned pregnancy in her senior year in high school, Mrs. Garcia remained in her childhood home with the financial, instrumental, and

(*continues*)

BOX 5.1

CASE FORMULATION PROCESS: APPLICATION TO THE GARCIA FAMILY (*Continued*)

emotional support of her parents in raising her son. Based on Mrs. Garcia's reports, the family roles and rules in the family did not change much after her son's birth. Specifically, her parents continued to maintain the household and support her education, and Mrs. Garcia continued her personal chores and took care of her son in the evenings. Whereas Mrs. Garcia largely remained in the child subsystem while residing with her parents, when she married her husband and moved into their marital home, she moved up in her new nuclear family hierarchy to the parental and couple/executive sub-systems. In collaboration with her husband, she became one of the family rulemakers and organizers of family life in their home. By contrast, her parents transitioned to grandparenthood and enjoyed being involved with their daughter's family and children.

In the context of a traumatic loss, Mrs. Garcia returned to the safety of her childhood home and the security of her parents' care, while her parents provided a safe haven for her and her children, apparently resuming many of the same household tasks and roles they had carried when Luke was first born. This time, however, Mrs. Garcia is working full-time and her retired mother is caring for Amelia at home, which reinforces Mrs. Smitt's role in the parental subsystem. Mr. Smitt, also now retired, is more involved with the children than previously and has taken on some of the child-related responsibilities of their deceased father, including transportation and involvement in Luke's after-school activities. Mrs. Garcia has stated that they spoil Luke and she resents her parents' interference, believing that inconsistencies in their rules and expectations have contributed to Luke's increasing misbehavior.

FAMILY FUNCTIONING

Structurally, this is a recently bereaved single-parent family currently residing in a multigenerational household. The Garcia family's life cycle stage as a family with young children has been disrupted by the unexpected suicide of a relatively young husband. This traumatic event contributed to posttraumatic symptoms among family members and resulted in several major transitions in the family system. During system-wide transitions, such as when a family loses (contraction) or adds (expansion) a member, the family system destabilizes and undergoes a reorganization to accommodate the loss or addition of a person. While family-wide evaluation was limited by Mrs. Garcia's reticence to allow her parents to fully participate in the assessment (excepting her mother's child behavior rating for Luke), examiners were able to gather family-level data from clinical interviews, the Family Environment Scale, genogram (see Box 4.3), and ecomap (see Box 4.4).

Current Family Functioning

On the Family Environment Scale, Mrs. Garcia and Luke agreed on some aspects of family functioning, including levels of organization, recreational activity (both high average), and emotional expression (low average). Like many parents and children, however, results in other areas suggested differing perceptions or response styles. For example, Mrs. Garcia endorsed high conflict and low levels of cohesion and independence in the family, whereas Luke reported average levels of these family dimensions. Luke may not be aware of conflict in the parental subsystem (or understand that his behaviors are perceived as conflictual), and he appears to feel relatively supported and independent in his home, unlike his mother, who is responsible for two young children and feels unsupported by her parents. Furthermore, Mrs. Garcia emphasized the importance of rules, whereas Luke's rating of this dimension was low average. This finding may reflect Luke's perception of a lack of clarity about rules in their current home, which is consistent with Mrs. Garcia's reports of inconsistent parenting practices between herself and her parents. For young children, it is also possible that social desirability plays a role in discrepant parent-child reports; in this case, Luke's pattern of responding produced average ratings across all family dimensions except Moral-Religious emphasis.

By all accounts, the grandparents are currently helping with many instrumental parenting duties, presumably shared previously between their daughter and deceased son-in-law. Both grandparents are now retired and spend quite a bit of time with their grandchildren. Providing emotional support and some structure/routine for the children may compensate for their mother's unavailability due to traumatic grief and PTSD symptoms. Despite clear support for the family, it is important to consider pretrauma family traits and the changes that are taking place now. For 5 years prior to moving back into her parents' home, Mrs. Garcia was in charge of her own nuclear family household, placing her and her husband at the top of the family hierarchy in the parental and couple/executive subsystems. She appeared to successfully differentiate from her family of origin while retaining friendly relationships with her parents and extended maternal relatives. In the space of 6 months, Mrs. Garcia witnessed her husband's suicide, literally abandoned forever by her primary attachment figure, and in a very real and painful way lost the family system she had spent the last 5 years developing, nurturing, and leading, along with many of the future hopes and dreams tied

(*continues*)

BOX 5.1

CASE FORMULATION PROCESS: APPLICATION TO THE GARCIA FAMILY (*Continued*)

to that family. Given the tragic circumstances and posttraumatic reactions, it is conceivable that when the grandparents stepped in to take care of their daughter and grandchildren, they unconsciously returned to the familiar interaction patterns around the time of Luke's birth and afterwards. As a result, Mrs. Garcia lost her prior executive position in the family and parental subsystem, and may find herself sometimes feeling that she is back in the child subsystem now. Recent family conflict may be related to Mrs. Garcia's need to reclaim parental authority and establish respectful boundaries with her parents.

When one or more family members experience a traumatic event, there is a risk for secondary traumatic stress in the family system. Mrs. Garcia reported increasing posttraumatic symptoms since her husband's death, which coincides with the return to her family of origin. Although she reported often retreating to her bedroom when the symptoms become overwhelming, it is nevertheless likely that other family members and the system itself have affected and been affected by her PTSD symptoms. In the immediate aftermath of trauma, diffuse internal boundaries are common as family members rally together in protective support of traumatized family members. Unfortunately, diffuse boundaries also create the opportunity for PTSD and grief symptoms to extend to other family members. Further assessment of boundaries is needed and will inform ongoing systemic hypothesizing. In addition, more information is needed about the biopsychosocial functioning of the grandparents and their roles in the family system.

Intergenerational Family Patterns

Results of the genogram indicated very different childhood experiences for Mrs. Garcia and her deceased husband. Looking first to the macrosystem, Mr. Garcia's father was an immigrant from Mexico with little education, and the family moved many times to follow construction jobs. This low-income Mexican-American family faced significant societal barriers to employment and advancement and may also have had multiple encounters with racism, discrimination, and other forms of oppression. Cultural norms regarding gender, dominance, and mental health care, as well as barriers to care, such as the lack of health insurance, should be considered as possible contributing factors to the functioning of his family of origin. At the family system level, Mrs. Garcia indicated that Mr. Garcia distanced himself from his family of origin and described his family as abusive with high levels of negative expressed emotion, conflict and violence, and problematic substance use. Mr. Garcia demonstrated resilience in many ways. With his family involved in construction, Mr. Garcia became an electrician and avoided the intergenerational risk of repeating many of his family's dysfunctional patterns himself. Nevertheless, his adverse childhood experiences may have contributed to the episodic depression that ultimately led to suicide.

Mrs. Garcia's family of origin was a middle-class White family that was stable and resided in the same suburban community for most of her childhood. Traditional gender roles were modeled by her father, who worked full-time outside of the home, and her mother, who was a full-time homemaker until she returned to work after her youngest child began elementary school. Even after she began work, her mother maintained primary responsibility for the children and the housework. Despite tension between her parents and older sister, her parents seem supportive of Mrs. Garcia, particularly during her unexpected pregnancy, and help with educational costs and childcare. Mrs. Garcia mentioned that her father stopped drinking alcohol when she was in elementary school because apparently he was a "belligerent drunk" according to her mother, though she did not remember this. Her father was reportedly somewhat disengaged from the family in Mrs. Garcia's childhood, but has become more involved with his grandchildren after his own retirement.

SYSTEMIC QUESTIONS AND HYPOTHESES

Relevant Systemic Questions

1. What are the effects of the mother's PTSD symptoms on family members and their interactions in the home, and how does the family help or hinder the mother's coping and symptom expression?
2. What was the structure of the Garcia family prior to the traumatic loss of the father (see Figure 5.1.1) and how has the Garcia family system changed since that time? How does the current multigenerational system compare to Mrs. Garcia's married family system? What were the roles/responsibilities of Mrs. Garcia and her deceased husband? Who has assumed Mr. Garcia's responsibilities and/or roles in the family system?
3. What does Luke's increased misbehavior represent and what function does it serve in the context of the family system? What is the family problem being expressed by his acting-out behaviors and anger?

Possible Systemic Hypotheses

1. Mrs. Garcia's PTSD symptoms represent a risk for secondary traumatization in the family unit, particularly if diffuse boundaries are present, as is often the case after a family tragedy (see Figure 5.1.2).

(*continues*)

BOX 5.1

CASE FORMULATION PROCESS: APPLICATION TO THE GARCIA FAMILY (*Continued*)

Luke may be particularly affected by his mother's emotions and symptoms, with Clinician-Administered PTSD Scale results suggesting subclinical posttraumatic symptoms that warrant ongoing observation. In turn, increased child misbehavior and family conflict may be exacerbating the mother's symptoms. No information is available on grandparent functioning, but if they are able to join therapy, exploring their psychosocial functioning in-session will be important to gain a complete picture of possible secondary traumatization.

2. The loss of their father and the relocation of Mrs. Garcia and her two children to her parents' home disrupted family organization, structure, and communication, thus contributing to a lack of clarity regarding subsystem boundaries, rules, and role expectations.

   Grief and PTSD symptoms have interfered with Mrs. Garcia's ability to fulfill maternal responsibilities. As a result of her tendency to withdraw, a rigid boundary between Mrs. Garcia and Luke may have formed, disrupting the mother-child attachment bond and creating higher levels of anxiety in both mother and child (see Figure 5.1.3).

   Lack of communication in the family system may be blocking healthy adaptation. With low emotional expression endorsed by Mrs. Garcia and Luke, it is important to note that research suggests that the subjects of death and trauma are often implicitly made "off limits" to protect the feelings/functioning of family members. Thus, the family may have unintentionally blocked communication about the suicide and death of the husband/father. Further exploration is needed.

   In an effort to help their daughter and grandchildren, the grandparents may be "overfunctioning," taking over household and childcare responsibilities. As a result, the grandparents have assumed the mother's role in the executive and parenting subsystems, and Mrs. Garcia's position may fluctuate between being part of the parental subsystem and the child subsystem.

   While intended to support their daughter, overfunctioning may extend to overprotection, which may paradoxically produce greater harm in terms of undermining their daughter's sense of competence and confidence in her recovery.

   If overprotection extends to the grandchildren, the grandparents' overfunctioning also creates the potential for diffuse boundaries between the (grand-)parental and child subsystems (see Figures 5.1.3 and 5.1.4).

   Recent reinvolvement of the grandparents in the parental subsystem has introduced inconsistencies in parenting practices and discipline, which has contributed to reported conflict between Mrs. Garcia and her parents about rules and parenting strategies for Luke.

3. Luke's current behavioral symptoms reflect traumatic grief and self-disorganization in response to his stepfather's death, the resulting disruption in family organization and communication, and/or potentially secondary traumatization processes.

   As part of the secondary traumatization process, Luke's escalating misbehavior may be an expression of unresolved and/or unexpressed grief that he does not talk about due to implicit family messages.

   Luke's misbehavior may reflect extreme attachment behaviors that function to regain his mother's attention for himself because she has become less accessible to him due to her own grief and traumatic stress reaction (see Figure 5.1.3).

   Luke's misbehavior succeeds in distracting himself and his mother from their grief, and may reflect an immature, paradoxical attempt to care for his mother.

   Tension between Mrs. Garcia and her parents may be detoured through Luke, contributing to higher conflict between mother and son (see Figure 5.1.4).

   Alternatively or simultaneously, Luke's misbehavior may interrupt/defuse mother-grandparent conflict and preserve family unity by refocusing the adults' attention toward himself.

Structural Maps Depicting Systemic Hypotheses

Below are structural family maps (see Box 4.1 for Key) depicting systemic hypotheses regarding child, parent, and couple/executive subsystems. Note that H = Husband, W = Wife, F = Father, M = Mother, CH = Child+age, GF = Grandfather, GM = Grandmother, mo = month, yr = year.

FIGURE 5.1.1. Pretrauma Family Map

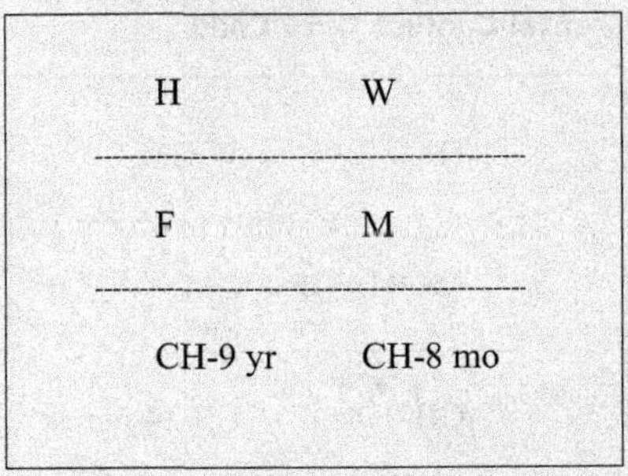

(*continues*)

BOX 5.1

CASE FORMULATION PROCESS: APPLICATION TO THE GARCIA FAMILY (*Continued*)

FIGURE 5.1.2. Posttrauma Hypothesis: Diffuse Boundaries Throughout System

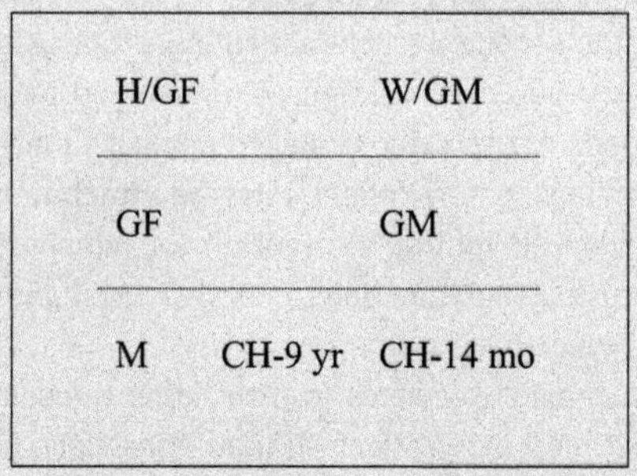

FIGURE 5.1.3. Posttrauma Hypothesis: Conflict in Parental Subsystem; Rigid Boundary Between Mother and Oldest Child; Diffuse Boundary Between Grandparents and Children; Child Focused on Mother

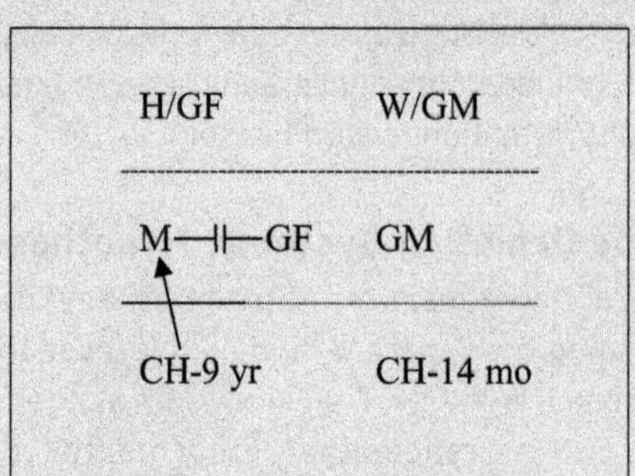

FIGURE 5.1.4. Posttrauma Hypothesis: Triangulation of Oldest Child, Detouring Interparental Conflict Onto Child

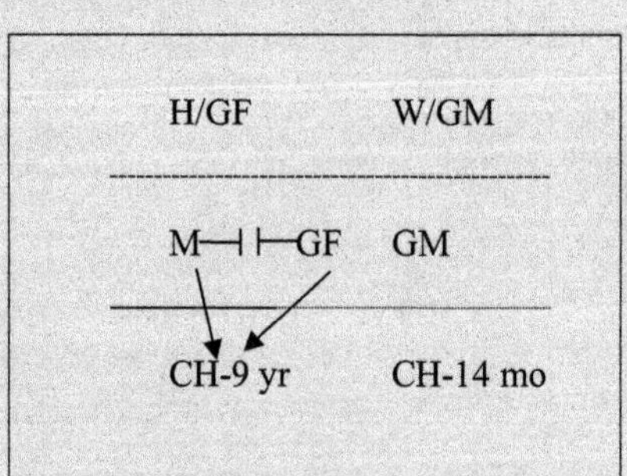

TREATMENT PLANNING: TARGETING SECOND-ORDER CHANGES

After a systemic family assessment and case formulation, the next step is treatment planning (Box 5.2 delineates the Garcia family's treatment plan). Part of treatment planning involves considering what therapeutic modality (or modalities) are most suitable for the case and deciding who should be involved, and in what ways. While clinicians may have specific intervention recommendations based on their formulation, these decisions must also be informed by the family's expressed preferences during the delivery of assessment feedback and as part of collaborative goal-setting. Given that the experience of trauma often includes being overpowered and losing one's agency, it is especially critical to support family members' wishes and perspectives throughout this process.

Deciding How to Intervene and Who to Involve . . . and Contraindications

Traditional family therapy approaches strongly encourage including the entire household in treatment, which often requires concentrated efforts to invite all family members to participate in therapy sessions. This general tenet must be adapted to the family's unique situation, however, considering members' availability and willingness, as well as the presence of violence, addiction, and other factors that may increase risk of harm to any family member. As noted above, when working with trauma-impacted families, it is especially vital to maintain a collaborative stance and be mindful of power dynamics, including how trying to convince or pressure members may unwittingly become a repetition of past trauma. A family may "fawn" with initial compliance while failing to authentically engage in the process, which will significantly limit progress.

In such situations, work with whoever in the family is open to meeting—whether that be one member, several members, or the entire household. While systemic treatment frequently involves couple and/or family sessions, it may take many forms and utilize a variety of treatment modalities (e.g., individual, dyadic, family, group) and methods (e.g., psychoeducation, coaching, consulting, psychotherapy). The important distinction is that treatment decisions are based on a systemic conceptualization of the case and are intended to broaden the scope of treatment beyond individuals to include their family relationships and other important contextual factors (Celano, 2019). After weighing the pros and cons of various approaches in relation to client characteristics and problems, systems-oriented clinicians may recommend one or more types of treatment simultaneously or in sequential fashion.

Just as stabilization and preparation of clients through skills training and titrated exposure is sometimes necessary before beginning intensive individual treatment of traumatic stress (Herman, 1992/2015), the same is true for trauma treatment with families. As such, an important question to be addressed as part of formulation and treatment planning is whether stabilization is required before working directly with trauma content in couple or family therapy (Sells & Souder, 2018). When severe symptoms interfere with the ability of a traumatized individual to function effectively and benefit from relational intervention, the treatment plan may recommend trauma-focused individual therapy to reduce symptoms and bolster self-regulation and grounding capacities before beginning couple or family treatment (Lebow, 2014). A treatment team of mental health professionals is ideal for this approach, whereby in consultation with one another, clinicians provide therapy to individual family members (i.e., a separate therapist for each family member who warrants individual treatment), while another practitioner treats the couple- or family-as-client (i.e., does not also act as an individual therapist to any family members). This approach prevents confusion and questions about therapist loyalty/allegiance, and also avoids the ethical risks inherent when therapists try to play multiple roles for clients. Clinicians can work with their consulting networks to refer family members for different types of treatment. With client consent, this practice can be enhanced systemically through collaboration and communication between providers to ensure common goals and prevent therapeutic contradictions or client confusion (see Chapter 6 in this volume).

Alternatively, in the context of less severe individual symptoms, the clinician may recommend family therapy with or without individual therapy in tandem. When the whole family experiences the same traumatic event or secondary traumatization, the entire family system or specific subsystems may be dysregulated and thus benefit from psychoeducation, skills training, and stabilization prior to beginning direct family work around trauma. Chapter 3 in this volume overviewed multiple frameworks relevant for this task, including Trauma Affect Regulation: Guide for Education and Therapy (Ford, 2020); Attachment, Regulation, and Competency (Blaustein & Kinniburgh, 2018); and Trust-Based Relational Intervention (Purvis et al., 2013), which can be implemented prior to more in-depth exploration and processing. It is important to emphasize, however, that every family's needs and situation are different; narratively processing the trauma together as an entire family is not always an appropriate or a relevant treatment goal.

For couples and families characterized by intense internal conflict and aggression, clinicians must carefully consider and prioritize the safety of all members before recommending treatment. The argument for systems-oriented treatment of family violence rests on the relational nature of abuse, conceptualized as a family system's extreme response to stress that often spans generations (Southern & Sullivan, 2021); the chief goal of trauma-informed family interventions is to alter the underlying systemic processes and interaction patterns that allow or perpetuate abuse of family members. There are many empirically supported interventions for families and parents who are at risk for or officially reported for child abuse and neglect (for reviews, see Carr, 2024; Malmberg-Heimonen et al., 2024; van IJzendoorn et al., 2020). Carr's umbrella synthesis of existing review and meta-analytic papers concluded that the most effective systemic interventions to reduce risk or occurrence of maltreatment are structured, family-based (often home visits), at least 6 months in duration, and intentionally attend to problems in various family subsystems (e.g., parenting skills, children's trauma reactions, parent's psychopathology, support from the family and social network). Clinicians must consider a number of factors, however, before making the determination that relational therapy is appropriate for families and identifying who should be involved. For example, in cases of child maltreatment, it may be productive to involve the offending parent/caregiver if it aligns with treatment goals, the child expresses a clear (uncoerced) desire for this, and the parent/caregiver has taken responsibility and is motivated to change their behavior. On the other hand, inclusion of offending parents/caregivers in session is contraindicated when abuse is ongoing or unacknowledged (e.g., parent denies the abuse, blames child) or when the child expresses fear or distress about the prospect. Another viable option in this case is to provide intervention services to family members without the presence of the abuser. In particular, professional guidelines for the treatment of children and adolescents affected by trauma recommend the involvement of at least the nonoffending caregiver (National Institute for Health and Care Excellence, 2018; Saunders et al., 2003). Child–caregiver interventions are well-established for use following traumatic experiences (McWey, 2022), with meta-analyses demonstrating greater symptom reduction (i.e., anxiety, depression, posttraumatic stress disorder [PTSD]) among children when treatment involves caregivers relative to individual child therapy (Gutermann et al., 2016) and control conditions (Szota et al., 2023).

In contrast to family-based interventions for children, couple therapy for IPV is still highly controversial due to ethical concerns for the safety of victims, as well as the potential for victim-blaming. Research has distinguished characterological from situational violence, with the former marked by consistent patterns of control and domination in the absence of remorse, and the latter stemming from difficulties in emotion regulation amid stress (Cleary Bradley & Gottman, 2012;

Stare & Fernando, 2014). Whether child abuse or IPV, ethical contraindications to couple and family therapy can generally be tied to characterological violence, including the presence of a high degree of physical danger; ongoing abuse of alcohol or other substances; control and domination motives for aggression; and a perpetrator's refusal to refrain from violence, accept responsibility, or agree to the treatment goal of ending violence (Antunes-Alves & De Stefano, 2014; Cooper & Vetere, 2005; Geffner & Mantooth, 2000; Geller, 1998). Under any of those conditions, therapists can refer both perpetrator and victim(s) to individual or group therapy programs designed for trauma intervention. Batterer intervention programs are by far the most common treatments recommended for IPV and are often mandated by courts, although research evidence on the effectiveness of these programs is mixed (Arias et al., 2013; Cheng et al., 2021). Several promising approaches to the treatment of male batterers have emerged in recent years, including Strength at Home (Taft et al., 2016) and Achieving Change through Values-Based Behavior (Lawrence et al., 2021; Zarling & Russell, 2022).

To be clear, couple or family therapy is contraindicated in cases of characterological violence, but it may be useful for treating situational violence characterized by low-frequency and noninjurious physical aggression (e.g., slapping, shoving, grabbing), based on systemic goals of creating change in the partners' interactions that can minimize the potential for more severe violence in the future (Stith et al., 2011). Meta-analytic evidence has found couple therapy effective in reducing IPV among couples with mild to moderate situational violence (Karakurt et al., 2016). Altogether, findings suggest that couple therapy can safely address family system or dyadic properties that impair relationship functioning, such as poor communication, lack of problem-solving skills, and patterns of conflict or coercion between partners or family members (Armenti & Babcock, 2016; Babcock et al., 2017; Bradley et al., 2011; Southern & Sullivan, 2021). If couple or family therapy is deemed ethical and appropriate, further conditions of treatment might include modifications to confidentiality agreements and implementation of no violence/intimidation agreements that, if violated, would terminate the therapeutic contract.

Family Feedback and Goal-Setting

Feedback to the family should discuss assessment results pertaining to individual, dyadic, and family system functioning, information regarding systemic processes and how they relate to the diagnosis or identified problem, and recommendations for intervention or other services (Stanton & Welsh, 2011). Systems-oriented therapists intentionally seek ways to extend attention beyond individual behavior or "expand the system" by framing behavior as one part of a pattern that involves multiple family members in a series of reciprocal interactions (Sprenkle et al., 2013). Informal psychoeducation may help family members understand an ecological systems perspective and facilitate the identification of additional sources of information or potential participation in therapy. *Expanding the system* effectively to the family household, significant extended family members, and sometimes school and other relevant systems can be critical in obtaining key information and getting the right people into therapy. As mentioned before, parents often bring in their children for individual therapy to address behavioral problems, explicitly defining the child as the "identified patient." Systemic formulation places the child within family and ecological contexts in order to examine interaction patterns that may unknowingly promote or maintain problematic behavior. In response to efforts to expand the system, parents can sometimes feel blamed for their child's problems. Sensitive and attuned therapists can alleviate this risk by highlighting nonlinear, multidetermined pathways that preclude blame on any one family member, while encouraging family members to help alter the system's homeostatic patterns by changing their own behavior rather than expecting and waiting for someone else to change.

Collaborative goal-setting invites the family's thoughts about the feedback, considers their preferences in prioritizing treatment goals, lays out various treatment options, and educates clients about the treatment process (Stanton & Welsh, 2011). The therapist's task is to facilitate a discussion of current challenges and desires for change, then help the family identify one or two initial goals that can be realistically achieved. At this stage, it is quite possible that some parents may be uninterested in individual treatment for themselves and/or do not see the need for family therapy despite the therapist's attempt to describe the connection of individual symptoms to family functioning and processes. In these cases, the clinician should be flexible and pivot to offer alternative types of treatment that nevertheless maintain a systemic conceptualization. If clients agree to family treatment, framing the goal in positive terms (i.e., increasing a behavior/activity) with concrete outcomes that would indicate progress can set an optimistic tone and instill hope and confidence in the family's ability to change. Goal-setting in systemically oriented therapy is an ongoing process, with collective refinement or modification of goals as treatment uncovers new family strengths, vulnerabilities, or understandings of current and past problems. Relatedly, clinicians should develop a plan for monitoring therapeutic progress on the identified goals, which might include periodic formal testing (e.g., The Systemic Therapy Inventory of Change;

Pinsof, 2017) and/or informal session-by-session observation and mapping of family processes and structure.

To be sure, it complicates goal-setting to have multiple people in the room, often with multiple perspectives that do not always align! The challenge of reconciling differences among family members can usually be met by identifying unifying language or themes, common "big picture" ideas or goals that family members can agree upon, or metaphors that all family members can engage with. Systemically oriented therapists must take care to navigate this multifaceted therapeutic alliance in a way that is perceived as fair to all (van den Bos & Miedema, 2000). Research on rupture and repair has delineated the importance of attending to each person's alliance with both the therapist and other family members, and every member's perception of each other's alliance with the therapist (Friedlander & Escudero, 2023). A family member's defensiveness, intense cross-complaining, or blame of others may indicate a faltering alliance, which should be proactively addressed to increase engagement and decrease risk for dropout. Once assessment feedback has been provided and treatment goals are mutually agreed upon, the therapist selects appropriate interventions to implement, drawing from both foundational trauma treatment skills and specialized therapeutic techniques common in couple and family therapy.

BOX 5.2

FAMILY THERAPY TREATMENT PLAN: THE GARCIA FAMILY

REASON FOR REFERRAL

The traumatic suicide death of a young father brought the Garcia family into therapy. The family is now living in the home of Mrs. Garcia's parents. Mrs. Garcia has been diagnosed with PTSD and referred for individual treatment. Her son, Luke, has demonstrated increasing misbehavior and emotional dysregulation since his stepfather's death; he has been working informally with the school counselor. In addition, the mother reported increasing conflict with her parents regarding parenting her son and daughter.

DIAGNOSTIC AND STATISTICAL MANUAL OF MENTAL DISORDER, FIFTH EDITION, DIAGNOSTIC IMPRESSIONS

- **Mrs. Garcia (27yo):** Posttraumatic stress disorder
- **Luke (9yo):** ADHD, inattentive subtype (per history)
- **Amelia (1yo):** None

MEDICATIONS

No prescription medication, although Mrs. Garcia reported taking over-the-counter sleeping medication 3-4 nights each week.

CLIENT STRENGTHS

Mrs. Garcia is currently employed, intelligent, and expresses desire for change to help son. The family has a good support system with grandparents, church, close friends.

CLIENT BARRIERS TO PROGRESS

Conflict with in-laws; school problems.

CURRENT SYMPTOMS

Mrs. Garcia—sleep disturbance and nightmares, irritability, avoidance of traumatic thoughts/reminders, withdrawal, hypervigilance; Luke—inattention (by history), increased emotional reactivity, anger, and misbehavior; family system—conflict and strained relationships between Mrs. Garcia and her father and son.

MODALITY

Mrs. Garcia will seek individual therapy to address PTSD symptoms. After maternal symptom reduction is achieved, family systems therapy will commence, with ongoing consultation with and support for Luke from school counselor.

FREQUENCY

1x per week for individual therapy; 1x per week for family therapy for approximately 3 months (12 sessions).

FAMILY THERAPY GOAL 1

To reduce symptoms, family will process emotions and thoughts related to the death of Mr. Garcia.

(continues)

BOX 5.2

FAMILY THERAPY TREATMENT PLAN: THE GARCIA FAMILY (*Continued*)

Measured by (as observed in session and reported by clients, family demonstrates):

- Positive indicators of rapport; for example, willingness to talk/interact with therapist.
- The family will engage together in grief and trauma work.
- Luke will better understand and express his negative emotions, as demonstrated in session and reported by mother.
- Mrs. Garcia will report fewer emotional outbursts and misbehavior by Luke.

Objective 1

Establish safety in family therapy setting.

Interventions

Join family by engaging with each family member; negotiate ground rules and structure for therapy sessions (e.g., child participation); collaborative goal-setting, prioritizing mother's concerns.

Objective 2

Learn about emotions and emotional regulation skills in the family context.

Interventions

Skills training in emotional regulation and coping strategies. Expand family system to include grandparents. For example, psychoeducation regarding emotional transmission in systems; homework for family movie night with mother, children, and grandparents to watch Disney's *Inside Out*, then discuss as a family immediately afterward and later in therapy.

Objective 3

Luke will recognize his own emotions and improve his emotional regulation skills.

Interventions

After movie night, explore Luke's understanding of emotions and self-soothing/coping habits he may have or wish to develop in session; invite mother to teach Luke relaxation techniques she has been learning in her individual therapy. Emotion-related drawing activity for Luke.

Review/strengthen parent behavioral management skills for ADHD that Mrs. Garcia learned in previous class.

Objective 4

Process traumatic grief reactions and identify changes in the family system due to the loss of a husband/parent.

Interventions

Open family communication and address avoidance by facilitating conversations about Mr. Garcia when he was alive, his death, and subsequent family changes.

Expand family system to include grandparents. Frame emotional/behavioral symptoms of mother and child as a family issue using psychoeducation regarding traumatic events/suicide and common secondary traumatic reactions of individual members and family systems.

Normalize the additional challenges inherent in moving to a new house/school and transitioning to a single-parent family residing in a grandparent household.

Encourage emotional and cognitive processing. Continue to explore and resolve issues of grief/loss as they arise.

FAMILY THERAPY GOAL 2

To assist family reorganization and cohesion after traumatic loss, the family will develop clear boundaries and communication about family roles, rules, and expectations.

Measured by (as observed in session and reported by clients, family demonstrates):

- Increased understanding of parenting and other family interactions.
- Improved communication and affection between all family members.
- Grandparents defer to mother in parenting decisions and practices.

Objective 1

Identify past and current family roles, rules, and expectations.

Interventions

Explore systemic hypotheses via circular questions about family rules, roles, and expectations in current household. Discuss how these characteristics are similar to / different from the previous family system including her husband and two children, as well as the previous family system including her parents, herself, and Luke for the first 5 years of his life.

(*continues*)

BOX 5.2

FAMILY THERAPY TREATMENT PLAN: THE GARCIA FAMILY (*Continued*)

Objective 2

Improve family communication and cohesion.

Interventions

Continue efforts to expand the system, that is, persuade mother to invite grandmother and grandfather to participate in family therapy, at least one session if not more.

Open lines of communication in the parental subsystem between mother, grandfather, and grandmother. Plan enjoyable activities for the whole family, including grandparents, once per week.

Objective 3

Clarify system and subsystem boundaries in the family system.

Interventions

Continue efforts to expand the system. Use structural maps to illustrate boundaries and relationships in the pre- and postsuicide family system in order to clarify intervention targets.

Objective 3a

Revision of parental subsystem to give executive authority to mother, while accepting coparental role of grandparents.

Interventions

Reframe perception of grandparents' interference in parenting as the grandparents' efforts to help mother and her children, linking current family structure to historical interaction patterns established when she was a teen mother residing in the grandparents' home with her son. Validate need to alter those patterns, which are no longer working because mother is now a fully grown adult and in need of a different kind of help.

Emphasize mother's authority in all parenting decisions while recognizing that her parents are functional members of the parenting subsystem currently.

Acknowledge grandparents' help and love, and validate their authority in their own home, while encouraging acceptance of daughter's authority with her children. Assess grandparents' ability/willingness to respect daughter's wishes regarding parenting.

Facilitate conversations between mother and her parents regarding her preferred parenting and disciplinary practices.

Utilize "Parenting Team" metaphor, with mother as head coach, grandparents as assistant coaches, and the children as the players.

Identify ways in which household/childcare duties and tasks can be shared and adjusted to the satisfaction of all parenting figures.

Objective 3b

Revise boundaries between the parental and child subsystems.

Interventions

Relax rigid boundary between mother and Luke by assigning homework for mother to spend special time individually with each of her children at least every other day, and plan an activity together with both her children at least once per week.

Strengthen diffuse boundary between grandparents and children to decrease their overinvolvement and increase mother's reengagement with children and household. Potentially block grandparents from disciplining children or speaking for mother in session and encourage mother to intervene.

SYSTEMICALLY ORIENTED INTERVENTION: GETTING DOWN TO BUSINESS!

After systemic case formulation has guided treatment planning for the family, it is time to choose and implement a therapeutic approach, while remaining open to adjustments along the way. The knowledge base needed for competency in couple and family intervention covers a wide range of empirically supported practices and specialized techniques applied to specific presenting concerns that emerge from the diverse sequelae of trauma. This section considers ways to organize and begin family treatment, including adapting basic counseling skills for working with multiple family members. We then explore a number of intervention techniques unique to the family therapy endeavor and the importance of pacing the processing of thoughts and emotions when trauma has disrupted family functioning. For reference, Table 5.1 summarizes common couple and family practices and techniques discussed below (highlighted with italics) and also provides specific examples relevant to the Garcia family case.

TABLE 5.1. Common Couple and Family Therapy Techniques

In-session technique	Action and purpose	Case example
Circular questions	Ask about connections and differences to gain information about relational patterns	"You've said that a lot of things stayed the same in the house before and after Luke was born. When reflecting on the household right after Luke was born compared to now that you're back living with your folks again, what is different and what is the same?"
Enactment	Facilitate in-session couple/family interactions to directly observe and address in-vivo unhealthy patterns and foster healthy ones	Recruited mother to tell Luke about the relaxation exercises learned in her individual therapy Asked mother and grandparents to discuss parenting roles, rules, disciplinary strategies, etc.
Expanding the system	Broaden conceptualization of problem to consider context and involve all family members in treatment	"It might be helpful to get all the adults on the same team when it comes to parenting and raising the children. The family environment affects everyone in the house, so reducing tension between you and your parents will make it easier for Luke to focus on and regulate his own emotions and behaviors. You will probably feel a lot better too. Would you be willing to bring your parents into session next week?"
Externalizing the problem	Frame the problem as separate from the person/family, enabling clients to see the problem as outside of themselves and then work together against it	"From what I hear, Daniel tried to fight off that nasty bug depression a lot of times, but in the end depression took him away."
Focusing the session	Provide direction and redirection in session to maintain productive conversation	"In the first part of the session, I thought we'd talk about family movie night and what y'all learned about emotions from *Inside Out*. And later I have a drawing activity for Luke, while we talk more about behavior management."
Intensifying emotion	Increase affective intensity aiming for "therapeutic window" to address avoidance and/or uncover and process underlying feelings	Discussion moved from easier, positive memories of the deceased to more difficult memories and the night of the suicide. When Luke became dysregulated, the therapist reminded Luke about the breathing exercises he learned earlier in therapy. Only after he regained his balance did therapy continue the family narrative

Joining	Connect with family members, gain access to system processes	Engaged fully with each family member; positive indicators of rapport and safety included the children's good behavior and quick acceptance of the therapist (e.g., son engaging in conversation with therapist, toddler showing toys to the therapist)
Making the covert overt	Directly state/explore rules or expectations that are unspoken	[to grandmother] "Because Jessica would cry and leave the room, you stopped trying to talk to her about Daniel so you wouldn't cause more pain. That's understandable. I wonder if Luke also thinks there is a family rule about not talking about Daniel or other bad stuff?"
Marking boundaries	Impose restrictions on participation to restructure system boundaries. For example, block interruptions, separate sessions, relocate members elsewhere in room	"Maybe we can start off with everyone present for the first part of the session, then send the children out to the playroom while the adults talk?" [to Luke] "You'll have to wait until your mom and grandparents are finished talking."
Metaphor	Suggest likeness between family or problem and other familiar systems or processes, to enhance understanding and buy-in	With family input, developed a baseball team metaphor to portray different roles and levels of authority in parenting
Negotiating ground rules	Explicitly establish expectations for in-session behavior, especially for children	"Sometimes young children can't concentrate the whole session, so how long would you like Luke to participate each time?"
Opening up communication	Directly address unspoken and/or taboo topics related to the problem; may be particularly vital for posttraumatic avoidance	"When tragedy affects the family, it's pretty common for people to avoid talking about it. I'm wondering if you all have talked much about Daniel's death?"
Positive reframing	Acknowledge problem, suggest constructive reinterpretation	"I wonder if your parents' 'interference' is part of them trying to help you and the kids without knowing your newer rules so they're just going with their old rules and 'take charge' ways of helping you, like right after Luke was born. Yet, as you say, you're older now, more mature,

(*continues*)

TABLE 5.1. Common Couple and Family Therapy Techniques (*Continued*)

In-session technique	Action and purpose	Case example
		and have developed your own parenting values and strategies that don't always match your parents' style, so those old ways aren't working any more."
Psychoeducation	Educate family to enhance understanding, normalize, correct misinformation/myths, etc.	Provided psychoeducation on depression, posttraumatic stress disorder, effects of trauma on families. "There is no doubt that talking about trauma and loss can be difficult and uncomfortable. Yet, the research suggests that it's probably better in the long run for everyone to talk about the loss and to grieve together than it is to avoid the pain and possibly let it build up to some sort of unspoken family rule that expects everyone to deal with their pain alone. Even young children can benefit from developmentally tailored discussions."
Skills training	Provide training in various skills to assist client in managing the problem	Provided training in emotional regulation for Luke and brief review of parent behavior management skills for mother and grandparents
Tracking family patterns	Noting sequential interactions and behaviors to understand underlying patterns that may contribute to or maintain the identified problem	"Tell me a little more about what it was like when you lived with your husband [or parents], like what were the chores, rules, parenting responsibilities, etc.?" "What typically happens when there are disagreements in your family? Who does what and when?"
Unbalancing	Interrupt power structure to destabilize ingrained patterns of interaction	Aligning with Mrs. Garcia on parenting issues unbalanced the power dynamics in the parental subsystem with the grandparents

Evidence-based practice often involves drawing from multiple therapeutic approaches, as one treatment model alone may not be suitable or effective for all families. Thus, practitioners should become familiar with multiple treatment approaches and models (see Chapter 3 in this volume), including their mechanisms of change, both common and model-specific factors (Stanton & Welsh, 2011). Beyond well-known common factors that substantially contribute to therapeutic effectiveness with individual clients (e.g., client factors, therapist factors, working alliance, placebo/hope; e.g., Wampold & Imel, 2015), Sprenkle et al. (2013) identified additional common factors within couple and family therapy: conceptualizing difficulties in relational terms, changing dysfunctional relationship patterns, extending the client unit to involve significant others and family members in treatment, and expanding the working alliance as a result of including multiple individuals and subsystems in the therapy process.

The field of couple and family therapy has generated many theories and treatment models, which vary in emphasis, but tend to share a conceptual foundation and accepted set of intervention strategies or techniques (Celano, 2019; Lebow, 2014). Here, we apply these to the population of trauma-impacted families, in particular. While the specific interventions (and their labels) that clinicians draw from depend on the presenting concern, client characteristics, and the therapist's choice of treatment model, core components and strategies of couple and family therapy that are relevant within trauma-informed and -responsive work include (Celano et al., 2010; Lebow, 2014; Midori-Hanna, 2018):

- psychoeducation about relevant issues, such as trauma impacts on neurobiology, relationships, child development, the family life cycle, and psychological disorders;
- skills training to alter ineffective communication, problem solving, parenting, or other family practices, particularly when these patterns are rooted in system-wide trauma responses (e.g., fight, flight, freeze, fawn);
- exploration of individual and family dynamics within and across generations (e.g., genogram) to promote an understanding of interpersonal and intergenerational influences, with attention to both transmission of trauma as well as strengths and resilience;
- efforts to improve family organization and structure, including consideration of the distribution of power and control (e.g., parental hierarchy, rules, discipline), explicit and implicit family roles or alliances, boundary rigidity or diffusion, and parent–child triangulation or other forms of boundary violation;

- attention to how cognitive (e.g., belief systems, meaning-making, blame, acceptance) and emotional (e.g., attachment, anger, hurt) aspects of family life have been affected by trauma, and how this contributes to family interaction patterns and problems; and
- strategies that foster therapeutic engagement with difficult behavioral patterns or emotional experiences through in-session coaching, enactments, and family sculpting, or prescribed home-based tasks and healing rituals.

Evidence-based systemic practice involves selecting interventions to address the presenting problem based on (a) the research evidence on treatment for specific issues and diverse populations; and (b) consideration of appropriateness—and potential modifications of interventions—in light of a family's culture, preferences, resources, motivation, and available time (N. Adams & Grieder, 2005; American Psychological Association [APA], 2021). These two "legs" of the evidence-based intervention are balanced by the third "leg" of the therapist's clinical expertise and competency in couple and family intervention. To assist with the development of this third leg, we offer a primer that describes common skills and techniques emerging from theories and models of couple and family therapy.

Organizing and Beginning Family Treatment Around Trauma

Beginning trauma-informed family therapy is in many ways similar to beginning any other type of treatment. For example, although often provided at intake, it never hurts to review ethical and legal obligations, agency policies, and other standard information. Discussing client expectations, establishing rapport, and asking questions are also customary at the onset of all types of psychotherapy. While similar, these interventions often must be adapted for effective trauma treatment and family therapy. Assuming that therapists and therapists-in-training are fluent in basic counseling skills, this section discusses ways in which these and other interventions can be modified and refined in working with traumatized families.

A particularly important ethical obligation here is the need to clarify with the client the roles of the therapist and family members in treatment, explicitly identifying who the client is before starting treatment (see Chapter 1 in this volume). These roles and the identification of the client may differ depending on the presenting concern, availability of collaborative treatment teams, agency organization and protocol, and so forth. It can also be helpful to give the client an idea of what to expect in therapy sessions. Providing organization or structure to treatment (with built-in flexibility, of course!) can often alleviate uncertainties and increase comfort with the frequently scary prospect of talking openly with other family members about difficult topics like trauma. When working with couples and families, a good place to start is to describe the therapy process in general, then begin *negotiating ground rules* for treatment and in-session behavior more specifically. For example, who is expected to attend, how many sessions and how often, are there rules to participation (e.g., listen without interruption), what are children expected to do (e.g., sit in a chair and participate for a certain amount of time before playing quietly with toys)? If not stated by the family, therapists can add additional rules to the agreement (e.g., turn off phones, refrain from name-calling). Setting ground rules in the first session is especially vital for families with young children or hostile/intrusive family members who tend to interrupt and speak over others.

Across theoretical models and treatment modalities, one of the most critical initial therapeutic tasks is to establish rapport with the client and work toward the development of a strong therapeutic alliance. When the client consists of multiple individuals, the task of building an alliance is complicated by the different personalities, developmental levels, and relationship dynamics within the family system (Celano et al., 2010). In addition to ordinary relationship-building elements (e.g., respect, empathy, understanding, instilling hope, highlighting strengths, validation), the *joining* process requires the therapist to connect empathically with each member of the family system, support and validate their individual and collective experiences, and honor their worldviews irrespective of disagreements between family members or with the therapist's viewpoint (Minuchin, 1974; Panichelli, 2013). Maintaining balance/neutrality toward family members' divergent views, while conveying that the therapist is on the "family's side," can promote fairness and trust, which contribute to a strong systemic alliance.

Traumatized individuals and families have good reason to be cautious and guarded, so therapists must exercise patience, gentle persistence, and careful pacing in the joining process, refraining from pushing too hard or too quickly discussing the traumatic event(s) and other difficult issues before the family is ready (Barnes & Figley, 2005). As its name implies, joining is an intentional therapeutic strategy that involves gaining temporary access to the family system, which confers invaluable flexibility to work from both within and outside of the family structure. If accepted by the family system, the clinician has greater freedom to explore authentic family functioning, challenge unhelpful or flawed perspectives, and restructure maladaptive interactions. One caveat to joining: Beware of being pulled into family dynamics unawares and unintentionally fulfilling some homeostatic mechanism (akin to systemic transference and countertransference processes). For instance, when witnessing one family member verbally attack another member, a therapist can sometimes be maneuvered by system processes into serving as the third point in a family triangle, for example, the "rescuer–victim–persecutor" triangle (Karpman, 1968). Our task is to join the family effectively, while also remaining differentiated, able to clearly see the family from the outside, and accessing our own subjectivity when needed. Like assessment, joining is an ongoing process throughout treatment, particularly when the alliance is challenged by difficult moments and ruptures (Knobloch-Fedders et al., 2007).

Circular questioning and positive reframing are practical and useful techniques in expanding the system. *Circular questions* provide a systemic frame to a problem by asking about connections and differences in the family system, which might include information about feelings, behaviors, or beliefs the family has observed and can compare between people, across time and generations, or between situations or settings (J. Brown, 2013; Feinberg, 1990). This shifts the focus to systemic relational patterns, making them explicit. As one example, circular questioning can be useful in tracking sequences of individual or relationship behavior by eliciting comparisons of behavior in relation to the ecological context, as well as behavioral patterns and exceptions over time, across settings, and with different relational partners. These types of questions draw attention to context and enable family members to identify and understand interaction patterns and communication processes, which in turn open up new ideas and possibilities for change and improvement. Circular questions are also handy tools for gathering information about family members who do not attend sessions (e.g., "What would [absent member] say about you and your brother's fighting?" "Who would [absent member] agree with?"). With respect to families exposed to an acute, one-time (vs. chronic) traumatic stressor, questions regarding each member's family roles and interactions both before and after the traumatic event can provide information essential to effective and respectful family treatment planning and intervention. In families with a complex history of multiple chronic stressors, circular questions can transform an ordinary linear trauma timeline into a more systemic overview of functioning in the family and its members across time.

Now widely used in many treatment approaches, therapeutic reframing has its origins in the communication research of the Mental Research Institute (Bateson et al., 1956; Satir, 1964; Watzlawick et al., 1967), one of the early leaders in family therapy research and intervention. The technique of *positive reframing* acknowledges a problem or negative situation while suggesting more constructive alternative views or interpretations for the family to consider. Satir assumed that members' hurtful/destructive communication and behavior was often the result of limited positive opportunities. For example, a spouse or parent's nagging might reflect deep concern for their spouse/child and a parent's punishment could be evidence of loving protection (Andreas, 1991). A gentle reframe that gives positive meaning to a client's problematic interactions with their environment can be a powerful intervention if the reframe is plausible and fits the situation. Although cognitive reframing is often part of individual trauma-focused therapy, caution is warranted to ensure that traumatic events are never minimized by a positive reframe in family treatment; indeed, sometimes families who avoid discussing traumatic experiences need to be challenged to face the significance and impact of the event(s). Explicitly acknowledging the adaptive nature of individual and family trauma responses as part of survival-oriented coping, while noting ways these same responses can impede recovery, helps counter shame and highlight strengths. Novel interpretations, or ways of seeing and talking about a situation, can loosen rigid thinking and open possibilities for new beliefs and behaviors, while acknowledging trauma effects and helping members process and expand on unhelpful views.

Systems-oriented intervention with trauma frequently incorporates psychoeducation and/or skills training. *Psychoeducation* targets areas of concern for the couple or family. For example, parents who have undue expectations of responsibility for 5-year-olds may benefit from education regarding child development and varying abilities at different ages. With families who have experienced trauma, therapists can normalize and contextualize young children's regressive behavior for parents as an acute stress reaction. In addition, education about the biopsychosocial effects of trauma exposure on individuals and families is a practical way to structure the beginning of treatment and slowly build tolerance before diving into more difficult cognitive, emotional, and systemic work (Briere & Scott, 2025). Couple and family practitioners utilize a broad range of *skills training* in their work. Parent behavioral management training is a widely used intervention that teaches parents basic principles of conditioning, models effective management strategies, and coaches the parent to implement these strategies with their child both in and out of therapy. Couple therapy often includes training in communication skills to help partners express themselves clearly, collaborate and compromise in problem solving and decision making, and better support one another. Systemically focused trauma intervention may also involve training in emotion regulation, coping strategies, and communication skills. Taken together, couple and family therapy with those impacted by trauma employs both foundational and unique techniques targeting second-order change in family organization and recurrent interaction patterns among members. We bring these concepts to life through following the Garcia family's therapy journey later in this chapter; here, we discuss the specifics of how second-order changes in trauma healing can be catalyzed within systemic treatment.

Trauma-Informed Techniques to Address Family Interactions and Structure

As treatment commences, the systemic hypotheses produced during assessment and formulation are tested in session through therapeutic discussion and exploration, as well as direct observations of spontaneous or directed interactions between family members. In the early stages particularly, observations of family members' real-time interactions in each session often yield new information that rules out (or in) previous hypotheses about how trauma may be impacting family functioning. Systemic therapists are continually looking for evidence that supports or challenges their hypotheses, discarding those that are unsupported or unhelpful to intervention and potentially forming new hypotheses based on additional evidence emerging in session as therapy progresses and changes begin occurring in the system. Throughout treatment, ongoing informal or formal assessment can track stuck points as well as changes in the family system (particularly second-order changes) and informs revision of the treatment plan or intentional shifts in therapeutic focus. These are some unique ways that interweaving systemic thinking with trauma treatment can facilitate therapeutic attention to the "forest" rather than getting lost in all the "trees." By bringing underlying family patterns and structure into focus, we have a unique vantage point from which to understand—and intervene—in order to help families adapt their ways of being to promote resilience and experience relationships as healing.

In a room with multiple people, the session can quickly turn chaotic if the therapist does not take the lead in *focusing the session*. Relative to individual psychotherapy, couple and family intervention requires clinicians to be more active and directive, because more people in the room translates to more voices—both literally in terms of the noise level and figuratively in the sense that different perspectives or experiences often manifest in tense, emotionally charged interactions among members (Thoburn et al., 2013). This is part and parcel of therapeutic work around trauma. Therapists working with multiple family members often have to manage their own emotions or countertransference (discussed further in Chapter 7 in this volume) while calmly asserting control in the session and defusing destructive conflict to maintain a safe environment (Lebow, 2014). To prevent wandering or active avoidance of traumatic material, clinicians can seek the family's agreement to a specific area of focus at the start of each session, then actively and consistently redirect the conversation back to that focus if the family goes off topic. It can also be clinically useful to listen for new insights emerging within content that may initially seem to be "off topic," as well as to pay attention to process aspects of how family members interact.

Discussion and exploration initially build on content the family provides, with an emphasis on *opening up communication* around the problem and *making the covert overt* to clarify vague communication, identify unspoken rules, and uncover implicit family role expectations or alliances. This is especially important because part of what makes something traumatic is its unspeakable nature. As systemic treatment continues, the focus of sessions often shifts to family interactions as described by members and observed in session. Family therapists must be at ease in vocalizing their observations of interaction patterns; this often amounts to "naming the elephant in the room" by drawing attention to what is being avoided or denied, which requires good doses of therapeutic curiosity, courage, humor, and the ability to tolerate discomfort. Similarly, a common component in PTSD treatment is "straight talk" (Silvern et al., 1995), which counteracts symptomatic avoidance by directly naming the traumatic event (instead of "it") and matter-of-factly talking about trauma without minimization or euphemisms (e.g., "died" or "murdered" instead of "passed away"). Within traumatized families, a "conspiracy of silence" can evolve into implicit or explicit rules not to talk about the traumatic event. In the short-term, this is understandable and possibly functional in protecting oneself and others from further pain, but ultimately prevents trauma processing and healing (Kerig & Alexander, 2012). Yet, attunement and pacing are critical, as clients sometimes initially use less direct language to approach trauma processing without being emotionally flooded. Clinicians should also be mindful of cultural, religious, and individual differences; for example, death is understood in diverse ways (e.g., afterlife, reincarnation) and highly religious families may understand their loved one as being "in heaven" or "with God."

Originating in structural family therapy as a way to observe and alter couple and family interactions in session, the use of *enactment* is now a common tool across a number of established clinical models for relational treatment, including emotionally focused couple therapy (S. M. Johnson, 1996/2019b), attachment-based family therapy (Tsvieli et al., 2022), and behavioral marital therapy (called "behavioral rehearsal"; Jacobson & Margolin, 1979). Enactments are direct, in-session interactions between family members, which can be initiated by the therapist (e.g., "Talk to each other about __") or can emerge organically in session and be leveraged by the therapist to facilitate more productive family engagement. Rather than speaking to or through the therapist, clients are instructed to speak to one another. At times, this is difficult for family members, who may continue to direct their comments to the therapist. Clinicians can address this by removing themselves from the dialogue, listening and observing while avoiding eye contact if necessary except to redirect, block other parties from interrupting, or potentially offer guidance and coaching in new ways of interacting (Butler & Gardner, 2003). Enactments help therapists observe and assess relational functioning and progress, facilitate communication, restructure relationships, and promote emotional disclosure and healing (Butler & Gardner, 2003).

Two other family therapy strategies, marking boundaries and unbalancing the system, target change in family organization, power, and structure. The goal of *marking boundaries* (also called "making boundaries") is to restructure (i.e., strengthen or reduce) boundaries between individuals, subsystems, and possibly between the family and larger external systems (Minuchin, 1974). Techniques used to mark boundaries in session include blocking interruption or participation in the therapeutic discussion through hand gestures, ignoring interjections, or giving directives (e.g., "Your parents are talking now, so you'll need to wait" to strengthen the parental hierarchy and boundary with the child subsystem), rearranging seating in the room (e.g., asking parents to sit next to each other on the couch to increase parental teamwork, instructing a child sitting between parents to move to another seat further away to reduce triangulation), and conducting separate sessions with certain subsystems/individuals (e.g., separate parent session without children present to strengthen subsystem boundaries). Disrupting maladaptive coalitions or triangles may also involve encouragement to strengthen relationships with other family members (Midori-Hanna, 2018). For example, when a child is being triangulated into spousal conflict and/or enlisted to perform parenting tasks while the other spouse/parent is operating as "one of the children," the therapist could meet with the couple separately to address their conflicts and parenting tasks directly. This structuring of who is/is not in session delineates boundaries between parental and child subsystems and loosens the role-reversal the child has been triangulated into.

The therapeutic strategy of *unbalancing* is geared toward interrupting power dynamics within the family system that are influencing the problem or preventing its resolution (Midori-Hanna, 2018). Keep in mind that families are more open to therapeutic intervention when the system is destabilized in some way, possibly due to normative transitions or external adversities. The same principle underlies the use of unbalancing, particularly when the family is stuck in unhealthy patterns that are not working in the family's best interest and other more direct interventions, such as enactments and challenging assumptions, have been ineffective in altering the dynamic (Gehart, 2018). Ordinarily, the therapist will strategically align with and support one family member temporarily to create disequilibrium in power dynamics, sometimes at the expense of others, but always in the service of changing the organizational structure to the benefit of all members. For example, a therapist may align with quieter, less powerful members to challenge typical family interaction patterns dominated by others, or conversely, align with more powerful members to support and validate them when responding to behaviors or changes they may not immediately welcome. Unbalancing is used only briefly and with considerable caution because selective alignment with certain family members may generate negative responses in others that require the therapist to realign and repair the systemic therapeutic alliance with all members. Therapists may also choose to align with the entire family against the symptom to reduce the power it has over the family, a narrative technique called *externalizing the problem* (Ramey et al., 2009; M. White & Epston, 1990). Families who have experienced a recent trauma may already be destabilized in that their normal operating processes are disrupted and in a state of change, making unbalancing strategies unnecessary. However, trauma exposure can often engender persistent maladaptive thoughts and either heightened or flattened emotions, which over time can contribute to dysfunctional interactions in the family that are difficult to change, so unbalancing can sometimes be useful in these cases. Thus, we turn our attention now to creative ways to address trauma-related cognitions and affects at both the individual and family level.

Thoughts and Emotions: Pacing in Systemic Treatment for Trauma

Therapists working with couples and families recognize the bidirectional influences between family relationships or interactions and each individual member's experience, including thoughts, beliefs, and emotions. The reciprocal nature of individual and family functioning should not be underestimated, particularly in cases of traumatic experiences that have cascading effects across the family system (Galano & Graham-Bermann, 2019), with trauma ripples flowing between family members, influencing individuals and other subsystems, and ultimately the functioning of the entire system. Traumatized individuals often develop beliefs and perceptions about self (e.g., I am bad, unworthy, and a failure) and other (e.g., the world is dangerous, no one can be trusted) that detrimentally affect their interactions with other family members (see Chapter 2 in this volume); likewise, families can hold inaccurate beliefs about trauma and mental health (e.g., my child just needs to try harder) that affect how they view and treat the traumatized family member. Uncovering the family's way of making meaning and their fundamental belief systems may be critical to understanding maladaptive behavior and interactions, as well as generating possible solutions.

Cognitive interventions might include identifying and possibly challenging current beliefs, reframing symptoms to offer a different interpretation that opens up new possibilities but can still be accommodated within the family's current worldview. One approach to help families make meaning of and heal from traumatic events together is coconstructing a trauma story or narrative, which involves inviting each family member to talk about their personal experiences related to the event(s). Therapists can encourage family members to help each other share their perspectives, identify both individual and family outcomes, clarify insights, correct distorted memories or thoughts, substitute new interpretations, and find new ways of completing their family's trauma story (Figley & Kiser, 2013). Developing metaphors is another way to help the family understand their situation and change it. *Metaphors* can be very powerful if selected to match the family's language and experience. As an example, a single mother with sole custody of two elementary school boys was referred for family therapy by her oldest son's school counselor for repeated misbehavior in class. The boys' father had been emotionally and physically abusive before abandoning the family 2 years prior. The maternal grandmother lived close by and was directly involved in raising the two boys their whole lives. The boys were rambunctious, loud, and undisciplined, and both were fascinated with anything military (e.g., movies, videogames, toys). The therapist developed a military metaphor for the family's functioning, highlighting parallels between military ranks and various family roles, authority, and responsibility in the family unit. The boys enthusiastically joined this metaphor, identifying their mother as the "General," the grandmother as the "Colonel," the oldest son as a "Captain" and the youngest a "Lieutenant." The therapist and family often returned to this metaphor throughout treatment to explain and reinforce the need for rules, parental authority, and child cooperation in order for their military/family unit to succeed. Similar metaphors for the family's structure and organization can be built around sports, videogames, occupations, school, dance and musical training, hobbies, and many more topics that are familiar to the family in your therapy room.

Couple and family therapists also deal directly with emotions in the family system, often in the context of enactments. Attachment relationships generate strong emotions like love, hurt, anxiety/fear, joy, and anger, which contribute to family interaction patterns for better or worse. While secure attachment is generally considered protective against individual and relational dysfunction (Riggs et al., 2002; Riggs & Riggs, 2011), the functioning of all families will be challenged by traumatic events encountered by one or more members. In the case of families with securely attached adults, help-seeking will be a natural coping strategy in the face of adversity, and they may very well end up in the therapist's office eager to accept assistance (Hindman et al., 2008; Riggs et al., 2002). Families without a secure attachment network may struggle to effectively and consistently meet the needs of their members on a daily basis, but seek therapy only as a last resort or when compelled by other factors, such as an ultimatum from a partner, court mandated treatment, or a traumatic event that overwhelms their capacity to adapt. Regardless of how they arrive in treatment, family members often can benefit from psychoeducation regarding the attachment system and therapeutic validation of attachment needs and patterns that encourages acceptance of and responsiveness to the emotions of all members.

Chronic anxiety in individuals and relationships, a common trauma response, can activate physiological and psychological processes that interfere with cognitive processing and self-regulation, which in turn contribute to relational dysfunction in the family system (Bowen, 1978; Papero, 2017). Families often develop coping strategies to reduce anxiety and preserve equilibrium in the system, including withdrawal, avoidance, denial, deflecting humor, or implicit family rules precluding the expression of anger, sadness, or other negative emotions. When necessary to uncover and process underlying emotional difficulties, couple and family therapists may seek to *intensify emotion* in session through repetition of questions/comments, selection of power words (i.e., words that provoke an emotional response), use of tone and volume, pacing and extending the duration of an interaction, or manipulation of physical space in the therapy room and between family members (Nichols & Schwartz, 2004). In encouraging the family to venture beyond their normal threshold for emotional expression, the therapist must be prepared to support members in effectively managing intense emotions in a way that can provide corrective emotional/attachment experiences and improve bonding and cohesion in the family.

The concepts of the "window of tolerance" (D. J. Siegel, 1999) and "therapeutic window" in trauma treatment (Briere & Scott, 2025) are important considerations when working with trauma-related thoughts and feelings in the family system. Rooted in neuroscience research, the window of tolerance refers to the range of emotional/physiological arousal within which a person's—or in this case a family system's—functioning is optimal. Outside of that window, underarousal can undermine motivation and efforts to change the status quo, whereas overarousal can overwhelm cognitive processes and emotion regulatory capacity, potentially triggering fight, flight, freeze, or fawn responses among trauma survivors. Briere and Scott (2025) recommended helping clients deepen their emotional experience in line with their unique window between inadequate versus excessive arousal. Traumatized individuals often have a small window of tolerance, and if this is not monitored in session, attempts at therapeutic processing may be retraumatizing.

Thus, careful attention to family affect is needed to balance challenging the avoidance of trauma-related material and supporting cognitive reorganization, emotion regulation, and grounding. Therapists must be careful not to exceed a client's window of tolerance by moving too quickly or failing to titrate the intensity of emotional activation associated with trauma-related material (Briere & Scott, 2016). In particular, when intensifying emotion, therapists must closely monitor and coregulate emotional arousal in the room to remain within the therapeutic window and provide the best opportunity for clients to benefit from interventions. Exposure to traumatic events can severely disrupt individual and family functioning, so when family members are so dysregulated that they are unable to remain within the therapeutic window, preliminary psychoeducation or skills training for the whole family and/or individual therapy for some members may be needed before family intervention proceeds. Box 5.3 presents several key clinical moments that illustrate systemic intervention strategies in the Garcia family's treatment.

BOX 5.3

KEY CLINICAL MOMENTS IN FAMILY THERAPY WITH THE GARCIA FAMILY

SESSION 4: OPENING COMMUNICATION ABOUT THE TRAUMA, ADDRESSING AVOIDANCE

After sustained efforts to expand the family system, Mrs. Jessica Garcia agreed to invite her parents to attend the fourth family therapy session and collaborated with the therapist to set the agenda for the session. The first part of this session included all family members and presented the metaphor of a baseball team, with family members working together for the children's benefit. Family discussion identified Mrs. Garcia as head coach, grandparents as assistant coaches, Luke as playing first base, and Amelia as the "batgirl" because she can't catch yet (humor). Everyone seemed to understand and get on board with this metaphor. Afterwards, the children were taken to the playroom to provide an opportunity for Mrs. Garcia to talk with her parents alone about her current struggles and concerns regarding how to help Luke. The therapist's primary goal in the following excerpt toward the end of session was to address avoidance and open up communication about the family's traumatic loss.

THERAPIST: When tragedy affects the family, it's pretty common for people to avoid talking about it. I'm wondering if y'all have talked much about Daniel's death? [shared looks between members]

JESSICA: No. [firmly] I don't want to talk about it any more than I have to in my own therapy. And I don't want to upset the kids. They're too young, don't you think? [neither grandparent responds]

THERAPIST: I'm wondering what you're learning in individual therapy about avoidance as part of PTSD, Jessica?

JESSICA: That it makes sense I'd want to push it all out of my mind, but the downside is there's no chance to process my feelings and thoughts and that's what causes the symptoms. That's why I'm always on edge and jump when I hear a car backfire and why I keep dreaming about it over and over again. But the nightmares are down to less than once a week now instead of every day.

THERAPIST: Yes, I can see how the work you're putting in to face and process Daniel's death is helping you heal. It's kind of the same thing in families. When we avoid talking about something that has fundamentally changed the family, we lose the opportunity to express ourselves, receive and provide support, and heal from the wound. Sometimes that's about finding meaning or hope, and sometimes it's about figuring out how to adjust to the big hole that's left when a family member dies. Especially a parent who is central to the family's functioning.

GRANDMA DEBBY: That's interesting. In the beginning, I tried talking to Jessica about it, but she only cried harder, shook her head and left the room, so I stopped trying cuz I didn't want to cause her any more pain.

THERAPIST: Of course. You're her mother and you wanted to protect her from that pain. It had to be tough for both of you [looking at grandfather to include him] watching your

(continues)

BOX 5.3

KEY CLINICAL MOMENTS IN FAMILY THERAPY WITH THE GARCIA FAMILY (*Continued*)

daughter hurt without being able to make her feel better. I'm betting that Jessica feels the same way about protecting her kids from the pain of losing their father.

JESSICA: Yes. Yes, I do. [choked up]

THERAPIST: There's no doubt that talking about trauma and loss can be difficult and uncomfortable. Yet, the research suggests that it's probably better in the long run for everyone to talk about the loss and to grieve together than it is to avoid the pain and possibly let it build up to some sort of unspoken family rule that expects everyone to deal with their pain alone. Even young children can benefit from developmentally tailored discussions. Jessica, you sought therapy to help your son. And Mr. and Mrs. Smitt, you've come in today to help your daughter and grandchildren. The love you have for each other is so evident here in this room, and I'm convinced that none of you want the children to be alone in their grief. Do I have that right?

JESSICA: [weeping, nodding head]

GRANDMA DEBBY: Yes, absolutely. I had no idea not talking could make it worse. Did you, John?

GRANDPA JOHN: Nope. Not much of a talker myself. We never talked about my mom after she passed when I was 10 or so. I just figured we weren't supposed to.

JESSICA: [surprised look at her father]

THERAPIST: That expectation of family silence is not uncommon after a death or a traumatic event and it sounds like you experienced that firsthand, Mr. Smitt. Sometimes kids are never even told what happened, so they guess all kinds of scenarios. I imagine it would have been pretty confusing to a 10-year-old to be unable to talk about his mom. So you were around Luke's age when you lost your mother?

GRANDPA JOHN: Yep.

JESSICA: I didn't know that, Daddy! Is that why you've been spending so much time with Luke?

GRANDPA JOHN: Girl, you know I love that boy like my own since he was a baby. I may not talk much, but I can listen pretty good.

GRANDMA DEBBY: That's God's truth, for sure. [patting her husband's arm] Always a good listener.

THERAPIST: So, Jessica, what do you think? Should we bring this up with the children next time and talk about what happened the night Daniel died? [pause] I know that's scary for you. Seems like your parents are eager to help and can be here to support you in that conversation.

JESSICA: Mom? Dad?

GRANDMA DEBBY: Of course, Jessie. [Grandpa John nods his head gravely.]

JESSICA: [to the therapist] Will you help me stay grounded?

THERAPIST: Yes, you're really growing in being able to ground yourself, and I'll be your backup to help out if you need me.

JESSICA: Ok, then.

SESSION 5: TRAUMA PROCESSING TOWARD A SHARED FAMILY NARRATIVE

The family entered the therapy room, with Grandpa John sitting in the big chair, and Jessica and Grandma Debby on either side of the couch with both children in between them. After greeting each person at the start of the session, the therapist asked how the family's teamwork went the past week. Amelia got off the couch and started wandering the room toward the toys in the corner, while Luke leaned on his mother. Jessica reported that she and both grandparents talked and agreed on specific parenting tasks and rules for the children. Luke added that as the first baseman, he was now in charge of playing with Amelia and "catching" her before she broke anything while his mother and grandma prepared dinner and cleaned up. The session proceeded to open opportunities for family members to share their memories of Daniel, and to explore their individual and collective experiences on the night of his death and afterwards.

THERAPIST: Jessica, have you told the children what we're going to talk about today?

JESSICA: Yes, Luke understands we're gonna talk about Daniel.

(continues)

BOX 5.3

KEY CLINICAL MOMENTS IN FAMILY THERAPY WITH THE GARCIA FAMILY (*Continued*)

THERAPIST: Luke, how do you feel about talking about your stepdad and how he died?

LUKE: [looks at mom, who nods her head, then he looks down and shrugs]

THERAPIST: Hmm, kinda mixed feelings? [Luke nods head] I suppose that's understandable cuz there are both good things and hard things that get talked about. [turning to everyone] How about we try, and see how it goes? [general nodding all around]

THERAPIST: I'd love to hear from each of you about some fun or happy memories of Daniel. Would anyone like to begin? [Each member shared a good memory; Luke twice followed up other people's stories with another story of his own; Grandpa's and Luke's memories involved baseball and fixing things; the family shared smiles and laughter at some of the funny stories.]

THERAPIST: Such great memories of Daniel! I feel like I know him a little better now. Sounds like he was a huge baseball fan, handy with tools, and a pretty funny guy. A loving and supportive husband, caring father, and good son-in-law. Clearly, that was recognized and appreciated by everyone in this room.

LUKE: I miss him.

JESSICA: We all do, honey. [putting arm around Luke] Very much. And it hurts cuz he's not here with us anymore. [Members continue to process sadness, missing, love.]

THERAPIST: I understand that Daniel was fun to be around most of the time, and there were also times he was sad and didn't feel up to having fun. Could you talk about that?

JESSICA: Daniel has always had periods when he withdraws a bit from everyone. Normally, it only lasted a day or two, but sometimes longer. One time when we were dating, it went on for a couple weeks and he finally explained that it didn't have anything to do with me, telling me a little about his childhood so I could understand why he got depressed and needed space every once in a while. So when he got that way, I would usually leave him alone and go do something with Luke, so I'm not sure he ever knew the difference? [looking at Luke]

LUKE: Was that why he didn't want to play ball with me last summer?

JESSICA: I'm not sure, but it could be. Sometimes he just didn't have the energy to do anything and seemed lost. He always came back though. [tearing up] I guess it just got too hard for him.

THERAPIST: It's quite possible that Daniel suffered clinical depression, [to Luke] which is an illness that makes people very sad. From what I hear, Daniel tried to fight off that nasty bug depression a lot of times, but in the end depression took him away. When someone we love is sick and dies, we can't help but feel sad, and maybe mad too. That's called grief. [to everyone] It can feel like a sharp wrench in our heart and gut. It can hurt a lot and be very confusing. It comes and goes like big waves of pain and longing, but over time, we can build a boat to ride on the waves, so they don't crash over us. And those waves can also bring up good memories to hold onto and reminisce about.

GRANDMA DEBBY: That's a beautiful way to look at it, and it makes me think about losing my dad. I'll never forget the sharp pain I felt in my body when I got the call that he'd died of a heart attack. It was so awful at the time, but now, I smile when I think of him. I miss him, but the missing is all mixed together with remembering the happy times.

THERAPIST: [smiling, nodding to Grandma] So remembering your father now brings you joy too instead of just pain. [pause, then to everyone] We're here together to help all of you on that journey. When we lose someone in our family traumatically, the grieving process gets complicated. Everybody reacts differently and the story can get confusing because we all remember something different. So, it might be helpful for us to talk about the night Daniel died. Putting all your memories together can help create a story that everyone shares and understands. [nodding by adults, Luke looking down, Amelia brings a toy to him, silence as family members look at each other]

(continues)

BOX 5.3

KEY CLINICAL MOMENTS IN FAMILY THERAPY WITH THE GARCIA FAMILY (*Continued*)

GRANDMA DEBBY: Would it help if I started?

THERAPIST: Sure, please do.

[Grandma describes the phone call from Jessica, her shock, and concern for Jessica and the kids. By the time she and Grandpa arrived, the ambulance and police were already there with Jessica. Grandma quickly hugged her then went to pack up the children when Jessica agreed that her mother should take them home while her father stayed with Jessica to sort things out. Amelia promptly fell asleep in the car, and her grandma transferred her to the portable crib at their house. She then laid down with Luke in his bed until he fell asleep.]

[Grandpa takes up the story about what happened after Grandma left. He describes sitting with Jessica as the officers questioned her, saying that he was "real proud" of Jessica for how she handled herself. Then he helped her pack up some things for herself and the children, and drove her to the grandparents' house where she immediately went to her old bedroom.]

THERAPIST: [to Luke] What do you remember about the night Daniel died?

LUKE: We had spaghetti and meatballs. I remember cuz Amelia got it all over everywhere and rolled a meatball off the table [smiles at mom, who returns smile], and we were laughing. Mama took a picture then took her straight to bath and bed when we were done and I got to watch TV for a while until bedtime.

THERAPIST: So after TV you went to bed and went to sleep?

LUKE: Well, I think I went to sleep, but when I opened my eyes it didn't seem like it.

THERAPIST: Why did you open your eyes?

LUKE: Heard something loud. Then running in hall. Peeked out door and heard Mama scream.

THERAPIST: That must've scared you. What did you do then?

LUKE: Tiptoed down the hall to look inside their room.

THERAPIST:	What did you see?
LUKE:	Mama came out of the bathroom crying real loud. Yelling nononononono, going in circles looking at her hands til she saw me and stopped. Then I ran back to my room and jumped under the covers.
THERAPIST:	You ran to your room?
LUKE:	[nodding] I was scared.
THERAPIST:	What scared you?
LUKE:	Mama's crying ... and her hands when she reached out.
THERAPIST:	I bet you're not used to seeing your mom so upset. [Luke shakes his head] And something about Mama's hands scared you . . . ?
LUKE:	They were all red and bloody, and her face and clothes had blood too. I knew something bad happened, but I don't think I wanted to know so I just curled up under the covers til Gramma came to get me.
JESSICA:	I'm so sorry you were scared, honey. I was really scared too and didn't know what to do. Thank goodness for Gramma and Grandpa, cuz you and I were kinda out of it, huh?
LUKE:	What happened, Mama?
JESSICA:	[takes deep, shaky breath] Well, Luke, I think Daniel was tired and worn out by a lot of hard things that happened to him. Like our therapist said, Daniel probably was sick with depression, which means he felt hopeless about things getting better, so he decided to stop living.
LUKE:	But why?
JESSICA:	[begins to tear up] I don't know, Luke. I wish I could tell you. It's hard to understand why someone would take their own life. Daniel's dad was pretty mean to him and everybody, and he had a hard time too when he came here from Mexico. All that made him feel terrible inside. Maybe it all just got to be too much for him, and he kind of shut down. In some ways I think he was trying to protect us, like somehow he didn't want us to be stuck in that dark and hopeless place with him . . .
LUKE:	[crying, standing up and facing mother] That's stupid! He was the best! Why would he think that? Why didn't you do

(*continues*)

BOX 5.3

KEY CLINICAL MOMENTS IN FAMILY THERAPY WITH THE GARCIA FAMILY (*Continued*)

something? [voice raised to yelling] I don't think he cared about us at all if he just decided to leave. Didn't he love us? Did I do something wrong? It's so unfair! [Luke continues to rant and has become emotionally dysregulated, Jessica is crying, the grandparents appear shocked, and Amelia is frightened and runs to Grandma, who picks her up.]

GRANDPA JOHN: [calm, deep, nonthreatening tone] Luke. [Luke spins toward him.] Take a deep breath, son. [Luke takes a deep breath.]

THERAPIST: Luke, do you remember those breathing exercises we talked about with your mother a couple weeks ago?

JESSICA: Look, Luke, I'm doing some of those slow, deep breaths right now. [Luke sees his mother, drops into a chair next to his grandfather, and begins mimicking his mother. Together, they do few cycles of deep breathing.] Remember the beach last summer when you got tumbled into shore by that huge wave? You lost your breath and I helped you stand back up? [She opens her arms and Luke immediately runs into her hug.]

THERAPIST: Yes, and when the waves get big, you can hold each other, and take deep breaths, and slow things down. Sometimes music can help, too ... do y'all have some favorite songs you like to listen to together? [family discusses briefly]

THERAPIST: To go back to what you were saying, Luke, we often feel guilt and anger when someone we love dies. Is anybody else feeling that way? [All the adults nod yes.]

JESSICA: Yes. I've been very angry at Daniel and I've wondered over and over what I could've done differently. But honestly, I'm not sure I could've stopped this ... I wish I could, but he was really sick. And sometimes people who are sick don't get better. In some ways, the depression stole him from us, Luke. [Session continues to process emotions and dispel dysfunctional cognitions, adding to the family narrative. Grandma brings in her faith, and describes how it helps her to imagine her own father looking down on her from heaven. This makes Luke curious and he asks if Daniel is in heaven, too. The therapist's focus is on helping family members draw from their spiritual beliefs to make meaning and cultivate an ongoing symbolic connection with the deceased member.]

LUKE: [to Grandma] Do you think your dad is playing baseball with Daniel now? [Everyone smiles.]

GRANDMA DEBBY: Now wouldn't that be something? Sure enough, I bet you're right.

SUMMARY AND KEY TAKEAWAYS

Just as a "trauma lens can be incorporated into existing family therapy practices" (James & MacKinnon, 2012, p. 189), so too can a family lens can be incorporated into existing trauma therapy practices. In working with traumatized families, part of the art of therapy is how the therapist integrates these two literatures and their respective interventions, utilizing the strategies, theoretical conceptualizations, and research evidence to create the best treatment plan for a particular individual, couple, or family. Systems-oriented therapists can draw from diverse treatment approaches and modalities to meet the needs of families who have experienced trauma. As with trauma treatment more generally, intervention includes multiple phases, beginning with an initial focus on stabilization and establishing safety before moving into the second phase of trauma processing (Herman, 1992). One benefit of couple and family modalities, however, is that Herman's third phase of integration and connection with others is inherently interwoven throughout the treatment process whenever multiple family members are involved as part of therapy. This can catalyze relational processes within the family system that support an upward spiral of healing, allowing members to validate each other's experiences and perspectives and walk with one another through dark places. Regardless of the specific approaches you draw from in a particular case, summarized below are some key elements common to trauma-focused family treatment:

- emphasis on all family members' safety (e.g., physical, emotional, psychological);
- maintaining a relational and systems perspective on the presenting problem;
- attending to the dynamic nature of the expanded therapeutic alliance, including repairing ruptures;

- in situations of child trauma, involvement of nonoffending caregiver(s);
- psychoeducation about trauma, acute stress responses and traumatic stress symptoms, effects on individuals and families, attachment, developmental considerations, grief, and so forth;
- normalization and reframing, often as part of psychoeducation;
- preliminary skills training (where indicated) before proceeding to the emotional and cognitive work of trauma intervention (e.g., self and emotion regulation, communication, problem solving, stress management, coping, and relational skills);
- opening communication about the trauma and addressing avoidance;
- narrative exposure and storytelling in order to facilitate integration/coherence and desensitization to trauma-related content:
  - cognitive processing and meaning-making,
  - emotional processing and soothing emotional reactivity,
  - healing attachment-related injuries through new relational experiences;
- a strengths-based focus that identifies individual, familial, and cultural resources to support healing and recovery;
- fostering within-family support as well as outside resources of support; and
- conveying optimism and hope for recovery.

Whether your professional role involves intervention with trauma-impacted couples and families, individual treatment with survivors, group therapy for individuals or families to provide skills training and facilitate meaning-making, or milieu intervention in a school or inpatient setting, a systemic approach to formulation, treatment planning, and intervention helps hold the complexity inherent in addressing the psychological, emotional, relational, structural, and spiritual/existential fallout of trauma. In our society, traumatized couples and families unfortunately often have a fairly disjointed and confusing experience seeking treatment, especially those with less access to resources. Many such families interact with multiple providers in different settings (e.g., adult therapists, child therapists, school counselors, pediatricians, primary care doctors, psychiatrists, speech and occupational therapists, CPS workers). Without regular and intentional coordination of care, providers may end up working at cross-purposes in ways that stymy family members' healing and recovery. Considering this, in the next chapter we turn our attention to systemic processes beyond the family alone.

6 BEYOND THE FAMILY

Consultation, Advocacy, and Creating Change in Larger Systems

Systems thinking is a discipline for seeing wholes. It is a framework for seeing interrelationships rather than things, for seeing "patterns of change" rather than "static snapshots."

—PETER M. SENGE (2006, P. 68)

Imagine sitting in the waiting room at the doctor's office . . . 3 months pregnant and feeling scattered and anxious. You didn't have best experience growing up and spent your childhood in not one, but many, households in the foster care system. As you embark on this journey of expectant motherhood, you envy women who have the support of their families . . . and whose partners can attend their appointments. Your boyfriend works an hourly job where it's not possible to step away.

As you wait for the nurse to call your name, you pass the time scrolling on social media, where your reels are increasingly filled with parenting advice. So. Much. Pressure.

This chapter contains a composite case vignette drawn from multiple clients and fictitious aspects. Details have been substantively changed to protect confidentiality.

https://doi.org/10.1037/0000487-007
Systemic Treatment of Trauma-Impacted Families: A Clinician's Guide to Assessment, Formulation, and Intervention, by S. A. Riggs and L. E. Captari

Your visit with the doctor lasts 9 minutes. He is all business. It's hard to remember what questions you'd hoped to ask. You feel awkward, rushed, and embarrassed when he raises his eyebrows about your weight gain. As you wait for the bus after your appointment, you feel more alone and overwhelmed than ever.

Now imagine entering a similar waiting room but being met by familiar faces. Your maternity appointments are scheduled alongside seven other women with similar due dates. In addition to weighing in, getting blood drawn, and being examined individually by the medical staff, you gather as a group. You talk, listen, laugh, cry, and support each other. The space is convened by a therapist you're beginning to trust, and there's room to talk about what you're anxious about in becoming a mom, how you want to create something different for your baby than what you've lived. You'll get to know these other women deeply as you continue to meet together regularly over the next 2 years. This space will hold you through the transition to parenthood and help you bond with your baby, in line with research about the critical importance of the first 1,000 days (Wardoyo et al., 2023).

By working upstream of perinatal mood disorders and traumatic stress during a pivotal transition period, this multisystemic approach holds both the mother and the baby in mind (Barlow & Svanberg, 2009). Rather than suggesting additional services or making referrals postpartum when mental health struggles emerge—or worse, intervening with this family if they emerge on Child Protective Services' radar due to concerns about child neglect or parental substance abuse—models of holistic care and capacity-building such as CenteringPregnancy (Crockett et al., 2019; R. Liu et al., 2017) and Expect With Me (Cunningham et al., 2017; Lewis & Ickovics, 2024) operate within a space that pregnant women already frequent. To help stem the tide of trauma's intergenerational impacts, we need more programs like this that proactively bolster early relational health and equip trauma survivors to parent with greater empathy, attunement, and responsiveness than they experienced in their own developmental histories. However, to actualize such a shift, we as professionals must expand our focus from trauma intervention to prevention, particularly during vulnerable time periods and transitions in the family life cycle. This goes against the grain of how the mental health care system in the United States is largely set up to intervene on a particular individual diagnosis.

In this chapter, we delve into the relevance of systemic influences beyond the family when treating trauma. This includes recognizing disparities in both trauma exposure and available treatment options, whereby families who have less access to resources and/or hold marginalized identities often experience a heavier trauma burden, and grappling as a field with how to substantively address this. We apply the multicultural orientation framework (MCO; D. E. Davis et al., 2018) to this context and discuss the complexities of intervening multisystemically, with a focus on helping readers develop competencies in coordination of care, interdisciplinary work, and advocacy. To bring these concepts to life, we track how the therapist working with the Garcia family supports their resilience and recovery through intervening at the level of multiple systems outside of sessions.

MENTALIZING FAMILIES' LIVED EXPERIENCES OF CARE

Multicultural perspectives orient us to families' diverse contexts and lived experiences. Larger societal factors can powerfully influence families' risk for trauma and recovery prognosis. In the United States, it is sobering that women and girls who are Black, Indigenous, and Persons of Color are at higher risk for rape, domestic violence, and other forms of abuse than their White counterparts, including maltreatment in the criminal justice system (Basile et al., 2022; Motz et al., 2020). This population is also almost three times more likely to die in childbirth (Hoyert, 2023; Women of Color Network, 2021). Young men of color are at notably higher risk of being targeted by police, and "one out of every three Black boys . . . can expect to go to prison in his lifetime, as can one of every six Latino boys—compared with one of every 17 White boys" (American Civil Liberties Union, 2024, para. 2). The burden of minority stress that LGBTQ+ individuals and their families face is reflected in heightened risk for suicidal thoughts and behaviors, among other areas; in one study, 42% reported suicidal ideation in the past 6 months (compared to 14% of non-LGBT youth) and 29% attempted suicide (compared to 9% of non-LGBT youth; Hatchel et al., 2019). Families who experience forced migration contend with multiple, overlapping stressors, both premigration, in flight, and following resettlement, with second-generation immigrants particularly at risk for mental health challenges (Captari et al., 2021; Tummala-Narra, 2021).

Sadly, this is not just society writ large. Evidence for iatrogenic treatment experiences testifies to the reality that encounters with medical and mental health care organizations can sometimes retraumatize these vulnerable populations, including experiences of racism and oppression (Aves, 2024; Ward-Ciesielski & Rizvi, 2021). Considering all this, it is critical that we consider families' lived experiences of seeking or being mandated to services. Many of the larger systems that traumatized families encounter (e.g., school, community, legal/court, health systems/hospitals, religious organizations, government agencies) are not well-versed in the complex sequelae of trauma. Added to that, such families often have their agency and autonomy taken away in situations of mandated treatment. Families labeled as resistant, noncompliant, disengaged, angry, or reactive can be understood with greater empathy when case formulations are trauma-informed, considering how the family's limited window of tolerance (Ogden et al., 2006) and perception of outsiders as threats can fuel physiological states of fight, flight, or freeze that manifest as challenging dynamics with providers. Furthermore, we must be careful not to conflate treatment engagement with physiological states of fawning, which involves dissociated compliance with providers' recommendations but a collapse of one's subjectivity and agency. Thus, practitioners should utilize careful attunement to ascertain the meaning and communication behind family members' behavior in treatment, especially when we are noticing intense countertransference in ourselves (more on this in Chapter 7 in this volume).

Among groups that are disadvantaged and vulnerable in society, cultural mistrust in the medical and mental health care system is real and important to acknowledge (Scott et al., 2011; R. E. Taylor & Kuo, 2019), particularly in light of increasing polarization in the United States. Families of color, immigrants, LGBTQ+ parents, and those who hold minority religious identities may have experienced racism, xenophobia, homo/transphobia, or other microaggressions from past providers. Fonagy and Allison (2014) framed such families' cautiousness and mistrust in terms of epistemic vigilance, that is, "the self-protective suspicion toward information coming from others that may be potentially damaging, deceptive, or inaccurate" (p. 373). In line with our understanding of trauma as inevitably impacting survivors' relational expectations and experiences, many of the families we interact with have life experiences that give them good reason to be vigilant and mistrustful of the health care system and mental health professionals. Seeking to understand families' hesitations about and frustrations in engaging with services expands our clinical formulation of what might be happening intersubjectively, informs empathic joining, and can help strengthen the alliance.

Sometimes a disposition and referral reveals notable worldview and cultural differences between a practitioner and family. For example, parents less acculturated to mental health frameworks might perceive a child who has attention-deficit/hyperactivity disorder (ADHD), a learning disorder, or executive functioning challenges stemming from complex trauma as "lazy," and thus be skeptical of the need for academic accommodations, psychotherapy, or medication. While our impulse might be to double down on psychoeducation, pacing and cultural humility are important in order to mentalize a family's experience, interweaving joining and validation with the presentation of another perspective. As part of this, we must consider how to align recommendations and referrals with a family's previously stated goals, as well as ways to creatively translate psychological terms into culturally accessible ideas and frames of reference (Owen & Tao, 2025).

APPLYING THE MULTICULTURAL ORIENTATION FRAMEWORK TO SYSTEMS

Every family is its own subculture, and many families encapsulate the melding of several distinct cultures of their members (which are sometimes perceived to be at odds with each other!). Therapists also each have their own cultural background and identities, which could be perceived by clients as an impediment to feeling understood and building a strong therapeutic alliance. At a larger level, each mental health care provision setting (e.g., clinic, hospital, therapeutic school, private practice) has a unique culture, history, and norms; within this, staff embody distinct professional subcultures that include particular language, roles, and expectations. Cultural differences at any of these levels can be a source of tension and conflict that, if not addressed, may compromise treatment. For example, based on lived experience and intersectionality of identities, a couple or family may hold vastly different perspectives from their therapist about trauma healing. Practitioners working with various members of the family system may offer conflicting treatment recommendations, rooted in what their professional discipline emphasizes. There are times, as well, that therapists experience values conflicts when their own worldview diverges from the systemic context they are working in.

How do we, as systemically oriented therapists, work across these differences in order to ensure the best quality of care for our patients? The MCO (D. E. Davis et al., 2018) offers an important counterpoint to the development of competencies alone by helping us attune to and invite these differences into the conversation. This requires the development of cultural humility, which "involves having an accurate view of oneself, particularly about one's limitations" and "being other-oriented rather than self-centered, marked especially by a lack of superiority" (D. E. Davis et al., 2018, p. 91). Cultural humility is especially critical when working with families who hold identities that have been historically (or are currently being) sidelined and subjugated in society, and sometimes, within the mental health care system. This sort of intentional awareness helps us to track and be mindful of power dynamics in order to cultivate "power with" rather than "power over" those who are already vulnerable to coercion and unwitting repetitions of trauma in treatment that does not honor and intentionally foster families' agency. Cultural humility is also a vital part of collaborating with professionals across diverse disciplines, and includes both owning our competence and being open to learning and taking in new perspectives from others.

Building from the foundation of cultural humility, the MCO framework orients therapists to seek out cultural opportunities, representing moments in which the other's (whether the client, another professional, or the clinic-as-a-whole) cultural identity, beliefs, and/or values can be engaged in meaningful dialogue (Owen et al., 2016). This is particularly salient to working with trauma. How a potentially traumatic experience and the ensuing recovery process is perceived, subjectively experienced, and understood relies heavily on family members' culturally embedded understandings of the self, the other, the world, the place of suffering in human experience, and so forth. Among families identifying as spiritual and/or religious, this aspect of culture is critical to integrate. Spiritual beliefs are often shaken or shattered by trauma, resulting in questions, doubts, and struggles (Sandage et al., 2020). Such spiritual struggles have been found to independently contribute to compromised well-being among trauma survivors, over and above symptom distress (Captari, Choe, Stein, & Sandage, 2024), perhaps in part because survivors may disaffiliate from (or not feel welcome in) their former faith community, representing a loss of belonging.

As explicated in Chapter 2 in this volume, there is no single objective narrative of trauma within a family—each member's perspectives and subjectivity must be listened to and honored. At the same time, therapeutic efforts to help a family come to a shared understanding (or at least respectful listening to understand each other's vantage points) can help increase cohesion and closeness. Cultural norms can reinforce shame and secrecy around what has occurred, and healing practices within families' cultural and spiritual communities may also play pivotal roles in catalyzing recovery. Beyond the therapy room, systems-oriented practitioners can seek out cultural opportunities when working interdisciplinarily and coordinating care. For example, this could involve inviting discussion around team members' different perspectives on a case.

Pursuing cultural opportunities requires the development of cultural comfort, that is, "feeling at ease, open, calm, or relaxed with diverse others" (D. E. Davis et al., 2018, p. 92). Cultural aspects of countertransference (discussed further in Chapter 7 in this volume) are important to consider and address as part of self-reflective practice. Our own intercultural development can be helped along by cultivating curiosity rather than judgement, learning to notice and regulate our own emotional reactions, and mentalizing others' perspectives (i.e., recognizing how they may be experiencing the current situation distinctly), rather than idealizing or minimizing the other (Hammer et al., 2003). Working with diverse families and coordinating care across professional disciplines and roles is challenging, requiring us to engage in self-reflection while navigating the multiple larger systems encountered by clients, including microsystem (e.g., family, peers, school), mesosystem (i.e., interactions between microsystems), and macrosystem (e.g., society, culture, economic status) levels.

In working with the Garcia family, for example, a clinician might incorporate these MCO tenets by being careful to validate Mrs. Garcia's initial reticence to involve her parents in therapy, rather than pressing her on this, as well as exploring across treatment how grief, mourning, and the afterlife are understood within the family culture, and being sensitive to the meaning of suicide for this family. On a larger systems level, the MCO orients practitioners toward a collaborative and culturally humble (rather than "expert") stance in coordinating care with multiple professionals involved with the family, including Mrs. Garcia's individual therapist, Luke's teacher and school counselor, and potentially Amelia's future daycare. All can offer valuable sources of information, as well as potential intervention points that work in tandem to support the family's healing and resilience.

TRAUMA-INFORMED CLINICAL INTERVENTION AT THE LEVEL OF MULTIPLE SYSTEMS

Mental health treatment is embedded within larger health care systems and community networks, which far too often are siloed from each other. This can create experiences of disjointed care for families, or worse, providers who are working at cross-purposes. For example, an individual therapist may be trying to support an adolescent's agency and encourage collaboration with parents, while another provider recommends a strict behavioral management protocol to the mother. Recent work in promoting early relational health, as described at the beginning of this chapter, is one example of innovative work being done that brings together medical, psychological, and educational professionals in joint momentum to support the dynamic developmental processes rooted in the caregiver–child relationship (Thomas, 2022; Tronick & Beeghly, 2011). By orienting toward healthy development and the prevention of the intergenerational transmission of trauma, these sorts of systemic interventions work upstream of individual psychological distress and represent an important future direction for our field. Whether or not you are personally working with multiple family members in treatment, a systemic approach to treatment prioritizes close coordination of care and collaboration with other professionals across disciplines who are involved with the family.

Consulting with other providers involved with a client sometimes functions as little more than a box to check, without substantively changing a family's treatment experience. This can be due to a variety of factors, including practitioner time demands and lack of infrastructure. Arguing for a systemic approach that attends to mind, body, and relationships as part of interprofessional team-based care, Ruddy and McDaniel (2024) noted how the "status quo too often stymies service integration efforts aimed at bringing a team approach to necessary services and gathering expertise" (p. 3). Systemically-oriented therapists have important roles outside of sessions with respect to the ecological context in which each family is situated. Holding the family system in mind, the work we do outside of formal psychotherapy sessions can be just as important as in-session intervention to support second-order change and growth. While this can vary significantly depending on work setting and population of care, it requires expanding our perspective beyond the individual and family to more broadly consider the macrosystem, both in terms of potential barriers and resources for our clients. Those in the macrosystem we interface with may include the following:

- mental health providers who are working with the same client(s) across therapeutic modalities (e.g., group or individual therapy, assessment) and levels of care (e.g., inpatient, intensive outpatient, partial hospitalization programs);
- mental health providers who are working with other family members or different family subsystems (e.g., couple, parent–child);
- medical providers who are working with one or more members of the family (e.g., primary care doctors, nurses, psychiatrists/psychopharmacologists, dietitians, physical therapists);
- health professionals who attend to the somatic impacts of trauma (e.g., therapeutic massage, yoga, reiki, physical trainers) and address developmental delays (e.g., speech and occupational therapy);
- school personnel (e.g., teachers, principal, Individualized Education Program team) and therapeutic staff (e.g., school counselor, school psychologist, milieu behavioral intervention team);
- investigators and case workers in relevant state offices (e.g., Child Protective Services, Department of Child and Family Services) that support families at risk and may act as guardians for children in foster care;
- legal and criminal justice personnel (e.g., guardian ad litem, court appointed special advocates, parole officers), particularly in situations of termination of parental rights, adoption, or youth with past criminal involvement; and

- other community networks and groups (e.g., clergy, chaplains, and spiritual leaders relevant for a particular family, 12-step and other peer-led programs, Boys' and Girls' Club or similar mentoring programs for at-risk youth)

Engaging with other professionals who are involved with a family can be challenging at times and necessitates intercultural awareness and flexibility, given the distinct values and culture within each discipline. Yet, this part of our work holds tremendous importance within a trauma-informed systemic approach to care. The New Haven trauma-focused competencies (Cook et al., 2014) emphasize the necessity of clinicians' attention to trauma-related relational and systems issues, including collaboration with families and care systems; the role of cultural, historical, and intergenerational factors; and the value of interdisciplinary consultation across systems to enhance treatment effectiveness and facilitate relational healing. Competencies in couple and family psychology delineate three specific application points in our professional work: (a) consultation, (b) engaging interprofessional systems, and (c) advocacy (Celano, 2019). Let's dive into these interrelated domains and consider their relevance to the case of the Garcia family.

Consultation and Coordination of Care

Consultation may involve gathering information, coordinating care, and advocating for a family's needs in interactions with other psychological and medical professionals (e.g., pediatricians, psychiatrists, other therapists involved with the family), as well as key stakeholders in educational (e.g., teachers, counselors/psychologists) and workplace (e.g., human resources) settings (Stanton & Welsh, 2011). Considering the Garcia family, Box 6.1 describes the therapist's initial consultation with Luke's school counselor and ongoing consultation with Mrs. Garcia individual therapist to gather information and support convergence in treatment, so that all practitioners are working in tandem to support the family system. Among families involved with Child Protective Services and/or the criminal justice system, coordinating with legal advocates may also be important. Beyond this, consultation also could involve coordinating with family members and others in their support network (e.g., neighbors, friends, clergy) at the family's request. Consultation may have multiple goals, depending on the situation; for example, exploring ways to increase the client's engagement in treatment, enhancing one's systemic formulation through hearing from other providers working with the family, supporting a holistic treatment approach through integrating psychological and medical health information, or streamlining families' care experiences and the effectiveness of treatment by ensuring all providers are working collaboratively (Celano, 2019).

BOX 6.1

CONSULTATION AND COORDINATION OF CARE WITH SCHOOL COUNSELOR ON BEHALF OF THE GARCIA FAMILY

After obtaining a release of information, the family therapist conducted a phone interview with Luke's school counselor, Ms. Linda Mayhew, MA, LPC, as part of gathering information for the initial assessment. Ms. Mayhew met Luke when he transferred to their school at the beginning of the school year. When registering him in late summer, Mrs. Garcia had informed her about Luke's ADHD-Inattentive diagnosis and the death of his stepfather. Documentation was transferred from the previous school and accommodations for ADHD included individual tutoring. Ms. Mayhew also made concerted efforts to monitor Luke and meet with him a couple times a month. She reported that initially Luke was fairly quiet, but friendly and liked to play with the toys in her office. In the first months of school, teachers noted some difficulties with concentration and distractibility, but Luke was relatively well-behaved until approximately 3 months ago when he began getting in trouble in class. In their individual meetings, Ms. Mayhew noted that Luke appeared increasingly angry and no longer wanted to talk or play in her office.

After several disciplinary referrals from his teacher, Ms. Mayhew met with Luke and Mrs. Garcia and made the referral for family therapy. The change in behavior reported by Ms. Mayhew matched Mrs. Garcia's description of change from Luke's pretrauma functioning to the recent escalating behavioral problems and noncompliance at home. The information from this initial conversation provided additional evidence that enabled the assessment examiner to parse out Luke's recent hyperactive agitation, emotion dysregulation, and difficulty adjusting to change, which could have been mistaken as being related to an ADHD diagnosis, and instead conclude that these behaviors likely represented reactions to the family trauma.

As a result of this consultation, the therapist and Ms. Mayhew decided to coordinate a meeting with Mrs. Garcia and Luke's teacher, Ms. Barnes. This especially made sense in order to avoid a game of "telephone" whereby Mrs. Garcia, who had limited cognitive and emotional resources amid acute grief, would be put in a position of trying to communicate to school personnel about how to help support Luke and address problematic behavior. Another outcome of this initial phone consultation was a plan for the family therapist to remain in regular contact with Ms. Mayhew to track Luke's functioning in the school milieu. See Box 6.2 for an overview of how interprofessional consultation with the school system played an ongoing role in the systemic treatment of the Garcia family.

CONSULTATION WITH CLINICAL TEAM

Given the severity of Mrs. Garcia's posttraumatic stress symptoms as indicated by the assessment results, the family therapist referred Mrs. Garcia to a colleague in the same clinic for trauma-focused individual therapy, Dr. Jamal Ahmad, LP. As part of the referral process, Mrs. Garcia consented for her individual therapist and the family therapist to share records and coordinate care in order to support treatment momentum and effectiveness across modalities. In this particular clinic, the medical record system enabled the individual therapist to access and review the family assessment report before meeting with Mrs. Garcia for intake. This decreased redundancy in paperwork/getting oriented to a new treatment context, as well as the questions the individual therapist needed to ask. Mrs. Garcia was also relieved that she didn't need to "start all over again" with another comprehensive intake.

Regular coordination of care was particularly important in this case because the treatment plan indicated that family intervention would commence after Mrs. Garcia had some time in individual therapy to focus on stabilization, resourcing, and skill-building to adaptively manage her trauma symptoms. The clinical rationale behind this decision was based on Mrs. Garcia's initial presentation as emotionally dysregulated and still reeling from her husband's suicide, which would make family work more difficult. When Dr. Ahmad and Mrs. Garcia concluded that she was managing her symptoms well enough to participate, the two therapists agreed that individual and family therapy could proceed concurrently.

Throughout the course of treatment, the family therapist and individual therapist met on a bimonthly basis to discuss progress and difficulties. This helped the individual therapist stay up-to-date with what recent family sessions were focusing on (e.g., establishing boundaries between subsystems, facilitating developmentally appropriate conversations with the children about the loss), so that these areas could be reinforced when they came up in individual sessions. Regular consultation with each other also helped the family therapist learn more about how Mrs. Garcia was processing feelings of shame, anger, and regret, which became increasingly important as family sessions moved toward engaging the loss directly and integrating grandparents.

While the Garcia family benefited from accessing multiple modes of mental health treatment within the same institutional context, practitioners working in private practice could incorporate a similar systemic approach by developing and maintaining a strong referral network, such that when a family presents with complex needs and multiple forms of therapy are

(continues)

BOX 6.1

CONSULTATION AND COORDINATION OF CARE WITH SCHOOL COUNSELOR ON BEHALF OF THE GARCIA FAMILY (*Continued*)

clinically indicated, the initial assessor can offer targeted referrals and maintain regular contact with these other clinicians.

In some cases, there may already be providers working with some members of a family when we encounter them. For example, if assessment suggested that Luke's problematic behavior was present before his stepfather's death, it might result in a recommendation to consult with Luke's primary care doctor about implementing psychopharmacotherapy to address ADHD symptoms.

Our professional experience has been that when we reach out to consult with providers already working with other family members, the initial response is sometimes surprise, given the health care field's emphasis on individual privacy rather than coordination of care across a family system. However, when we explain our focus on coordinating with other practitioners working with the family to stimulate therapeutic momentum, the response is usually curiosity and openness. Given the back-to-back schedules common in clinical practice, it takes intentionality to find time to jump on the phone or Zoom; doing so signifies belief in and commitment to how collaborating with other providers can improve outcomes for families who may otherwise get lost in the shuffle.

Putting on our consultant hat necessitates zooming out to visualize the network of relationships, other providers, and contexts that touch a family's life, and seeking to work in tandem with them rather than "reinventing the wheel." An ecomap, such as the one conducted as part of the Garcias' intake assessment, can bring into focus key stakeholders that therapists may not have otherwise considered. Part of competency in this area involves conducting systemic needs assessments that help elucidate stressors/strains, gaps in services, and strengths that can be built on at both family and organizational levels. Of course, given confidentiality, consultation must always be preceded by documented client consent, and any information shared should be done for the purposes of meeting the family's needs. Yet, our experience has been that some therapists are unfamiliar with the importance of coordinating systemically and tend to hide behind confidentiality, rather than entering this terrain thoughtfully and wisely.

Engaging Interprofessional and Interdisciplinary Systems

Working with families necessitates navigating interdisciplinary and interprofessional systems, as part of, but not limited to, consultation. Returning to the Garcia family, Box 6.2 describes the therapist's interdisciplinary collaboration with Luke's teacher and school counselor to support the use of trauma-informed practices and effectively address his misbehavior. Within mental health treatment, team-based approaches to care have shown promise in "catching" families that would otherwise fall through the cracks or drop out prematurely, as well as reducing provider burnout and secondary traumatic stress. Trauma systems therapy (Saxe et al., 2015) and multisystemic therapy (Henggeler et al., 2009), as discussed in Chapter 3 in this volume, are two models that place significant focus on the importance of a coherent organizational process for family services and utilization of resources. Dialectical behavior therapy's (Linehan, 2014) emphasis on the treatment team is a worthy reminder about the value of working collaboratively with other colleagues on a particular case and relying on them to process intense transferences and countertransferences, in order to increase client engagement and treatment effectiveness. However, team-based work also increases the potential for trauma-related dynamics, such as splitting (e.g., one provider idealized, the other derogated), making it even more important to foster team cohesion, track dynamics across providers, and cultivate a stance of reflective—rather than reactive—practice.

BOX 6.2

ENGAGING INTERPROFESSIONAL SYSTEMS IN WORKING WITH THE GARCIA FAMILY

After the initial consultation with the school counselor, Ms. Mayhew, the family therapist obtained written permission from Mrs. Garcia and made contact with Luke's teacher, Ms. Barnes, by sending an introductory letter and requesting she complete a symptom checklist about Luke's behavior and functioning at school as part of the assessment process. The letter also mentioned coordination with the school counselor and the hope for a family-school meeting in the near future. Ms. Barnes completed and returned the Behavior Assessment System for Children-Teacher Rating Scale promptly, including a brief note that she would be happy to talk with us.

Prior to the onset of family therapy, after Mrs. Garcia had completed her fourth session of individual therapy, the family-school meeting took place in

(*continues*)

BOX 6.2

ENGAGING INTERPROFESSIONAL SYSTEMS IN WORKING WITH THE GARCIA FAMILY (*Continued*)

Ms. Mayhew's private office at Luke's school. At this time, both Ms. Mayhew and Ms. Barnes reported that Luke's disruptive behavior continued to interfere with his learning and the therapist used this information when family treatment commenced to inform the focus of early sessions on helping Luke learn how to identify and regulate emotions. One important insight from this family-school meeting was that Luke seemed to struggling with the transition to his new school and never warmed up to his teacher, so he was still somewhat shy and guarded with her. Ms. Barnes noted finding it very helpful to gain a broader understanding of what was happening in the family, especially the context for Luke's stepfather's death. She hadn't known these details but sensed that something was "off" for Luke recently. Rather than attributing it to ADHD alone, she was now able to "see" Luke inside the larger family system and discuss trauma-informed education practices that could help Luke stay within his window of tolerance in class. Further, Ms. Barnes was curious to hear more from Luke's mother about the things he liked so she could look for ways to strengthen their student-teacher relationship and put him more at ease.

"I assumed he'd just been goofing off and not caring about school," Ms. Barnes acknowledged, "but all this is making me think that maybe some of what he's doing is a trauma response." Luke's teacher referenced learning about trauma-informed education as part of a recent continuing education training and expressed that this new perspective would definitely change how she responded to Luke, including using playful and collaborative redirections that helped coregulate his emotion rather than only focusing on behavioral compliance.

The team also identified that it could be helpful for Luke to have some extra support between arriving at school and going to the classroom, as Ms. Mayhew noted Luke seemed more withdrawn in the mornings, typically sitting in a corner of the gym reading rather than engaging with peers. Ms. Barnes noted that Luke has decent social skills and had friends in class, so this isolating behavior seemed intentional. Ms. Mayhew also mentioned that she'd been hoping to start a Pokémon group focused on socioemotional development and suggested that maybe Luke would like to join. Mrs. Garcia was excited about this possibility and noted that Luke "loves all things Pokémon." These changes were noted in Luke's 504 educational plan.

During a phone consultation about midway through family therapy, Ms. Mayhew reported a decrease in disciplinary issues but expressed continuing concern about Luke's low mood and apparent lack of interest in tutoring sessions. The family therapist counted this as progress in behavioral control and hypothesized that Luke's ongoing sadness and poor motivation was related to the therapeutic grieving process currently taking place in family therapy. Toward the end of family therapy, the therapist reached out again to schedule another consultation with Mrs. Garcia and the school personnel via an online meeting platform. In the meeting, Ms. Barnes noted that Luke was much more engaged in class and was trying hard to follow instructions, although he still struggled to concentrate on difficult assignments. She expressed gratitude for helping her understand his behavior from a trauma-informed perspective and noted that she now pays much more attention to this sort of thing when involved in creating 504 plans with the counselor. Ms. Mayhew reported that Luke was doing better in tutoring but needed to catch up with some of the work and concepts he had missed in the past few months. She added that the Pokémon group had also been a smashing success and Luke had made several new friends. Ms. Mayhew no longer needed to provide extra support to Luke at the beginning of the day, as Luke and his friends were usually busy trading cards. Nevertheless, she planned to continue monitoring Luke's functioning and would contact Mrs. Garcia if any further problems arose.

Overall, Mrs. Garcia reported that this collaborative experience with the school gave her a lot of confidence to support Luke in the school setting. She noted that, growing up, her parents were not that involved in her schooling due to their demanding work schedules, and while she really wanted to be involved with Luke's school experience, sometimes she got intimidated and worried that school officials would think she was a bad parent if she told them what had really been going on. Having a positive experience whereby school personnel were able to make use of contextual information about the family to be more attuned to her child's needs changed her perspective.

Many families presenting for mental health treatment have complex needs that go well beyond the scope of therapy. Thus, systemically focused intervention requires situating individual, couple, or family therapy work within the larger context of a family's vulnerabilities, strengths, needs, and potential resources. Therapy doesn't fix everything. It is important that we "right size" our efforts and level of influence, collaborating with each client and family to spark reflection on their part about what they need and anticipate being most helpful. As part of a holistic bio-psycho-social-spiritual approach, well-timed referrals for adjunctive services can play vital roles in the larger arc of trauma healing for a family. This might include psychological assessment, medical care, working with a dietitian, trauma-focused yoga or other somatic practices, and speech or occupational therapies. How we go about making referrals matters significantly, beginning with understanding a client's perspective, including potential hesitations and concerns. Many survivors of sexual trauma, for example, understandably avoid gynecological care or even seeing a primary care doctor because of trauma reminders. Those who have experienced poor treatment, medical trauma, or racism in medical settings also have good reason to be cautious about seeking care. Acknowledging and validating these realities, while collaborating with clients to disrupt avoidance and consider how best to advocate for themselves, can help address this.

Advocacy and Working Toward Larger Changes

Advocacy is "baked in" to thinking and working systemically. This may include specific actions taken within a particular case, such as helping parents navigate the bureaucracy of IEPs/504 plans to increase their child's access to educational resources, assisting a working family member in advocating for their needs with the Human Resource department for making use of Family Medical Leave Act benefits, or writing a letter in support of expediting an extended family member's visa process so that they can be present with and assist the family during a vulnerable time (e.g., childbirth, chronic illness). Box 6.3 details the therapist's advocacy and community involvement stemming from her work with the Garcia family. This included providing in-service training for the local school district about trauma-informed teaching practices, as well as getting connected with a nonprofit in her community focused on suicide prevention in immigrant communities.

BOX 6.3

ADVOCACY AND COMMUNITY INVOLVEMENT BEYOND THE GARCIA FAMILY

In addition to advocating for trauma-informed education practices with Luke's school, the therapist's work with the Garcias and several other families with school-aged children made her increasingly aware of how 504 plans often fail to address the sequelae of trauma. Especially when students do not have a trauma-related diagnosis, school personnel might miss the trauma responses underlying difficult classroom behaviors. Encouraged by the school personnel's receptivity to integrating trauma-informed practices in their educational approach and classroom norms during the family-school consultation, the clinician reached out to a colleague who was on the faculty of the education department at the local university. This colleague was delighted to hear of the therapist's interest in this area and invited her to guest lecture in her class for teachers-in-training who were completing their field placement. Over time, the therapist and her colleague expanded beyond the undergraduate context and began facilitating in-service training on trauma-informed classroom practices in the local school district. The therapist felt tremendous energy in the systemic convergence between the ways she intervened with families in treatment and the ecosystem changes she was helping to support through equipping teachers and school staff.

A few years later, the therapist saw a flyer for a local nonprofit focused on mental health awareness and suicide prevention among immigrant communities. Recalling that she had worked with multiple families where a member who had experienced immigration ultimately died by suicide (as was the case for Mr. Garcia), she was deeply saddened to see the social determinants of health within her own clinical practice. She e-mailed the nonprofit to introduce herself and learn more about their work and was pleased to hear that they hoped to adapt Mental Health First Aid (MHFA) and the Question, Persuade, and Refer (QPR) training programs for work with immigrant communities, particularly families who were less acculturated to the U.S. mental health care system. The therapist ultimately became part of an advisory board that provided consultation to key stakeholders (including first- and second-generation immigrants, local religious leaders, and community organizers) as the nonprofit was exploring how the MHFA/QPR frameworks could be incorporated in daily life interactions between community members. The nonprofit was able to obtain grant funding for using a novel community-based prevention and early intervention (CBPI) approach, equipping community members to deliver frontline social and emotional support following training in culturally adapted MHFA/QPR.

The therapist's role in all this was facilitating one of the CBPI community consultation groups, available for free to community members who had completed the MHFA/QPR trainings and were in contexts that involved caring for and supporting others (e.g., their neighbors, congregants, etc.). Group members brought their questions and dilemmas, with the therapist offering guidance about how to apply the MHFA/QPR frameworks to provide psychosocial support to those around them, while also identifying more serious mental health problems warranting a higher level of care and providing guidance on the referral process. The discussion usually turned to helping immigrant families explore and appreciate the strengths and

(*continues*)

BOX 6.3

ADVOCACY AND COMMUNITY INVOLVEMENT BEYOND THE GARCIA FAMILY (*Continued*)

grounding of their cultural background, given that many felt pressure to assimilate in order to blend in and decrease risk for discrimination. In a very real sense, these families lost their homes and livelihoods when they moved to the United States. Some families also lost their bearings and feeling of belonging, which sometimes extended to loss of identity and loss of hope. To address this, the community decided to sponsor regular cultural celebrations that provided "a taste of home" for immigrants from diverse places and encouraged increased dialogue and friendship with people throughout the community.

Importantly, while this therapist is deeply engaged in her community, she is not operating as a lone ranger or trying to "do it all." Rather, she identified key stakeholders and organizations in the community and is collaborating thoughtfully and intentionally with them. While the therapist brings advanced training and expertise in systems-oriented trauma intervention and prevention, she adopts a stance of curiosity, openness, learning, and collaboration, creating a culture of "power with" rather than "power over." From a systemic perspective, her efforts in the community are focused on equipping others to create a long continuum of care that extends well beyond mental health treatment and helps families thrive.

"This work is really changing me," she reflects to her partner one evening over dinner. "I can't imagine just being limited to the therapy room now. I've met such amazing, passionate, skillful people in our community who are out there supporting families who are struggling . . . long before they'd ever find my office. And hopefully, many of them never need to!"

Our experience is that, in the context of a strong therapeutic alliance, families often ask for input and help navigating macrosystem challenges, and yet, many of our supervisees—and we ourselves sometimes—can freeze up when this happens, wondering, is this part of my role? While differentiating our role and establishing clear boundaries is foundational to being a therapist, it seems that training often stops there. Developing competencies in working systemically behooves us to be guided by a different question: In what ways might I use my role to support and facilitate this family's flourishing? Beyond any single case, advocacy in our professional work also entails bringing a systemic orientation that honors families' strengths and healing potential into our supervision, teaching, research and dissemination of research to policymakers, as well as administrative/organizational practices. Our role as advocates can encompass diverse areas, including

> promot[ing] organizational practices that prioritize the needs of families and facilitate evidence-based systemic practice, ... argu[ing] for incorporation of relational processes and diagnosis into the *DSM*, and challeng[ing] medical models and associated funding and reimbursement policies that marginalize a systemic conceptualization of human behavior in favor of a view of problems as brain disorders. (Celano, 2019, p. 445)

The lens of advocacy orients us beyond any single family to consider creative ways we might use our professional influence and expertise to increase care providers' and community members' awareness about the influential role of family context and dynamics—as well as broader relational networks—in both the experience of trauma and the process of healing and recovery.

Community-Based Prevention and Early Intervention Amid Adversity

The complex contextual situations that we encounter in working with traumatized families can sometimes leave us feeling helpless, discouraged, or demoralized after witnessing, for example, our clients' lack of or denial of access to resources and treatment, history of adversity and/or discrimination, or other types of unfair or unreasonable circumstances beyond their control (Crabtree et al., 2025). A systemic understanding of trauma and its impacts orients us beyond psychotherapy alone to consider creative ways to help prevent traumatization through targeting underlying social and societal determinants. Adjacent fields such as public health, prevention science, environmental studies, emergency management, and religion are important partners in exploring how to bolster culturally and spiritually embedded strengths and healing practices, promote healthy development across the family lifecycle (especially during transition periods such as parenting, divorce, death of a loved one, etc.), and support community resilience in times of stress and adversity. In this section, we delve into what community-level efforts might look like practically and how this type of work fits within our professional identity.

As Part of Cultural Responsiveness

CBPI efforts can help support the natural resilience and capacity-building of families and communities who are at risk for or have endured trauma (Reese & Vera, 2007). Systemically oriented clinicians are well-suited to serve as consultants in developing CBPI programs, helping key stakeholders and cultural insiders identify spaces and activities around which the community of concern naturally gathers. This might include schools, workplaces, recreational facilities, and/or houses of worship, along with the rituals, gatherings, and cultural events that unfold therein and might be integrated with CBPI (Aten et al., 2011, 2020; Captari et al., 2023). Depending on the nature of the trauma, certain places that were the site of a mass trauma (frequently experienced as "desecrated") could play a role in collective healing. For example, following the mass shootings at Mother Emanuel African Methodist Episcopal Church and Tree of Life Congregation synagogue, communal gatherings at these sites provided a collective space to grieve and a needed receptacle for collective rage, lament, and memorializing.

Rather than focusing on the diagnosis and treatment of particular mental health disorders, a CBPI paradigm taps into and reinforces culturally embedded healing practices and spaces that have existed long before psychotherapy as we know it developed. Across time, people have come together, told stories, danced, drummed, wailed, prayed, eaten and drunk together, and conducted a variety of healing rituals. A holistic and culturally responsive approach to trauma healing includes listening for, honoring, and centering such culturally embedded healing practices—the diverse ways that communities regulate trauma-related emotions, make meaning, transcend suffering, claim a sense of agency, and reestablish a collective identity. As part of this, we must take the intergenerational transmission of strengths and resilience (L. Liu et al., 2018; Tesfai et al., 2023) just as seriously as the intergenerational transmission of trauma. For example, Native American and other Indigenous spiritual traditions understand trauma recovery as a holistic journey that involves healing "soul wounds" (Duran, 2019). As Ringland (2019) described,

> Experiences that propel a person into a state of terror and dissociation are seen as "soul loss," meaning that the person is no longer fully present in ordinary reality, because parts of his or her spirit have split off, fled, or gotten lost. (p. 3)

In such traditions, restoring a sense of wholeness to the psyche/spirit and mending these splits are central to trauma healing, not just coping or reducing symptoms. As part of an APA presidential initiative in this area, Bryant (2024) noted the centrality of reclamation of self and community to many survivors' healing process, beyond psychotherapy alone. Novel pathways to this end within prevention and early intervention may include helping a family reengage with their culture and its resources as medicine, strengthen community support and belonging, draw hope and strength from their spirituality, and/or engage with expressive arts as a means of symbolizing that for which there is no words (Bryant, 2024; Gone, 2019).

Given evidence that families who are more religious and/or non-Western are often less acculturated to mental health terminology and less likely to enter psychotherapy (Amri & Bemak, 2013; Lefevor et al., 2022), religion-specific and culture-specific interventions fill an important gap in promoting family- and community-level resilience. There is tremendous potential for collaborating with clergy and community leaders to develop group healing spaces rooted in emic language, narrative, and theologies. For example, Coffee/Tea and Family Education and Support (Walsh, 2007) utilized a 9-week multifamily group format to support families in Bosnia and Kosovo impacted by war, "offering a compassionate setting to share stories of suffering and struggle . . . [and] affirm family strengths and resources" (Walsh, 2007, p. 221). The groups met in a neighborhood storefront over tea (in Kosovo) or coffee (in Bosnia), incorporating cultural practices around which people gather. Another initiative, Healing the Wounds of Trauma (Hill et al., 2021), was designed to meet the unique needs of Christian survivors in low-resource contexts. In collaboration with local faith leaders, 8-week Healing the Wounds of Trauma groups have been implemented in over 150 cultures and found to be efficacious in reducing trauma-related symptoms and promoting adaptive coping (Worthington et al., 2024).

In more collectivistic cultures and particularly in situations of mass trauma, healing may not be something that any one person or family pursues or experiences individually, but rather recovery emerges out of the community bearing witness to and joining the sufferers in carrying the weight of trauma's impact (Saul, 2022). Becoming well-versed in the research on relational, affective, cognitive, and behavioral mechanisms of change underlying trauma-focused psychotherapies (see Chapter 3 in this volume) equips us to listen for and notice the resources that already exist within a family or community and can be capitalized on to promote healing. This is true evidence-based practice, not implementing an empirically supported treatment manual in a one-size-fits-all manner. In collaborating with community leaders, we might ask questions like, "In your neighborhood, how do people make sense of, move through, and heal from terrible life experiences?" As part of this, we must be mindful that even the language of trauma itself is less relevant in some cultural contexts (Schnyder et al., 2016), and some communities may use other words that more aptly capture their felt experience. Taken together, psychosocial, educational, spiritual, and other community-based interventions can play important roles in helping increase access and breaking down barriers to care when we are sensitive to diverse worldviews, and ensure we are working within or in cooperation with already trusted support networks (López-Zerón & Parra-Cardona, 2015; Reese & Vera, 2007).

As Part of Early Intervention Following Crisis and Disaster

A majority of trauma-focused interventions seek to ameliorate clinical levels of distress. Sometimes this can feel like plugging holes in a colander, given how the effects of trauma spill over across family systems, communities, and generations. Research has shown that adverse childhood experiences "may beget later stressors and alter life-course trajectories of stressor exposure" (Bürgin et al., 2021, p. 124). This begs the question: Why do we wait until someone meets criteria for posttraumatic stress disorder or another mental health disorder before taking action? Substantively tackling this public health issue necessitates working upstream of symptomology to (a) address individual and family vulnerabilities that predispose survivors to future traumatization; (b) alter societal conditions that set the stage for victimization and abuses of power; and (c) provide appropriate and accessible supports before, during, and after stressful experiences that a family or community encounters.

This larger vantage point is imperative in light of crises and disaster situations arising in the communities in which we live. Climate changes are resulting in increased frequency and intensity of natural disasters, including forest fires, tornados, earthquakes, flooding, and other extreme weather (Benevolenza & DeRigne, 2019). Human-caused disasters, such as mass shootings, industrial accidents, terrorism, and armed conflict, have ripple effects across communities and can change children's developmental trajectories, as do chronic conditions of police violence, high crime, and lack of safety (Halpern & Vermeulen, 2017). In situations of crisis and disaster, it is children, the elderly, and people with disabilities who are most vulnerable to long-lasting negative impacts (Andrade et al., 2023; Mann et al., 2021). Survivors who have less access to resources and social capital (e.g., undocumented and migrant families) are often overlooked in government relief efforts (Méndez et al., 2020).

In the midst of all this, formal mental health treatment may not be clinically indicated and/or desired, but secondary prevention strategies embedded within larger relief efforts can be incredibly timely and helpful: "Upset, stressed, and anxious survivors are usually not looking for a 'shrink,' psychologist, or social worker. They're often reluctant to ask for or accept professional services. What they are looking for is human contact and support" (Halpern & Vermeulen, 2017, p. 8). Mental health professionals with a systemic understanding of trauma and healing are uniquely equipped to partner with community stakeholders (e.g., government officials, emergency response teams, religious leaders, school administration) to create a multipronged disaster mental health response strategy. We know from research that there are diverse trajectories of posttrauma adjustment (Galatzer-Levy et al., 2018). Disaster mental health efforts seek to bolster a community's recovery in the first days, weeks, and months after a distinct event. This represents a sensitive period that can lay the groundwork for longer-term recovery trajectories by connecting people with social resources, meaning-making practices, and narratives that incorporate a larger perspective (and counter self-blame).

Normative human responses to highly distressing experiences in the immediate days and weeks following a disaster include physical, emotional, behavioral, and even existential/spiritual components, like feeling anxious and on edge, experiencing anger or guilt, disruptions in eating and sleeping, ruminating about the situation, and looking for someone to blame. Such acute stress reactions are common and often resolve without professional intervention. This is not to suggest that survivors are unaffected, but rather that "like the physiological immune system that fights threats to physical health, people have a psychological immune system that fights threats to emotional well-being," including psychological defenses, coping, and attempting to make sense of what has occurred (T. D. Wilson & Gilbert, 2005, p. 133). Family systems and community networks similarly operate as a sort of social immune system to help counter the effects of stress, with immune system responses ranging from more adaptive (e.g., collective mourning, meaning-making, and altruism) to less adaptive (e.g., collective minimization and denial).

Our role might involve drawing from psychological science and systemic principles to advise and assist community leadership in providing clear, developmentally appropriate information about what occurred and what resources are available, as well as normalizing the acute stress responses that people are experiencing instead of overemphasizing positive messaging like "we are resilient!" A multipronged intervention approach might include maintaining a mental health presence at shelters or other gathering places to provide real-time support and risk assessments, and collaborating with local spiritual leaders to create communal gatherings for mourning and comfort. Social media campaigns, school collaborations, and fact sheets can inform and/or reinforce adaptive individual and family coping strategies. Community opportunities to engage in the creative arts (e.g., murals, memorials, music) may help members symbolize the raw psychic experience related to mass trauma. Clinicians might also be involved in providing support to first responders (e.g., firefighters, police, emergency medical technicians) who experience secondary trauma and potential moral injury in their professional roles.

As Part of Equipping Community Members

One does not need to be a mental health professional to provide empathic and effective support following a stressful experience, yet appropriate training is certainly important. Well-meaning people say all sorts of things that can be experienced as unhelpful and sometimes cause harm (Van den Eynde & Veno, 2013). Part of intervening multisystemically includes equipping spiritual leaders, lay helpers, administrators, community members, and parents with knowledge about acute stress responses and basic helping skills to respond to these vulnerabilities. This goes far beyond simply having counselors available at school, for example, to talk to kids after a shooting occurs. Tapping into trusted relationships and leaders' cultural expertise can help bolster communal care networks, leading to much broader dissemination and accessibility of effective strategies to cope with mass trauma. Here, we review three research-supported intervention frameworks that can be flexibly applied by individuals in a variety of helping and supportive roles following community crisis and disaster: Psychological First Aid, Skills for Psychological Recovery, and Spiritual First Aid. Key tenets from these models can be interwoven with culture-specific healing and coping practices (e.g., dance, music, the arts) to meet the needs of a particular community.

Psychological First Aid (PFA; National Child Traumatic Stress Network & National Center for PTSD, 2006) emphasizes early intervention in order to decrease distress and increase adaptive coping. PFA delineates eight core actions that providers can flexibly draw from based on survivors' needs and the context of support. For example, initiating contact with survivors should be done in a nonintrusive, empathic manner, with immediate attention to physical and emotional safety. This sort of community work often involves providing real-time emotional support to families who are disoriented and emotionally overwhelmed; of note, this is distinct from asking survivors what happened or trying to engage with trauma processing, which is contraindicated in the immediate aftermath of the traumatic event. While it is inadvisable to "shut down" someone who spontaneously begins to share elements of their disaster story unless the context is inappropriate, critical incident stress debriefing has not been found to be effective (Stileman & Jones, 2023; van Emmerik et al., 2002). In the early postdisaster phases, stabilization is the overriding goal, not processing. PFA orients us to support families' sense of agency through exploring their current concerns and needs. Depending on the context, we might offer some type of practical assistance, help connect survivors with social supports, provide information about stress reactions and coping, and link them with government or other community services.

Given that community recovery is a process that ultimately unfolds across months and years, Skills for Psychological Recovery (SPR; National Child Traumatic Stress Network & National Center for PTSD, 2010) focuses on survivors' adjustment beyond the initial phase of stabilization. For example, SPR might be helpful when people are trying to resume "normal life"—going back to school or work, but still contending with disaster impacts. SPR outlines six key skills, namely, supporting survivors' self-awareness about their needs, fostering adaptive problem solving, promoting positive activities, managing acute stress reactions, strengthening social connections, and promoting balanced perspectives. These principles are well-suited to discussions with multiple family members, given that each person's reaction affects others in the family, and that (as discussed in Chapter 2 in this volume) members' lived experiences of a disaster can vary greatly.

Often, faith communities are on the frontlines of volunteer recovery efforts and are eager to gain information about how to be responsive to acute stress reactions and help disenfranchised community members without inadvertently hurting them (Aten & Boan, 2016). The Spiritual First Aid (SFA; Aten et al., 2020) framework integrates PFA/SPR principles with existential and spiritual domains, given that doubts, questions, and the search for meaning are frequent following disaster and that spiritual/religious resources and coping strategies can support resilience (Zhang et al., 2021). SFA orients care providers to assess for and respond to survivors' needs and gaps in belonging, livelihood, emotional support, spirituality/meaning, and safety.

Equipping key personnel in administrative and leadership roles, schools, religious communities, and other networks to integrate these key principles of disaster recovery and trauma healing within their milieus can help move the needle on creating change at a societal level. At the same time, it is important to clearly distinguish this peer support from clinical assessment or therapy; training should always include attention to recognizing the scope and limitations of one's knowledge and referring survivors in acute distress to the appropriate level of mental health care. Beyond crisis and disaster situations alone, there are a number of well-established CBPIs that readers may be interested in incorporating into their community work. For example, the therapist working with the Garcia family partnered with a local nonprofit to help adapt MHFA (Kitchener & Jorm, 2008) and the QPR suicide prevention framework (Quinnett, 2012) to meet the needs of local families less acculturated to mental health care who may be struggling with similar challenges to the Garcias, but who are unlikely to show up in her office. By providing training and consultation to key stakeholders in implementing MHFA/QPR principles in several different contexts, this clinician is truly thinking and working systemically . . . holding individual families in mind, but not stopping there.

SUMMARY AND KEY TAKEAWAYS

This chapter has explored terrain that is often neglected in psychotherapy training, seen as the purview of social work or adjacent fields. We argue that addressing trauma multisystemically is critical in order to facilitate second-order changes, particularly in situations of mass or collective trauma, but also more broadly as part of changing conditions that set the stage for traumatization (e.g., economic inequity, structural racism, minority stress). When practitioners fail to invest the time and energy to hold the entire family in mind and collaborate in ongoing ways with other service providers, traumatized families often end up being overtreated, but underhelped. This can increase risk for lack of engagement, therapeutic ruptures, early dropout, or even iatrogenic outcomes:

> Multistressed families can easily become multitreated families, with no one provider having a systemic, comprehensive view of family strengths and resilience . . . , potentially engendering anger, reinforcing powerlessness, and leading to reluctance to engage in treatment. (Celano, 2019, p. 437)

Yet, truly engaging in multisystemic intervention can be uniquely challenging for several reasons. First, many of us work in roles where we are only financially compensated for "billable hours," that is, hours providing psychotherapy services. The current structure of the insurance system is not aligned with research showing that when professionals utilize team-based and family-centered approaches in working with those who have experienced trauma, treatment is often more effective and payors can actually experience cost savings (Gaebel et al., 2020; Sinkler et al., 2022). Importantly, healthy systemic dynamics among providers are necessary in order for such team-based care to be effective. As long as consultation, interdisciplinary collaboration, and advocacy fall under the nebulous umbrella of (often unpaid) administrative work, these competencies will continue to be disincentivized in clinical practice.

Second, meaningful collaboration across systems not only takes time but also necessitates working effectively across difference, which can be taxing. Each profession has a distinct subculture, treatment philosophy, and language. Synthesizing these divergent vantage points—like pieces of a puzzle to reveal a more holistic perspective on the family—requires high levels of executive functioning, dialectical thinking, and interpersonal skills. Intercultural awareness, flexibility, and humility are necessary in order to hold multiple (and at times, seemingly opposing) formulations in mind. Too often, team-based care is stymied by providers digging in their heels concerning differing recommendations or formulations, becoming territorial or ego-driven. Families deserve better.

Third, the potential momentum of team-based work can be stalled by power dynamics, poor leadership, and lack of clarity concerning each person's tasks, roles, and authority. This may be especially the case in postdisaster situations, where team members' own acute stress responses fuel reactivity, rigidity, or individualistic heroism. Familiarity with systems thinking and dynamics can help us understand—and proactively develop more differentiated and balanced—treatment team dynamics. It behooves those who are in leadership and administrative roles to analyze the systemic patterns of their teams and consider how to strengthen cohesion, direct communication, and clarity about tasks/roles/authority, as well as how to effectively navigate workplace conflicts, polarization, and potential detouring/scapegoating. In situations where multiple independent providers are working with a family, frank discussion about who is "taking lead" on what parts of the case and addressing potential or active splitting can ensure that practitioners are working in tandem, rather than against each other.

Taken together, working at a community level requires building deep relationships of trust and goodwill, yet it unlocks unique opportunities to tackle the roots of trauma. In a world where there are not enough providers to keep up with mental health need, CBPIs are largely an untapped resource. While ultimately more fiscally responsible in the long run, investing in CBPIs requires a paradigm shift beyond the family alone as well as a commitment to tackling risk factors of chronic traumatization and supporting protective factors at a community level. Systemically oriented therapists have the opportunity to be on the leading edge of helping bolster communities' resilience through collaborating with key stakeholders to infuse what we know from psychological science with culturally embedded healing practices. How do we do this work in a sustainable way?

We turn our attention now to the self of the therapist, exploring risks for vicarious/secondary trauma and identifying ways practitioners—and the organizations they work within—can cultivate career longevity in trauma-focused systemic work.

7 CHALLENGES AND POSSIBILITIES AS A FAMILY TRAUMA THERAPIST

A Communal Approach to Cultivating Resilience and Sustainability

Can we accept as a given that the self-of-the-therapist is an essential factor in the therapeutic process?

—VIRGINIA SATIR (2000, P. 26)

"Have you ever stopped to consider—and actually write down—what you're exposed to every day? The stories you're living with your clients and their families . . . and how that impacts you as a person?" The question came from a mentor of mine (LC), who started her career working with survivors of abuse well before posttraumatic stress disorder (PTSD) was even part of the *DSM*. She shared with me a regular practice that had helped sustain her in trauma work across decades, rooted in the presupposition that it is simply not possible to step into the "eye of the storm" with traumatized families without being personally impacted. As a young therapist, I found this so helpful and validating. My training had emphasized self-care and good boundaries, but it felt way more complicated in real life. The stories and experiences of my clients were tragic and unforgettable. I could not (and did not want to) just push them out of my

This chapter contains a composite case vignette drawn from multiple clients and fictitious aspects. Details have been substantively changed to protect confidentiality.

https://doi.org/10.1037/0000487-008
Systemic Treatment of Trauma-Impacted Families: A Clinician's Guide to Assessment, Formulation, and Intervention, by S. A. Riggs and L. E. Captari

mind when I got home at night. I did not yet know how to hold, metabolize, and release the suffering I was encountering.

I was fresh out of my master's program and working as an intensive in-home therapist with children and teens who had been discharged from inpatient psychiatric hospitalization. In our rural community, many of the families I worked with were living in poverty and had very few resources. I remember shivering with cold in one home as I tried to make therapeutic contact with Max, a selectively mute little boy. His mother noted they did not have money to run the heat. I sat with this boy and his mother for several hours a week, for months, engaging in a variety of expressive and play interventions, before he uttered his first word in session. By then it was spring, and not so cold. I discovered that Max had good reasons not to talk. His home held many secrets, including harboring a family member hiding from the law.

Another of my clients, Jackie, experienced persistent suicidal thoughts and was severely depressed. But she seemed to come alive when we engaged with the family animals. Chickens. Goats. Sheep. I'll never forget the day I felt warm liquid spray across my legs mid-conversation and looked down to see one of the goats peeing on me. (No class prepared me for that!) We both couldn't help laughing. Later, Jackie confided in me as we sat in her bedroom that a family member was abusing her and her siblings. The Child Protective Services report unfortunately led to the family terminating services, so I'm not sure what happened next for Jackie.

Then there was Candace, a young mother with severe PTSD, who had grown up in the foster care system. Her son, Theo, was living with grandparents due to behavior problems and school refusal, with the goal of reunification. Theo often screamed "no" and stomped his feet whenever I showed up. As I tried to remain calm and steadfast, I wondered about all this little boy might be holding for the family. Over time, I learned through working with Candace that she had been keeping her son home from school to protect him from "the evils of the world" and as a buffer against her abusive husband. Despite a restraining order in place, I often felt on edge when there, given that her husband had made threats against "any professional who comes near my family."

Years later, these stories remain vivid and poignant, making my heart hurt and my stomach churn. The unique gift—and challenge—of meeting with these families in their home environment was that I swam in the waters of their trauma states, dynamics, and secrets. The emotional and psychological currents of trauma registered in my own body and nervous system. I felt the chaos, the powerlessness, and a profound sense of despair; the desperation, darkness, rage, and shame; the unspeakability of what had happened (and was continuing to). Some days, it felt like I was drowning . . . as if the walls of these homes were closing in and there was no way out. Added to that, I was often up against insurance bureaucracy . . . having to substantiate medical necessity for services to be able to continue. While I was lucky to have a wonderfully skilled and supportive supervisor, I was physically alone most of my day . . . often driving an hour or more between clients' homes.

I loved my work and the families I met with. I could not imagine a more meaningful job. And yet, it took its toll. Thankfully, supervision and mentorship helped me self-reflect and track my experiences and needs at a deeper level. As we begin this chapter, we invite you to take a few moments to engage with this personal reflection for yourself.

First, grab a piece of paper and fold it in half. On the left side, write down everything that comes to mind that you encounter and experience in your role as a therapist. Just a word or phrase for each idea is sufficient. The point is to capture the essence of your experience.

Second, on the right half of the paper, see if you can identify and describe the opposite of each of the phenomena you listed on the left. For example:

Chaos—a sense of order, predictability
Powerlessness—agency, freedom
Despair—hope, possibility, creativity
Rage, fear—calm, safety
Shame—acceptance, compassion
Unspeakability—coherence, narrative, curiosity

"Unless you actively cultivate these things in your life," my mentor admonished, pointing to the righthand column, "You won't be able to enter into and companion others in these dark places for long." She had my attention. Her tone was serious, grave even.

Supervision, mentoring, and our own psychotherapy can all play critical roles in exploring what brings each of us to this work, and what comes up personally when we bear witness to clients' trauma, tragedy, and resilience. In the face of the too-muchness inherent in trauma intervention, therapists are vulnerable to becoming heroes or robots. The pull to cast ourselves as the hero of our clients' lives is rooted in a sense of grandiosity that idealizes our role and contributions (as a defense against helplessness). On the opposite extreme, we might start to feel like robots—deflated, diminished, and a bit dissociated from both ourselves and our clients.

Working with trauma is inevitably existential, requiring that we face and grapple with our own motivations for, and limitations around, being a helper. As a beginning therapist, I was idealistic and a bit naïve. I wanted to make a difference—to "be the change you wish to see in the world," as they say. But this was also an altruistic reframe for my own fantasies of being powerful and effectual to help and heal others . . . to create for others some of what I needed and hadn't had. Particularly as graduate training increasingly focuses on skills, competencies, and treatment manuals, it is vital that therapists also have developmentally focused spaces to reflect on their motivations for pursuing this career, and working with trauma in particular. This chapter delves into the challenges and possibilities of working therapeutically with traumatized families. We start by discussing the professional competency of reflective practice and explore the role of the self-of-the-therapist—including countertransference and use of self, as well as personal psychological dynamics that may increase the risk of occupational hazards. An exploration of ways to develop personal and professional resilience in this line of work follows, including self-care practices, social and professional support, and supervision/consultation. The chapter ends by considering the ethical responsibility of therapists to maintain their mental health and competence to practice psychotherapy, the difficulties inherent in self-assessment, and the need to move beyond self-care to develop systems of care that support therapists' longevity.

WE NEVER "ARRIVE": THE CRITICAL IMPORTANCE OF REFLECTIVE PRACTICE

The training and everyday work of being a systemically oriented psychotherapist engages both our professional and personal selves. Personal experiences, beliefs, attributes, and capacity for empathy are directly connected to our deep-seated desire to help and the ways we interact with clients, supervisors, and professional colleagues. Most readers likely remember the intense emotions they experienced in early practicum field experiences—the excited highs of success when clients improved in treatment and the distressing lows triggered by their painful, sometimes traumatic stories, as well as personal self-doubts in response to supervisory feedback. Especially when working with couples and families, the relational nature of intervention inevitably entails intense emotional exchanges; thus, it is essential for therapists to learn to recognize and manage not only their clients' emotions in session, but also their own emotional reactions to the therapeutic process both inside and outside of session (Karam et al., 2015). Like other professional organizations for mental health practitioners, the American Psychological Association (APA) has codified the significance of therapists' self-awareness in a foundational professional competency emphasizing reflective practice, as well as self-assessment and self-care (Fouad et al., 2009; Hatcher et al., 2013).

The value of reflective practice is not new, and writers in various disciplines have traced its ethos to the ancient Greek maxim "Know thyself" (Bolton, 2010;

Lilienfeld & Basterfield, 2020; D. Taylor, 2020). In the mental health field, many definitions have been proposed over the years; J. Brown (2019) described reflective practice as "the personal experience of meaning-making for self-awareness, cultural sensitivity, enhancement of the therapeutic relationship, as well as personal, professional, and social change" (p. 1). Reflective practice helps us avoid the pitfalls of becoming a robot or a hero in clinical interactions. This requires an openness to introspection and self-evaluation on a personal level, as well as taking initiative to build in space and time professionally for supervision and/or consultation. Personal and professional self-awareness includes active and ongoing self-reflection, self-assessment of strengths and limitations in professional competencies, appropriate self-monitoring and self-care, along with a readiness to take appropriate action when needed, such as seeking supervision and/or training, obtaining treatment, reducing caseloads, etc. In the APA Competency Benchmarks (Fouad et al., 2009; Hatcher et al., 2013), reflective practice also comprises "self used as therapeutic tool" (Fouad et al., 2009, p. S10). The use of self in psychotherapy practice attends to and utilizes overlapping spheres of the personal self (e.g., personality, beliefs, life experiences) and the professional self (e.g., training, skills, knowledge, techniques; Dewane, 2006; Omylinska-Thurston & James, 2011). The science of psychotherapy highlights the critical importance of the therapeutic alliance and therapist factors in effective treatment (Baldwin & Imel, 2013; Horvath et al., 2011), with some scholars arguing that the therapist, rather than any particular intervention model, is the key change ingredient in effective treatment (Blow et al., 2007). The art of psychotherapy, on the other hand, involves the skillful blending of our professional knowledge and competencies with vital facets of our personal selves in a real relationship with clients and families in order to offer hope and assistance in healing from trauma.

While we have overviewed specific competencies relevant for systemically oriented practitioners treating the broad sequelae of trauma throughout this book, it is equally important to acknowledge and critique the field's primary focus on competencies. This language can suggest there is an arrival point, such that once you demonstrate a competency, you are now "competent" and ready to enter professional practice without further training. Competency-based training ensures that students develop specific skills prior to becoming licensed practitioners; however, scholars have suggested that it is also important to emphasize *capability*—the ability to learn how things are connected, to use the self to generate new perspectives, and to adapt professional competencies in flexible, creative ways to dynamic and novel clinical situations (Fraser & Greenhalgh, 2001; Kaslow et al., 2022). Capability highlights the process of lifelong learning and improvement in the science and skills of systemic psychotherapy, as well as the art and creativity brought to the endeavor by our unique personality and selfhood.

ATTENDING TO THE SELF-OF-THE-THERAPIST

In the early years of psychotherapy, there were mixed perspectives on the importance of the person-of-the-therapist, with a primary emphasis on correcting personal deficits in order to treat clients effectively. Originating with Freud (1910/1957), the concept of countertransference referred to therapists' unconscious reactions to their clients' transference due to unresolved personal conflicts. Since that time, the meaning of countertransference has evolved to more broadly represent the therapist's thoughts, emotions, reactions, associations, and values that emerge in the psychotherapeutic context (Niño & Zeytinoglu-Saydam, 2020). The "use of self" in contemporary psychodynamic therapy is a finely tuned clinical skill that facilitates an understanding of interpersonal themes in the therapeutic relationship and how these themes play out in the client's world outside of therapy. For example, upon reflecting internally on their own annoyance with the client, a therapist might ask themselves, "If I am feeling annoyed by this client's behavior in session, what could that reveal about how they interact with other people in their life?" and subsequently use that question, sparked by self-experience, to help the client explore interpersonal behaviors and social interactions. As a learned clinical skill, the use of self employs the therapist's self-reflective understanding of countertransference, which begins with an intimate knowledge of one's own psychology and relational dynamics.

The concept of self-of-the-therapist (aka, person-of-the-therapist) has a long tradition in couple and family therapy. From the perspective of systems theory, the self is conceived as relational and interdependent, so reciprocal and mutually influential interactions are inevitable in all relationships, including the client–therapist relationship. Couple and family therapy training has emphasized the need for therapists to explore their own family of origin issues in order to avoid possible blind spots or disruptions in their ability to remain objective and manage intense emotions in session (e.g., Bowen, 1978; McGoldrick, 1982). Self-of-the-therapist training and exploration are intended to help therapists understand how their personal experiences, relationships, family, and cultural background have shaped their sense of self, personal values, and biases, and then recognize how these factors may affect their clinical interactions with clients. With this in mind, a common training exercise in the field involves students creating their own family's genogram and analyzing intergenerational patterns of relationships, personalities/roles, occupations, education, medical/psychological conditions, and strengths and vulnerabilities. Ecomaps are another way to expand our vantage point about the world each of us lives in—including friends, community, workplace, collegial relationships, and other kinship networks (e.g., extended and chosen family, faith community)—identifying where we receive support and where we experience strain and expend a lot of energy.

Aponte (2022), who developed the person-of-the-therapist training model, emphasized the need for self-awareness to guide "the conscious, active and purposeful use of self as is in the moment of the therapeutic engagement with clients" (p. 136), describing the therapist's use of self in treatment as "the soul of therapy" (p. 136). As implied by Satir's words at the opening of this chapter, early pioneers in systemic intervention saw the value of understanding the self-of-the-therapist for a variety of reasons. For example, Bowen (Kerr & Bowen, 1988) suggested that therapists' differentiation of self is critical in order to preserve therapeutic objectivity and reduce emotional reactivity, and empirical research has borne this out (Captari et al., 2025). Other family scholars noted that if therapists' family of origin issues are unresolved, a clinician might be pulled unwittingly into the family system during the joining process and lose their clinical vantage point, or might be unable to manage intense emotions within themselves when seeking to increase or de-escalate intensity in session (Minuchin & Fishman, 1981; Napier & Whitaker, 1978). Minuchin and Fishman (1981) encouraged family therapists to be curious about how their actions in session affect and are affected by the family, and to use their own position in the system to help facilitate change in family patterns.

When unrecognized, unresolved, or denied, countertransference and self-of-the-therapist aspects can interfere with the therapeutic alliance and clinical effectiveness. This is particularly true for trauma therapists whose own unresolved issues and experiences may be triggered by trauma-related session content (Leung et al., 2023). However, when recognized and utilized in a differentiated manner, even trauma-related countertransference can be a powerful force in facilitating deeper empathic understanding and connection, particularly given its utility to orient clinicians to what is unspeakable and disavowed in the family (Bromberg, 2014). Drawing from Greek mythology, Jung (1951/1976) proposed the notion of the "wounded healer," arguing that "it is [a therapist's] own hurt that gives a measure of [their] power to heal" (p. 116). This describes a therapist whose own vulnerabilities and exposure to adverse events serve as personal resources for understanding and empathizing with clients' struggles. Most of us have suffered at some point in our lives, and many gifted psychotherapists are attracted to this profession precisely because of difficult personal experiences that generate a heartfelt determination to prevent or lessen the emotional pain of others facing adversity. Trials, tribulations, and tragedy can paradoxically yield personal strength, empathy, wisdom, and growth that reflective psychotherapists successfully draw from in their work with traumatized clients. Thus, we caution readers against misinterpreting the literature to presume that one's own trauma history is a blight on professional competence. Scholars have noted that there are many possible therapeutic strengths arising from childhood adversity and other formative experiences in clinicians' lives, such as potentially greater capacity to sit with difficult emotions, bear witness to suffering, and companion others on their healing journey (Captari et al., 2025; Timm & Blow, 1999; Whittenbury et al., 2025). However, as discussed below, wounded healers who have unresolved personal vulnerabilities may encounter considerable personal and professional strain in working with trauma-impacted families.

CHALLENGES AND RISKS OF TRAUMA-FOCUSED SYSTEMIC THERAPY

Journeying with traumatized couples and families in therapy can be physically, cognitively, emotionally, and existentially demanding, and, as graduate training increasingly focuses on competencies and skills, self-of-the-therapist aspects can easily fall by the wayside. In *Trauma Stewardship*, van Dernoot Lipsky and Burk (2009) elucidated how chronic exposure to suffering, tragedy, and the dark side of life can fan the flames of personal psychological vulnerabilities. In fact, scholars have argued that it is not possible to not be impacted in some manner by such heart-rending work, and called for greater attention to clinicians' ongoing personal and professional development as part of reflective practice (Captari, Choe, Crabtree, et al., 2024; Crabtree et al., 2025). This requires understanding our internal dynamics and motivations, processing complex countertransference reactions, and proactively recognizing risks to our well-being and clinical effectiveness, each of which we explore below.

Therapist Strengths and Vulnerabilities in Trauma Work

Self-reflective therapists understand their personal strengths and weaknesses, and how these characteristics play out in their work. Also important to therapist self-awareness is an understanding that some personal strengths, while admirable and even noble, can also at times represent potential self-of-the-therapist vulnerabilities, particularly when working with individuals and families exposed to traumatic events. For example, on the one hand, the capacity for empathy is a key ingredient for effective therapy, and on the other hand, empathic connection to traumatized clients can come at a heavy emotional cost to the psychotherapist (Figley, 1995). When out of balance, these personal psychological dynamics may interfere with clinical judgement and can lead therapists to lose sight of the client's system, blinding us to the influential role of interactions among family members and between the family and outside systems, as well as the intergenerational transmission of these patterns. This can result in difficulties with the working alliance, client–therapist boundary violations or rigidity, avoidance of salient client material, and increased work stress or personal distress. In the therapeutic setting, personal characteristics that can act as a proverbial double-edged sword include a sense of calling, selflessness and self-sacrifice, and a strong work ethic, each of which we explore below.[1]

A deep sense of calling or personal mission to help others can be exhilarating and profoundly motivating. At the same time, if not embodied with differentiation and wisdom, our commitment to this purpose may set the stage for overextending ourselves, ignoring personal needs, and minimizing warning signs of burnout as "just being tired" (Bunderson & Thompson, 2009; Sussman, 1995, 2007). Experiencing our work as a moral duty rooted in our core values, and for some, spirituality, can fuel tremendous passion, but we must be mindful to not lose sight of our humanness and realistic limitations. This is especially important when working in low-resource clinics and communities characterized by hardship and deprivation, where staff are often expected to set their own needs aside for the "greater good."

Historically, acts of selfless giving and prioritizing the well-being of others have also been highly commendable virtues across many cultures. Self-sacrifice involves a motivation or readiness to give, a cost to the giver, and a worthy cause or end-goal, with evidence suggesting that costlier self-sacrifice increases both the willingness to sacrifice and commitment to the cause (Bélanger et al., 2018). A balanced perspective recognizes that sometimes the "giving well" needs to be replenished, with our ability to care for others dependent on taking care of and giving to ourselves. Without balance, compulsive self-sacrifice

---

[1] The concepts in this section are drawn from the Catalyzing Helping professionals' Resilience, vitalitY, Spirituality, Authentic Living, and Inner Strength (CHRYSALIS) framework (Captari, Choe, Crabtree, et al., 2024), a depth-oriented and culturally responsive approach that orients therapists to the cultivation of strengths to address self-of-the-therapist vulnerabilities. CHRYSALIS has been shown to be effective in decreasing risks for therapist burnout and traumatization, and enhancing well-being.

represents the extreme of a "caregiver identity," which might manifest in difficulty saying no, lack/loss of personal interests, or feeling selfish for any focus on the self, resulting in unmet needs and exhaustion. This may have an element of moral masochism, meaning that we extract a sense of meaning and satisfaction from caring for others' needs to the extent that we deprive ourselves. Always putting ourselves last is a recipe for disaster, and burdens clients with countertransference pressure to make our sacrifice "worth it" and "get better." Consequences of a self-sacrificing defense style in the therapy room might include rescue attempts, boundary violations, or controlling behaviors (Herman, 1992). When we rely on our work to define our core sense of meaning and selfhood, this sets the stage for resentment, exhaustion, and expecting others to be equally giving and self-effacing. Even within more communal and collectivistic cultures, each of us must still take personal ownership to acknowledge our needs and limits.

Finally, a strong work ethic inspires us to maintain high standards for our work and to exert substantial efforts to "do right by" our clients. This same principle, however, may fuel shame, isolation, and workaholism if we have a predisposition toward perfectionism. High standards for ourselves and our work sometimes operate in tandem with feeling like an imposter. The more we doubt ourselves and lack a good-enough sense of professional efficacy, the more we as therapists are going to feel the need to prove ourselves. This can manifest in diverse ways, including difficulty acknowledging our missteps in sessions (which does not bode well for repairing ruptures!), less self-awareness about when consultation or supervision might be needed, and spending inordinate time on work-related tasks (Holden & Jeanfreau, 2023; Richardson et al., 2020). For example, in the face of feeling helpless and stuck with a family, we might be pulled toward grandiosity, throwing ourselves into overfunctioning to ward off feelings that we aren't doing enough.

Common Countertransference With Trauma-Impacted Families

Negative countertransference refers to therapists' unfavorable emotional reactions and behavioral responses to clients and their stories, often arising from natural outrage at the depths of human cruelty and sometimes stemming from a therapist's own unresolved issues or past experiences. Feelings of anger, shock, loathing, disgust, and deep sorrow in response to trauma narratives are frequently intense and completely understandable, stirring our personal needs and motives to help and protect. Psychotherapists may be particularly vulnerable to problematic countertransference and self-of-the-therapist issues when they have a personal history of unresolved trauma that is triggered by vicarious engagement with a client's traumatic experience. By and large, it is not uncommon for psychotherapists with trauma cases to experience negative countertransference that contributes to feelings of helplessness, frustration, inadequacy, or even shame and abandonment (McElroy & McElroy, 1991; Neumann & Gamble, 1995). It is what we as therapists do with these feelings that makes an important difference in our longevity and effectiveness. Can we reflect on our countertransference, and possibly use the information derived to improve our case formulation and interventions? Should we increase our efforts at self-care, and process our reactions with mentors, colleagues, or a therapist? Answers to these questions will be based on the therapist's self-awareness, as well as their familiarity with trauma and psychotherapy science, which have identified common types of countertransference that clinicians might experience when treating trauma.

Countertransference challenges when working with traumatized families may take many forms. Common countertransference roles that therapists can be pulled into when treating trauma include protector, rescuer, comforter, perpetrator, or another significant figure in the traumatic event (Shubs, 2008; J. P. Wilson & Lindy, 1994). Rescuer fantasies and idealization of our role often occur when personal wounds and vulnerabilities are unconsciously disowned and projected into the client/family. They are "broken," and we are the "expert" or "hero" who can bring relief. Working with children who have experienced trauma or abuse from caregivers can especially set the stage for this dynamic, whereby we cast ourselves as the "perfect parent" they never had and derogate their caregivers as irredeemable. This undermines clients' agency, resources, and subjectivity (possibly a reenactment of trauma itself), ignores the inherent human potential for healing, and interferes with effectively engaging parents and caregivers in the treatment process (Malawista, 2004; Vaknin & Wiseman, 2021).

When treating cases of violence or trauma, another frequent countertransference response is "walking on eggshells" (Shubs, 2008), or the "hostage syndrome" (Kauffman, 1992), whereby clients are defensive or volatile in session to the extent that clinicians feel controlled, silenced, or attacked. When therapists continue to press client defenses or confront denial/avoidance, clients may view them as cruel or exploitive, and therapists may feel tremendous guilt or experience themselves as a perpetrator (Shubs, 2008). Psychotherapists who work with abusing or violent families encounter additional types of countertransference in relation to specific family members, including disapproval or disbelief of a nonoffending parent (e.g., "How could they not know?"), a strong reluctance to confront a defensive parent that blocks productive therapeutic communication, and overidentification with an abused child that reminds the therapist of a sibling, their own son or daughter, or possibly the therapist as a child (McElroy & McElroy, 1991).

Overidentification and fusion with clients' emotions may, at first glance, look like empathy. After all, we are putting ourselves in our clients' shoes, right? Actually, no ... we are *losing* ourselves in our clients' shoes. This is an important distinction, which is reflected in mixed findings regarding the link between therapist empathy and well-being (Moosman, 2002; Wolosky, 2022). If we are totally swept up in a family's emotions, we lose our objectivity and ability to stand outside the system, which is necessary in order to help a family expand on their current ways of relating and being. Overidentifying with clients' experience can sometimes be a way of unconsciously trying to work through personal emotional injuries via our vocation (Compton & Patterson, 2024; Halevi & Idisis, 2018).

When clinicians overidentify with a client's traumatic experiences, therapeutic boundaries can easily slip and blur as the therapist's sense of responsibility and desire to help are heightened and further fueled by the pain and anguish of the entire family in session. Thus, trauma-informed couple and family practitioners must actively attend to therapeutic boundaries, metaphorically trying to keep one empathic foot in the family's world in order to create connection, trust, and safety for the client, while standing on the other well-trained foot in the professional world in order to maintain self-reflective capacity, emotional control, behavioral flexibility, and cognitive clarity. Differentiation of self supports a strong sense of identity that enables therapists to distinguish and separate their own experiences, emotions, and reactions from those of their clients. Therapeutic boundaries enable clinicians to empathically engage with client emotions while holding a separate sense of identity that reduces the risk of being drawn into maladaptive family interaction patterns and unhelpful transference–countertransference roles. In clinical work with traumatized individuals and families, the psychotherapist's boundaries must be balanced—open enough to allow authentic connection with the client, and firm enough to filter out potentially harmful effects and limit adverse reactions to stress-triggering client situations.

Potential Occupational Hazards of Trauma Intervention

Most psychotherapists who treat trauma demonstrate resilience and differ little from psychotherapists who do not treat trauma (Elwood et al., 2011; Velasco et al., 2023); some even experience vicarious posttraumatic growth as a result of their work (Cleary et al., 2024; Samios et al., 2012). However, a large literature has documented potential harmful effects on psychotherapists and other professionals who work directly with traumatized individuals (for reviews, e.g., K. Cohen & Collens, 2013; Hensel et al., 2015). Professional burnout is a psychological state resulting from chronic on-the-job stressors and is characterized by physical and/or emotional exhaustion, cynicism and detachment, and feelings of ineffectiveness (Maslach & Leiter, 2016). Because burnout is a potential risk across many stressful occupations, we focus here on occupational hazards specific to mental health professionals working with traumatized couples and families. Psychological distress associated with the therapist's indirect exposure to trauma includes various manifestations of empathy-based stress (Rauvola et al., 2019), such as compassion fatigue (Joinson, 1992), secondary traumatic stress (Ludick & Figley, 2016), and vicarious traumatization/trauma (Pearlman & Saakvitne, 1995). While the definitions of these constructs differ somewhat, they are clearly interrelated and share significant overlap in terms of associated experiences and symptoms that result from working with the trauma of others.

As its name implies, compassion fatigue in the helping professions is characterized by exhaustion and the loss of compassion as a cumulative consequence of empathic connection with clients affected by trauma exposure. Common symptoms of compassion fatigue include sleeping difficulties, emotional reactivity (e.g., irritability, anxiety), hypervigilance, and diminished interest in regular activities (Figley, 1995). Studies have documented increased risks for compassion fatigue associated with the helper's younger age (Ghahramanlou & Brodbeck, 2000), higher trauma caseload (Craig & Sprang, 2010), and personal history of maltreatment (Nelson-Gardell & Harris, 2003). On the other hand, possible protective factors include training (Rich, 1997), supervision, self-care, social support (Chrestman, 1999), work satisfaction (Figley, 2002; Ludick & Figley, 2016), and the use of evidence-based practice (Craig & Sprang, 2010).

Secondary traumatic stress is not confined to family members and other close relationships, as discussed earlier in this book. Members of many helping professions, including psychotherapists, can also develop PTSD-like symptoms after prolonged personal interactions with people directly affected by a traumatic event. Figley (2003) noted that compassion fatigue and secondary traumatic stress are parallel phenomena with intersecting symptom patterns and are often used interchangeably in the literature. Meta-analytic findings suggest that risk factors for secondary traumatic stress, like those for compassion fatigue, include a higher trauma caseload and a personal history of trauma, whereas trauma-specific training, greater clinical experience, and workplace and social support appeared to have buffering effects (Hensel et al., 2015), as well as the proactive cultivation of therapist strengths (Whittenbury et al., 2025).

Vicarious traumatization is more specifically defined as a negative transformation in the therapist's inner experience that results from engagement with the client's trauma material; this might include alterations in therapists' views of themselves and others, their spirituality, emotional regulation, and core schemas about safety, trust, esteem, control, and intimacy (McCann & Pearlman, 1990; Pearlman & Saakvitne, 1995). In a research synthesis, Baird and Kracen (2006) concluded that there is persuasive evidence that personal history of trauma is a risk factor for vicarious trauma through the mediator of self-neglect, as well as some evidence that coping ability and supervision can protect against vicarious trauma. Other findings suggest that maladaptive defense styles, especially a self-sacrificing defense style, are risk factors (Aafjes-Van Doorn et al., 2021; S. A. Adams & Riggs, 2008), while differentiation of self is a protective factor against vicarious trauma (Halevi & Idisis, 2018) and compassion fatigue (Finzi-Dottan & Kormosh, 2018).

Each of these factors frequently intersects with the intense countertransference that emerges in working with such clients and families. How might we meaningfully address and counter these potentially detrimental dynamics? First, we must commit to ongoing reflective practice to promote self-awareness and clarity regarding how we are honestly feeling and functioning. We can also make concerted efforts to intentionally build strengths and capacities that allow us to navigate these complexities and counter unhealthy "pulls." The next section describes various strategies that therapists can implement to support their well-being and competence, and further, to develop greater resilience against the possible negative effects of trauma-informed systemic intervention.

CULTIVATING AWARENESS AND RESILIENCE AS A TRAUMA THERAPIST

The self-of-the-therapist is where resilience against and amelioration of potential occupational hazards begin. Self-reflection informs our self-care activities and allows us to recognize our limitations and counteract potential difficulties. As therapists, most of us have worked with clients to identify strengths and weaknesses, develop self-care and self-compassion practices, and build coping strategies to adaptively navigate times of adversity. Yet, it is so easy to neglect these endeavors ourselves (Mavridis et al., 2019). A systemic formulation of this dilemma illuminates what can become a perfect storm of interrelated factors that promote a sense of powerlessness and exhaustion: the immensity of clients' needs, what this activates in each of us, and how the health care systems we work within often reinforce "pushing harder" and "doing more" to our own detriment (Captari, Choe, Crabtree, et al., 2024). To help counter these forces, we explore here a multifaceted approach to resilience and professional longevity, with the goal of not just avoiding becoming traumatized ourselves, but rather, cultivating a sense of thriving, even as we are bearing witness to families' adversity, tragedy, and recovery day after day.

Resilience to Compassion Fatigue and Secondary Trauma

Ludick and Figley (2016; Figley & Ludick, 2017) proposed that resilience against compassion fatigue is driven by four components: self-care, psychological detachment, sense of satisfaction, and social support. First, it is the therapist's ethical responsibility to establish an effective self-care routine that allows time for the therapist to rejuvenate and continue competent practice. Self-care, as it is most often operationalized, tends to be rooted in Eurocentric understandings of personhood and behavior (Barnett & Homany, 2022); as such, it is important to think expansively about what this might entail. Self-care practices vary widely among therapists as they are uniquely determined by the individual therapist's view of what is relaxing and/or enjoyable and what will improve their emotional and physical well-being. Some clinicians may feel revitalized after strenuous outdoor activities or fun get-togethers with friends and family, while others may prefer quiet time reading an enjoyable book or watching a favorite show in the comfort of their own home. Self-care can also take the form of practicing gratitude and mindfulness in the present moment and taking the time to notice and appreciate everyday acts of kindness, love, and respect observed at the neighborhood park, grocery store, or restaurant. With respect to physical self-care, psychotherapists can monitor their eating habits, sleep patterns, and physical exercise or activity, and find ways to reconnect with their bodies and attend to their physical senses as a way to "remind one of the joys of being alive and help to ground one in the physical world" (Neumann & Gamble, 1995, p. 346).

Psychological detachment is about setting firm boundaries between sessions. More than just a behavioral practice, this is rooted in underlying capacities for differentiation. Systemic therapists must strive to leave families' traumatic stories and worries at work by drawing clear boundaries around their work and home lives (Negash & Sahin, 2011). Given that this profession inherently involves both our personal and professional selves, this is not an easy task to accomplish and may require active and intentional efforts to draw effective boundaries. For example, to mark the transition from work to home, psychotherapists might find it helpful to implement after-work decompression rituals (Neumann & Gamble, 1995), such as listening to an audiobook or music on the way home, stopping at the gym to exercise, or grabbing 10–15 minutes of "me time" to shift gears by taking a walk, playing with the dogs, watering the plants, or another outdoor physical activity. Importantly, psychological detachment does not support avoidant coping in either the work or home setting; instead, it promotes a healthy work–life balance that contributes to overall well-being and relies on the therapist's reflective practice and active, problem-focused coping strategies to resolve any personal or professional difficulties arising from trauma work.

Satisfaction with the work of helping others, or compassion satisfaction, and a sense of mastery or competency can also contribute to the resilience of clinicians working with traumatized couples and families. Work fulfillment and compassion satisfaction are positively related to self-compassion (Babenko et al., 2019; Duarte et al., 2016) and negatively related to compassion fatigue and secondary traumatic stress (Conrad & Kellar-Guenther, 2006; Figley & Ludick, 2017). Additional research suggests that a sense of mastery, professional self-esteem, and empowerment may reduce the risk of secondary traumatic stress among therapists with caseloads involving family violence and trauma (Choi, 2017; Finzi-Dottan & Kormosh, 2018; Gil & Weinberg, 2015). Consistent with the idea that evidence-based practice may contribute to therapist competence by providing structure and boundaries to the therapeutic process (Fonagy, 1999), Craig and Sprang (2010) found that the use of such practices is associated with decreased compassion fatigue and increased compassion satisfaction among clinicians.

Social support is another important part of cultivating resilience, yet effectively accessing such support may depend in part on clinicians' own attachment dynamics, personality factors, and energy level (particularly in situations of burnout). Meta-analytic results support the protective role of social support and work-related support, showing small significant effect sizes on secondary traumatic stress in therapeutic work with trauma survivors (Hensel et al., 2015). Seeking social support from friends and family can reduce vulnerability to mental health distress in the general population, and is especially important for those who are affected directly or indirectly by trauma. Relationships with a partner and/or family can be a tremendous source of rejuvenation, meaning, and joy, yet our work as trauma therapists also has the potential to spill over into these personal domains of life, creating additional stress and tension at home. For example, feeling burnt out at work has been shown to impact therapists' own family functioning and relational satisfaction;

conversely, feeling stretched thin at home from parenting young children or caring for aging parents can drain empathic resources to connect with families experiencing traumatic stress (Agarwal & Simon, 2024; Jia & Li, 2022; Rupert et al., 2009, 2013). The toll is not simply about hours worked, but also includes the interplay between deep empathic involvement with traumatized families and deep empathic involvement with one's own partner, children, and/or family. The exhausting realities of family responsibilities are often sidelined in the professional space. Greater dialogue about work-to-family and family-to-work spillover and the complexities of integrating work and family life can help normalize and provide support in this domain.

Work support from colleagues, supervisors, agency staff, and leaders can also potentially reduce the risk of secondary traumatic stress. The literature consistently highlights the importance of regular supervision and specialized training for therapists who treat trauma (Chrestman, 1999; Gil & Weinberg, 2015; McElroy & McElroy, 1991; Soloski & Deitz, 2016). Practical supports from within one's workplace might include being mindful of the makeup of a therapist's caseload (i.e., avoiding a full caseload of traumatized families), training in empirically supported interventions for family trauma, increasing staff support time, providing additional trauma-specific supervision grounded in a clear understanding of self-of-therapist and countertransference issues common to trauma therapy, and increasing opportunities for self-care (e.g., longer clinician leave time, workplace autonomy, access to mental health services). In agency and hospital settings, a team treatment approach provides invaluable access to specialized consultation and support, as well as professional resources and learning opportunities.

Self-Awareness, Self-Monitoring, and Personal Growth

When working with trauma-impacted populations, therapists should carefully self-monitor potential cognitive and existential changes in their trauma-related schemas as well as emotion regulation capacities both in and out of session, and also attend to the ways clinical work is impacting their views of self, others, the world, the future, and the sacred (Saakvitne et al., 1996). If we identify personal issues that could interfere or are interfering with our ability to be emotionally present and attuned with clients, mindful acceptance and self-compassion for our normal human responses to tragedy are an important first step to combat empathy fatigue and burnout (Beaumont et al., 2016; Neff et al., 2020) and potentially spur reparative action to ensure our well-being and clinical effectiveness. Rather than minimizing the psychological effects of our work or judging ourselves as "weak," acknowledging signs of secondary traumatic stress or other occupational hazards can serve as an impetus to seek out personal psychotherapy, advocate for additional supports at work (e.g., more supervision, changes in caseload), and make changes in our personal and vocational life to counter these risks.

Personal therapy has long been considered a fundamental element of psychotherapists' professional development, with the goal of raising clinicians' self-awareness to the benefit of their own well-being and the quality of their professional practice (Orlinsky et al., 2011). Psychoanalytic training traditionally prescribes personal analysis, and many present-day graduate trainers in programs for mental health professionals continue to recommend that students seek personal therapy (Åstrand & Sandell, 2019). Fortunately, the experience of personal therapy among mental health therapists is not uncommon, with research demonstrating generally positive effects on both personal and professional development (Åstrand & Sandell, 2019; Bike et al., 2009; Orlinsky et al., 2011). By creating a regular, protected space to explore one's own feelings, reactions, and needs, personal therapy may be the best preventative and resilience-building strategy that therapists have at their disposal, particularly when their daily work schedule includes regular interactions with highly distressed clients and families.

Since the 1990s, when secondary traumatization was first recognized, a number of interventions have been developed for professionals exposed to trauma at work. In addition to self-help books and workbooks (e.g., Bush, 2015; Mathieu, 2012; B. C. Miller, 2021; Saakvitne et al., 1996), available interventions include psychoeducation, mindfulness, art and recreational programs, and alternative medicine (Kim et al., 2022). Psychoeducation and mindfulness interventions tend to overlap somewhat, focusing on symptom reduction, skills training for stress management, and self-care plans. Short-term interventions have also been designed to increase self-compassion, with evidence suggesting effectiveness in increasing self-compassion and reducing the risk of psychological distress, burnout, and secondary traumatization among health professionals (Delaney, 2018; Germer & Neff, 2019; Neff et al., 2020). While largely effective in decreasing helper stress and other key outcomes, scholars have noted that existing programs tend to focus on general stress reduction and self-care rather than specific effects of vicarious trauma and secondary traumatic stress (Kim et al., 2022; Sprang et al., 2019).

There is a need for more holistic frameworks that account for and address how systemic dynamics might contribute to trauma therapists' functioning and take a more preventative, strengths-focused, and communal approach. Beyond formal intervention, we invite readers to consider how you can proactively build in greater attention to your ongoing growth and development as a systemically oriented practitioner. For example, rooting ourselves in self-compassion can help us honor our calling while also honoring ourselves as human beings who are worthy of care and attention. Self-compassion is linked to lower depression, burnout, and compassion fatigue among therapists (Beaumont et al., 2016; Richardson et al., 2020) and other health professionals (Neff et al., 2020), yet do we actively cultivate self-compassion in our daily professional lives when we make mistakes or become tired and upset? Understanding our own vulnerabilities and having grace toward ourselves after difficult sessions and/or self-perceived failures may help counter harsh self-critique and burnout among trauma therapists. Rather than ignoring, avoiding, or shaming ourselves, self-compassion begins with mindfulness or in-the-moment acknowledgement of our painful emotions and thoughts, grounded in a sense of common humanity and conscious efforts to extend kindness to ourselves as we would to a friend, colleague, or client (Germer & Neff, 2013). Scholars have argued that wisdom operates as a meta-virtue for therapists, helping us identify and draw from strengths to meet the clinical challenge at hand (Levitt & Piazza-Bonin, 2016, 2017). Wisdom "allows us to view problems from many different angles, realize that circumstances are constantly changing, and understand that how we relate to our experience (tenderly–harshly, accepting–resisting, curious–avoidant) affects our sense of well-being" (Germer & Siegel, 2012, p. 3). As we will discuss below, such self-compassion and wisdom do not develop in isolation, but rather, as part of a larger community with colleagues whose input and feedback foster our ongoing personal and professional growth.

FROM SELF-CARE TO SYSTEMS OF CARE

In the mental health care fields, there often tends to be an overemphasis on the responsibility of individual therapists to maintain their well-being and clinical effectiveness, without acknowledging relational, organizational, and contextual contributions. How would any of us know if our therapeutic effectiveness is at risk of being compromised? Although self-awareness and self-monitoring are core clinical competencies, research has shown that we are not always the most accurate at assessing our effectiveness across career stages, particularly in the context of stress and strain (Dunning et al., 2003, 2004; Walfish et al., 2012). As therapists, we can never outrun our own humanness . . . and to be human is to have blind spots. Importantly, the point at which our competence is "slipping" is when we are most vulnerable to overappraising our functioning, potentially coping with stress by unconsciously minimizing or denying the fact that we are struggling, or by externalizing blame (Dunning et al., 2003, 2004; W. B. Johnson & Barnett, 2011). In short, self-care and self-monitoring are easier said than done, and may very likely be insufficient and somewhat inaccurate. In the spirit of this book's focus on thinking and working systemically, we extend accountability beyond individual practitioners to also include the reciprocal and influential roles of various systems in which each of us is embedded.

What might a more communal approach to caring for the self-of-therapist entail that honors individual and cultural differences and also accounts for systemic influences? While postgraduate training to remain up-to-date on current standards and practices in the United States is largely structured by continuing education requirements, we envision the necessity of a more relational emphasis, including communities of practice for therapists working with traumatized couples and families. Our functioning as therapists—whether we are thriving or traumatized—is dynamic and inextricably interconnected with our relational lives and organizational contexts. Thus, current professional recommendations are just the tip of the iceberg. Beyond therapists' self-care or lack thereof, the expectations and dynamics of our particular professional home, the pressures and realities within the mental health care system, and larger relational and societal conditions are all implicated in professional competence. Each of these domains is in dynamic interplay with one other, in line with Bronfenbrenner's (1979) ecological model. Here, we explore possibilities for creating shifts in the field toward developing systems of care that support therapists, including the influential roles of workplace and organizational dynamics.

Communitarianism to Fortify Professional Competence

Given evidence suggesting some degree of inaccuracy in self-assessment, Barnett and Homany (2022) argued that it is critical for psychotherapists, particularly those in private practice, to seek out a professional network of colleagues and peers to provide case consultation and feedback on a regular basis. Trauma-informed systemically oriented therapists understand the fundamental interdependence of their clients' sense of self, as well as their own, with their respective relationships and the world they live in. Trauma is a complex phenomenon with manifold etiologies and consequences, which can disrupt clinicians' sense of competence, psychological coherence, and identity as a healer. Considering the limits of confidentiality, professional relationships are a critical source of support, community, and belonging, as well as clinical input, mentoring, and consultation to counter the limitations of self-monitoring.

Lack of professional support has been associated with increased vicarious traumatization (Finklestein et al., 2015), and its presence has been acknowledged as a key contributor to longevity in working with traumatized children and their families (Pistorius et al., 2008). Given that meaning-making is an inherently relational process, we are more likely to experience negative inner transformations as part of vicarious trauma when we are left to try to process and metabolize the toll of our work in isolation.

W. Brad Johnson et al. (2012, 2013) proposed a professional competence model that represents a significant expansion of ethical obligations, reaching beyond individual accountability to community responsibility. Consistent with systems theory, communitarian and ethics of care perspectives recognize the interdependence of the self and reciprocal interactions among psychotherapists and their communities, emphasizing relational ethics whereby some degree of acting as our brethren's keeper is needed for healthy functioning. This requires a spirit of humility and collaboration that challenges our individualistic culture and the norms for clinical practice, in which most of us receive little input from peers following licensure. While concern for others is already an established norm among psychotherapists and included in professional competencies (e.g., Fouad et al., 2009), W. B. Johnson et al. (2012, 2013) encouraged formal modifications to ethical standards of competence in psychology, specifically to add that practitioners are obligated to interact and consult regularly with colleagues and professional networks about their clinical skills and performance, and in turn offer care and support to struggling colleagues and assist them in evaluating the current state of their professional competence.

The "competence constellation" (W. B. Johnson et al., 2012, 2013) is conceptualized as a professional ecosystem of interconnected subsystems. The individual psychotherapist is the basic unit, nested within the therapist's inner circle or "core," made up of the therapist's closest colleagues and mentors, whose reciprocal relationships provide high levels of emotional support in each clinician's daily professional life. The inner core might also include a personal therapist, who can validate painful emotions evoked by clients' traumatic stories and explore self-of-therapist issues contributing to negative countertransference. Surrounding the inner core are the expanding layers of the therapist's collegial community (caring colleagues providing moderate support) and collegial acquaintances (professional friendships and connections), all situated within the broad professional culture that sets standards for practice and ethical behavior. Working together, the people and groups in this constellation are actively interested in fostering the individual therapist's well-being, success, and professional competence. As part of this larger system, the individual therapist is reciprocally involved with colleagues in a similar manner.

For therapists who regularly treat clients with trauma histories, the inner core in this model takes on an invaluable role in consistently offering case consultation and social support, as well as peer supervision, to the members of this subsystem. One of the key roadblocks to the communitarian model is the general reluctance to deliver constructive feedback and address problems of professional competence in colleagues, despite ethical guidance to the contrary (Barnett, 2008; Kruger & Dunning, 1999). Hesitancy to intervene is influenced by many different factors, including concerns regarding lack of evidence, how well the professional in question is known, fear of reprisals or accusations of betrayal from peers, and negative professional consequences for a distressed colleague who may very well be a close friend or respected collaborator (W. B. Johnson et al., 2012). To develop a strong and effective competence constellation, mental health professionals need to demonstrate self-awareness and self-care; other-oriented empathy, vulnerability, and nondefensiveness; fluid expertise (i.e., easily shifting from learner to teacher/expert); and collegial assertiveness that allows one to initiate difficult conversations in a caring and supportive manner (W. B. Johnson et al., 2013).

Thus, therapists doing trauma work benefit from having a strong collegial network outside of their workplace alone. As such, we argue that a professional consultation group with whom therapists can discuss challenging trauma cases is indispensable for processing difficult countertransference and enhancing our capacities to think and work systemically, as well as for providing communal support and guidance. Connecting with colleagues can also spark creativity and generativity through natural opportunities that emerge for collaboration, and such relationships also facilitate a sense of continuity when therapists experience employment changes. Broader professional networks enable therapists to build connections with other professionals across disciplines, which is vital given that systemically oriented practitioners often work collaboratively with those in other disciplines (see Chapter 6 in this volume) and may refer clients to other forms of therapy, medication management, and adjunctive supports.

Workplace and Organizational Dynamics

How we fare as trauma therapists is significantly influenced by our relational and organizational context. Unfortunately, given the nature of training, we often encounter some of our most complex and severe clinical cases early on in our careers (Buechler, 2012). Public institutions and community clinics are often underresourced and flooded with those seeking care, even more-so since the COVID-19 pandemic (Ghafari et al., 2022; Kader et al., 2024). This can lead to situations where therapists' personhood and human limitations are totally neglected ... and they are told to "figure it out" as caseload sizes and work hours continue to rise (Crabtree et al., 2025). Such work environments actually make use of and reinforce therapists' personal bent toward over-functioning, self-sacrifice, or living out a sacred calling. Through a systemic understanding of trauma, we might begin to notice that many mental health care institutions are operating in survival mode, marked by organizational dynamics of reactivity, mistrust, unclear communication, and/or cutoff. The result can be rigid and/or unclear policies, detouring of responsibility, the silencing of staff with less power, and sometimes even scapegoating. A systems lens helps us understand all this as an organization's attempt to create and maintain homeostasis, while a trauma lens reminds us that we can never evade our own nervous systems, with the clinic itself representing a "hive" nervous system of sorts that can fuel states of fight, flight, freeze, or fawn.

In such workplace environments, "the recommendation to 'take care of yourself' may actually compound [therapist] distress because it sets the stage for attributions of failure, inadequacy, and the imposter syndrome (e.g., something is wrong with *me*)" and also fails to acknowledge and address systemic contributors (Captari, Choe, Crabtree, et al., 2024, p. 181). What may at first glance look like encouragement often amounts to organizational minimization of unsustainable policies and workplace expectations—detouring the responsibility for burnout or secondary traumatization to individual practitioners. Therapeutic work with complex, chronic, and severe forms of trauma is often most effective when therapists utilize a team-based and interdisciplinary approach. In its absence, vulnerable families are much more likely to fall through the cracks. Yet, collaborating effectively will never be more than an aspiration if administrators and treatment team members do not respect and trust each other, are caught up in power struggles, avoid conflict by sidelining divergent perspectives, or simply do not cross paths because they are running around helter-skelter. Quality supervision is also often short-changed in low-resource settings—because of "increased pressure due to an exponentially growing list of clients to see, practitioners often are not given the platform to evolve and mend any past conflicts and struggles" (Davies et al., 2022, p. 66). Supervisory relationships in an overstressed organizational milieu face additional hurdles in establishing trust and openness.

How can we expect families to be "open systems" that value, listen to, and incorporate multiple perspectives when the systems they are seeking care within are often "closed systems"? The negative spillover of dysfunctional organizational dynamics on quality of care and therapists' own well-being must be attended to. When treatment team members experience their co-workers as having their back, feel valued, heard, and supported, are taken seriously by leadership when it comes to feedback and change, have reasonable workplace expectations, and are recognized as whole people (including organizational commitment to staff growth and development), a collective momentum can emerge that bolsters therapists in the face of daily clinical exposure to trauma. Research increasingly reveals that risks for burnout, vicarious trauma, and secondary traumatic stress are significantly shaped by workplace environment (Rollins et al., 2021; Sutton et al., 2022); if a therapist is carrying a complex caseload of families in distress, and on top of that feels isolated from peers, undervalued by leadership, and receives the message to "push through" when they are struggling, that context is in and of itself a significant occupational hazard. APA's healthy workplace initiative highlights the interplay between organizational functioning, employee well-being, and quality of care (Grawitch & Ballard, 2016). The shift from "fixing the worker" to "fixing the workplace" includes creating a collaborative and values-driven culture (embodying and reinforcing the character strengths discussed above, such as humility, differentiation, courage, etc.), reducing job demands and increasing available resources, cocreating solutions with staff (rather than simply implementing wellness programs), increasing worker flexibility and autonomy, and creating regular opportunities for peer support (Sinsky et al., 2020).

This discussion would not be complete without also considering how the mental health care system at large and broader societal influences affect our work with traumatized families. Insurance bureaucracy, health care policies, and systemic inequities are often barriers to providing the care we hope to. In some situations, we may experience moral distress or injury when it feels like our hands are tied (Austin et al., 2005)—for example, a family is motivated to continue treatment beyond initial stabilization, but we cannot continue working with them due to program constraints or perceived lack of medical necessity by their insurance provider. These sorts of complex contextual situations that are beyond our control can feel discouraging and demoralizing, and larger systems-level changes are needed to address the social determinants of health, through which marginalized and socially disenfranchised families (e.g., families of color, immigrant/refugee families, LGBTQ+ families) carry a greater burden of unresolved trauma and its sequelae. In addition to advocacy for more equitable policies, working with key stakeholders in low-resource communities to cocreate community-based programs that support families is critical. As discussed in Chapter 6 in this volume, this necessitates stepping outside our offices and recognizing that systemically oriented trauma therapy may look vastly different from traditional sessions. Given their holistic and developmental foci, family intervention principles are uniquely suited to be creatively intertwined in community milieus (e.g., schools, faith communities).

SUMMARY AND KEY TAKEAWAYS

When it comes to working with families impacted by trauma, your personhood cannot be "bracketed out." Most of us are wounded healers, in some way or another. If we minimize and ignore our distinct psychological makeup and family/life history, we are significantly more vulnerable to being negatively impacted in our work with traumatized families. Despite the presumption that a personal history of trauma increases risk for outcomes like vicarious trauma in clinical work, key mediators such as self-sacrifice and self-neglect reveal that presumably, it is the unprocessed "ghosts" of our own adversity that can most increase vulnerability, not just the experience itself (Aafjes-Van Doorn et al., 2021; S. A. Adams & Riggs, 2008; Baird & Kracen, 2006). This knowledge is vital in shaping a deeper understanding of our ongoing development as psychotherapists working with couples and families, focused on who each of us is and is becoming, and how that is inextricably intertwined with context—the "water" we swim in at work, with colleagues, and in larger society. Given the inherent emotional complexity of working with multiple family members, who may be dysregulated and/or disengaged, clinicians must take time to intentionally reflect on and process personal experiences of trauma and adversity, as well as ways these themes can get reactivated in session, in order to cultivate wisdom, self-compassion, differentiation of self, and other strengths to navigate clinical challenges that arise.

This chapter has reviewed and critiqued current best practices, applying systemic principles to understand trauma therapists' vulnerabilities and needs in light of larger relational, organizational, and societal contexts. For all those interested and/or involved in trauma work with couples and families, knowing ourselves is especially critical. As we seek to develop specialized competencies in the areas discussed throughout this book, we must also attend to our psychological makeup and vulnerabilities. This involves going beyond behavioral recommendations around self-care to understand the unique values, motivations, relational dynamics, and cultural contexts that inform how we as therapists, for example, readily show up for others but often tend to minimize and set aside our own needs. One way we can work upstream of occupational hazards is by watering the soil of the personal strengths, virtues, and values that are embedded within our unique cultural and spiritual contexts. Cultivating capacities to ground our own nervous systems when we are exposed to trauma-related affects and then metabolize the raw psychic material (e.g., images, stories, gut feelings) that lingers after sessions can help us avoid feeling emotionally flooded and disoriented. Cultivating humility—a realistic sense of both our strengths and limitations—can help us "right-size" our contributions and create a collaborative, empowering therapeutic space, releasing "rescuer" fantasies. Embodying differentiated empathy can enable us to be present in the moment with families in their healing journey, without fusing with their experience. Drawing from a deep well of courage can help us challenge ingrained family patterns, and patience enables us to meet families where they are at rather than needing them to change quickly so that we feel better about ourselves! Hope can ground us in clinical situations where all seems lost, and embodying creativity and curiosity can "keep us alive" as we engage family systems that are deadened by dissociation and denial.

Beyond this, rather than placing the onus on therapists alone (as the "identified patient" who needs to make lifestyle changes), thinking systemically stipulates greater responsibility from the professional community. We argue for the necessity of a communitarian ethos around cultivating and maintaining clinical effectiveness in trauma-focused systemic work. Regular consultation with colleagues can alleviate unrealistic burdens on therapists and provide needed feedback for maintaining competence. Working systemically also necessitates tracking, understanding, and making changes at the level of organizations and the mental health care system to increase quality of care and buffer occupational hazards. Thus, we invite those in teaching, training, and leadership roles within clinical contexts serving populations impacted by trauma to consider the systemic dynamics and norms that your staff and trainees are operating within. In what ways might you attend to the holistic development and flourishing of each professional providing care to couples and families in your setting? Taking a systemic approach to therapist well-being and effectiveness intervenes upstream of each session to help practitioners continue to develop and grow holistically, and thus competently provide evidence-based mental health services. Couples and families seeking treatment to heal from trauma deserve the best possible care we can offer, even if it means rethinking some of the ways that mental health care has been structured. Helping our clinical workforce thrive and have longevity increases treatment accessibility in the community and can begin to bridge the gap to meet the needs of trauma-impacted families.

CONCLUSION

A Shift in Trauma-Informed Care That Holds the Family in Mind

Traumatic stress can spread to anyone with whom the sufferers share their lives. Trauma begets trauma.

—SHAILI JAIN (2019)

Attention to trauma increasingly pervades public consciousness, and one doesn't have to look far to find the terminology of trauma-informed, trauma-responsive, and trauma-focused ... not only in mental health care, but also in medicine, education, business, sports, and congregational life. Growing recognition of how trauma shapes—and can contort—the soma, psyche, and soul is incredibly heartening, particularly given the cultural-level dissociation and historical conflicts that stymied attention to these realities for many decades (Herman, 1992/2015; Rix, 2000). Yet, progress does not come without potential vulnerabilities. Primary among these is the risk that practitioners, researchers, scholars, and funders may drill down into the individual experience of trauma, while neglecting relational and systemic contexts that can be profoundly influential as sources of both exacerbation and healing. If researchers presume to have mapped the etiology of trauma and shift our focus to elucidating brain mechanisms that create and maintain posttraumatic

https://doi.org/10.1037/0000487-009
Systemic Treatment of Trauma-Impacted Families: A Clinician's Guide to Assessment, Formulation, and Intervention, by S. A. Riggs and L. E. Captari

stress disorder, we are liable to lose sight of the interplay between an individual and their context. Our focus on the intrapsychic and neurobiological must always be counterbalanced with exploration of the systemic and environmental when it comes to trauma healing.

The field's emphasis on the diagnosis and treatment of trauma-related psychopathology at an individual level, in line with the medical model, is evident in calls for grant funding focused on "neurobiological, behavioral, cognitive, and other risk and protective factors for psychopathology after traumatic events" (National Institutes of Mental Health, n.d., para. 1). What gets funded gets researched, and what gets researched ultimately informs clinical practice. Couple and family therapy is more difficult to get funding for, and lack of research attention to systemic interventions often spills over into how the next generation of therapists are trained, and thus, the treatment options available in the community.

We highlight several notable limitations of individual trauma therapy. First, people in many cultures who are negatively impacted by trauma may not be able (or willing) to access individual trauma-focused psychotherapy. In low-resource settings, there is a lack of trained providers, leaving community and faith leaders on the front line of supporting traumatized families. Second, in collectivist societies where relational life is central, the idea of going off privately to meet with a professional to talk about one's trauma—stripped of the context of family and close relationships—just doesn't fit. Third, not all traumas are individual. Communities and subpopulations who experience collective trauma, such as mass shootings, racial violence, natural disasters, police brutality, war, terrorist attacks, and forced displacement, to name a few areas, need more than just individual treatment options. As we have discussed throughout this book, a family also represents a relational community that may experience collective trauma and/or be indirectly impacted by a relative's trauma and its aftereffects across family relationships and generations. Scholars argue that collective trauma necessitates holistic, communal processes of meaning-making, mourning, and healing (Hübl, 2020; Saul, 2022), and research is starting to bear this out. Yet, the vast majority of trauma treatment options available in routine mental health care settings are still limited to individual therapy.

At the same time, in line with the movement toward prevention and early intervention, as well as recognition of the need to personalize treatment in light of cultural differences and client preferences, the National Institute of Mental Health (n.d.) does emphasize the importance of "models for delivering care effectively and efficiently across settings, contexts, and populations (e.g., children, adolescents, and adults)" (para. 1). In this book, we have argued that systemically oriented treatment offers one such model for delivering trauma-focused care. Greater attention to and investment in clinical research is critical in order to move systemic models forward. Especially when there has been a shared trauma, working with a couple and/or family can be more clinically effective and efficient in facilitating recovery than individual treatment, creating systemic momentum for change and facilitating adaptive adjustment to adversity. This is consistent with Indigenous cultures and spiritual traditions across history that have emphasized the need to come together to heal. Yet, in many communities there are few practitioners with advanced couple/family and trauma-specific competencies to provide such treatment.

A substantial part of the problem underlying the shortage and inaccessibility of systemically oriented psychotherapy for the treatment of trauma is lack of training. Some graduate programs offer a course in couple and family therapy, but outside of marriage and family therapy training programs, this rarely involves a clinical practicum component and doesn't typically cover the unique challenges of working with traumatized families (Celano, 2018; Riggs, 2017). Thus, systemic interventions remain theoretical for most clinicians entering the field. While graduate coursework in trauma therapy is thankfully becoming more prevalent, such training generally covers individual, empirically supported treatments , with little mention of substantive involvement of other family members, a systemic conception of traumatization and healing, or the intricacies of working with complex trauma (Kumar et al., 2022). Furthermore, the widespread dissemination of information made possible by technology increases the risk for misinformation about trauma (O'Connor et al., 2025); popularized (and frequently monetized) frameworks for healing may become fads, with little attention to the empirical base. Trauma can wreak havoc on survivors' lives, and people who are suffering understandably want and are sometimes desperate for relief, which can leave them vulnerable to gimmicks and promises of quick fixes.

Throughout the writing of this book, we have noticed the frequent (almost daily!) referral requests appearing on professional listservs for systems-oriented trauma treatment, often with mention of just how hard it is to find a practitioner skilled in working with multiple family members around trauma impacts. It doesn't have to stay this way! In these pages, we have only scratched the surface of the well-developed body of research, theory, and professional literature at the intersection of family systems and trauma science. By sending this book out into the world, we hope to begin to address these problems by piquing mental health professionals' interest in systemic formulation and intervention as a unique lens to track, understand, and address how trauma often spills over across relationships, and the unique healing potential of these contexts.

Why systemic therapy? Virginia Satir (1964) pointed out that this mode of therapeutic intervention is vital because it deals with family pain. When we as therapists have the opportunity to work with multiple family members on the journey of healing, or when we incorporate a systemic perspective to support an individual client in second-order relational change, we are offering an intervention with distinctive healing possibilities beyond just symptom reduction. Treating trauma systemically has the potential to activate stalled developmental processes, catalyze an upward spiral of relational healing, put to rest ghosts of untreated trauma, and in some way change the course of the next generation, breaking the cycle of intergenerational trauma. At the same time, we do not put forth couple and family modalities per se as the be-all and end-all. Traumatized family systems are often operating in a manner that is reactive, rigid, and/or denies the existence of the trauma itself; thus, practitioners should not equate systemic intervention with simply inviting all family members to sit down together and talk about the trauma(s) they have endured. (If only it were that simple!) Rather, a systemically oriented approach to working with trauma equips therapists to identify and formulate the underlying trauma-related dynamics that are "living" within the family system, and work flexibly with whoever is open to treatment . . . whether that is one person or multiple individuals. We will all encounter cases where the use of couple and family modalities is significantly limited by family members' reticence to engage and/or lack of motivation to change. Luckily, systemically oriented treatment can help both support individual trauma healing of any involved member and set the stage for second-order changes in a couple or family's ways of relating, regardless of who is physically in the therapy room.

If you're still reading, chances are this approach to clinical practice intrigues and enlivens you . . . even as it may also confuse, frustrate, and exhaust you at times! Perhaps, like us, this sort of work "found" you . . . like the wand choosing the wizard. Couple and family therapy isn't magic; on the contrary, it's really hard work. We carry a lot. We doubt ourselves. But then there are those profound moments where something shifts . . . where family members really hear each other, collaborate in a new way . . . lean in to grieving what's not possible and building what is.

Welcome to the journey of lifelong learning as we collaborate with families to spark healing potential. What might your next step be in actualizing systemic work in your clinical practice? We invite you to seek out supervision, consultation, and ongoing training in these areas to continue to equip yourself to meet the needs of trauma-impacted families. May you find deep wells of connection, wisdom, courage, and creativity in your ongoing formation.

References

Aafjes-Van Doorn, K., Békés, V., Luo, X., Prout, T. A., & Hoffman, L. (2021). What do therapist defense mechanisms have to do with their experience of professional self-doubt and vicarious trauma during the COVID-19 pandemic? *Frontiers in Psychology, 12*, Article 647503. https://doi.org/10.3389/fpsyg.2021.647503

Abidin, R. R. (1990). *Parenting Stress Index* [Database record]. APA PsycTests. https://doi.org/10.1037/t02445-000

Abidin, R. R. (1995). *Parenting Stress Index: Professional manual.* Psychological Assessment Resources.

Accreditation Council for Graduate Medical Education. (2023). *ACGME program requirements for graduate medical education in psychiatry.* https://www.acgme.org/globalassets/pfassets/programrequirements/400_psychiatry_2023.pdf

Achenbach, T. M., & Rescorla, L. A. (2001). *Manual for the ASEBA school-age forms and profiles.* University of Vermont Research Center for Children, Youth, and Families.

Acklin, M. W., & Cho-Stutler, L. (2006). The science and art of parent–child observation in child custody evaluation. *Journal of Forensic Psychology Practice, 6*(1), 51–62. https://doi.org/10.1300/J158v06n01_03

Adams, N., & Grieder, D. (2005). *Treatment planning for person-centered care: The road to mental health and addiction recovery.* Academic Press.

Adams, S. A., & Riggs, S. A. (2008). An exploratory study of vicarious trauma among therapist trainees. *Training and Education in Professional Psychology, 2*(1), 26–34. https://doi.org/10.1037/1931-3918.2.1.26

Adler-Tapia, R., & Settle, C. (2023). *EMDR and the art of psychotherapy with children: Guidebook and treatment manual.* Springer.

Agarwal, M., & Simon, S. (2024). When work whispers at home: Spillover of occupational stress, supervisor support, and stigma towards occupational stress among Indian mental health professionals. In B. Alareeni & A. Hamdan (Eds.), *Navigating the technological tide: The evolution and challenges of business model innovation* (pp. 399–410). Springer. https://doi.org/10.1007/978-3-031-67434-1_38

Alderfer, M. A., Fiese, B. H., Gold, J. I., Cutuli, J. J., Holmbeck, G. N., Goldbeck, L., Chambers, C. T., Abad, M., Spetter, D., & Patterson, J. (2008). Evidence-based assessment in pediatric psychology: Family measures. *Journal of Pediatric Psychology, 33*(9), 1046–1064. https://doi.org/10.1093/jpepsy/jsm083

Allen, D. N., & Becker, M. L. (2019). Clinical interviewing. In G. Goldstein, D. N. Allen, & J. DeLuca (Eds.), *Handbook of psychological assessment* (4th ed., pp. 307–336). Academic Press. https://doi.org/10.1016/B978-0-12-802203-0.00010-9

American Academy of Child and Adolescent Psychiatry. (1997). Practice parameters for the forensic evaluation of children and adolescents who may have been physically or sexually abused. *Journal of the American Academy of Child and Adolescent Psychiatry, 36*(3), 423–442. https://doi.org/10.1097/00004583-199703000-00026

American Academy of Child and Adolescent Psychiatry. (2007). Practice parameter for the assessment of children and adolescents with anxiety disorders. *Journal of the American Academy of Child & Adolescent Psychiatry, 46*(2), 267–283. https://doi.org/10.1097/01.chi.0000246070.23695.06

American Association for Marriage and Family Therapy. (2015). *AAMFT code of ethics*. https://www.aamft.org/AAMFT/Legal_Ethics/Code_of_Ethics.aspx

American Civil Liberties Union. (2024). *Mass incarceration*. https://www.aclu.org/issues/smart-justice/mass-incarceration

American Counseling Association. (2014). *ACA code of ethics* (Rev. ed.). https://www.counseling.org/docs/default-source/default-document-library/ethics/2014-aca-code-of-ethics.pdf

American Mental Health Counselors Association. (2020). *AMHCA code of ethics*. https://www.amhca.org/viewdocument/2020-amhca-code-of-ethics

American Psychiatric Association. (2022). *Diagnostic and statistical manual of mental disorders* (5th ed., text rev.). https://doi.org/10.1176/appi.books.9780890425787

American Psychological Association. (2001). Guidelines for test user qualifications. *American Psychologist, 56*(12), 1099–1113. https://doi.org/10.1037/0003-066X.56.12.1099

American Psychological Association. (2003). Guidelines on multicultural education, training, research, practice, and organizational change for psychologists. *American Psychologist, 58*(5), 377–402. https://doi.org/10.1037/0003-066X.58.5.377

American Psychological Association. (2007). Record keeping guidelines. *American Psychologist, 62*(9), 993–1004. https://doi.org/10.1037/0003-066X.62.9.993

American Psychological Association. (2010). Guidelines for child custody evaluations in family law proceedings. *American Psychologist, 65*(9), 863–867. https://doi.org/10.1037/a0021250

American Psychological Association. (2013a). Guidelines for psychological evaluations in child protection matters. *American Psychologist, 68*(1), 20–31. https://doi.org/10.1037/a0029891

American Psychological Association. (2013b). Specialty guidelines for forensic psychology. *American Psychologist, 68*(1), 7–19. https://doi.org/10.1037/a0029889

American Psychological Association. (2015a). *Guidelines on trauma competencies for education and training*. https://doi.org/10.1037/e528872015-001

American Psychological Association. (2015b). *Standards of accreditation for health service psychology*. https://www.apa.org/ed/accreditation/standards-of-accreditation.pdf

American Psychological Association. (2017a). *Clinical practice guideline for the treatment of posttraumatic stress disorder (PTSD) in adults*. https://www.apa.org/ptsd-guideline/ptsd.pdf

American Psychological Association. (2017b). *Ethical principles of psychologists and code of conduct* (2002, amended effective June 1, 2010, and January 1, 2017). https://www.apa.org/ethics/code

American Psychological Association. (2017c). *Multicultural guidelines: An ecological approach to context, identity, and intersectionality*. https://www.apa.org/about/policy/multicultural-guidelines.pdf

American Psychological Association. (2021). *APA guidelines on evidence-based psychological practice in health care*. https://www.apa.org/about/policy/psychological-practice-health-care.pdf

American Psychological Association. (2022). *Guidelines for child custody evaluations in family law proceedings*. https://www.apa.org/about/policy/child-custody-evaluations.pdf

American Psychological Association. (2024). *Advisory steering committee statement on the evidentiary bases of clinical practice guidelines*. https://www.apa.org/about/offices/directorates/guidelines/evidentiary-basis-statement

American Psychological Association, Presidential Task Force on Evidence-Based Practice. (2006). Evidence-based practice in psychology. *American Psychologist, 61*(4), 271–285. https://doi.org/10.1037/0003-066x.61.4.271

American Psychological Association, Task Force on Psychological Assessment and Evaluation Guidelines. (2020). *APA guidelines for psychological assessment and evaluation*. https://www.apa.org/about/policy/guidelines-psychological-assessment-evaluation.pdf

Amri, S., & Bemak, F. (2013). Mental health help-seeking behaviors of Muslim immigrants in the United States: Overcoming social stigma and cultural mistrust. *Journal of Muslim Mental Health, 7*(1), 43–63. https://doi.org/10.3998/jmmh.10381607.0007.104

Andrade, E. L., Jula, M., Rodriguez-Diaz, C. E., Lapointe, L., Edberg, M. C., Rivera, M. I., & Santos-Burgoa, C. (2023). The impact of natural hazards on older adult health: Lessons learned from Hurricane Maria in Puerto Rico. *Disaster Medicine and Public Health Preparedness, 17*, Article e52. https://doi.org/10.1017/dmp.2021.305

Andreas, S. (1991). *Virginia Satir: The patterns of her magic.* Science and Behavior Books.

Anker, M. G., Duncan, B. L., & Sparks, J. A. (2009). Using client feedback to improve couple therapy outcomes: A randomized clinical trial in a naturalistic setting. *Journal of Consulting and Clinical Psychology, 77*(4), 693–704. https://doi.org/10.1037/a0016062

Antunes-Alves, S., & De Stefano, J. (2014). Intimate partner violence: Making the case for joint couple treatment. *The Family Journal, 22*(1), 62–68. https://doi.org/10.1177/1066480713505056

Aponte, H. J. (1994). *Bread and spirit: Therapy with the new poor, diversity of race, culture and values.* W. W. Norton.

Aponte, H. J. (2022). The soul of therapy: The therapist's use of self in the therapy relationship. *Contemporary Family Therapy, 44*(2), 136–143. https://doi.org/10.1007/s10591-021-09614-5

Aponte, H. J., & Kissel, K. (2016). *The person of the therapist training model: Mastering the use of the self.* Routledge.

Arias, E., Arce, R., & Vilarino, M. (2013). Batterer intervention programmes: A meta-analytic review of effectiveness. *Psychosocial Intervention, 22*(2), 153–160. https://doi.org/10.5093/in2013a18

Armenti, N. A., & Babcock, J. C. (2016). Conjoint treatment for intimate partner violence: A systematic review and implications. *Couple and Family Psychology: Research and Practice, 5*(2), 109–123. https://doi.org/10.1037/cfp0000060

Aspland, H., & Gardner, F. (2003). Observational measures of parent–child interaction: An introductory review. *Child and Adolescent Mental Health, 8*(3), 136–143. https://doi.org/10.1111/1475-3588.00061

Association of Family and Conciliation Courts. (2006). *Model standards of practice for child custody evaluation.* https://www.afccnet.org/Portals/0/Committees/ModelStdsChildCustodyEvalSept2006.pdf

Åstrand, K., & Sandell, R. (2019). Influence of personal therapy on learning and development of psychotherapeutic skills. *Psychoanalytic Psychotherapy, 33*(1), 34–48. https://doi.org/10.1080/02668734.2019.1570546

Aten, J. D., & Boan, D. M. (2016). *Disaster ministry handbook.* InterVarsity Press.

Aten, J. D., Shannonhouse, L., Davis, D. E., Davis, E. B., Hook, J. N., Van Tongeren, D. R., Hwang, J., McElroy-Heltzel, S. E., Schruba, A., & Annan, K. (2020). *Spiritual first aid manual.* Humanitarian Disaster Institute.

Aten, J. D., Topping, S., Denney, R. M., & Hosey, J. M. (2011). Helping African American clergy and churches address minority disaster mental health disparities: Training needs, model, and example. *Psychology of Religion and Spirituality, 3*(1), 15–23. https://doi.org/10.1037/a0020497

Atlas, G. (2022). *Emotional inheritance: A therapist, her patients, and the legacy of trauma.* Hachette UK.

Attachment, Regulation and Competency. (2024). *What is ARC?* https://arcframework.org/what-is-arc/

Austin, W., Rankel, M., Kagan, L., Bergum, V., & Lemermeyer, G. (2005). To stay or to go, to speak or stay silent, to act or not to act: Moral distress as experienced by psychologists. *Ethics & Behavior, 15*(3), 197–212. https://doi.org/10.1207/s15327019eb1503_1

Aves, W. (2024). Escaping iatrogenic harm: A journey into mental health service avoidance. *Journal of Psychiatric and Mental Health Nursing, 31*(4), 668–673. https://doi.org/10.1111/jpm.13020

Axberg, U., & Petitt, B. (2023). Systemic perspectives and psychiatric diagnosis: Mutually exclusive or mutually inclusive? In S. M. Myra, T. Grover, & U. Axberg (Eds.), *New horizons in systemic practice with children and families* (pp. 105–128). Springer.

Babcock, J. C., Armenti, N. A., & Warford, P. (2017). The trials and tribulations of testing couples-based interventions for intimate partner violence. *Partner Abuse, 8*(1), 110–122. https://doi.org/10.1891/1946-6560.8.1.110

Babcock, J. C., Waltz, J., Jacobson, N. S., & Gottman, J. M. (1993). Power and violence: The relation between communication patterns, power discrepancies, and domestic violence. *Journal of Consulting and Clinical Psychology, 61*(1), 40–50. https://doi.org/10.1037/0022-006X.61.1.40

Babenko, O., Mosewich, A. D., Lee, A., & Koppula, S. (2019). Association of physicians' self-compassion with work engagement, exhaustion, and professional life satisfaction. *Medical Sciences, 7*(2), Article 29. https://doi.org/10.3390/medsci7020029

Bailey, B., Tabone, J., Smith, B., Monnin, J., Hixon, B., Williams, K., & Rishel, C. (2024). State of the evidence of attachment regulation and competency framework and adaptions: A rapid scoping review. *Journal of Child & Adolescent Trauma, 17*(2), 571–583. https://doi.org/10.1007/s40653-023-00575-5

Baird, K., & Kracen, A. C. (2006). Vicarious traumatization and secondary traumatic stress: A research synthesis. *Counselling Psychology Quarterly, 19*(2), 181–188. https://doi.org/10.1080/09515070600811899

Baldwin, S. A., & Imel, Z. E. (2013). Therapist effects: Findings and methods. In M. J. Lambert (Ed.), *Bergin and Garfield's handbook of psychotherapy and behavior change* (6th ed., pp. 258–297). Wiley.

Bolton, G. (2010). *Reflective practice: Writing and professional development*. Sage Publications.

Barker, P. (1995). *The child and adolescent psychiatry evaluation: Basic child psychiatry*. Blackwell Scientific.

Barlow, J., & Svanberg, P. O. (2009). *Keeping the baby in mind: Infant mental health in practice*. Routledge.

Barnes, M., & Figley, C. R. (2005). Family therapy: Working with traumatized families. In J. Lebow (Ed.), *Handbook of clinical family therapy* (pp. 309–326). Wiley.

Barnett, J. E. (2008). The ethical practice of psychotherapy: Easily within our reach. *Journal of Clinical Psychology, 64*(5), 569–575. https://doi.org/10.1002/jclp.20473

Barnett, J. E., & Homany, G. (2022). The new self-care: It's not all about you. *Practice Innovations, 7*(4), 313–326. https://doi.org/10.1037/pri0000190

Barnett, J. E., & Jacobson, C. H. (2019). Ethical and legal issues in family and couple therapy. In B. H. Fiese, M. Celano, K. Deater-Deckard, E. N. Jouriles, & M. A. Whisman (Eds.), *APA handbook of contemporary family psychology: Vol. 3. Family therapy and training* (pp. 53–68). American Psychological Association. https://doi.org/10.1037/0000101-004

Bartlett, J. D., Griffin, J. L., Spinazzola, J., Fraser, J. G., Noroña, C. R., Bodian, R., Todd, M., Montagna, C., & Barto, B. (2018). The impact of a statewide trauma-informed care initiative in child welfare on the well-being of children and youth with complex trauma. *Children and Youth Services Review, 84*, 110–117. https://doi.org/10.1016/j.childyouth.2017.11.015

Basile, K. C., Smith, S. G., Kresnow, M., Khatiwada, S., & Leemis, R. W. (2022). *The National Intimate Partner and Sexual Violence Survey: 2016/2017 report on sexual violence*. National Center for Injury Prevention and Control, Centers for Disease Control and Prevention. https://www.cdc.gov/nisvs/documentation/nisvsReportonSexualViolence.pdf

Bateman, A., Fonagy, P., Campbell, C., Luyten, P., & Debbané, M. (2023). *Cambridge guide to mentalization-based treatment (MBT)*. Cambridge University Press.

Bateson, G., Jackson, D. D., Haley, J., & Weakland, J. (1956). Toward a theory of schizophrenia. *Behavioral Science, 1*(4), 251–254. https://doi.org/10.1002/bs.3830010402

Bauch, J., Hefti, S., Oeltjen, L., Pérez, T., Swenson, C. C., Fürstenau, U., Rhiner, B., & Schmid, M. (2022). Multisystemic therapy for child abuse and neglect: Parental stress and parental mental health as predictors of change in child neglect. *Child Abuse & Neglect, 126*, Article 105489. https://doi.org/10.1016/j.chiabu.2022.105489

Beasley, C. C., & Ager, R. (2019). Emotionally focused couples therapy: A systematic review of its effectiveness over the past 19 years. *Journal of Evidence-Based Social Work, 16*(2), 144–159. https://doi.org/10.1080/23761407.2018.1563013

Beaumont, E., Durkin, M., Hollins Martin, C. J., & Carson, J. (2016). Measuring relationships between self-compassion, compassion fatigue, burnout and well-being in student counsellors and student cognitive behavioural psychotherapists: A quantitative survey. *Counselling & Psychotherapy Research, 16*(1), 15–23. https://doi.org/10.1002/capr.12054

Beavers, R. W., & Hampson, R. B. (1990). *Successful families: Assessment and intervention*. W. W. Norton.

Beavers, R. W., & Hampson, R. B. (2000). The Beavers systems model of family functioning. *Journal of Family Therapy, 22*(2), 128–143. https://doi.org/10.1111/1467-6427.00143

Beck, J. G., & Sloan, D. M. (Eds.). (2022). *The Oxford handbook of traumatic stress disorders* (2nd ed.). Oxford University Press. https://doi.org/10.1093/oxfordhb/9780190088224.013.41

Becvar, R. J., Becvar, D. S., & Reif, L. V. (2023). *Systems theory and family therapy: A primer* (4th ed.). Rowman & Littlefield.

Beebe, B., Hoven, C. W., Kaitz, M., Steele, M., Musa, G., Margolis, A., Ewing, J., Sossin, K. M., & Lee, S. H. (2020). Urgent engagement in 9/11 pregnant widows and their infants: Transmission of trauma. *Infancy, 25*(2), 165–189. https://doi.org/10.1111/infa.12323

Bélanger, J. J., Schumpe, B. M., Menon, B., Ng, J., Nociti, N., Zeigler-Hill, V., & Shackelford, T. K. (2018). Self-sacrifice for a cause: A review and an integrative model. In V. Zeigler-Hill & T. K. Shackelford (Eds.), *The Sage handbook of personality and individual differences* (pp. 465–483). Sage Publications. https://doi.org/10.4135/9781526470317.n25

Bellak, L., & Abrams, D. M. (1993). *The Thematic Apperception Test, the Children's Apperception Test, and the Senior Apperception Technique in clinical use* (5th ed.). Allyn & Bacon.

Bellak, L., & Bellak, S. S. (1949). *Children's Apperception Test.* CPS Co.

Benazzo, Z., & Benazzo, M. (Directors). (2021). *The wisdom of trauma* [Film]. Science and Nonduality. https://vimeo.com/762456491

Benevolenza, M. A., & DeRigne, L. (2019). The impact of climate change and natural disasters on vulnerable populations: A systematic review of literature. *Journal of Human Behavior in the Social Environment, 29*(2), 266–281. https://doi.org/10.1080/10911359.2018.1527739

Benjet, C., Bromet, E., Karam, E. G., Kessler, R. C., McLaughlin, K. A., Ruscio, A. M., Shahly, V., Stein, D. J., Petukhova, M., Hill, E., Alonso, J., Atwoli, L., Bunting, B., Bruffaerts, R., Caldas-de-Almeida, J. M., de Girolamo, G., Florescu, S., Gureje, O., Huang, Y. . . . Koenen, K. C. (2016). The epidemiology of traumatic event exposure worldwide: Results from the World Mental Health Survey Consortium. *Psychological Medicine, 46*(2), 327–343. https://doi.org/10.1017/S0033291715001981

Bennett, J. (2022, February 4). If everything is 'trauma,' is anything? *The New York Times*. https://www.nytimes.com/2022/02/04/opinion/caleb-love-bombing-gaslighting-trauma.html

Benzies, K., & Mychasiuk, R. (2009). Fostering family resiliency: A review of the key protective factors. *Child & Family Social Work, 14*(1), 103–114. https://doi.org/10.1111/j.1365-2206.2008.00586.x

Berger, R., & Weiss, T. (2009). The posttraumatic growth model: An expansion to the family system. *Traumatology, 15*(1), 63–74. https://doi.org/10.1177/1534765608323499

Berkowitz, S. J., Stover, C. S., & Marans, S. R. (2011). The child and family traumatic stress intervention: Secondary prevention for youth at risk of developing PTSD. *Journal of Child Psychology and Psychiatry, 52*(6), 676–685. https://doi.org/10.1111/j.1469-7610.2010.02321.x

Bernard, D. L., Calhoun, C. D., Banks, D. E., Halliday, C. A., Hughes-Halbert, C., & Danielson, C. K. (2021). Making the "C-ACE" for a culturally-informed adverse childhood experiences framework to understand the pervasive mental health impact of racism on Black youth. *Journal of Child & Adolescent Trauma, 14*(2), 233–247. https://doi.org/10.1007/s40653-020-00319-9

Berns, S. B., Jacobson, N. S., & Gottman, J. M. (1999). Demand–withdraw interaction in couples with a violent husband. *Journal of Consulting and Clinical Psychology, 67*(5), 666–674. https://doi.org/10.1037/0022-006X.67.5.666

Bhana, A., & Bachoo, S. (2011). The determinants of family resilience among families in low- and middle-income contexts: A systematic literature review. *South African Journal of Psychology, 41*(2), 131–139. https://doi.org/10.1177/008124631104100202

Bigner, J. J., & Wetchler, J. L. (Eds.). (2012). *Handbook of LGBT-affirmative couple and family therapy*. Routledge.

Bike, D. H., Norcross, J. C., & Schatz, D. M. (2009). Processes and outcomes of psychotherapists' personal therapy: Replication and extension 20 years later. *Psychotherapy, 46*(1), 19–31. https://doi.org/10.1037/a0015139

Black, K., & Lobo, M. (2008). A conceptual review of family resilience factors. *Journal of Family Nursing, 14*(1), 33–55. https://doi.org/10.1177/1074840707312237

Blaustein, M. E., & Kinniburgh, K. M. (2018). *Treating traumatic stress in children and adolescents: How to foster resilience through attachment, self-regulation, and competency*. Guilford Press.

Blow, A. J., & Karam, E. A. (2017). The therapist's role in effective marriage and family therapy practice: The case for evidence based therapists. *Administration and Policy in Mental Health and Mental Health Services Research, 44*(5), 716–723. https://doi.org/10.1007/s10488-016-0768-8

Blow, A. J., Sprenkle, D. H., & Davis, S. D. (2007). Is who delivers the treatment more important than the treatment itself? The role of the therapist in common factors. *Journal of Marital and Family Therapy, 33*(3), 298–317. https://doi.org/10.1111/j.1752-0606.2007.00029.x

Bograd, M. (1992). Values in conflict: Challenges to family therapists' thinking. *Journal of Marital and Family Therapy, 18*(3), 245–256. https://doi.org/10.1111/j.1752-0606.1992.tb00937.x

Bograd, M., & Mederos, F. (1999). Battering and couples therapy: Universal screening and selection of treatment modality. *Journal of Marital and Family Therapy, 25*(3), 291–312. https://doi.org/10.1111/j.1752-0606.1999.tb00249.x

Borgogno, F. (2019). Sándor Ferenczi, a classical and contemporary psychoanalyst. *The American Journal of Psychoanalysis, 79*(4), 453–467. https://doi.org/10.1057/s11231-019-09222-1

Boszormenyi-Nagy, I., & Spark, G. M. (1973). *Invisible loyalties: Reciprocity in intergenerational family therapy*. Harper & Row.

Bowen, M. (1978). *Family therapy in clinical practice*. Jason Aronson.

Bradley, R. P. C., Friend, D. J., & Gottman, J. M. (2011). Supporting healthy relationships in low-income, violent couples: Reducing conflict and strengthening relationship skills and satisfaction. *Journal of Couple & Relationship Therapy, 10*(2), 97–116. https://doi.org/10.1080/15332691.2011.562808

Brand, B. L., Schielke, H., Brams, J., & DiComo, R. A. (2017). Assessing trauma-related dissociation in forensic contexts: Addressing trauma-related dissociation as a forensic psychologist, Part II. *Psychological Injury and Law, 10*(4), 298–312. https://doi.org/10.1007/s12207-017-9305-7

Brand, B. L., Webermann, A. R., & Frankel, A. S. (2016). Assessment of complex dissociative disorder patients and simulated dissociation in forensic contexts. *International Journal of Law and Psychiatry, 49*(Pt. B), 197–204. https://doi.org/10.1016/j.ijlp.2016.10.006

Brandt, K., Perry, B. D., Seligman, S., & Tronick, E. (Eds.). (2013). *Infant and early childhood mental health: Core concepts and clinical practice.* American Psychiatric Association.

Brave Heart, M. Y. H. (2003). The historical trauma response among natives and its relationship with substance abuse: A Lakota Illustration. *Journal of Psychoactive Drugs, 35*(1), 7–13. https://doi.org/10.1080/02791072.2003.10399988

Brave Heart, M. Y. H., Chase, J., Elkins, J., & Altschul, D. B. (2011). Historical trauma among Indigenous peoples of the Americas: Concepts, research, and clinical considerations. *Journal of Psychoactive Drugs, 43*(4), 282–290. https://doi.org/10.1080/02791072.2011.628913

Bray, J. H. (2013). Couple and family assessment. In J. H. Bray & M. Stanton (Eds.), *Wiley-Blackwell handbook of family psychology* (pp. 165–182). Wiley-Blackwell. https://doi.org/10.1002/9781444310238.ch10

Brennan, K. A., Clark, C. L., & Shaver, P. R. (1998). Self-report measurement of adult attachment: An integrative overview. In J. A. Simpson & W. S. Rholes (Eds.), *Attachment theory and close relationships* (pp. 46–76). Guilford Press.

Briere, J. (1996). *Trauma Symptom Checklist for Children (TSCC): Professional manual.* Psychological Assessment Resources.

Briere, J. (2011). *Trauma Symptom Inventory–2 (TSI-2)*. Psychological Assessment Resources.

Briere, J., & Lanktree, C. B. (2013). *Integrative treatment of complex trauma for adolescents (ITCT-A): A guide for the treatment of multiply-traumatized youth* (2nd ed.). USC Adolescent Trauma Treatment Training Center, National Child Traumatic Stress Network, U.S. Department of Substance Abuse and Mental Health Services Administration.

Briere, J., & Scott, C. (2025). *Principles of trauma therapy: A guide to symptoms, evaluation, and treatment* (3rd ed.). Sage Publications.

Bright, C. L., Farrell, J., Winters, A. M., Betsinger, S., & Lee, B. R. (2018). Family centered treatment, juvenile justice, and the grand challenge of smart decarceration. *Research on Social Work Practice, 28*(5), 638–645. https://doi.org/10.1177/1049731517730127

Brom, D., Stokar, Y., Lawi, C., Nuriel-Porat, V., Ziv, Y., Lerner, K., & Ross, G. (2017). Somatic experiencing for posttraumatic stress disorder: A randomized controlled outcome study. *Journal of Traumatic Stress, 30*(3), 304–312. https://doi.org/10.1002/jts.22189

Bromberg, P. M. (2014). *Standing in the spaces: Essays on clinical process, trauma, and dissociation*. Routledge.

Bronfenbrenner, U. (1977). Toward an experimental ecology of human development. *American Psychologist, 32*(7), 513–531. https://doi.org/10.1037/0003-066X.32.7.513

Bronfenbrenner, U. (1979). *The ecology of human development: Experiments by nature and design*. Harvard University Press.

Brown, E. J., Cohen, J. A., & Mannarino, A. P. (2020). Trauma-focused cognitive-behavioral therapy: The role of caregivers. *Journal of Affective Disorders, 277*, 39–45. https://doi.org/10.1016/j.jad.2020.07.123

Brown, J. (2013). Circular questioning: An introductory guide. *Australian and New Zealand Journal of Family Therapy, 18*(2), 109–114. https://doi.org/10.1002/j.1467-8438.1997.tb00276.x

Brown, J. (2019). *Reflective practice of counseling and psychotherapy in a diverse society*. Springer.

Bruce, A. E., Cole, D. A., Dallaire, D. H., Jacquez, F. M., Pineda, A. Q., & LaGrange, B. (2006). Relations of parenting and negative life events to cognitive diatheses for depression in children. *Journal of Abnormal Child Psychology, 34*(3), 321–333. https://doi.org/10.1007/s10802-006-9019-x

Bryant, T. (2024). Lessons from decolonial and liberation psychologies for the field of trauma psychology. *American Psychologist, 79*(5), 683–696. https://doi.org/10.1037/amp0001393

Buck, J. N. (1966). *The house-tree-person technique: Revised manual*. Western Psychological Services.

Buderer, C., Hefti, S., Fux, E., Pérez, T., Swenson, C. C., Fürstenau, U., Rhiner, B., & Schmid, M. (2020). Effects of multisystemic therapy for child abuse and neglect on severity of neglect, behavioral and emotional problems, and attachment disorder symptoms in children. *Children and Youth Services Review, 119*, Article 105626. https://doi.org/10.1016/j.childyouth.2020.105626

Buechler, S. (2012). *Still practicing: The heartaches and joys of a clinical career*. Routledge.

Bunderson, J. S., & Thompson, J. A. (2009). The call of the wild: Zookeepers, callings, and the double-edged sword of deeply meaningful work. *Administrative Science Quarterly, 54*(1), 32–57. https://doi.org/10.2189/asqu.2009.54.1.32

Bürgin, D., Boonmann, C., Schmeck, K., Schmid, M., Tripp, P., Nishimi, K., & O'Donovan, A. (2021). Compounding stress: Childhood adversity as a risk factor for adulthood trauma exposure in the health and retirement study. *Journal of Traumatic Stress, 34*(1), 124–136. https://doi.org/10.1002/jts.22617

Burns, R. C., & Kaufman, S. H. (1987). *Kinetic Family Drawings (K-F-D): An introduction to understanding children through kinetic drawings*. Brunner/Mazel.

Busby, D. M., Christensen, C., Crane, D. R., & Larson, J. H. (1995). A revision of the Dyadic Adjustment Scale for use with distressed and nondistressed couples: Construct hierarchy and multidimensional scales. *Journal of Marital and Family Therapy, 21*(3), 289–308. https://doi.org/10.1111/j.1752-0606.1995.tb00163.x

Bush, A. D. (2015). *Simple self-care for therapists: Restorative practices to weave through your workday*. W. W. Norton.

Busch, F., Milrod, B., Chen, C., & Singer, M. (2021). *Trauma focused psychodynamic psychotherapy: A step-by-step treatment manual*. Oxford University Press.

Butler, M. H., & Gardner, B. C. (2003). Adapting enactments to couple reactivity: Five developmental stages. *Journal of Marital and Family Therapy, 29*(3), 311–327. https://doi.org/10.1111/j.1752-0606.2003.tb01209.x

Byng-Hall, J. (1995). *Rewriting family scripts: Improvisation and systems change*. Guilford Press.

Byng-Hall, J. (2008a). The crucial roles of attachment in family therapy. *Journal of Family Therapy, 30*(2), 129–146. https://doi.org/10.1111/j.1467-6427.2008.00422.x

Byng-Hall, J. (2008b). The significance of children fulfilling parental roles: Implications for family therapy. *Journal of Family Therapy, 30*(2), 147–162. https://doi.org/10.1111/j.1467-6427.2008.00423.x

Callaghan, E. M., Fellin, L. C., Alexander, J. H., Mavrou, S., & Papathanasiou, M. (2017). Children and domestic violence: Emotional competencies in embodied and relational contexts. *Psychology of Violence, 7*(3), 333–342. https://doi.org/10.1037/vio0000108

Captari, L. E. (2020). *Childhood emotional maltreatment and the developing self: Examining the roles of attachment, affect regulation, and dissociation in psychological functioning* [Unpublished doctoral dissertation]. University of North Texas. https://digital.library.unt.edu/ark:/67531/metadc1707247/?q=CAPTARI

Captari, L. E., Choe, E. J. Y., Crabtree, S. A., Sandage, S. J., Gerstenblith, J. A., Stein, L. B., Hydinger, K. R., & Stavros, G. (2024). The development and feasibility of a novel group intervention to support helping professionals in metabolizing suffering and engaging strengths: The CHRYSALIS program. *International Journal of Group Psychotherapy, 74*(2), 177–216. https://doi.org/10.1080/00207284.2024.2329565

Captari, L. E., Choe, E. J. Y., Stein, L. B., & Sandage, S. J. (2024). Trauma survivors' spiritual struggles and the anger of hope: A practice-based clinical study examining links with mental health symptoms and well-being. *Spirituality in Clinical Practice, 11*(3), 235–249. https://doi.org/10.1037/scp0000376

Captari, L. E., Gerstenblith, J. A., Guterres, K., Choe, E. J. Y., Crabtree, S. A., & Sandage, S. A. (in press). Psychotherapists' burnout, traumatization, and sense of flourishing: A scoping review examining the role of character strengths and virtues. *Clinical Psychology and Psychotherapy*.

Captari, L. E., Nyiransekuye, H., Shelton Zaremba, J., Gerber, M., Hook, J. N., Davis, D. E., Owen, J., & Van Tongeren, D. R. (2021). Engaging refugees with cultural humility. In J. Aten & J. Hwang (Eds.), *Refugee mental health* (pp. 45–75). American Psychological Association. https://doi.org/10.1037/0000226-003

Captari, L. E., Shannonhouse, L., Aten, J. D., & Snyder, J. D. (2023). Building spiritual fortitude and resilience following disaster: Synthesizing the contributions of positive psychology and religion/spirituality. In E. B. Davis, E. L. Worthington, Jr., & S. A. Schnitker (Eds.), *Handbook of positive psychology, religion, and spirituality* (pp. 475–492). Springer Nature. https://doi.org/10.1007/978-3-031-10274-5_30

Captari, L. E., & Worthington, E. L., Jr. (2024). Assessing and treating trauma impacts in religious and spiritual populations: Introduction to the special issue. *Spirituality in Clinical Practice*, *11*(3), 195–202. https://doi.org/10.1037/scp0000380

Carlson, C. I. (1995). Families as the focus of assessment: Theoretical and practical issues. In J. C. Conoley & E. Werth (Eds.), *Family assessment* (pp. 19–63). Buros Institute of Mental Measurement.

Carr, A. (2018). Couple therapy, family therapy and systemic interventions for adult-focused problems: The current evidence base. *Journal of Family Therapy*, *41*(4), 492–536. https://doi.org/10.1111/1467-6427.12225

Carr, A. (2024). Family therapy and systemic interventions for child-focussed problems: The evidence base. *Journal of Family Therapy*, *47*(1), Article e12476. https://doi.org/10.1111/1467-6427.12476

Celano, M. P. (2018). *Children with emotional and behavioral disorders: Systemic practice*. Momentum Press.

Celano, M. (2019). Competencies in couple and family psychology for health service psychologists. In B. H. Fiese, M. Celano, K. Deater-Deckard, E. N. Jouriles, & M. A. Whisman (Eds.), *APA handbook of contemporary family psychology: Vol. 3. Family therapy and training* (pp. 427–448). American Psychological Association. https://doi.org/10.1037/0000101-026

Celano, M. P., Smith, C. O., & Kaslow, N. J. (2010). A competency-based approach to couple and family therapy supervision. *Psychotherapy*, *47*(1), 35–44. https://doi.org/10.1037/a0018845

Charney, D. S., & Keane, T. M. (1990). A clinician rating scale for assessing current and lifetime PTSD: The CAPS-1. *Behavior Therapist*, *13*, 187–188.

Charuvastra, A., & Cloitre, M. (2008). Social bonds and posttraumatic stress disorder. *Annual Review of Psychology*, *59*(1), 301–328. https://doi.org/10.1146/annurev.psych.58.110405.085650

Cheng, S. Y., Davis, M., Jonson-Reid, M., & Yaeger, L. (2021). Compared to what? A meta-analysis of batterer intervention studies using nontreated controls or comparisons. *Trauma, Violence & Abuse, 22*(3), 496–511. https://doi.org/10.1177/1524838019865927

Cho, A., & Lee, S. (2019). Exploring effects of childhood parentification on adult-depressive symptoms in Korean college students. *Journal of Clinical Psychology, 75*(4), 801–813. https://doi.org/10.1002/jclp.22737

Choi, G. Y. (2017). Secondary traumatic stress and empowerment among social workers working with family violence or sexual assault survivors. *Journal of Social Work, 17*(3), 358–378. https://doi.org/10.1177/1468017316640194

Chou, F., & Buchanan, M. J. (2021). Intergenerational trauma: A scoping review of cross-cultural applications from 1999 to 2019. *Canadian Journal of Counselling and Psychotherapy, 55*(3), 363–395. https://doi.org/10.47634/cjcp.v55i3.71456

Chou, F., Buchanan, M. J., Mcdonald, M., Westwood, M., & Huang, C. (2023). Narrative themes of Chinese Canadian intergenerational trauma: Offspring perspectives of trauma transmission. *Counselling Psychology Quarterly, 36*(2), 321–349. https://doi.org/10.1080/09515070.2022.2093165

Chrestman, K. R. (1999). Secondary exposure to trauma and self-reported distress among therapists. In B. H. Stamm (Ed.), *Secondary traumatic stress: Self-care issues for clinicians, researchers, and educators* (2nd ed., pp. 29–36). Sidran Press.

Christensen, A. (1988). Dysfunctional interaction patterns in couples. In P. Noller & M. A. Fitzpatrick (Eds.), *Perspectives on marital interaction* (pp. 31–52). Multilingual Matters.

Christl, M. E., Pham, K. C. T., Rosenthal, A., & DePrince, A. P. (2024). When institutions harm those who depend on them: A scoping review of institutional betrayal. *Trauma, Violence, & Abuse, 25*(4), 2797–2813. https://doi.org/10.1177/15248380241226627

Cicchetti, D., Rogosch, F. A., & Toth, S. L. (2006). Fostering secure attachment in infants in maltreating families through preventive interventions. *Development and Psychopathology, 18*(3), 623–649. https://doi.org/10.1017/S0954579406060329

Cleary, E., Curran, D., Dyer, K., Simms, J., & Hanna, D. (2024). Contributing factors to secondary traumatic stress and vicarious posttraumatic growth in therapists. *Journal of Traumatic Stress, 37*(1), 103–112. https://doi.org/10.1002/jts.22995

Cleary Bradley, R. P., Friend, D. J., & Gottman, J. M. (2011). Supporting healthy relationships in low-income, violent couples: Reducing conflict and strength ening relationship skills and satisfaction. *Journal of Couple & Relationship Therapy, 10*(2), 97–116. https://doi.org/10.1080/15332691.2011.562808

Cleary Bradley, R. P., & Gottman, J. M. (2012). Reducing situational violence in low-income couples by fostering healthy relationships. *Journal of Marital and Family Therapy, 38*(s1), 187–198. https://doi.org/10.1111/j.1752-0606.2012.00288.x

Cloitre, M., Cohen, L. R., Ortigo, K. M., Jackson, C., & Koenen, K. C. (2020). *Treating survivors of childhood abuse and interpersonal trauma: STAIR narrative therapy*. Guilford Press.

CNA Military Advisory Board. (2007, April). *National security and the threat of climate change*. Center for Naval Analyses. https://www.cna.org/archive/CNA_Files/pdf/national%20security%20and%20the%20threat%20of%20climate%20change.pdf

Coe, J. L., Davies, P. T., Hentges, R. F., & Sturge-Apple, M. L. (2020). Detouring in the family system as an antecedent of children's adjustment problems. *Journal of Family Psychology, 34*(7), 814–824. https://doi.org/10.1037/fam0000727

Cohen, J. A., Mannarino, A. P., & Deblinger, E. (Eds.). (2016). *Trauma-focused CBT for children and adolescents: Treatment applications*. Guilford Press.

Cohen, K., & Collens, P. (2013). The impact of trauma work on trauma workers: A metasynthesis on vicarious trauma and vicarious posttraumatic growth. *Psychological Trauma: Theory, Research, Practice, and Policy, 5*(6), 570–580. https://doi.org/10.1037/a0030388

Cole, D. A., Goodman, S. H., Garber, J., Cullum, K. A., Cho, S. J., Rights, J. D., Felton, J. W., Jacquez, F. M., Korelitz, K. E., & Simon, H. F. M. (2018). Validating parent and child forms of the Parent Perception Inventory. *Psychological Assessment, 30*(8), 1065–1081. https://doi.org/10.1037/pas0000552

Commission on Accreditation for Marriage and Family Education. (2021). *Accreditation standards*. https://www.coamfte.org/Common/Uploaded%20files/COAMFTE/Accreditation%20Resources/COAMFTE%20Standards%20Version%2012.5%20-%20Published%20August%202021%20-%208.26.21%20(with%20links).pdf

Compton, L., & Patterson, T. (2024). Absorption vulnerability: A new look at compassion fatigue. *Traumatology, 31*(1), 65–73. https://doi.org/10.1037/trm0000503

Conrad, D., & Kellar-Guenther, Y. (2006). Compassion fatigue, burnout, and compassion satisfaction among Colorado child protection workers. *Child Abuse & Neglect, 30*(10), 1071–1080. https://doi.org/10.1016/j.chiabu.2006.03.009

Constantino, M. J., Coyne, A. E., & Muir, H. J. (2020). Evidence-based therapist responsivity to disruptive clinical process. *Cognitive and Behavioral Practice, 27*(4), 405–416. https://doi.org/10.1016/j.cbpra.2020.01.003

Cook, J. M., Newman, E., & the New Haven Trauma Competency Group. (2014). A consensus statement on trauma mental health: The New Haven Competency Conference process and major findings. *Psychological Trauma: Theory, Research, Practice, and Policy, 6*(4), 300–307. https://doi.org/10.1037/a0036747

Cook, J. M., Rehman, O., Bufka, L., Dinnen, S., & Courtois, C. (2011). Responses of a sample of practicing psychologists to questions about clinical work with trauma and interest in specialized training. *Psychological Trauma: Theory, Research, Practice, and Policy, 3*(3), 253–257. https://doi.org/10.1037/a0025048

Cook, J. M., Simiola, V., Ellis, A. E., & Thompson, R. (2017). Training in trauma psychology: A national survey of doctoral graduate programs. *Training and Education in Professional Psychology, 11*(2), 108–114. https://doi.org/10.1037/tep0000150

Cooper, J., & Vetere, A. (2005). *Domestic violence and family safety: A systemic approach to working with violence in families*. Wiley.

Cordukes, K., U'Ren, G., Katz, E. C., & McIntosh, J. E. (2024). Working with adult families of origin: On the nature of rupture and repair. *Australian and New Zealand Journal of Family Therapy, 45*(3), 279–291. https://doi.org/10.1002/anzf.1600

Cornett, N., & Bratton, S. C. (2014). Examining the impact of child parent relationship therapy (CPRT) on family functioning. *Journal of Marital and Family Therapy, 40*(3), 302–318. https://doi.org/10.1111/jmft.12014

Council for Accreditation of Counseling and Related Educational Programs. (2024). *CACREP standards*. https://www.cacrep.org/wp-content/uploads/2024/04/2024-Standards-Combined-Version-4.11.2024.pdf

Council on Social Work Education. (2022). *Educational policy and accreditation standards*. https://www.cswe.org/getmedia/bb5d8afe-7680-42dc-a332-a6e6103f4998/2022-Educational-Policy-and-Accreditation-Standards-(EPAS).pdf

Coupland, S. K., Serovich, J., & Glenn, J. E. (1995). Reliability in constructing genograms: A study among marriage and family therapy doctoral students. *Journal of Marital and Family Therapy, 21*(3), 251–263. https://doi.org/10.1111/j.1752-0606.1995.tb00160.x

Cowan, P. A., & Cowan, C. P. (2012). Normative family transitions, couple relationship quality, and healthy child development. In F. Walsh (Ed.), *Normal family processes: Growing diversity and complexity* (4th ed., pp. 428–451). Guilford Press.

Cox, M. J., & Paley, B. (1997). Families as systems. *Annual Review of Psychology, 48*(1), 243–267. https://doi.org/10.1146/annurev.psych.48.1.243

Crabtree, S. A., Captari, L. E., Guterres, K., & Sandage, S. A. (2025). Mental health clinician functioning emerging from the COVID-19 pandemic: A mixed methods study. *Traumatology*. Advance online publication. https://doi.org/10.1037/trm0000576

Craig, C. D., & Sprang, G. (2010). Compassion satisfaction, compassion fatigue, and burnout in a national sample of trauma treatment therapists. *Anxiety, Stress, & Coping, 23*(3), 319–339. https://doi.org/10.1080/10615800903085818

Crenshaw, K. (1989). Demarginalizing the intersection of race and sex: A Black feminist critique of antidiscrimination doctrine, feminist theory, and antiracist politics. *University of Chicago Legal Forum, 140*, 139–167.

Crockett, A. H., Heberlein, E. C., Smith, J. C., Ozluk, P., Kindred, L., & Tanner-Smith, E. E. (2019). Effects of a multi-site expansion of group prenatal care on birth outcomes. *Maternal and Child Health Journal, 23*(10), 1424–1433. https://doi.org/10.1007/s10995-019-02795-4

Cronholm, P. F., Forke, C. M., Wade, R., Bair-Merritt, M. H., Davis, M., Harkins-Schwarz, M., Pachter, L. M., & Fein, J. A. (2015). Adverse childhood experiences: Expanding the concept of adversity. *American Journal of Preventive Medicine, 49*(3), 354–361. https://doi.org/10.1016/j.amepre.2015.02.001

Cui, M., Donnellan, M. B., & Conger, R. D. (2007). Reciprocal influences between parents' marital problems and adolescent internalizing and externalizing behavior. *Developmental Psychology, 43*(6), 1544–1552. https://doi.org/10.1037/0012-1649.43.6.1544

Cuijpers, P., Reijnders, M., & Huibers, M. J. (2019). The role of common factors in psychotherapy outcomes. *Annual Review of Clinical Psychology, 15*(1), 207–231. https://doi.org/10.1146/annurev-clinpsy-050718-095424

Cunningham, S. D., Ickovics, J. R., Lewis, J. B., Grilo, S. A., & Ickovics, J. R. (2017). Expect with me: Development and evaluation design for an innovative model of group prenatal care to improve perinatal outcomes. *BMC Pregnancy and Childbirth, 17*(1), Article 147. https://doi.org/10.1186/s12884-017-1327-3

Curtis, M. G., Ellis, E. M., Ann, S., Dai, Y., & Bermudez, J. M. (2020). Intersectionality within family sciences and family therapy journals from 2010 to 2020. *Journal of Family Theory & Review, 12*(4), 510–528. https://doi.org/10.1111/jftr.12399

Dalton, E. J., Greenman, P. S., Classen, C. C., & Johnson, S. M. (2013). Nurturing connections in the aftermath of childhood trauma: A randomized controlled trial of emotionally focused couple therapy for female survivors of childhood abuse. *Couple and Family Psychology: Research and Practice, 2*(3), 209–221. https://doi.org/10.1037/a0032772

D'Aniello, C., & Fife, S. T. (2020). A 20-year review of common factors research in marriage and family therapy: A mixed methods content analysis. *Journal of Marital and Family Therapy, 46*(4), 701–718. https://doi.org/10.1111/jmft.12427

Danielson, C. K., Adams, Z. W., & Hanson, R. (2019). Risk reduction through family therapy (RRFT): Exposure-based treatment for co-occurring PTSD and substance use problems among adolescents. In A. A. Vujanovic & S. E. Back (Eds.), *Posttraumatic stress and substance use disorders: A comprehensive clinical handbook* (pp. 165–182). Routledge.

Danielson, C. K., Adams, Z., McCart, M. R., Chapman, J. E., Sheidow, A. J., Walker, J., Smalling, A., & de Arellano, M. A. (2020). Safety and efficacy of exposure-based risk reduction through family therapy for co-occurring substance use problems and posttraumatic stress disorder symptoms among adolescents: A randomized clinical trial. *JAMA Psychiatry, 77*(6), 574–586. https://doi.org/10.1001/jamapsychiatry.2019.4803

Danielson, C. K., McCart, M., Walsh, K., de Arellano, M. A., White, D., & Resnick, H. S. (2012). Reducing substance use risk and mental health problems among sexually assaulted adolescents: A pilot randomized controlled trial. *Journal of Family Psychology, 26*(4), 628–635. https://doi.org/10.1037/a0028862

Danylchuk, L. S., & Connors, K. J. (2023). *Treating complex trauma and dissociation: A practical guide to navigating therapeutic challenges*. Routledge.

Darling Rasmussen, P., Storebø, O. J., Løkkeholt, T., Voss, L. G., Shmueli-Goetz, Y., Bojesen, A. B., Simonsen, E., & Bilenberg, N. (2019). Attachment as a core feature of resilience: A systematic review and meta-analysis. *Psychological Reports, 122*(4), 1259–1296. https://doi.org/10.1177/0033294118785577

Davey, M. P., Davey, A., Tubbs, C., Savlad, J., & Anderson, S. (2012). Second order change and evidence-based practice. *Journal of Family Therapy, 34*(1), 72–90. https://doi.org/10.1111/j.1467-6427.2010.00499.x

Davidson, J. R. T., Tupler, L. A., Wilson, W. H., & Connor, K. M. (1998). A family study of chronic post-traumatic stress disorder following rape trauma. *Journal of Psychiatric Research, 32*(5), 301–309. https://doi.org/10.1016/s0022-3956(98)00016-8

Davies, S. M., Sriskandarajah, S., Staneva, A. S., Boulton, H. C., Roberts, C., Shaw, S. H., & Silverio, S. A. (2022). Factors influencing 'burn-out' in newly qualified counsellors and psychotherapists: A cross-cultural, critical review of the literature. *Counselling and Psychotherapy Research, 22*(1), 64–73. https://doi.org/10.1002/capr.12485

Davis, D. E., DeBlaere, C., Owen, J., Hook, J. N., Rivera, D. P., Choe, E., Van Tongeren, D. R., Worthington, E. L., Jr., & Placeres, V. (2018). The multicultural orientation framework: A narrative review. *Psychotherapy, 55*(1), 89–100. https://doi.org/10.1037/pst0000160

Davis, L. W., Luedtke, B. L., Monson, C., Siegel, A., Daggy, J. K., Yang, Z., Bair, M. J., Brustuen, B., & Ertl, M. (2021). Testing adaptations of cognitive-behavioral conjoint therapy for PTSD: A randomized controlled pilot study with veterans. *Couple and Family Psychology: Research and Practice, 10*(2), 71–86. https://doi.org/10.1037/cfp0000148

Davis, S. D., & Hsieh, A. L. (2019). What does it mean to be a common factors informed family therapist? *Family Process, 58*(3), 629–640. https://doi.org/10.1111/famp.12477

De Los Reyes, A., & Makol, B. A. (2022). Informant reports in clinical assessment. In G. Asmundson (Ed.), *Comprehensive clinical psychology* (2nd ed., Vol. 4, pp. 105–122). Elsevier. https://doi.org/10.1016/B978-0-12-818697-8

Dekel, R., & Goldblatt, H. (2008). Is there intergenerational transmission of trauma? The case of combat veterans' children. *American Journal of Orthopsychiatry, 78*(3), 281–289. https://doi.org/10.1037/a0013955

Dekel, S., Papadakis, J. E., Quagliarini, B., Jagodnik, K. M., & Nandru, R. (2023). *A systematic review of interventions for prevention and treatment of post-traumatic stress disorder following childbirth*. medRxiv. https://doi.org/10.1101/2023.08.17.23294230

DeKlyen, M., & Greenberg, M. T. (2018). Attachment and psychopathology in childhood. In J. Cassidy & P. R. Shaver (Eds.), *Handbook of attachment:*

Theory, research, and clinical applications (3rd ed., pp. 639–666). Guilford Press.

Delaney, M. C. (2018). Caring for the caregivers: Evaluation of the effect of an eight-week pilot mindful self-compassion (MSC) training program on nurses' compassion fatigue and resilience. *PLOS One, 13*(11), Article 0207261. https://doi.org/10.1371/journal.pone.0207261

Demby, K. P., Riggs, S. A., & Kaminski, P. L. (2017). Attachment and family processes in children's emotional adjustment. *Family Process, 56*(1), 234–249. https://doi.org/10.1111/famp.12145

Derogatis, L. R. (1993). *Brief Symptom Inventory (BSI): Administration, scoring, and procedures manual* (4th ed.). National Computer Systems.

Dewane, C. J. (2006). Use of self: A primer revisited. *Clinical Social Work Journal, 34*(4), 543–558. https://doi.org/10.1007/s10615-005-0021-5

Diamond, G., Diamond, G. M., & Levy, S. (2021). Attachment-based family therapy: Theory, clinical model, outcomes, and process research. *Journal of Affective Disorders, 294*, 286–295. https://doi.org/10.1016/j.jad.2021.07.005

Diamond, G., Russon, J., & Levy, S. (2016). Attachment-based family therapy: A review of the empirical support. *Family Process, 55*(3), 595–610. https://doi.org/10.1111/famp.12241

Doğan, C. K., Yaşar, A. B., & Gündoğmuş, İ. (2021). Effects of the EMDR couple protocol on relationship satisfaction, depression, and anxiety symptoms. *Journal of EMDR Practice and Research, 15*(4), 218–230. https://doi.org/10.1891/EMDR-D-21-00008

Dorahy, M. J., Lewis-Fernández, R., Krüger, C., Brand, B. L., Şar, V., Ewing, J., Martínez-Taboas, A., Stavropoulos, P., & Middleton, W. (2017). The role of clinical experience, diagnosis, and theoretical orientation in the treatment of posttraumatic and dissociative disorders: A vignette and survey investigation. *Journal of Trauma & Dissociation, 18*(2), 206–222. https://doi.org/10.1080/15299732.2016.1225626

Dorsey, S., McLaughlin, K. A., Kerns, S. E., Harrison, J. P., Lambert, H. K., Briggs, E. C., Cox, J. R., & Amaya-Jackson, L. (2017). Evidence base update for psychosocial treatments for children and adolescents exposed to traumatic events. *Journal of Clinical Child & Adolescent Psychology, 46*(3), 303–330. https://doi.org/10.1080/15374416.2016.1220309

Drozd, L., & Flens, J. R. (2014). *Psychological testing in child custody evaluations*. Routledge.

Duarte, J., Pinto-Gouveia, J., & Cruz, B. (2016). Relationships between nurses' empathy, self-compassion and dimensions of professional quality of life: A cross-sectional study. *International Journal of Nursing Studies, 60*, 1–11. https://doi.org/10.1016/j.ijnurstu.2016.02.015

Dubowitz, H. (1997). Ethical issues in professionals' response to child maltreatment. *Child Maltreatment, 2*(4), 348–355. https://doi.org/10.1177/1077559597002004008

Duncan, J. M., Garrison, M. E., & Killian, T. S. (2021). Measuring family resilience: Evaluating the Walsh Family Resilience Questionnaire. *The Family Journal, 29*(1), 80–85. https://doi.org/10.1177/1066480720956641

Dunn, J. (2002). Sibling relationships. In P. K. Smith & C. H. Hart (Eds.), *Blackwell handbook of childhood social development* (pp. 223–237). Wiley-Blackwell.

Dunning, D., Heath, C., & Suls, J. M. (2004). Flawed self-assessment: Implications for health, education, and the workplace. *Psychological Science in the Public Interest, 5*(3), 69–106 https://doi.org/10.1111/j.1529-1006.2004.00018.x

Dunning, D., Johnson, K., Ehrlinger, J., & Kruger, J. (2003). Why people fail to recognize their own incompetence. *Current Directions in Psychological Science, 12*(3), 83–87. https://doi.org/10.1111/1467-8721.01235

Dunst, C. J. (2021). Family strengths, the circumplex model of family systems, and personal and family functioning: A meta-analysis of the relationships among study measures. *Journal of Behavior, Health & Social Issues, 13*(2), 1–16. https://doi.org/10.22201/fesi.20070780e.2021.13.2.77837

Duran, E. (2019). *Healing the soul wound: Trauma-informed counseling for Indigenous communities*. Teachers College Press.

Dutton, D. G., Starzomski, A., Saunders, K., & Bartholomew, K. (1994). Intimacy-anger and insecure attachment as precursors of abuse in intimate relationships. *Journal of Applied Social Psychology, 24*(15), 1367–1386. https://doi.org/10.1111/j.1559-1816.1994.tb01554.x

Dye, H. L. (2020). Is emotional abuse as harmful as physical and/or sexual abuse? *Journal of Child & Adolescent Trauma, 13*(4), 399–407. https://doi.org/10.1007/s40653-019-00292-y

Economidis, G., Pilkington, R., Lynch, J., Dobbins, T., Shakeshaft, A., Powell, M., Eades, A. M., & Falster, K. (2023). The effect of family-based therapy on child physical abuse and neglect: A narrative systematic review. *International Journal on Child Maltreatment: Research, Policy and Practice, 6*(4), 633–674. https://doi.org/10.1007/s42448-023-00170-z

Eddy, J. M., Dishion, T. J., & Stoolmiller, M. (1998). The analysis of intervention change in children and families: Methodological and conceptual issues embedded in intervention studies. *Journal of Abnormal Child Psychology, 26*(1), 53–69. https://doi.org/10.1023/A:1022634807098

Ellis, B. H., Fogler, J., Hansen, S., Forbes, P., Navalta, C. P., & Saxe, G. (2012). Trauma systems therapy: 15-month outcomes and the importance of effecting environmental change. *Psychological Trauma: Theory, Research, Practice, and Policy, 4*(6), 624–630. https://doi.org/10.1037/a0025192

Elwood, L. S., Mott, J., Lohr, J. M., & Galovski, T. E. (2011). Secondary trauma symptoms in clinicians: A critical review of the construct, specificity, and implications for trauma-focused treatment. *Clinical Psychology Review, 31*(1), 25–36. https://doi.org/10.1016/j.cpr.2010.09.004

Epstein, N. B., Baldwin, L. M., & Bishop, D. S. (1983). The McMaster family assessment device. *Journal of Marital and Family Therapy, 9*(2), 171–180. https://doi.org/10.1111/j.1752-0606.1983.tb01497.x

Eubanks, C. F., Samstag, L. W. E., & Muran, J. (2023). Conclusion: Don't be afraid to get messy—Points of convergence in rupture and repair. In C. F. Eubanks, L. W. Samstag, & J. C. Muran (Eds.), *Rupture and repair in psychotherapy: A critical process for change* (pp. 305–317). American Psychological Association. https://doi.org/10.1037/0000306-013

Evans, K. E., Bender, A. E., Rolock, N., Hambrick, E. P., Bai, R., White, K., Diamant-Wilson, R., & Bailey, K. A. (2024). Exploring adherence to client treatment recommendations in the neurosequential model of therapeutics. *Research on Social Work Practice, 34*(2), 222–233. https://doi.org/10.1177/10497315231160588

Eyberg, S. M. (1988). Parent–child interaction therapy: Integration of traditional and behavioral concerns. *Child & Family Behavior Therapy, 10*(1), 33–46. https://doi.org/10.1300/J019v10n01_03

Fairbairn, W. R. D. (1943). The repression and the return of bad objects (with special reference to the 'war neuroses'). *British Journal of Medical Psychology, 19*(3–4), 327–341. https://doi.org/10.1111/j.2044-8341.1943.tb00328.x

Fehrenbach, T., Sax, R. M., Urban, T. H., Simon-Roper, L., Novacek, J., Aaby, D. A., & Hodgdon, H. B. (2022). Trauma treatment for youth in community-based settings: Implementing the Attachment, Regulation, and Competency (ARC) framework. *Journal of Child and Family Studies, 31*(2), 434–446. https://doi.org/10.1007/s10826-021-02096-x

Feinberg, P. H. (1990). Circular questions: Establishing the relational context. *Family Systems Medicine, 8*(3), 273–277. https://doi.org/10.1037/h0089070

Felitti, V. J., Anda, R. F., Nordenberg, D., Williamson, D. F., Spitz, A. M., Edwards, V., & Marks, J. S. (1998). Relationship of childhood abuse and household dysfunction to many of the leading causes of death in adults: The adverse childhood experiences (ACE) study. *American Journal of Preventive Medicine, 14*(4), 245–258. https://doi.org/10.1016/S0749-3797(98)00017-8

Ferenczi, S. (1926). *Further contributions to the theory and technique of psychoanalysis*. Hogarth Press.

Ferenczi, S. (1931). *Final contributions to the problems and methods of psychoanalysis*. Hogarth Press.

Ferenczi, S. (Ed.). (1988). *The clinical diary of Sándor Ferenczi* (J. Dupont, Ed.; M. Balint & N. Z. Jackson, Trans.). Harvard University Press. (Original work published 1932)

Fernández-Álvarez, H., Consoli, A. J., & Gómez, B. (2016). Integration in psychotherapy: Reasons and challenges. *American Psychologist, 71*(8), 820–830. https://doi.org/10.1037/amp0000100

Figley, C. R. (1989). *Helping traumatized families*. Jossey-Bass.

Figley, C. R. (1995). *Compassion fatigue: Coping with secondary traumatic stress disorder in those who treat the traumatized*. Brunner/Mazel.

Figley, C. R. (2002). Compassion fatigue: Psychotherapists' chronic lack of self care. *Journal of Clinical Psychology, 58*(11), 1433–1441. https://doi.org/10.1002/jclp.10090

Figley, C. R. (2003). *Compassion fatigue: An introduction*. Green Cross Foundations' Gift From Within. https://www.giftfromwithin.org/ptsd/what-is-compassion-fatigue-dr-charles-figley/

Figley, C. R., & Barnes, M. (2005). External trauma and families. In P. C. McKenry & S. J. Price (Eds.), *Families and change* (pp. 379–401). Sage Publications.

Figley, C. R., & Kiser, L. (2013). *Helping traumatized families* (2nd ed.). Routledge. https://doi.org/10.4324/9780203813508

Figley, C. R., & Ludick, M. (2017). Secondary traumatization and compassion fatigue. In S. N. Gold (Ed.), *APA handbook of trauma psychology: Vol. 1. Foundations in knowledge* (pp. 573–593). American Psychological Association. https://doi.org/10.1037/0000019-029

Finklestein, M., Stein, E., Greene, T., Bronstein, I., & Solomon, Z. (2015). Posttraumatic stress disorder and vicarious trauma in mental health professionals. *Health & Social Work, 40*(2), e25–e31. https://doi.org/10.1093/hsw/hlv026

Finzi-Dottan, R., & Kormosh, M. B. (2018). The spillover of compassion fatigue into marital quality: A mediation model. *Traumatology, 24*(2), 113–122. https://doi.org/10.1037/trm0000137

Fite, P. J., Colder, C. R., Lochman, J. E., & Wells, K. C. (2006). The mutual influence of parenting and boys' externalizing behavior problems. *Journal of Applied Developmental Psychology, 27*(2), 151–164. https://doi.org/10.1016/j.appdev.2005.12.011

Fitzgerald, H. E., Johnson, D. J., Allen, J., Villaruel, F. A., & Qin, D. B. (2021). Historical and race-based trauma: Resilience through family and community. *Adversity and Resilience Science, 2*(2), 215–223. https://doi.org/10.1007/s42844-021-00048-4

Fitzgerald, M., London-Johnson, A., & Gallus, K. L. (2020). Intergenerational transmission of trauma and family systems theory: An empirical investigation. *Journal of Family Therapy, 42*(3), 406–424. https://doi.org/10.1111/1467-6427.12303

Foa, E. B., Chrestman, K. R., & Gilboa-Schechtman, E. (2009). *Prolonged exposure therapy for adolescents with PTSD: Emotional processing of traumatic experiences: Therapist guide*. Oxford University Press.

Foa, E. B., Hembree, E. A., Rothbaum, B. O., & Rauch, S. (2007). *Prolonged exposure therapy for PTSD: Emotional processing of traumatic experiences: Therapist guide*. Oxford University Press.

Fogarty, T. (1979). The distancer and the pursuer. *The Family, 7*, 11–16.

Fonagy, P. (1999). Achieving evidence-based psychotherapy practice: A psychodynamic perspective on the general acceptance of treatment manuals. *Clinical*

Psychology: Science and Practice, 6(4), 442–444. https://doi.org/10.1093/clipsy.6.4.442

Fonagy, P. (2018). Attachment, trauma, and psychoanalysis: Where psychoanalysis meets neuroscience. In J. Canestri, M. Leuzinger-Bohleber, & M. Target (Eds.), *Early development and its disturbances* (pp. 53–75). Routledge. https://doi.org/10.4324/9780429474057-2

Fonagy, P., & Allison, E. (2014). The role of mentalizing and epistemic trust in the therapeutic relationship. *Psychotherapy, 51*(3), 372–380. https://doi.org/10.1037/a0036505

Ford, J. D. (2020). Trauma affect regulation: Guide for education and therapy. In J. D. Ford & C. A. Courtois (Eds.), *Treating complex traumatic stress disorders in adults: Scientific foundations and therapeutic models* (2nd ed., pp. 390–412). Guilford Press.

Ford, J. D., & Courtois, C. A. (2020). *Treating complex traumatic stress disorders in adults: Scientific foundations and therapeutic models* (2nd ed.). Guilford Press.

Ford, J. D., Steinberg, K., Hawke, J., Levine, J., & Zhang, W. (2012). Randomized trial comparison of emotion regulation and relational psychotherapies for PTSD with girls involved in delinquency. *Journal of Clinical Child & Adolescent Psychology, 41*(1), 27–37. https://doi.org/10.1080/15374416.2012.632343

Ford, J. D., Steinberg, K., & Zhang, W. (2011). A randomized clinical trial comparing affect regulation and social problem-solving psychotherapies for mothers with victimization-related PTSD. *Behavior Therapy, 42*(4), 561–578. https://doi.org/10.1016/j.beth.2010.12.005

Fortin, A., Doucet, M., & Damant, D. (2011). Children's appraisals as mediators of the relationship between domestic violence and child adjustment. *Violence and Victims, 26*(3), 377–392. https://doi.org/10.1891/0886-6708.26.3.377

Fouad, N. A., Grus, C. L., Hatcher, R. L., Kaslow, N. J., Hutchings, P. S., Madson, M. B., Collins, F. L., Jr., & Crossman, R. E. (2009). Competency benchmarks: A model for understanding and measuring competence in professional psychology across training levels. *Training and Education in Professional Psychology, 3*(4, Suppl.), S5–S26. https://doi.org/10.1037/a0015832

Fox, D. J. (2024). The integration of somatic-based strategies into couples therapy. *Clinical Social Work Journal, 52*(1), 79–88. https://doi.org/10.1007/s10615-023-00905-y

Fraiberg, S., Adelson, E., & Shapiro, V. (1975). Ghosts in the nursery: A psychoanalytic approach to the problems of impaired infant–mother relationships. *Journal of American Academy of Child Psychiatry, 14*(3), 387–421. https://doi.org/10.1016/s0002-7138(09)61442-4

Fraser, S. W., & Greenhalgh, T. (2001). Coping with complexity: Educating for capability. *BMJ, 323*(7316), 799–803. https://doi.org/10.1136/bmj.323.7316.799

Freud, S. (1953). Inhibitions, symptoms and anxiety. In J. Strachey (Ed. & Trans.), *The standard edition of the complete psychological works of Sigmund Freud* (Vol. 20, pp. 75–176). Hogarth Press. (Original work published 1926)

Freud, S. (1955). Beyond the pleasure principle. In J. Strachey (Ed. & Trans.), *The standard edition of the complete psychological works of Sigmund Freud* (Vol. 18, pp. 1–64). Hogarth Press. (Original work published 1920)

Freud, S. (1957). The future prospects of psycho-analytic therapy. In J. Strachey (Ed. & Trans.), *The standard edition of the complete psychological works of Sigmund Freud* (Vol. 11, pp. 139–152). Hogarth Press. (Original work published 1910)

Freud, S. (1958). Remembering, repeating and working-through (further recommendations on the technique of psycho-analysis II). In J. Strachey (Ed. & Trans.), *The standard edition of the complete psychological works of Sigmund Freud* (Vol. 12, pp. 145–156). Hogarth Press. (Original work published 1914)

Friedlander, M. L., & Escudero, V. (2023). A close look at the complex rupture and repair process in family therapy. In C. F. Eubanks, L. W. Samstag, & J. C. Muran (Eds.), *Rupture and repair in psychotherapy: A critical process for change* (pp. 73–94). American Psychological Association. https://doi.org/10.1037/0000306-004

Funderburk, B. W., & Eyberg, S. (2011). Parent–child interaction therapy. In J. C. Norcross, G. R. VandenBos, & D. K. Freedheim (Eds.), *History of psychotherapy: Continuity and change* (2nd ed., pp. 415–420). American Psychological Association. https://doi.org/10.1037/12353-021

Furrow, J. L., Palmer, G., Johnson, S. M., Faller, G., & Palmer-Olsen, L. (2019). *Emotionally focused family therapy: Restoring connection and promoting resilience*. Routledge. https://doi.org/10.4324/9781315669649

Gaebel, W., Kerst, A., Janssen, B., Becker, T., Musalek, M., Rössler, W., Ruggeri, M., Thornicroft, G., Zielasek, J., & Stricker, J. (2020). EPA guidance on the quality of mental health services: A systematic meta-review and update of recommendations focusing on care coordination. *European Psychiatry, 63*(1), Article e75. https://doi.org/10.1192/j.eurpsy.2020.75

Galano, M. M., & Graham-Bermann, S. A. (2019). Traumatic stress within the family. In B. H. Fiese, M. Celano, K. Deater-Deckard, E. N. Jouriles, & M. A. Whisman (Eds.), *APA handbook of contemporary family psychology: Vol. 2. Applications and broad impact of family psychology* (pp. 539–554). American Psychological Association. https://doi.org/10.1037/0000100-033

Galatzer-Levy, I. R., Huang, S. H., & Bonanno, G. A. (2018). Trajectories of resilience and dysfunction following potential trauma: A review and statistical evaluation. *Clinical Psychology Review, 63*, 41–55. https://doi.org/10.1016/j.cpr.2018.05.008

Gallup. (2024, March 29). *How religious are Americans?* https://news.gallup.com/poll/358364/religious-americans.aspx#:~:text=At%20its%20peak%20in%20theslightly%20higher%2C%20at%2032%25

Galovski, T., & Lyons, J. A. (2004). Psychological sequelae of combat violence: A review of the impact of PTSD on the veteran's family and possible interventions. *Aggression and Violent Behavior, 9*(5), 477–501. https://doi.org/10.1016/S1359-1789(03)00045-4

Garcia, E. S., & Johnson, C. M. (2019). Using feminist family therapy and a multidisciplinary collaboration to address issues regarding sexism in gamers. *Journal of Feminist Family Therapy, 31*(1), 19–39. https://doi.org/10.1080/08952833.2018.1526512

Garland, C. (Ed.). (1998). *Understanding trauma: A psychoanalytical approach*. Karnac.

Gates, G. J. (2013). *LGBT parenting in the United States*. Williams Institute, UCLA School of Law. https://williamsinstitute.law.ucla.edu/wp-content/uploads/LGBT-Parenting.pdf

Gates, G. J. (2015). Marriage and family: LGBT individuals and same-sex couples. *The Future of Children, 25*(2), 67–87. https://doi.org/10.1353/foc.2015.0013

Gee, D. G., & Cohodes, E. M. (2023). Leveraging the developmental neuroscience of caregiving to promote resilience among youth exposed to adversity. *Development and Psychopathology, 35*(5), 2168–2185. https://doi.org/10.1017/S0954579423001128

Geffner, R., & Mantooth, C. (2000). *Ending spouse/partner abuse: A psychoeducational approach for individuals and couples*. Springer.

Gehart, D. (2018). *Mastering competencies in family therapy* (3rd ed.). Cengage.

Geller, J. A. (1998). Conjoint therapy for treatment of partner abuse: Indications and contraindications. In A. R. Roberts (Ed.), *Battered women and their families: Intervention strategies and treatment programs* (pp. 76–96). Springer.

Germer, C., & Neff, K. D. (2013). Self-compassion in clinical practice. *Journal of Clinical Psychology, 69*(8), 856–867. https://doi.org/10.1002/jclp.22021

Germer, C., & Neff, K. D. (2019). Mindful self-compassion (MSC). In I. Itvzan (Ed.). *The handbook of mindfulness-based programs: Every established intervention, from medicine to education* (pp. 357–367). Routledge.

Germer, C., & Siegel, R. D. (Eds.). (2012). *Wisdom and compassion in psychotherapy: Deepening mindfulness in clinical practice*. Guilford Press.

Ghafari, M., Nadi, T., Bahadivand-Chegini, S., & Doosti-Irani, A. (2022). Global prevalence of unmet need for mental health care among adolescents: A systematic review and meta-analysis. *Archives of Psychiatric Nursing, 36*, 1–6. https://doi.org/10.1016/j.apnu.2021.10.008

Ghahramanlou, M., & Brodbeck, C. (2000). Predictors of secondary trauma in sexual assault trauma counselors. *International Journal of Emergency Mental Health, 2*(4), 229–240.

Ghosh Ippen, C. G., Harris, W. W., Van Horn, P., & Lieberman, A. F. (2011). Traumatic and stressful events in early childhood: Can treatment help those at highest risk? *Child Abuse & Neglect, 35*(7), 504–513. https://doi.org/10.1016/j.chiabu.2011.03.009

Giardino, A. P., Lyn, M. A., & Giardino, E. R. (Eds.). (2018). *A practical guide to the evaluation of child physical abuse and neglect*. Springer.

Gil, S., & Weinberg, M. (2015). Secondary trauma among social workers treating trauma clients: The role of coping strategies and internal resources. *International Social Work, 58*(4), 551–561. https://doi.org/10.1177/0020872814564705

Giladi, L., & Bell, T. S. (2013). Protective factors for intergenerational transmission of trauma among second and third generation Holocaust survivors. *Psychological Trauma: Theory, Research, Practice, and Policy, 5*(4), 384–391. https://doi.org/10.1037/a0028455

Gilbert, P., & Simos, G. (Eds.). (2022). *Compassion focused therapy: Clinical practice and applications*. Routledge.

Giuliani, D. (2016). *Sociology of family*. Utah Valley University.

Goff, B. S. N., Ruhlmann, L. M., Dekel, R., & Huxman, S. A. (2020). Trauma, posttraumatic stress, and family systems. In K. S. Wampler, M. Rastogi, & R. Singh (Eds.), *The handbook of systemic family therapy* (Vol. 4, pp. 267–296). Wiley. https://doi.org/10.1002/9781119438519.ch93

Goldner, V. (1998). The treatment of violence and victimization in intimate relationships. *Family Process, 37*(3), 263–286. https://doi.org/10.1111/j.1545-5300.1998.00263.x

Gomez, A. M. (2012). *EMDR therapy and adjunct approaches with children: Complex trauma, attachment, and dissociation*. Springer.

Gómez, A. M., & Hosey, J. (Eds.). (2025). *The handbook of complex trauma and dissociation in children: Theory, research, and clinical applications*. Taylor & Francis.

Gone, J. P. (2019). "The thing happened as he wished": Recovering an American Indian cultural psychology. *American Journal of Community Psychology, 64*(1–2), 172–184. https://doi.org/10.1002/ajcp.12353

Goodman, R. D. (2013). The transgenerational trauma and resilience genogram. *Counselling Psychology Quarterly, 26*(3–4), 386–405. https://doi.org/10.1080/09515070.2013.820172

Gottlieb, M. C. (1995). Ethical dilemmas in change of format and live supervision. In R. H. Mikesell, D. D. Lusterman, & S. H. McDaniel (Eds.), *Integrating family therapy: Handbook of family psychology and systems theory* (pp. 561–569). American Psychological Association. https://doi.org/10.1037/10172-032

Gottlieb, M. C., Lasser, J., & Simpson, G. L. (2008). Legal and ethical issues in couple therapy. In A. S. Gurman (Ed.), *Clinical handbook of couple therapy* (4th ed., pp. 698–717). Guilford Press.

Gottman, J. M. (1993). A theory of marital dissolution and stability. *Journal of Family Psychology, 7*(1), 57–75. https://doi.org/10.1037/0893-3200.7.1.57

Grawitch, M. J., & Ballard, D. W. (Eds.). (2016). *The psychologically healthy workplace: Building a win–win environment for organizations and employees*. American Psychological Association. https://doi.org/10.1037/14731-000

Greenberg, L. S. (2011). *Emotion-focused therapy*. American Psychological Association.

Greenberg, L. S., & Johnson, S. M. (1988). *Emotionally focused therapy for couples*. Guilford Press.

Greenblatt-Kimron, L., Shrira, A., Ben-Ezra, M., & Palgi, Y. (2025). Echoes of ancestral trauma: Russo-Ukrainian War salience and psychological distress among subsequent generations in Holocaust survivor families. *Psychological Trauma: Theory, Research, Practice, and Policy, 17*(4), 750–757. https://doi.org/10.1037/tra0001633

Grove, D. R., Greene, G. J., & Lee, M. Y. (2020). *Family therapy for treating trauma: An integrative family and systems treatment (I-FAST) approach*. Oxford University Press.

Grych, J. H., Raynor, S. R., & Fosco, G. M. (2004). Family processes that shape the impact of interparental conflict on adolescents. *Development and Psychopathology, 16*(3), 649–665. https://doi.org/10.1017/S0954579404004717

Grych, J. H., Seid, M., & Fincham, F. D. (1992). Assessing marital conflict from the child's perspective: The children's perception of interparental conflict scale. *Child Development, 63*(3), 558–572. https://doi.org/10.2307/1131346

Guerney, B., Jr. (1964). Filial therapy: Description and rationale. *Journal of Consulting Psychology, 28*(4), 304–360. https://doi.org/10.1037/h0041340

Guild, D. J., Toth, S. L., Handley, E. D., Rogosch, F. A., & Cicchetti, D. (2017). Attachment security mediates the longitudinal association between child–parent psychotherapy and peer relations for toddlers of depressed mothers. *Development and Psychopathology, 29*(2), 587–600. https://doi.org/10.1017/S0954579417000207

Gurwitch, R. H., & Warner-Metzger, C. M. (2022). Trauma-directed interaction (TDI): An adaptation to parent–child interaction therapy for families with a history of trauma. *International Journal of Environmental Research and Public Health, 19*(10), Article 6089. https://doi.org/10.3390/ijerph19106089

Gutermann, J., Schreiber, F., Matulis, S., Schwartzkopff, L., Deppe, J., & Steil, R. (2016). Psychological treatments for symptoms of posttraumatic stress disorder in children, adolescents, and young adults: A meta-analysis. *Clinical Child and Family Psychology Review, 19*(2), 77–93. https://doi.org/10.1007/s10567-016-0202-5

Hahn, A. M., Adams, Z. W., Chapman, J., McCart, M. R., Sheidow, A. J., de Arellano, M. A., & Danielson, C. K. (2020). Risk reduction through family therapy (RRFT): Protocol of a randomized controlled efficacy trial of an integrative treatment for co-occurring substance use problems and posttraumatic stress disorder symptoms in adolescents who have experienced interpersonal violence and other traumatic events. *Contemporary Clinical Trials, 93*, Article 106012. https://doi.org/10.1016/j.cct.2020.106012

Hahn, H., Putnam, K., Epstein, C., Marans, S., & Putnam, F. (2019). Child and family traumatic stress intervention (CFTSI) reduces parental posttraumatic stress symptoms: A multi-site meta-analysis (MSMA). *Child Abuse & Neglect, 92,* 106–115. https://doi.org/10.1016/j.chiabu.2019.03.010

Haines, S. K. (2019). *The politics of trauma: Somatics, healing, and social justice.* North Atlantic Books.

Haladjian, L. (2020). *Intergenerational trauma among second, third, and fourth generation Armenian genocide survivors* [Doctoral dissertation, Fielding Graduate University]. ProQuest Dissertations and Theses Global.

Halevi, E., & Idisis, Y. (2018). Who helps the helper? Differentiation of self as an indicator for resisting vicarious traumatization. *Psychological Trauma: Theory, Research, Practice, and Policy, 10*(6), 698–705. https://doi.org/10.1037/tra0000318

Halpern, J., & Vermeulen, K. (2017). *Disaster mental health interventions: Core principles and practices.* Routledge.

Hamilton, E., & Carr, A. (2016). Systematic review of self-report family assessment measures. *Family Process, 55*(1), 16–30. https://doi.org/10.1111/famp.12200

Hammer, M. R., Bennett, M. J., & Wiseman, R. (2003). Measuring intercultural sensitivity: The Intercultural Development Inventory. *International Journal of Intercultural Relations, 27*(4), 421–443. https://doi.org/10.1016/S0147-1767(03)00032-4

Hampson, R. B., & Beavers, W. R. (2004). Observational assessment of couples and families. In L. Sperry (Ed.), *Assessment of couples and families: Contemporary and cutting-edge strategies* (pp. 77–98). Brunner-Routledge. https://doi.org/10.4324/9780203308271

Harris, J., Loth, E., & Sethna, V. (2024). Tracing the paths: A systematic review of mediators of complex trauma and complex post-traumatic stress disorder. *Frontiers in Psychiatry, 15,* Article 1331256. https://doi.org/10.3389/fpsyt.2024.1331256

Hartman, A. (1978). Diagrammatic assessment of family relationships. *Social Casework, 60*(8), 465–476.

Harway, M., Kadin, S., Gottlieb, M. C., Nutt, R. L., & Celano, M. (2012). Family psychology and systemic approaches: Working effectively in a variety of contexts. *Professional Psychology: Research and Practice, 43*(4), 315–327. https://doi.org/10.1037/a0029134

Haslam, N., & McGrath, M. J. (2020). The creeping concept of trauma. *Social Research: An International Quarterly, 87*(3), 509–531. https://doi.org/10.1353/sor.2020.0052

Hatchel, T., Ingram, K. M., Mintz, S., Hartley, C., Valido, A., Espelage, D. L., & Wyman, P. (2019). Predictors of suicidal ideation and attempts among LGBTQ adolescents: The roles of help-seeking beliefs, peer victimization, depressive symptoms, and drug use. *Journal of Child and Family Studies, 28*(9), 2443–2455. https://doi.org/10.1007/s10826-019-01339-2

Hatcher, R. L., Fouad, N. A., Grus, C. L., Campbell, L. F., McCutcheon, S. R., & Leahy, K. L. (2013). Competency benchmarks: Practical steps toward a culture of competence. *Training and Education in Professional Psychology, 7*(2), 84–91. https://doi.org/10.1037/a0029401

Haxhe, S. (2016). Parentification and related processes: Distinction and implications for clinical practice. *Journal of Family Psychotherapy, 27*(3), 185–199. https://doi.org/10.1080/08975353.2016.1199768

Hazzard, A., Christensen, A., & Margolin, G. (1983). Children's perceptions of parental behaviors. *Journal of Abnormal Child Psychology, 11*(1), 49–59. https://doi.org/10.1007/BF00912177

Health Service Psychology Education Collaborative. (2013). Professional psychology in health care services: A blueprint for education and training. *American Psychologist, 68*(6), 411–426. https://doi.org/10.1037/a0033265

Henggeler, S. W., Schoenwald, S. K., Borduin, C. M., Rowland, M. D., & Cunningham, P. B. (2009). *Multisystemic therapy for antisocial behavior in children and adolescents*. Guilford Press.

Henning, J. A., Brand, B., & Courtois, C. A. (2022). Graduate training and certification in trauma treatment for clinical practitioners. *Training and Education in Professional Psychology, 16*(4), 362–375. https://doi.org/10.1037/tep0000326

Hensel, J. M., Ruiz, C., Finney, C., & Dewa, C. S. (2015). Meta-analysis of risk factors for secondary traumatic stress in therapeutic work with trauma victims. *Journal of Traumatic Stress, 28*(2), 83–91. https://doi.org/10.1002/jts.21998

Herbine-Blank, T., & Sweezy, M. (2021). *Internal family systems: Couple therapy skills manual: Healing relationships with intimacy from the inside out*. PESI Publishing.

Herman, J. L. (1992). *Trauma and recovery: The aftermath of violence—From domestic abuse to political terror*. Hachette UK.

Hetherington, E. M. (1999). Should we stay together for the sake of the children? In E. M. Hetherington (Ed.), *Coping with divorce, single parenting, and remarriage: A risk and resiliency perspective* (pp. 93–116). Lawrence Erlbaum.

Heyman, R. E., Feldbau-Kohn, S. R., Ehrensaft, M. K., Langhinrichsen-Rohling, J., & O'Leary, K. D. (2001). Can questionnaire reports correctly classify relationship distress and partner physical abuse? *Journal of Family Psychology, 15*(2), 334–346. https://doi.org/10.1037/0893-3200.15.2.334

Heyman, R. E., & Slep, A. M. S. (2006). Creating and field-testing diagnostic criteria for partner and child maltreatment. *Journal of Family Psychology, 20*(3), 397–408. https://doi.org/10.1037/0893-3200.20.3.397

Heyman, R. E., & Slep, A. M. S. (2019). Relational disorders and beyond. In B. H. Fiese, M. Celano, K. Deater-Deckard, E. N. Jouriles, & M. A. Whisman (Eds.), *APA handbook of contemporary family psychology: Vol. 3. Family therapy and training* (pp. 19–34). American Psychological Association. https://doi.org/10.1037/0000101-002

Hicks, S. R. (2015). *A critical analysis of post traumatic slave syndrome: A multigenerational legacy of slavery* [Doctoral dissertation, California Institute of Integral Studies]. ProQuest Dissertations and Theses Global.

Hill, M., Baggé, R., & Miersma, P. (2021). *Healing the wounds of trauma: How the church can help*. American Bible Society.

Hindman, J. M., Riggs, S. A., Clark, C., Sexton, S., & Stephenson, L. (2008, November). *Attitudes toward therapy and adult attachment style* [Conference session]. Texas Psychological Association Annual Convention, Austin, TX, United States.

Hindman, J. M., Riggs, S. A., & Hook, J. (2013). Contributions of executive, parent–child, and sibling subsystems to children's psychological functioning. *Couple and Family Psychology: Research and Practice, 2*(4), 294–308. https://doi.org/10.1037/a0034419

Hipwell, A. E., Tung, I., Northrup, J., & Keenan, K. (2019). Transgenerational associations between maternal childhood stress exposure and profiles of infant emotional reactivity. *Development and Psychopathology, 31*(3), 887–898. https://doi.org/10.1017/S0954579419000324

Hirschberger, G. (2018). Collective trauma and the social construction of meaning. *Frontiers in Psychology, 9*, Article 351992. https://doi.org/10.3389/fpsyg.2018.01441

Holden, C. L., & Jeanfreau, M. M. (2023). Are perfectionistic standards associated with burnout? Multidimensional perfectionism and compassion experiences among professional MFTs. *Contemporary Family Therapy, 45*(2), 207–217. https://doi.org/10.1007/s10591-021-09605-6

Holtzworth-Munroe, A., Smutzler, N., & Stuart, G. L. (1998). Demand and withdraw communication among couples experiencing husband violence. *Journal of Consulting and Clinical Psychology, 66*(5), 731–743. https://doi.org/10.1037/0022-006X.66.5.731

Horvath, A. O., Del Re, A. C., Flückiger, C., & Symonds, D. (2011). Alliance in individual psychotherapy. *Psychotherapy, 48*(1), 9–16. https://doi.org/10.1037/a0022186

Howard, A. R., Parris, S. R., Nielsen, L. E., Lusk, R., Bush, K., Purvis, K. B., & Cross, D. R. (2014). Trust-based relational intervention (TBRI) for adopted children receiving therapy in an outpatient setting. *Child Welfare, 93*(5), 47–64. https://www.jstor.org/stable/48623452

Howell, K. H., Barrett-Becker, E. P., Burnside, A., Wamser-Nanney, R., Layne, C. M., & Kaplow, J. B. (2016). Children facing parental cancer versus parental death: The buffering effects of positive parenting and emotional expression. *Journal of Child and Family Studies, 25*(1), 152–164. https://doi.org/10.1007/s10826-015-0198-3

Howell, K. H., Kaplow, J. B., Layne, C. M., Benson, M. A., Compas, B. E., Katalinski, R., Pasalic, H., Bosankic, N., & Pynoos, R. (2014). Predicting adolescent posttraumatic stress in the aftermath of war: Differential effects of coping strategies across trauma reminder, loss reminder, and family conflict domains. *Anxiety, Stress, & Coping, 28*(1), 88–104. https://doi.org/10.1080/10615806.2014.910596

Hoyert, D. (2023). *Maternal mortality rates in the United States, 2021*. Centers for Disease Control and Prevention/National Center for Health Statistics. https://doi.org/10.15620/cdc:124678

Hübl, T. (2020). *Healing collective trauma: A process for integrating our intergenerational and cultural wounds*. Sounds True.

Hunsley, J., & Mash, E. J. (2007). Evidence-based assessment. *Annual Review of Clinical Psychology, 3*, 29–51. https://doi.org/10.1146/annurev.clinpsy.3.022806.091419

Institute of Medicine, & National Research Council. (2014). *New directions in child abuse and neglect research*. The National Academies Press.

Ivey, A. E., Ivey, M. B., & Zalaquett, C. P. (2017). *Intentional interviewing and counseling: Facilitating client development in a multicultural society* (9th ed.). Cengage Learning.

Jacobson, N. S., & Margolin, G. (1979). *Marital therapy*. Brunner/Mazel.

Jacobvitz, D. B., & Bush, N. F. (1996). Reconstructions of family relationships: Parent–child alliances, personal distress, and self-esteem. *Developmental Psychology, 32*(4), 732–743. https://doi.org/10.1037/0012-1649.32.4.732

Jacobvitz, D. B., Hazen, N., Curran, M., & Hitchens, K. (2004). Observations of early triadic family interactions: Boundary disturbances in the family predict symptoms of depression, anxiety, and attention-deficit/hyperactivity disorder in middle childhood. *Development and Psychopathology, 16*(3), 577–592. https://doi.org/10.1017/s0954579404004675

Jacobvitz, D. B., Riggs, S. A., & Johnson, E. (1999). Cross-sex and same-sex family alliances: Immediate and long-term effects on sons and daughters. In N. Chase (Ed.), *Parentified children: Theory, research, and treatment* (pp. 34–55). Sage Publications.

Jain, S. (2019). *The unspeakable mind: Stories of trauma and healing from the frontlines of PTSD science*. HarperCollins Publishers.

Jain, S., Reno, R., Cohen, A. K., Bassey, H., & Master, M. (2019). Building a culturally-responsive, family-driven early childhood system of care: Understanding the needs and strengths of ethnically diverse families of children with social-emotional and behavioral concerns. *Children and Youth Services Review, 100*, 31–38. https://doi.org/10.1016/j.childyouth.2019.02.034

James, K., & MacKinnon, L. (2012). Integrating a trauma lens into a family therapy framework: Ten principles for therapists. *Australian and New Zealand Journal of Family Therapy, 33*(03), 189–209. https://doi.org/10.1017/aft.2012.25

Janoff-Bulman, R. (1992). *Shattered assumptions: Towards a new psychology of trauma*. Free Press.

Jegarl, A. M., Jegede, O., Isom, J., Ciarleglio, N., & Black, C. (2023). Psychotic misdiagnosis of racially minoritized patients: A case-based ethics, equity, and educational exploration. *Harvard Review of Psychiatry, 31*(1), 28–36. https://doi.org/10.1097/HRP.0000000000000353

Jia, C. X., & Li, J. C. M. (2022). Work-family conflict, burnout, and turnover intention among Chinese social workers: The moderating role of work support. *Journal of Social Service Research, 48*(1), 12–27. https://doi.org/10.1080/01488376.2021.1942393

Johannessen, K. N., Bakken, A. K., Hambrick, E. P., & Solbakken, O. A. (2024). Treatment effects of introducing the neurosequential model of therapeutics in a Norwegian residential treatment facility for children aged 7–13. *Children, 11*(5), Article 503. https://doi.org/10.3390/children11050503

Johns, A. N., Brown, L. S., & Cromer, L. D. (2022). Examining intergenerational transmission of Holocaust trauma as it relates to Jewish identity, communication type, and mental well-being. *Journal of Traumatic Stress, 35*(5), 1497–1507. https://doi.org/10.1002/jts.22856

Johnson, J. H., & McCutcheon, S. (1980). *Life Events Checklist*. Hemisphere Publishing.

Johnson, S. M. (2002). *Emotionally focused couple therapy with trauma survivors: Strengthening attachment bonds*. Guilford Press.

Johnson, S. M. (2019a). *Attachment theory in practice: Emotionally focused therapy (EFT) with individuals, couples, and families*. Guilford Press.

Johnson, S. M. (2019b). *The practice of emotionally focused marital therapy: Creating connection*. Brunner/Mazel/Routledge. (Original work published 1996)

Johnson, S. M., & Lee, A. C. (2005). Emotionally focused family therapy: Restructuring attachment. In C. E. Bailey (Ed.), *Children in therapy: Using the family as a resource* (pp. 112–133). W. W. Norton.

Johnson, W. B., & Barnett, J. E. (2011). Preventing problems of professional competence in the face of life-threatening illness. *Professional Psychology: Research and Practice, 42*(2), 285–293. https://doi.org/10.1037/a0024433

Johnson, W. B., Barnett, J. E., Elman, N. S., Forrest, L., & Kaslow, N. J. (2012). The competent community: Toward a vital reformulation of professional ethics. *American Psychologist, 67*(7), 557–569. https://doi.org/10.1037/a0027206

Johnson, W. B., Barnett, J. E., Elman, N. S., Forrest, L., & Kaslow, N. J. (2013). The competence constellation model: A communitarian approach to support professional competence. *Professional Psychology: Research and Practice, 44*(5), 343–354. https://doi.org/10.1037/a0033131

Joinson, C. (1992). Coping with compassion fatigue. *Nursing, 22*(4), 116–120. https://doi.org/10.1097/00152193-199204000-00035

Jordan, K. (2004). The color-coded timeline trauma genogram. *Brief Treatment and Crisis Intervention, 4*(1), 57–70. https://doi.org/10.1093/brief-treatment/mhh005

Jung, C. G. (1976). Aion: Phenomenology of the self (R. F. C. Hull, Trans.). In J. Campbell (Ed.), *The portable Jung* (pp. 139–162). Penguin Classics. (Original work published 1951)

Kader, M. R., Rahman, M. M., Bristi, P. D., & Ahmmed, F. (2024). Change in mental health service utilization from pre- to post-COVID-19 period in the United States. *Heliyon, 10*(22), Article e40454. https://doi.org/10.1016/j.heliyon.2024.e40454

Kailanko, S., Wiebe, S. A., Tasca, G. A., Laitila, A. A., & Allan, R. (2022). Somatic experience of emotion in emotionally focused couple therapy: Experienced trainer therapists' views and experiences. *Journal of Marital and Family Therapy, 48*(3), 677–692. https://doi.org/10.1111/jmft.12543

Kalmakis, K. A., & Chandler, G. E. (2015). Health consequences of adverse childhood experiences: A systematic review. *Journal of the American Association of Nurse Practitioners, 27*(8), 457–465. https://doi.org/10.1002/2327-6924.12215

Kaplin, D., Parente, K., & Santacroce, F. A. (2019). A review of the use of trauma systems therapy to treat refugee children, adolescents, and families. *Journal of Infant, Child, and Adolescent Psychotherapy, 18*(4), 417–431. https://doi.org/10.1080/15289168.2019.1687220

Kaplow, J. B., Layne, C. M., Saltzman, W. R., Cozza, S. J., & Pynoos, R. S. (2013). Using multidimensional grief theory to explore the effects of deployment, reintegration, and death on military youth and families. *Clinical Child and Family Psychology Review, 16*(3), 322–340. https://doi.org/10.1007/s10567-013-0143-1

Karakurt, G., Whiting, K., van Esch, C., Bolen, S. D., & Calabrese, J. R. (2016). Couples therapy for intimate partner violence: A systematic review and meta-analysis. *Journal of Marital and Family Therapy, 42*(4), 567–583. https://doi.org/10.1111/jmft.12178

Karam, E. A., Blow, A. J., Sprenkle, D. H., & Davis, S. D. (2015). Strengthening the systemic ties that bind: Integrating common factors into marriage and family therapy curricula. *Journal of Marital and Family Therapy, 41*(2), 136–149. https://doi.org/10.1111/jmft.12096

Karl, A., Schaefer, M., Malta, L. S., Dörfel, D., Rohleder, N., & Werner, A. (2006). A meta-analysis of structural brain abnormalities in PTSD. *Neuroscience & Biobehavioral Reviews, 30*(7), 1004–1031. https://doi.org/10.1016/j.neubiorev.2006.03.004

Karpman, S. (1968). Fairy tales and script drama analysis. *Transactional Analysis Bulletin, 7*, 39–43.

Kaslow, N. J., Celano, M. P., & Stanton, M. (2005). Training in family psychology: A competencies-based approach. *Family Process, 44*(3), 337–353. https://doi.org/10.1111/j.1545-5300.2005.00063.x

Kaslow, N. J., Farber, E. W., Ammons, C. J., Graves, C. C., Hampton-Anderson, J. N., Lewis, D. E., Lim, N., McKenna, B. G., Penna, S., & Cattie, J. E. (2022). Capability-informed competency approach to lifelong professional development. *Training and Education in Professional Psychology, 16*(2), 182–189. https://doi.org/10.1037/tep0000392

Kaslow, N. J., Kaslow, F. W., & Farber, E. W. (1999). Theories and techniques of marital and family therapy. In M. B. Sussman, S. K. Steinmetz, & G. W. Peterson (Eds.), *Handbook of marriage and the family* (2nd ed., pp. 767–793). Plenum Press. https://doi.org/10.1007/978-1-4757-5367-7_29

Kauffman, C. M. (1992, October). *Countertransference hostage syndrome in the treatment of trauma survivors* [Conference session]. Annual Meeting of the International Society for Traumatic Stress Studies, Los Angeles, CA, United States.

Keilholtz, B. M., & Spencer, C. M. (2022). Couples therapy and intimate partner violence: Considerations, assessment, and treatment modalities. *Practice Innovations, 7*(2), 124–137. https://doi.org/10.1037/pri0000176

Keith, D. V., & Whitaker, C. A. (1982). Experiential-symbolic family therapy. In A. M. Horne & M. M. Ohlsen (Eds.), *Family counseling and therapy* (pp. 43–74). Peacock.

Kelledy, L., & Lyons, B. (2019). Circular causality in family systems theory. In J. L. Lebow, A. L. Chambers, & D. C. Breunlin (Eds.), *Encyclopedia of couple and family therapy* (pp. 1–4). Springer. https://doi.org/10.1007/978-3-319-49425-8_248

Kerig, P. K. (1995). Triangles in the family circle: Effects of family structure on marriage, parenting, and child adjustment. *Journal of Family Psychology, 9*(1), 28–43. https://doi.org/10.1037/0893-3200.9.1.28

Kerig, P. K. (2016). Family systems from a developmental psychopathology perspective. In D. Cicchetti (Ed.), *Developmental psychopathology: Theory and method* (3rd ed., Vol. 1, pp. 580–630). Wiley.

Kerig, P. K., & Alexander, J. F. (2012). Family matters: Integrating trauma treatment into functional family therapy for traumatized delinquent youth. *Journal of Child & Adolescent Trauma, 5*(3), 205–223. https://doi.org/10.1080/19361521.2012.697103

Kerig, P. K., & Lindahl, K. M. (Eds.). (2001). *Family observational coding systems: Resources for systemic research*. Lawrence Erlbaum.

Kerig, P. K., & Swanson, J. A. (2010). Ties that bind: Triangulation, boundary dissolution, and the effects of interparental conflict on child development. In M. S. Schulz, M. K. Pruett, P. K. Kerig, & R. D. Parke (Eds.), *Strengthening couple relationships for optimal child development: Lessons from research and intervention* (pp. 59–76). American Psychological Association. https://doi.org/10.1037/12058-005

Kerr, M. E., & Bowen, M. (1988). *Family evaluation: An approach based on Bowen theory*. W. W. Norton.

Kessler, R. C., Aguilar-Gaxiola, S., Alonso, J., Benjet, C., Bromet, E. J., Cardoso, G., Degenhardt, L., de Girolamo, G., Dinolova, R. V., Ferry, F., Florescu, S. E., Gal, G., Gureje, O., Haro, J. M., Huang, Y., Karam, E. G., Kawakami, N., Lee, S., Lepine, J. P., . . . Koenen, K. C. (2017). Trauma and PTSD in the WHO world mental health surveys. *European Journal of Psychotraumatology, 8*(Suppl. 5), Article 1353383. https://doi.org/10.1080/20008198.2017.1353383

Keyes, C. L. (2007). Promoting and protecting mental health as flourishing: A complementary strategy for improving national mental health. *American Psychologist, 62*(2), 95–108. https://doi.org/10.1037/0003-066X.62.2.95

Keyes, C. L. (2024). *Languishing: How to feel alive again in a world that wears us down*. Crown.

Khafi, T. Y., Yates, T. M., & Luthar, S. S. (2014). Ethnic differences in the developmental significance of parentification. *Family Process, 53*(2), 267–287. https://doi.org/10.1111/famp.12072

Kilmer, R. P., Cook, J. R., & Palamaro Munsell, E. (2010). Moving from principles to practice: Recommended policy changes to promote family-centered care. *American Journal of Community Psychology, 46*(3–4), 332–341. https://doi.org/10.1007/s10464-010-9350-9

Kim, J., Chesworth, B., Franchino-Olsen, H., & Macy, R. J. (2022). A scoping review of vicarious trauma interventions for service providers working with people who have experienced traumatic events. *Trauma, Violence, & Abuse, 23*(5), 1437–1460. https://doi.org/10.1177/1524838021991310

Kiser, L., Connors, K., Gardner, S., Strieder, F., Dowling, L., & Lyons, J. S. (2009). *Family Assessment of Needs and Strengths—Trauma version manual*. https://www.aztrauma.org/wp-content/uploads/2018/01/FANS-Trauma.pdf

Kisiel, C., Conradi, L., Fehrenbach, T., Torgersen, E., & Briggs, E. (2014). Assessing the effects of trauma in children and adolescents in practice settings. *Child and Adolescent Psychiatric Clinics of North America, 23*(2), 223–242. https://doi.org/10.1016/j.chc.2013.12.007

Kisiel, C., Fehrenbach, T., Conradi, L., & Weil, L. (2021). *Trauma-informed assessment with children and adolescents: Strategies to support clinicians*. American Psychological Association. https://doi.org/10.1037/0000233-000

Kisiel, C., Lyons, J. S., Blaustein, M., Fehrenbach, T., Griffin, G., Germain, J., Saxe, G., Ellis, H., & the National Child Traumatic Stress Network. (2013). *Child and adolescent needs and strengths (CANS) manual: The NCTSN CANS Comprehensive—Trauma version*. Praed Foundation.

Kisiel, C., Torgersen, E., Weil, L. E. G., & Fehrenbach, T. (2018). Use of a structured approach to assessment within child welfare: Applications of the child and adolescent needs and strengths-trauma comprehensive (CANS-trauma). In V. Strand & G. Sprang (Eds.), *Trauma responsive child welfare systems* (pp. 105–126). Springer. https://doi.org/10.1007/978-3-319-64602-2_7

Kissane, D. W., & Bloch, S. (2002). *Family focused grief therapy: A model of family-centred care during palliative care and bereavement*. Open University Press.

Kissane, D. W., McKenzie, M., Bloch, S., Moskowitz, C., McKenzie, D. P., & O'Neill, I. (2006). Family focused grief therapy: A randomized, controlled trial in palliative care and bereavement. *American Journal of Psychiatry, 163*(7), 1208–1218. https://doi.org/10.1176/ajp.2006.163.7.1208

Kitchener, B. A., & Jorm, A. F. (2008). Mental health first aid: An international programme for early intervention. *Early Intervention in Psychiatry, 2*(1), 55–61. https://doi.org/10.1111/j.1751-7893.2007.00056.x

Knobloch, L. K., & Theiss, J. A. (2012). Experiences of U.S. military couples during the postdeployment transition: Applying the relational turbulence model. *Journal of Social and Personal Relationships, 29*(4), 423–450. https://doi.org/10.1177/0265407511431186

Knobloch-Fedders, L. M., Pinsof, W. M., & Mann, B. J. (2007). Therapeutic alliance and treatment progress in couple psychotherapy. *Journal of Marital and Family Therapy, 33*(2), 245–257. https://doi.org/10.1111/j.1752-0606.2007.00019.x

Kolko, D. J., Simonich, H., & Loiterstein, A. (2014). Alternatives for families: A cognitive behavioral therapy: An overview and a case example. In S. Timer & A. Urquiza (Eds.), *Evidence-based approaches for the treatment of maltreated children: Considering core components and treatment effectiveness* (pp. 187–212). Springer.

Kolko, D. J., & Swenson, C. C. (2002). *Assessing and treating physically abused children and their families: A cognitive-behavioral approach*. Sage Publications.

Koocher, G. P., & Daniel, J. H. (2012). Treating children and adolescents. In S. J. Knapp, M. C. Gottlieb, M. M. Handelsman, & L. D. VandeCreek (Eds.), *APA handbook of ethics in psychology: Vol. 2. Practice, teaching, and research* (pp. 3–14). American Psychological Association. https://doi.org/10.1037/13272-001

Koocher, G. P., & Keith-Spiegel, P. (2008). *Ethics in psychology and the mental health professions: Standards and cases* (3rd ed.). Oxford University Press.

Kozlowska, K., & Hanney, L. (2002). The network perspective: An integration of attachment and family systems theories. *Family Process, 41*(3), 285–312. https://doi.org/10.1111/j.1545-5300.2002.41303.x

Kruger, J., & Dunning, D. (1999). Unskilled and unaware of it: How difficulties in recognizing one's own incompetence lead to inflated self-assessments. *Journal of Personality and Social Psychology, 77*(6), 1121–1134. https://doi.org/10.1037/0022-3514.77.6.1121

Kuhfuß, M., Maldei, T., Hetmanek, A., & Baumann, N. (2021). Somatic experiencing—Effectiveness and key factors of a body-oriented trauma therapy: A scoping literature review. *European Journal of Psychotraumatology, 12*(1), Article 1929023. https://doi.org/10.1080/20008198.2021.1929023

Kumar, S. A., Brand, B. L., & Courtois, C. A. (2022). The need for trauma training: Clinicians' reactions to training on complex trauma. *Psychological Trauma: Theory, Research, Practice, and Policy, 14*(8), 1387–1394. https://doi.org/10.1037/tra0000515

Landreth, G. L., & Bratton, S. (2019). *Child parent relationship therapy (CPRT) manual: An evidence based 10-session filial therapy model for training parents*. Routledge.

Lanktree, C. B., Briere, J., Godbout, N., Hodges, M., Chen, K., Trimm, L., Adams, B., Maida, C. A., & Freed, W. (2012). Treating multitraumatized, socially marginalized children: Results of a naturalistic treatment outcome study. *Journal of Aggression, Maltreatment & Trauma, 21*(8), 813–828. https://doi.org/10.1080/10926771.2012.722588

La Roche, M. J., & Christopher, M. S. (2009). Changing paradigms from empirically supported treatment to evidence-based practice: A cultural perspective. *Professional Psychology: Research and Practice, 40*(4), 396–402. https://doi.org/10.1037/a0015240

Lawrence, E., Barry, R. A., Brock, R. L., Bunde, M., Langer, A., Ro, E., Fazio, E., Mulryan, L., Hunt, S., Madsen, L., & Dzankovic, S. (2011). The relationship quality interview: Evidence of reliability, convergent and divergent validity, and incremental utility. *Psychological Assessment, 23*(1), 44–63. https://doi.org/10.1037/a0021096

Lawrence, E., Brock, R. L., Barry, R. A., Langer, A., & Bunde, M. (2009). Assessing relationship quality: Development of an interview and implications for couple assessment and intervention. In E. Cuyler & M. Ackhart (Eds.), *Psychology of relationships* (pp. 173–189). Nova Science Publishers.

Lawrence, E., Mazurek, C., & Reardon, K. W. (2021). Comparing recidivism rates among domestically violent men enrolled in ACTV versus Duluth/CBT. *Journal of Consulting and Clinical Psychology, 89*(5), 469–475. https://doi.org/10.1037/ccp0000649

Layne, C. M., Pynoos, R. S., Saltzman, W. R., Arslanagic, B., Black, M., Savjak, N., & Houston, R. (2001). Trauma/grief-focused group psychotherapy: School-based postwar intervention with traumatized Bosnian adolescents. *Group Dynamics: Theory, Research, and Practice, 5*(4), 277–290. https://doi.org/10.1037/1089-2699.5.4.277

Lazarus, R. S., & Folkman, S. (1984). *Stress, appraisal, and coping*. Springer.

Lebow, J. (2005). Integrative family therapy for families experiencing high-conflict divorce. In J. L. Lebow (Ed.), *Handbook of clinical family therapy* (pp. 516–542). Wiley.

Lebow, J. (2014). *Couple and family therapy: An integrative map of the territory*. American Psychological Association. https://doi.org/10.1037/14255-000

Lebow, J., & Stroud, C. B. (2012). Assessment of effective couple and family functioning: Prevailing models and instruments. In F. Walsh (Ed.), *Normal family processes: Growing diversity and complexity* (4th ed., pp. 501–528). Guilford Press.

Lee, A. T., Chin, P., Nambiar, A., & Haskins, N. H. (2023). Addressing intergenerational trauma in Black families: Trauma informed and culturally attuned family therapy. *Journal of Marital and Family Therapy, 49*(2), 447–462. https://doi.org/10.1111/jmft.12632

Lee, M. Y., Greene, G. J., Fraser, J. S., Edwards, S. G., Grove, D., Solovey, A. D., & Scott, P. (2013). Common and specific factors approaches to home-based treatment: I-FAST and MST. *Research on Social Work Practice, 23*(4), 407–418. https://doi.org/10.1177/104973151348318

Lee, M. Y., Greene, G. J., Hsu, K. S., Solovey, A., Grove, D., Fraser, J. S., Washburn, P., & Teater, B. (2009). Utilizing family strengths and resilience: Integrative family and systems treatment with children and adolescents with severe emotional and behavioral problems. *Family Process, 48*(3), 395–416. https://doi.org/10.1111/j.1545-5300.2009.01291.x

Lee, M. Y., Hsu, K. S., Liu, C., Greene, G. J., Fraser, J. S., Grove, D., Solovey, A., Edwards, S. G., & Scott, P. (2016). Treatment efficacy of Integrative Family and Systems Treatment (I-FAST) with and without consultation: The role of model training in the sustainability of evidence-based family treatments. *Administration and Policy in Mental Health and Mental Health Services Research, 43*(4), 579–591. https://doi.org/10.1007/s10488-015-0644-y

Lefevor, G. T., Paiz, J. Y., Milburn, H. E., Sheffield, P. E., & Tamez Guerrero, N. A. (2022). Religiousness and help seeking: Individual, congregational, and clergy factors. *Counselling Psychology Quarterly, 35*(1), 89–109. https://doi.org/10.1080/09515070.2021.1874297

Le Poire, B. A. (2006). *Family communication: Nurturing and control in a changing world.* Sage Publications. https://doi.org/10.4135/9781452233048.n10

Leung, T., Schmidt, F., & Mushquash, C. (2023). A personal history of trauma and experience of secondary traumatic stress, vicarious trauma, and burnout in mental health workers: A systematic literature review. *Psychological Trauma: Theory, Research, Practice, and Policy, 15*(Suppl. 2), S213–S221. https://doi.org/10.1037/tra0001277

Levine, H. B. (2014). Psychoanalysis and trauma. *Psychoanalytic Inquiry, 34*(3), 214–224. https://doi.org/10.1080/07351690.2014.889475

Levine, P. A. (2010). *In an unspoken voice: How the body releases trauma and restores goodness.* North Atlantic Books.

Levitt, H. M., & Piazza-Bonin, E. (2016). Wisdom and psychotherapy: Studying expert therapists' clinical wisdom to explicate common processes. *Psychotherapy Research, 26*(1), 31–47. https://doi.org/10.1080/10503307.2014.937470

Levitt, H. M., & Piazza-Bonin, E. (2017). The professionalization and training of psychologists: The place of clinical wisdom. *Psychotherapy Research, 27*(2), 127–142. https://doi.org/10.1080/10503307.2015.1090034

Lev-Wiesel, R. (2007). Intergenerational transmission of trauma across three generations: A preliminary study. *Qualitative Social Work, 6*(1), 75–94. https://doi.org/10.1177/1473325007074167

Lewis, J. B., & Ickovics, J. R. (2024). Expect with me—Group prenatal care to reduce disparities. *New England Journal of Medicine, 390*(22), 2039–2040. https://doi.org/10.1056/NEJMp2400482

Liddle, H. A. (2009). Multidimensional family therapy: A science-based treatment system for adolescent drug abuse. In J. H. Bray & M. Stanton (Eds.), *The Wiley-Blackwell handbook of family psychology* (pp. 341–354). Wiley-Blackwell. https://doi.org/10.1002/9781444310238.ch23

Lieberman, A. F., Diaz, M. A., Castro, G., & Bucio, G. O. (2020). *Make room for baby: Perinatal child–parent psychotherapy to repair trauma and promote attachment.* Guilford Press.

Lieberman, A. F., Ippen, C. G., & Van Horn, P. (2006). Child–parent psychotherapy: 6-month follow-up of a randomized controlled trial. *Journal of the American Academy of Child & Adolescent Psychiatry, 45*(8), 913–918. https://doi.org/10.1097/01.chi.0000222784.03735.92

Lieberman, A. F., Padrón, E., Van Horn, P., & Harris, W. W. (2005). Angels in the nursery: The intergenerational transmission of benevolent parental influences. *Infant Mental Health Journal: Infancy and Early Childhood, 26*(6), 504–520. https://doi.org/10.1002/imhj.20071

Liebman, R. E., Whitfield, K. M., Sijercic, I., Ennis, N., & Monson, C. M. (2020). Harnessing the healing power of relationships in trauma recovery: A systematic review of cognitive-behavioral conjoint therapy for PTSD. *Current Treatment Options in Psychiatry, 7*(3), 203–220. https://doi.org/10.1007/s40501-020-00211-1

Lilienfeld, S. O., & Basterfield, C. (2020). Reflective practice in clinical psychology: Reflections from basic psychological science. *Clinical Psychology: Science and Practice, 27*(4), Article e12352. https://doi.org/10.1111/cpsp.12352

Lind, C., Anderson, B., & Oberle, K. (2003). Ethical issues in adolescent consent for research. *Nursing Ethics, 10*(5), 504–511. https://doi.org/10.1191/0969733003ne632oa

Lindblad-Goldberg, M., Dore, M., & Stern, L. (1998). *Creating competence from chaos: A comprehensive guide to home-based services*. W. W. Norton.

Lindblad-Goldberg, M., & Northey, W. F. (2013). Ecosystemic structural family therapy: Theoretical and clinical foundations. *Contemporary Family Therapy, 35*(1), 147–160. https://doi.org/10.1007/s10591-012-9224-4

Linehan, M. (2014). *DBT skills training manual*. Guilford Press.

Litvin, J. M., Kaminski, P. L., & Riggs, S. A. (2017). The Complex Trauma Inventory: A self-report measure of posttraumatic stress disorder and complex posttraumatic stress disorder. *Journal of Traumatic Stress, 30*(6), 602–613. https://doi.org/10.1002/jts.22231

Litvin, J. M., Kaminski, P. L., & Ryals, A. (2024). Development of the complex trauma screener: A brief measure of *ICD-11* PTSD and complex PTSD. *Psychiatry Research, 334*, Article 115819. https://doi.org/10.1016/j.psychres.2024.115819

Liu, L., Xu, L., Luo, F., & Li, Y. (2018). Intergenerational transmission of interpersonal strengths: The role of parent gender, family processes, and child characteristics. *Journal of Adolescence, 67*(1), 66–76. https://doi.org/10.1016/j.adolescence.2018.06.005

Liu, R., Chao, M. T., Jostad-Laswell, A., & Duncan, L. G. (2017). Does CenteringPregnancy group prenatal care affect the birth experience of underserved women? A mixed methods analysis. *Journal of Immigrant and Minority Health, 19*(2), 415–422. https://doi.org/10.1007/s10903-016-0371-9

Lohrasbe, R. S., & Ogden, P. (2017). Somatic resources: Sensorimotor psychotherapy approach to stabilising arousal in child and family treatment. *Australian and New Zealand Journal of Family Therapy, 38*(4), 573–581. https://doi.org/10.1002/anzf.1270

Longo, V., Saadati, N., & Karakus, M. (2024). Exploring the role of extended family in child rearing practices across different cultures. *Journal of Psychosociological Research in Family and Culture, 2*(4), 4–12. https://doi.org/10.61838/kman.jprfc.2.4.2

López-Zerón, G., & Blow, A. (2017). The role of relationships and families in healing from trauma. *Journal of Family Therapy, 39*(4), 580–597. https://doi.org/10.1111/1467-6427.12089

López-Zerón, G., & Parra-Cardona, J. R. (2015). Elements of change across community-based trauma interventions. *Journal of Systemic Therapies, 34*(3), 60–76. https://doi.org/10.1521/jsyt.2015.34.3.60

Ludick, M., & Figley, C. M. (2016). Toward a mechanism for secondary trauma induction and reduction: Reimagining a theory of secondary traumatic stress. *Traumatology, 23*(1), 112–123. https://doi.org/10.1037/trm0000096

Lyons, J. S., Uziel-Miller, N. D., Reyes, F., & Sokol, P. T. (2000). Strengths of children and adolescents in residential settings: Prevalence and associations with psychopathology and discharge placement. *Journal of the American Academy of Child & Adolescent Psychiatry, 39*(2), 176–181. https://doi.org/10.1097/00004583-200002000-00017

Lyons-Ruth, K., & Jacobvitz, D. (2018). Attachment disorganization from infancy to adulthood: Neurobiological correlates, parenting contexts, and pathways to disorder. In J. Cassidy & P. R. Shaver (Eds.), *Handbook of attachment: Theory, research, and clinical applications* (3rd ed., pp. 667–695). Guilford Press.

Magruder, K. M., McLaughlin, K. A., & Elmore Borbon, D. L. (2017). Trauma is a public health issue. *European Journal of Psychotraumatology, 8*(1), Article 1375338. https://doi.org/10.1080/20008198.2017.1375338

Main, M., & Hesse, E. (1990). Parents' unresolved traumatic experiences are related to infant disorganized attachment status: Is frightened and/or frightening parental behavior the linking mechanism? In M. T. Greenberg, D. Cicchetti, & E. M. Cummings (Eds.), *Attachment in the preschool years: Theory, research, and intervention* (pp. 161–182). University of Chicago Press.

Malarbi, S., Abu-Rayya, H. M., Muscara, F., & Stargatt, R. (2017). Neuropsychological functioning of childhood trauma and post-traumatic stress disorder: A meta-analysis. *Neuroscience & Biobehavioral Reviews, 72*, 68–86. https://doi.org/10.1016/j.neubiorev.2016.11.004

Malawista, K. L. (2004). Rescue fantasies in child therapy: Countertransference/transference enactments. *Child and Adolescent Social Work Journal, 21*(4), 373–386. https://doi.org/10.1023/b:casw.0000035222.16367.32

Malberg, N., Jurist, E., Bate, J., & Dangerfield, M. (2023). *Working with parents in therapy: A mentalization-based approach*. American Psychological Association. https://doi.org/10.1037/0000341-000

Malda-Castillo, J., Browne, C., & Perez-Algorta, G. (2019). Mentalization-based treatment and its evidence-base status: A systematic literature review. *Psychology and Psychotherapy: Theory, Research and Practice, 92*(4), 465–498. https://doi.org/10.1111/papt.12195

Malmberg–Heimonen, I., Finne, J., Grete Tøge, A., Pontoppidan, M., Dion, J., Truls Tømmerås, T., & Pedersen, E. (2024). Interventions to reduce child maltreatment: A systematic review with a narrative synthesis. *International Journal on Child Maltreatment, 7,* 459–475. https://doi.org/10.1007/s42448-024-00196-x

Mann, M., McMillan, J. E., Silver, E. J., & Stein, R. E. (2021). Children and adolescents with disabilities and exposure to disasters, terrorism, and the COVID-19 pandemic: A scoping review. *Current Psychiatry Reports, 23*(12), Article 80. https://doi.org/10.1007/s11920-021-01295-z

Marrow, M. T., Knudsen, K. J., Olafson, E., & Bucher, S. E. (2014). The value of implementing TARGET within a trauma-informed juvenile justice setting. In P. Kerig (Ed.), *Psychological trauma and juvenile delinquency* (pp. 174–187). Routledge.

Masiran, R., Ibrahim, N., Awang, H., & Lim, P.Y. (2023). The positive and negative aspects of parentification: An integrated review. *Children and Youth Services Review, 144,* Article 106709. https://doi.org/10.1016/j.childyouth.2022.106709

Maslach, C., & Leiter, M. P. (2016). Understanding the burnout experience: Recent research and its implications for psychiatry. *World Psychiatry, 15*(2), 103–111. https://doi.org/10.1002/wps.20311

Masten, A. S., Tyrell, F. A., & Cicchetti, D. (2023). Resilience in development: Pathways to multisystem integration. *Development and Psychopathology, 35*(5), 2103–2112. https://doi.org/10.1017/S0954579423001293

Masterson, M. P., Schuler, T. A., & Kissane, D. W. (2013). Family focused grief therapy: A versatile intervention in palliative care and bereavement. *Bereavement Care, 32*(3), 117–123. https://doi.org/10.1080/02682621.2013.854544

Mathieu, F. (2012). *The compassion fatigue workbook: Creative tools for transforming compassion fatigue and vicarious traumatization.* Routledge/Taylor & Francis Group.

Matulis, S., Resick, P. A., Rosner, R., & Steil, R. (2014). Developmentally adapted cognitive processing therapy for adolescents suffering from posttraumatic stress disorder after childhood sexual or physical abuse: A pilot study. *Clinical Child and Family Psychology Review, 17*(2), 173–190. https://doi.org/10.1007/s10567-013-0156-9

Maurović, I., Liebenberg, L., & Ferić, M. (2020). A review of family resilience: Understanding the concept and operationalization challenges to inform research and practice. *Child Care in Practice, 26*(4), 337–357. https://doi.org/10.1080/13575279.2020.1792838

Mavridis, C., Harkness, S., Super, C. M., & Liu, J. L. (2019). Family workers, stress, and the limits of self-care. *Children and Youth Services Review, 103,* 236–246. https://doi.org/10.1016/j.childyouth.2019.06.011

Maxey, V. A. (2021). The intersectional growth model: The Satir growth model informed by intersectional feminism. *Contemporary Family Therapy, 43*(1), 54–68. https://doi.org/10.1007/s10591-020-09553-7

McCann, I. L., & Pearlman, L. A. (1990). Vicarious traumatization: A framework for understanding the psychological effects of working with victims. *Journal of Traumatic Stress, 3*(1), 131–149. https://doi.org/10.1007/BF00975140

McConaughy, S. H. (2005). *Clinical interviews for children and adolescents: Assessment to intervention*. Guilford Press.

McDonald, R., & Grych, J. H. (2006). Young children's appraisals of interparental conflict: Measurement and links with adjustment problems. *Journal of Family Psychology, 20*(1), 88–99. https://doi.org/10.1037/0893-3200.20.1.88

McDowell, T. (2015). *Applying critical social theories to family therapy practice*. Springer.

McElroy, L. P., & McElroy, R. A., Jr. (1991). Countertransference issues in the treatment of incest families. *Psychotherapy: Theory, Research, Practice, Training, 28*(1), 48–54. https://doi.org/10.1037/0033-3204.28.1.48

McGauran, A., Brooks, M., & Khan, R. (2019). The role of emotional resilience, childhood parentification, and attachment style on antisocial behavior in adulthood: A comparison of an offender and normative population. *Journal of Criminal Psychology, 9*(2), 75–87. https://doi.org/10.1108/JCP-08-2018-0035

McGoldrick, M. (1982). Through the looking glass: Supervision of a trainee's "trigger" family. In R. Wiffen & J. Byng-Hall (Eds.), *Family therapy supervision* (pp. 17–37). Academic Press.

McGoldrick, M., & Gerson, R. (1985). *Genograms in family assessment*. W. W. Norton.

McGoldrick, M., Gerson, R., & Petry, S. (2008). *Genograms in family assessment* (3rd ed.). W. W. Norton.

McGoldrick, M., Preto, N. A. G., & Carter, B. A. (2015). *The expanding family life cycle: Individual, family, and social perspectives*. Pearson Education.

McGoldrick, M., & Shibusawa, T. (2012). The family life cycle. In F. Walsh (Ed.), *Normal family processes: Growing diversity and complexity* (4th ed., pp. 375–398). Guilford Press.

McIntosh, J. M., Lyon, A. R., Carlson, G. A., Everette, C. D. B., & Loera, S. (2008). Measuring the mesosystem: A survey and critique of approaches to cross setting measurement for ecological research and models of collaborative care. *Families, Systems, & Health, 26*(1), 86–104. https://doi.org/10.1037/1091-7527.26.1.86

McLaughlin, K. D. (2017). Ethical considerations for clinicians treating victims and perpetrators of intimate partner violence. *Ethics and Behavior, 27*(1), 43–52. https://doi.org/10.1080/10508422.2016.1185012

McWey, L. M. (2022). Systemic interventions for traumatic event exposure: A 2010–2019 decade review. *Journal of Marital and Family Therapy, 48*(1), 204–230. https://doi.org/10.1111/jmft.12547

Mencken, H. L. (1917, November 16). The divine afflatus. *New York Evening Mail, 16*.

Méndez, M., Flores-Haro, G., & Zucker, L. (2020). The (in)visible victims of disaster: Understanding the vulnerability of undocumented Latino/a and indigenous immigrants. *Geoforum*, *116*, 50–62. https://doi.org/10.1016/j.geoforum.2020.07.007

Merali, N. (2002). Culturally informed ethical decision making in situations of suspected child abuse. *Canadian Journal of Counselling*, *36*(3), 233–244.

Messer, E. P., Eismann, E. A., Folger, A. T., Grass, A., Bemerer, J., & Bensman, H. (2024). Comparative effectiveness of parent–child interaction therapy based on trauma exposure and attrition. *Psychological Trauma: Theory, Research, Practice, and Policy*, *16*(Suppl. 1), S97–S105. https://doi.org/10.1037/tra0001259

Messer, E. P., Greiner, M. V., Beal, S. J., Eismann, E. A., Cassedy, A., Gurwitch, R. H., Boat, B. W., Bensman, H., Bemerer, J., Hennigan, M., Greenwell, S., & Eiler-Sims, P. (2018). Child adult relationship enhancement (CARE): A brief, skills-building training for foster caregivers to increase positive parenting practices. *Children and Youth Services Review*, *90*, 74–82. https://doi.org/10.1016/j.childyouth.2018.05.017

Midori-Hanna, S. (2018). *The practice of family therapy: Key elements across models* (5th ed.). Routledge. https://doi.org/10.4324/9781351051460

Mikulincer, M., & Shaver, P. R. (2016). *Attachment in adulthood: Structure, dynamics, and change* (2nd ed.). Guilford Press.

Mikulincer, M., Shaver, P. R., & Solomon, Z. (2015). An attachment perspective on traumatic and posttraumatic reactions. In M. Safir, H. Wallach, & A. Rizzo (Eds.), *Future directions in post-traumatic stress disorder* (pp. 79–96). Springer. https://doi.org/10.1007/978-1-4899-7522-5_4

Miller, B. C. (2021). *Reducing secondary traumatic stress: Skills for sustaining a career in the helping professions*. Routledge.

Miller, D. A. (1981). The “sandwich” generation: Adult children of the aging. *Social Work*, *26*(5), 419–423. https://www.jstor.org/stable/23712207

Miller, I. W., Ryan, C. E., Keitner, G. I., Bishop, D. S., & Epstein, N. B. (2000). The McMaster approach to families: Theory, assessment, treatment and research. *Journal of Family Therapy*, *22*(2), 168–189. https://doi.org/10.1111/1467-6427.00145

Minuchin, S. (1974). *Families and family therapy*. Harvard University Press.

Minuchin, S., & Fishman, H. C. (1981). *Family therapy techniques*. Harvard University Press.

Misevičė, M., Gervinskaitė-Paulaitienė, L., Lesinskienė, S., & Grauslienė, I. (2024). Trust-Based Relational Intervention (TBRI) impact for traumatized children—Meaningful change on attachment security and mental health after one year. *Children*, *11*(4), Article 411. https://doi.org/10.3390/children11040411

Mones, A. G., & Schwartz, R. C. (2007). The functional hypothesis: A family systems contribution toward an understanding of the healing process of the common factors. *Journal of Psychotherapy Integration*, *17*(4), 314–329. https://doi.org/10.1037/1053-0479.17.4.314

Monson, C. M., & Fredman, S. J. (2012). *Cognitive-behavioral conjoint therapy for PTSD: Harnessing the healing power of relationships*. Guilford Press.

Monson, C. M., & Fredman, S. J. (2021). Couple/family interventions for PTSD. *PTSD Research Quarterly, 32*(3), 1–9.

Monson, C. M., Fredman, S. J., & Dekel, R. (2010). Posttraumatic stress disorder in an interpersonal context. In J. G. Beck (Ed.), *Interpersonal processes in the anxiety disorders: Implications for understanding psychopathology and treatment* (pp. 179–208). American Psychological Association. https://doi.org/10.1037/12084-007

Montgomery, E., Just-Østergaard, E., & Jervelund, S. S. (2019). Transmitting trauma: A systematic review of the risk of child abuse perpetrated by parents exposed to traumatic events. *International Journal of Public Health, 64*(2), 241–251. https://doi.org/10.1007/s00038-018-1185-4

Moos, R. H., & Moos, B. S. (2002). *Family environment scale manual: Development, applications, research* (3rd ed.). Center for Health Care Evaluation, Department of Veterans Affairs and Stanford University Medical Centers.

Moosman, J. L. (2002). *Vicarious traumatization: The effects of empathy and trait arousability* [Unpublished doctoral dissertation]. George Mason University.

Motz, A., Dennis, M., & Aiyegbusi, A. (2020). *Invisible trauma: Women, difference and the criminal justice system*. Routledge. https://doi.org/10.4324/9781315390000

Muntigl, P., & Horvath, A. O. (2016). A conversation analytic study of building and repairing the alliance in family therapy. *Journal of Family Therapy, 38*(1), 102-119. https://doi.org/10.1111/1467-6427.12109

Murphy, C. M., & O'Farrell, T. J. (1997). Couple communication patterns of maritally aggressive and nonaggressive male alcoholics. *Journal of Studies on Alcohol, 58*(1), 83–90. https://doi.org/10.15288/jsa.1997.58.83

Murray, C. E. (2006). Controversy, constraints, and context: Understanding family violence through family systems theory. *The Family Journal, 14*(3), 234–239. https://doi.org/10.1177/1066480706287277

Murry, V. M., & Lippold, M. A. (2018). Parenting practices in diverse family structures: Examination of adolescents' development and adjustment. *Journal of Research on Adolescence, 28*(3), 650–664. https://doi.org/10.1111/jora.12390

Napier, A. Y., & Whitaker, C. A. (1978). *The family crucible*. Harper & Row.

Narimani, M., & Taghizadeh Hir, S. (2021). Effectiveness of child–parent relationship therapy (CPRT) on parenting stress and child–parent relationship of mothers of children with attention deficit/hyperactivity disorder. *Scientific Research Quarterly of Woman and Culture, 13*(48), 83–98.

National Association of Social Workers. (2021). *Code of ethics*. https://www.socialworkers.org/About/Ethics/Code-of-Ethics/Code-of-Ethics-English

National Child Traumatic Stress Network. (2019). *FCT: Family centered treatment*. https://www.nctsn.org/interventions/family-centered-treatment

National Child Traumatic Stress Network, Complex Trauma Task Force. (2003). *Complex trauma in children and adolescents* [White paper]. https://www.nctsn.org/sites/default/files/resources/complex_trauma_in_children_and_adolescents.pdf

National Child Traumatic Stress Network, Family Systems Collaborative Group. (2011). *Family trauma assessment: Tip sheet for clinicians*. National Center for Child Traumatic Stress. https://www.nctsn.org/resources/family-trauma-assessment-tips-clinicians

National Child Traumatic Stress Network, & National Center for PTSD. (2006). *Psychological first aid: Field operations guide* (2nd ed.). https://www.nctsn.org/resources/psychological-first-aid-pfa-field-operations-guide-2nd-edition

National Child Traumatic Stress Network, & National Center for PTSD. (2010). *Skills for psychological recovery: Field operations guide*. https://www.nctsn.org/resources/skills-for-psychological-recovery

National Institute for Health and Care Excellence. (2018). *Guideline no. 116: Post-traumatic stress disorder*. https://www.nice.org.uk/guidance/ng116/evidence/supplement-1-methods-chapter-pdf-6773944429

National Institutes of Mental Health. (n.d.). *Traumatic stress research program*. U.S. Department of Health and Human Services, National Institutes of Health. Retrieved August 2025, from https://www.nimh.nih.gov/about/organization/dtr/traumatic-stress-research-and-dimensional-measurement-and-intervention-program

Neff, K. D., Knox, M. C., Long, P., & Gregory, K. (2020). Caring for others without losing yourself: An adaptation of the mindful self-compassion program for healthcare communities. *Journal of Clinical Psychology, 76*(9), 1543–1562. https://doi.org/10.1002/jclp.23007

Negash, S., Carlson, S. H., & Linder, J. N. (2018). Emotionally focused therapy and eye movement desensitization and reprocessing: An integrated treatment to heal the trauma of infidelity. *Couple and Family Psychology: Research and Practice, 7*(3–4), 143–157. https://doi.org/10.1037/cfp0000107

Negash, S., & Sahin, S. (2011). Compassion fatigue in marriage and family therapy: Implications for therapists and clients. *Journal of Marital and Family Therapy, 37*(1), 1–13. https://doi.org/10.1111/j.1752-0606.2009.00147.x

Nelson-Gardell, D., & Harris, D. (2003). Childhood abuse history, secondary traumatic stress, and child welfare workers. *Child Welfare, 82*(1), 5–26. https://www.jstor.org/stable/45390105

Neumann, D. A., & Gamble, S. J. (1995). Issues in the professional development of psychotherapists: Countertransference and vicarious traumatization in the new trauma therapist. *Psychotherapy, 32*(2), 341–347. https://doi.org/10.1037/0033-3204.32.2.341

Newby, L. W., Brown, R. T., Pawletko, T. M., Gold, S. H., & Whitt, J. K. (2000). Social skills and psychological adjustment of child and adolescent cancer survivors. *Psychooncology, 9*(2), 13–126. https://doi.org/10.1002/(sici)1099-1611(200003/04)9:2<113::aid-pon432>3.0.co;2-f

Nichols, M., & Schwartz, R. (2004). *Family therapy: Concepts and methods* (6th ed.). Allyn & Bacon.

Nielsen, L. E. (2014). *Trust-based relational intervention (TBRI) for adopted children receiving therapy in an outpatient setting* [Honors project]. Illinois Wesleyan University. https://digitalcommons.iwu.edu/psych_honproj/165

Niño, A., & Zeytinoglu-Saydam, S. (2020). Helping supervisees use their self in their clinical work: The person-of-the-therapist training model (POTT) in supervision. *Journal of Family Psychotherapy, 31*(3–4), 96–113. https://doi.org/10.1080/08975353.2020.1804799

Norcross, J. C., & Wampold, B. E. (2018). A new therapy for each patient: Evidence-based relationships and responsiveness. *Journal of Clinical Psychology, 74*(11), 1889–1906. https://doi.org/10.1002/jclp.22678

O'Connor, C., Brown, G., Debono, J., Suty, L., & Joffe, H. (2025). How trauma is represented on social media: Analysis of #trauma content on TikTok. *Psychological Trauma: Theory, Research, Practice, and Policy, 17*(Suppl. 1), S132–S138. https://doi.org/10.1037/tra0001792

Office of the Surgeon General. (2024). *Parents under pressure: The U.S. Surgeon General's advisory on the mental health & well-being of parents*. U.S. Department of Health and Human Services. https://www.ncbi.nlm.nih.gov/books/NBK606662/

Ogden, P., & Fisher, J. (2015). *Sensorimotor psychotherapy: Interventions for trauma and attachment*. W. W. Norton.

Ogden, P., Minton, K., & Pain, C. (2006). *Trauma and the body: A sensorimotor approach to psychotherapy*. W. W. Norton.

Olson, D. H. (1993). Circumplex model of marital and family systems: Assessing family functioning. In F. Walsh (Ed.), *Normal family processes* (2nd ed., pp. 104–137). Guilford Press.

Olson, D. H. (2000). Circumplex model of marital and family systems. *Journal of Family Therapy, 22*(2), 144–167. https://doi.org/10.1111/1467-6427.00144

Olson, D. H. (2011). FACES IV and the circumplex model: Validation study. *Journal of Marital and Family Therapy, 37*(1), 64–80. https://doi.org/10.1111/j.1752-0606.2009.00175.x

Olson, D. H., & Gorall, D. M. (2003). Circumplex model of marital and family systems. In F. Walsh (Ed.), *Normal family processes: Growing diversity and complexity* (3rd ed., pp. 514–548). Guilford Press. https://doi.org/10.4324/9780203428436_chapter_19

Omylinska-Thurston, J., & James, P. E. (2011). The therapist's use of self: A closer look at the processes within congruence. *Counselling Psychology Review, 26*(3), 20–33. https://doi.org/10.53841/bpscpr.2011.26.3.20

Orlinsky, D. E., Schofield, M. J., Schroder, T., & Kazantzis, N. (2011). Utilization of personal therapy by psychotherapists: A practice-friendly review and a new study. *Journal of Clinical Psychology, 67*(8), 828–842. https://doi.org/10.1002/jclp.20821

Owen, J., & Tao, K. W. (2025, May 28). *Cultivating connection through multicultural orientation in a polarized world* [Webinar]. The Albert and Jessie Danielsen Institute Speaker Series, Boston University.

Owen, J., Tao, K. W., Drinane, J. M., Hook, J., Davis, D. E., & Kune, N. F. (2016). Client perceptions of therapists' multicultural orientation: Cultural (missed) opportunities and cultural humility. *Professional Psychology: Research and Practice*, *47*(1), 30–37. https://doi.org/10.1037/pro0000046

Painter, W. E., Jr., & Smith, L. B. (2020). *The definitive report for family centered treatment*. Family Centered Treatment Foundation. https://static1.squarespace.com/static/57850a09d2b857904415f3fb/t/60400b501b4f33542c6f2ac0/1614809937985/The+Definitive+Report+for+Family+Centered+Treatment+R2020+%281%29.pdf

Paivio, S. C., & Pascual-Leone, A. (2023). *Emotion-focused therapy for complex trauma: An integrative approach* (2nd ed.). American Psychological Association. https://doi.org/10.1037/0000336-000

Panichelli, C. (2013). Humor, joining, and reframing in psychotherapy: Resolving the auto-double-bind. *American Journal of Family Therapy*, *41*(5), 437–451. https://doi.org/10.1080/01926187.2012.755393

Papero, D. V. (2017). Trauma and the family: A systems-oriented approach. *Australian and New Zealand Journal of Family Therapy*, *38*(4), 582–594. https://doi.org/10.1002/anzf.1269

Park, C. L. (2022). Meaning making following trauma. *Frontiers in Psychology*, *13*, Article 844891. https://doi.org/10.3389/fpsyg.2022.844891

Patterson, G. R., & Forgatch, M. S. (1995). Predicting future clinical adjustment from treatment outcome and process variables. *Psychological Assessment*, *7*(3), 275–285. https://doi.org/10.1037/1040-3590.7.3.275

Patterson, T. (2013). Ethical and legal considerations in family psychology. In J. H. Bray & M. Stanton (Eds.), *Wiley-Blackwell handbook of family psychology* (pp. 165–182). Wiley-Blackwell.

Pearlman, L. A., & Saakvitne, K. W. (1995). *Trauma and the therapist: Countertransference and vicarious traumatization in psychotherapy with incest survivors*. W. W. Norton.

Peebles-Kleiger, M. J. (2000). Pediatric and neonatal intensive care hospitalization as traumatic stressor: Implications for intervention. *Bulletin of the Menninger Clinic*, *64*(2), 257–280.

Peltz, J. S., Rogge, R. D., Rogosch, F. A., Cicchetti, D., & Toth, S. L. (2015). The benefits of child–parent psychotherapy to marital satisfaction. *Families, Systems, & Health*, *33*(4), 372–382. https://doi.org/10.1037/fsh0000149

Perilloux, C., Duntley, J. D., & Buss, D. M. (2012). The costs of rape. *Archives of Sexual Behavior*, *41*(5), 1099–1106. https://doi.org/10.1007/s10508-011-9863-9

Perry, B. D. (2019). The neurosequential model. In J. Tucci, J. Mitchell, & E. Tronick (Eds.), *The handbook of therapeutic care for children: Evidence-informed approaches to working with traumatized children and adolescents in foster, kinship and adoptive care* (pp. 137–158). Jessica Kingsley Publishers.

Pew Research Center. (2019). *First- and second-generation share of the population, 1900–2017*. https://www.pewresearch.org/chart/first-and-second-generation-share-of-the-population/

Piccolo, M. S. (2019). Listening to somatosensory states in psychoanalysis: Body, trauma, and poetry. *Psychoanalytic Inquiry, 39*(8), 557–570. https://doi.org/10.1080/07351690.2019.1671070

Pickover, A. M., Lipinski, A. J., Dodson, T. S., Tran, H. N., Woodward, M. J., & Beck, J. G. (2017). Demand/withdraw communication in the context of intimate partner violence: Implications for psychological outcomes. *Journal of Anxiety Disorders, 52*, 95–102. https://doi.org/10.1016/j.janxdis.2017.07.002

Pino, C., Simons, N., & Slowinowski, M. J. (1984). The Children's Family Environment Scale (CFES). *Family Therapy. 11*(1), 85–86.

Pinsof, W. M. (2017). The Systemic Therapy Inventory of Change—STIC: A multi-systemic and multi-dimensional system to integrate science into psychotherapeutic practice. In T. Tilden & B. E. Wampold (Eds.), *Routine outcome monitoring in couple and family therapy: The empirically informed therapist* (pp. 85–101). Springer. https://doi.org/10.1007/978-3-319-50675-3_5

Pistorius, K. D., Feinauer, L. L., Harper, J. M., Stahmann, R. F., & Miller, R. B. (2008). Working with sexually abused children. *The American Journal of Family Therapy, 36*(3), 181–195. https://doi.org/10.1080/01926180701291204

Plant, D. T., Pawlby, S., Pariante, C. M., & Jones, F. W. (2018). When one childhood meets another—Maternal childhood trauma and offspring child psychopathology: A systematic review. *Clinical Child Psychology and Psychiatry, 23*(3), 483–500. https://doi.org/10.1177/1359104517742186

Platt, L. F., & Skowron, E. A. (2013). The Family Genogram Interview: Reliability and validity of a new interview protocol. *The Family Journal, 21*(1), 35–45. https://doi.org/10.1177/1066480712456817

Porges, S. W. (2011). *The polyvagal theory: Neurophysiological foundations of emotions, attachment, communication, and self-regulation*. W. W. Norton.

Prescott, A., Bank, L., Reid, J. B., Knutson, J. F., Burraston, B. O., & Eddy, J. M. (2000). The veridicality of punitive childhood experiences reported by adolescents and young adults. *Child Abuse & Neglect, 24*(3), 411–423. https://doi.org/10.1016/s0145-2134(99)00153-2

Prins, A., Bovin, M. J., Kimerling, R., Kaloupek, D. G., Marx, B. P., Pless Kaiser, A., & Schnurr, P. P. (2015). The Primary Care PTSD Screen for *DSM-5* (PC-PTSD-5). *Journal of General Internal Medicine, 31*(10), 1206–1211. https://doi.org/10.1007/s11606-016-3703-5

Pu, D. F., & Rodriguez, C. M. (2021). Spillover and crossover effects: Mothers' and fathers intimate partner violence, parent–child aggression risk, and child behavior problems. *Child Maltreatment, 26*(4), 420–430. https://doi.org/10.1177/1077559520985936

Pukay-Martin, N. D., Fredman, S. J., Martin, C. E., Le, Y., Haney, A., Sullivan, C., Monson, C. M., & Chard, K. M. (2022). Effectiveness of cognitive behavioral conjoint therapy for posttraumatic stress disorder (PTSD) in a U.S. Veterans Affairs PTSD clinic. *Journal of Traumatic Stress, 35*(2), 644–658. https://doi.org/10.1002/jts.22781

Purvis, K. B., Cross, D. R., Dansereau, D. F., & Parris, S. R. (2013). Trust-based relational intervention (TBRI): A systemic approach to complex developmental trauma. *Child & Youth Services, 34*(4), 360–386. https://doi.org/10.1080/0145935X.2013.859906

Quinnett, P. (2012). *QPR gatekeeper training for suicide prevention: The model, theory and research.* QPR Institute. https://qprinstitute.com/uploads/QPR%20Theory%20Paper.pdf

Rambo, A., & Hibel, J. (2013). What is family therapy? Underlying premises. In A. Rambo, C. West, A. Schooley, & T. V. Boyd (Eds.), *Family therapy review: Contrasting contemporary models* (pp. 3–8). Routledge, Taylor & Francis Group.

Ramey, H. L., Tarulli, D., Frijters, J. C., & Fisher, L. (2009). A sequential analysis of externalizing in narrative therapy with children. *Contemporary Family Therapy, 31*(4), 262–279. https://doi.org/10.1007/s10591-009-9095-5

Rauvola, R. S., Vega, D. M., & Lavigne, K. N. (2019). Compassion fatigue, secondary traumatic stress, and vicarious traumatization: A qualitative review and research agenda. *Occupational Health Science, 3*(3), 297–336. https://doi.org/10.1007/s41542-019-00045-1

Reese, L. R. E., & Vera, E. M. (2007). Culturally relevant prevention: The scientific and practical considerations of community-based programs. *The Counseling Psychologist, 35*(6), 763–778. https://doi.org/10.1177/0011000007304588

Reis, B. E. (2019). *Creative repetition and intersubjectivity: Contemporary Freudian explorations of trauma, memory, and clinical process.* Routledge.

Resnick, P. A., Monson, C. M., & Chard, K. M. (2016). *Cognitive processing therapy for PTSD: A comprehensive manual.* Guilford Press.

Reynolds, C. R., & Kamphaus, R. W. (1992). *Behavior assessment system for children.* American Guidance Service.

Rich, K. D. (1997). Vicarious traumatization: A preliminary study. In S. B. Edmunds (Ed.), *Impact: Working with sexual abusers* (pp. 75–88). Safer Society Press.

Richardson, C. M., Trusty, W. T., & George, K. A. (2020). Trainee wellness: Self-critical perfectionism, self-compassion, depression, and burnout among doctoral trainees in psychology. *Counselling Psychology Quarterly, 33*(2), 187–198. https://doi.org/10.1080/09515070.2018.1509839

Ridenour, T. A., Greenberg, M. T., & Cook, E. T. (2006). Structure and validity of people in my life: A self-report measure of attachment in late childhood. *Journal of Youth and Adolescence, 35*(6), 1037–1053. https://doi.org/10.1007/s10964-006-9070-5

Riggs, S. A. (2010). Childhood emotional abuse and the attachment system across the life cycle: What theory and research tell us. *Journal of Aggression,*

Maltreatment & Trauma, 19(1), 5–51. https://doi.org/10.1080/10926770903475968

Riggs, S. A. (2017). Tasks for CFP educators and trainers. *The Family Psychologist, 33*(3), 5–6.

Riggs, S. A., Gomez, J., Pollard, S., Sanford, G., & Wise, C. (2020). *Couple and family psychology education and training guidelines*. American Psychological Association Society for Couple and Family Psychology.

Riggs, S. A., Jacobvitz, D., & Hazen, N. (2002). Adult attachment and history of psychotherapy in a normative sample. *Psychotherapy: Theory, Research, Practice, Training, 39*(4), 283–296. https://doi.org/10.1037/0033-3204.39.4.344

Riggs, S. A., Raiche, E., Creech, S., McGuffin, J., & Romero, D. (2020). Attachment, couple communication, and family functioning in relation to psychological distress among service members and veterans. *Couple and Family Psychology: Research and Practice, 9*(4), 239–255. https://doi.org/10.1037/cfp0000154

Riggs, S. A., & Riggs, D. S. (2011). Risk and resilience in military families experiencing deployment: The role of the family attachment network. *Journal of Family Psychology, 25*(5), 675–687. https://doi.org/10.1037/a0025286

Ringland, V. (2019). Indigenous trauma healing: A modern model. *Australian Counselling Research Journal, 13*(1), 1–7.

Rix, R. (2000). Trauma, science, and the law: A brief history of trauma research and the social response. *Journal of Aggression, Maltreatment & Trauma, 3*(2), 1–47. https://doi.org/10.1300/J146v03n02_01

Rober, P., & Seltzer, M. (2010). Avoiding colonizer positions in the therapy room: Some ideas about the challenges of dealing with the dialectic of misery and resources in families. *Family Process, 49*(1), 123–137. https://doi.org/10.1111/j.1545-5300.2010.01312.x

Rollins, A. L., Eliacin, J., Russ-Jara, A. L., Monroe-Devita, M., Wasmuth, S., Flanagan, M. E., Morse, G. A., Leiter, M., & Salyers, M. P. (2021). Organizational conditions that influence work engagement and burnout: A qualitative study of mental health workers. *Psychiatric Rehabilitation Journal, 44*(3), 229–237. https://doi.org/10.1037/prj0000472

Rosenthal, M. (2021). Intergenerational trauma: An embodied experience. *International Body Psychotherapy Journal, 20*(2), 80–86.

Roulon-Arroyo, B., Oosterhoff, B., Layne, C. M., Steinberg, A. M., Pynoos, R. S., & Kaplow, J. B. (2019). The UCLA PTSD Reaction Index for *DSM-5* brief form: A screening tool for trauma-exposed youth. *Journal of the American Academy of Child and Adolescent Psychiatry, 59*(3), 434–443. https://doi.org/10.1016/j.jaac.2019.06.015

Rowa, K., Kerig, P. K., & Geller, J. (2001). The family and anorexia nervosa: Examining parent–child boundary problems. *European Eating Disorders Review, 9*(2), 97–114. https://doi.org/10.1002/erv.383

Ruddy, N. B., & McDaniel, S. H. (2024). *A systemic approach to behavioral healthcare integration: Context matters*. American Psychological Association. https://doi.org/10.1037/0000381-000

Runyon, M. K., & Deblinger, E. (2013). *Combined parent–child cognitive behavioral therapy: An approach to empower families at-risk for child physical abuse*. Oxford University Press.

Rupert, P. A., Hartman, E. R. T., & Miller, A. S. O. (2013). Work demands and resources, work–family conflict, and family functioning among practicing psychologists. *Professional Psychology: Research and Practice, 44*(5), 283–289. https://doi.org/10.1037/a0034494

Rupert, P. A., Stevanovic, P., & Hunley, H. A. (2009). Work–family conflict and burnout among practicing psychologists. *Professional Psychology: Research and Practice, 40*(1), 54–61. https://doi.org/10.1037/a0012538

Saakvitne, K. W., Pearlman, L. A., & the Traumatic Stress Institute, Center for Adult & Adolescent Psychotherapy. (1996). *Transforming the pain: A workbook on vicarious traumatization*. W. W. Norton.

Sabourin, T. C., Infante, D. A., & Rudd, J. E. (1993). Verbal aggression in marriages: A comparison of violent, distressed but nonviolent, and nondistressed couples. *Human Communication Research, 20*(2), 245–267. https://doi.org/10.1111/j.1468-2958.1993.tb00323.x

Sachser, C., Berliner, L., Holt, T., Jensen, T. K., Jungbluth, N., Risch, E., Rosner, R., & Goldbeck, L. (2017). International development and psychometric properties of the Child and Adolescent Trauma Screen (CATS). *Journal of Affective Disorders, 210*, 189–195. https://doi.org/10.1016/j.jad.2016.12.040

Saltzman, W., Layne, C., Pynoos, R., Olafson, E., Kaplow, J., & Boat, B. (2017). *Trauma and grief component therapy for adolescents: A modular approach to treating traumatized and bereaved youth*. Cambridge University Press.

Samarah, E. M. S. (2024). Narrative exposure therapy to address PTSD symptomology with refugee and migrant children and youth: A review. *Traumatology, 30*(3), 260–273. https://doi.org/10.1037/trm0000427

Samios, C., Pakenham, K. I., & Sofronoff, K. (2012). Sense making and benefit finding in couples who have a child with Asperger syndrome: An application of the actor–partner interdependence model. *Autism, 16*(3), 275–292. https://doi.org/10.1177/1362361311418691

Sandage, S. J., Rupert, D., Stavros, G., & Devor, N. G. (2020). *Relational spirituality in psychotherapy: Healing suffering and promoting growth*. American Psychological Association. https://doi.org/10.1037/0000174-000

Satir, V. (1964). *Conjoint family therapy*. Science and Behavior Books.

Satir, V. (1988). *The new peoplemaking*. Science and Behavior Books.

Satir, V. (2000). The therapist story. In M. Baldwin (Ed.), *The use of self in therapy* (2nd ed., pp. 17–27). Haworth.

Sattler, J. M. (2001). *Assessment of children: Cognitive applications* (4th ed.). Jerome M. Sattler Publisher.

Saul, J. (2022). *Collective trauma, collective healing: Promoting community resilience in the aftermath of disaster*. Routledge.

Saunders, B. E., Berliner, L., & Hanson, R. F. (Eds.). (2003). *Child physical and sexual abuse: Guidelines for treatment*. National Crime Victims Research and Treatment Center.

Savell, S. M., Saini, R., Ramos, M., Wilson, M. N., Lemery-Chalfant, K., & Shaw, D. S. (2023). Family processes and structure: Longitudinal influences on adolescent disruptive and internalizing behaviors. *Family Relations, 72*(1), 361–382. https://doi.org/10.1111/fare.12728

Saxe, G. N., Ellis, B. H., & Brown, A. D. (2015). *Trauma systems therapy for children and teens*. Guilford Press.

Saxe, G. N., Ellis, B. H., Fogler, J., Hansen, S., & Sorkin, B. (2005). Comprehensive care for traumatized children: An open trial examines treatment using trauma systems therapy. *Psychiatric Annals, 35*(5), 443–448. https://doi.org/10.3928/00485713-20050501-10

Schauer, M., & Elbert, T. (2010). Dissociation following traumatic stress: Etiology and treatment. *Journal of Psychology, 218*(2), 109–127. https://doi.org/10.1027/0044-3409/a000018

Schauer, M., Neuner, F., & Elbert, T. (2011). *Narrative exposure therapy: A short-term treatment for traumatic stress disorders*. Hogrefe Publishing.

Schauer, M., Neuner, F., & Elbert, T. (2017). Narrative exposure therapy for children and adolescents (KIDNET). In M. A. Landolt, M. Cloitre, & U. Schnyder (Eds.), *Evidence-based treatments for trauma related disorders in children and adolescents* (pp. 227–250). Springer. https://doi.org/10.1007/978-3-319-46138-0_11

Schnyder, U., Bryant, R. A., Ehlers, A., Foa, E. B., Hasan, A., Mwiti, G., Kristensen, C. H., Neuner, F., Oe, M., & Yule, W. (2016). Culture-sensitive psychotraumatology. *European Journal of Psychotraumatology, 7*(1), Article 31179. https://doi.org/10.3402/ejpt.v7.31179

Schulz, M. S., Pruett, M. K., Kerig, P. K., & Parke, R. D. (Eds.). (2010). *Strengthening couple relationships for optimal child development: Lessons from research and intervention*. American Psychological Association. https://doi.org/10.1037/12058-000

Schwartz, R. C., & Sweezy, M. (2020). *Internal family systems therapy*. Guilford Press.

Scott, L. D., McCoy, H., Munson, M. R., Snowden, L. R., & McMillen, J. C. (2011). Cultural mistrust of mental health professionals among Black males transitioning from foster care. *Journal of Child and Family Studies, 20*(5), 605–613. https://doi.org/10.1007/s10826-010-9434-z

Sells, S. P., & Souder, E. (2018). *Treating the traumatized child: A step-by-step family systems approach*. Springer.

Selvini Palazzoli, M., Boscolo, L., Cecchin, G., & Prata, G. (1978). *Paradox and counterparadox: A new model in the therapy of the family in schizophrenic transaction*. Jason Aronson.

Senge, P. M. (2006). *The fifth discipline: The art and practice of the learning organization* (Rev. ed.). Doubleday.

Sensorimotor Psychotherapy Institute. (2024). *What is sensorimotor psychotherapy?* https://sensorimotorpsychotherapy.org/about/

Sexton, T. L. (2011). *Functional family therapy in clinical practice: An evidence-based treatment model for working with troubled adolescents*. Routledge.

Sexton, T. L., & Stanton, M. (2016). Systems theories. In J. C. Norcross, G. R. VandenBos, & D. K. Freedheim (Eds.), *APA handbook of clinical psychology: Vol. 2. Theory and research* (pp. 213–239). American Psychological Association. https://doi.org/10.1037/14773-008

Shapiro, F. (1989). Efficacy of the eye movement desensitization procedure in the treatment of traumatic memories. *Journal of Traumatic Stress, 2*(2), 199–223. https://doi.org/10.1002/jts.2490020207

Shapiro, F. (2017). *Eye movement desensitization and reprocessing (EMDR) therapy: Basic principles, protocols, and procedures*. Guilford Press.

Shapiro, F., Kaslow, F. W., & Maxfield, L. (Eds.). (2007). *Handbook of EMDR and family therapy processes*. Wiley.

Sharpley, C. F., & Rogers, H. J. (1984). Preliminary validation of the abbreviated Spanier Dyadic Adjustment Scale: Some psychometric data regarding a screening test of marital adjustment. *Educational and Psychological Measurement, 44*(4), 1045–1049. https://doi.org/10.1177/0013164484444029

Shellenberger, S., Dent, M. M., Davis-Smith, M., Seale, J. P., Weintraut, R., & Wright, T. (2007). Cultural genogram: A tool for teaching and practice. *Families, Systems, & Health, 25*(4), 367–381. https://doi.org/10.1037/1091-7527.25.4.367

Shengold, L. (2011). Trauma, soul murder, and change. *The Psychoanalytic Quarterly, 80*(1), 121–138. https://doi.org/10.1002/j.2167-4086.2011.tb00080.x

Sheras, P. L., Abidin, R. R., & Konold, T. R. (1998). *Stress Index for Parents of Adolescents: Professional manual*. Psychological Assessment Resources.

Sherman, M., Smith, J. G., Straits-Troster, K., Larsen, J., & Gewirtz, A. (2016). Veterans' perceptions of the impact of PTSD on their parenting and children. *Psychological Services, 13*(4), 401–410. https://doi.org/10.1037/ser0000101

Shubs, C. H. (2008). Countertransference issues in the assessment and treatment of trauma recovery with victims of violent crime. *Psychoanalytic Psychology, 25*(1), 156–180. https://doi.org/10.1037/0736-9735.25.1.156

Siegel, D. J. (1999). *The developing mind: Toward a neurobiology of interpersonal experience*. Guilford Press.

Siegel, J. P. (2013). Breaking the links in intergenerational violence: An emotional regulation perspective. *Family Process, 52*(2), 163–178. https://doi.org/10.1111/famp.12023

Silvern, L., Karyl, J., & Landis, T. Y. (1995). Individual psychotherapy for the traumatized children of abused women. In E. Peled, P. G. Jaffe, & J. L. Edleson (Eds.), *Ending the cycle of violence: Community responses to children of battered women* (pp. 43–76). Sage Publications. https://doi.org/10.4135/9781483326894.n4

Silvestre, M., & Tarquinio, C. L. (2022). Systemic family therapy and EMDR therapy: An integrative approach. *European Journal of Trauma & Dissociation, 6*(4), Article 100291. https://doi.org/10.1016/j.ejtd.2022.100291

Simpson, J. A., & Rholes, W. S. (2002). Fearful-avoidance, disorganization, and multiple working models: Some directions for future theory and research. *Attachment & Human Development, 4*(2), 223–229. https://doi.org/10.1080/14616730210154207

Sinkler, M. A., Furdock, R. J., & Vallier, H. A. (2022). Treating trauma more effectively: A review of psychosocial programming. *Injury, 53*(6), 1756–1764. https://doi.org/10.1016/j.injury.2022.04.022

Sinsky, C. A., Biddison, L. D., Mallick, A., Dopp, A. L., Perlo, J., Lynn, L., & Smith, C. D. (2020). Organizational evidence-based and promising practices for improving clinician well-being. *NAM Perspectives*. 1–15. https://doi.org/10.31478/202011a

Skinner, H. A., Steinhauer, P. D., & Santa-Barbara, J. (1995). *The Family Assessment Measure–III manual*. Multi-Health Systems.

Skinner, H. A., Steinhauer, P. D., & Sitarenios, G. (2000). Family Assessment Measure (FAM) and process model of family functioning. *Journal of Family Therapy, 22*(2), 190–210. https://doi.org/10.1111/1467-6427.00146

SmithBattle, L., Loman, D. G., Yoo, J. H., Cibulka, N., & Rariden, C. (2022). Evidence for revising the adverse childhood experiences screening tool: A scoping review. *Journal of Child & Adolescent Trauma, 15*(1), 89–103. https://doi.org/10.1007/s40653-021-00358-w

Smits, M. L., Luyten, P., Feenstra, D. J., Bales, D. L., Kamphuis, J. H., Dekker, J. J. M., Verheul, R., & Busschbach, J. J. V. (2022). Trauma and outcome in mentalization-based therapy for borderline personality disorder. *American Journal of Psychotherapy, 75*(1), 12–20. https://doi.org/10.1176/appi.psychotherapy.20210027

Snyder, D. K., & Aikman, G. G. (1999). Marital Satisfaction Inventory–Revised. In M. E. Maruish (Ed.), *The use of psychological testing for treatment planning and outcomes assessment* (2nd ed., pp. 1173–1210). Lawrence Erlbaum.

Snyder, D. K., Heyman, R. E., Haynes, S. N., Carlson, C. I., & Balderrama-Durbin, C. (2019). Couple and family assessment. In B. H. Fiese, M. Celano, K. Deater-Deckard, E. N. Jouriles, & M. A. Whisman (Eds.), *APA handbook of contemporary family psychology: Vol. 3. Family therapy and training* (pp. 35–51). American Psychological Association. https://doi.org/10.1037/0000101-003

Solms, M., & Turnbull, O. (2002). *The brain and the inner world: An introduction to the neuroscience of subjective experience*. Karnac Books.

Soloski, K. L., & Deitz, S. L. (2016). Managing emotional responses in therapy: An adapted EFT supervision approach. *Contemporary Family Therapy, 38*(4), 361–372. https://doi.org/10.1007/s10591-016-9392-8

Sommers-Flanagan, J., & Sommers-Flanagan, R. (2016). *Clinical interviewing* (6th ed.). Wiley.

Southern, S., & Sullivan, R. D. (2021). Family violence in context: An intergenerational systemic model. *The Family Journal, 29*(3), 260–291. https://doi.org/10.1177/10664807211006274

Spanier, G. B. (1976). Measuring dyadic adjustment: New scales for assessing the quality of marriage and similar dyads. *Journal of Marriage and the Family, 38*(1), 15–28. https://doi.org/10.2307/350547

Spengler, P. M., Lee, N. A., Wiebe, S. A., & Wittenborn, A. K. (2024). A comprehensive meta-analysis on the efficacy of emotionally focused couple therapy. *Couple and Family Psychology: Research and Practice, 13*(2), 81–99. https://doi.org/10.1037/cfp0000233

Sperry, L. (2005). Case conceptualization: A strategy for incorporating individual, couple and family dynamics in the treatment process. *The American Journal of Family Therapy, 33*(5), 353–364. https://doi.org/10.1080/01926180500341598

Spiegel, L. (2017). *Internal family systems therapy with children*. Routledge.

Sprang, G., Ford, J., Kerig, P., & Bride, B. (2019). Defining secondary traumatic stress and developing targeted assessments and interventions: Lessons learned from research and leading experts. *Traumatology, 25*(2), 72–81. https://doi.org/10.1037/trm0000180

Sprenkle, D. H., & Blow, A. J. (2004). Common factors are not islands—They work through models: A response to Sexton, Ridley, and Kleiner. *Journal of Marital and Family Therapy, 30*(2), 151–157. https://doi.org/10.1111/j.1752-0606.2004.tb01228.x

Sprenkle, D. H., Davis, S. D., & Lebow, J. L. (2013). *Common factors in couple and family therapy: The overlooked foundation for effective practice*. Guilford Press.

Stanton, M., & Harway, M. (2019). Graduate education in couple and family psychology. In B. H. Fiese, M. Celano, K. Deater-Deckard, E. N. Jouriles, & M. A. Whisman (Eds.), *APA handbook of contemporary family psychology: Vol. 3. Family therapy and training* (pp. 469–482). American Psychological Association. https://doi.org/10.1037/0000101-028

Stanton, M., & Welsh, R. (2011). *Specialty competencies in couple and family psychology*. Oxford University Press. https://doi.org/10.1093/med:psych/9780195387872.001.0001

Stare, B. G., & Fernando, D. M. (2014). Intimate partner violence typology and treatment: A brief literature review. *The Family Journal, 22*(3), 298–303. https://doi.org/10.1177/1066480714529747

Stein, J. A., Rotheram-Borus, M. J., & Lester, P. (2007). Impact of parentification on long-term outcomes among children of parents with HIV/AIDS. *Family Process, 46*(3), 317–333. https://doi.org/10.1111/j.1545-5300.2007.00214.x

Steinhauer, P. D., Santa-Barbara, J., & Skinner, H. (1984). The process model of family functioning. *The Canadian Journal of Psychiatry, 29*(2), 77–88. https://doi.org/10.1177/070674378402900202

Stephenson, E., & Yost, H. (2023). Exploring the effectiveness and sustainability of Trust Based Relational Intervention (TBRI) as a trauma-informed approach in two Tasmanian child and family learning centres. *Journal of Child & Adolescent Trauma, 17*(2), 1–14. https://doi.org/10.1007/s40653-023-00574-6

Stileman, H. M., & Jones, C. A. (2023). Revisiting the debriefing debate: Does psychological debriefing reduce PTSD symptomology following work-related trauma? A meta-analysis. *Frontiers in Psychology, 14*, Article 1248924. https://doi.org/10.3389/fpsyg.2023.1248924

Stith, S. M., McCollum, E. E., & Rosen, K. H. (2011). *Couples therapy for domestic violence: Finding safe solutions*. American Psychological Association. https://doi.org/10.1037/12329-000

Stith, S. M., Rosen, K. H., Middleton, K. A., Busch, A. L., Lundeberg, K., & Carlton, R. P. (2000). The intergenerational transmission of spouse abuse: A meta-analysis. *Journal of Marriage and Family, 62*(3), 640–654. https://doi.org/10.1111/j.1741-3737.2000.00640.x

Stith, S. M., Spencer, C. M., & Mittal, M. (2020). Trauma, posttraumatic stress, and family systems. In K. S. Wampler, M. Rastogi & R. Singh (Eds.), *The handbook of systemic family therapy* (Vol. 3, pp. 990–121). Wiley.

Stolorow, R. D. (2007). *Trauma and human existence: Autobiographical, psychoanalytic, and philosophical reflections*. Routledge.

Stover, C. S., Hahn, H., Maciejewski, K. R., Epstein, C., & Marans, S. (2022). The child and family traumatic stress intervention: Factors associated with symptom reduction for children receiving treatment. *Child Abuse & Neglect, 134*, Article 105886. https://doi.org/10.1016/j.chiabu.2022.105886

Strathearn, L., Giannotti, M., Mills, R., Kisely, S., Najman, J., & Abajobir, A. (2020). Long-term cognitive, psychological, and health outcomes associated with child abuse and neglect. *Pediatrics, 146*(4), Article e20200438. https://doi.org/10.1542/peds.2020-0438

Stratton, P. (2016). *The evidence base of family therapy and systemic practice*. Association for Family Therapy and Systemic Practice.

Stratton, P., Bland, J., Janes, E., & Lask, J. (2010). Developing an indicator of family function and a practicable outcome measure for systemic family and couple therapy: The SCORE. *Journal of Family Therapy, 32*(3), 232–258. https://doi.org/10.1111/j.1467-6427.2010.00507.x

Straus, M. A., & Douglas, E. M. (2004). A short form of the Revised Conflict Tactics Scales, and typologies for severity and mutuality. *Violence and Victims, 19*(5), 507–520. https://doi.org/10.1891/vivi.19.5.507.63686

Straus, M. A., Hamby, S. L., Boney-McCoy, S., & Sugarman, D. B. (1996). The Revised Conflict Tactics Scales (CTS2): Development and preliminary psychometric data. *Journal of Family Issues, 17*(3), 283–316. https://doi.org/10.1177/019251396017003001

Straus, M. A., Hamby, S. L., Finkelhor, D., Moore, D. W., & Runyan, D. (1998). Identification of child maltreatment with the parent–child conflict tactics scales: Development and psychometric data for a national sample of American parents. *Child Abuse & Neglect, 22*(4), 249–270. https://doi.org/10.1016/s0145-2134(97)00174-9

Sturge-Apple, M. L., Davies, P. T., & Cummings, E. M. (2010). Typologies of family functioning and children's adjustment during the early school years. *Child Development, 81*(4), 1320–1335. https://doi.org/10.1111/j.1467-8624.2010.01471.x

Substance Abuse and Mental Health Services Administration. (2014). *Trauma-informed care in behavioral health services* (Treatment Improvement Protocol (TIP) Series 57, HHS Publication No. (SMA) 13-4801). https://www.ncbi.nlm.nih.gov/books/NBK207201/

Sullivan, M. B., & Bennear, L. S. (2021). *A quasi-experimental evaluation of family centered treatment in the Maryland Department of Juvenile Services community based non-residential program: Child permanency and well-being*. Family Centered Treatment Foundation. https://static1.squarespace.com/static/57850a09d2b857904415f3fb/t/6047b2f92088591138b3b18a/1615311610418/A+Quasi-experimental+Evaluation+of+Family+Centered+Treatment%C2%AE+in+the+Maryland+Department+of+Juvenile+Services+Community+Based+Non-residential+Program-Child+Permanency+and+Well-being.pdf

Sullivan, M. B., Bennear, L. S., Honess, K. F., Painter, W. E., Jr., & Wood, T. J. (2012). Family centered treatment—An alternative to residential placements for adjudicated youth: Outcomes and cost-effectiveness. *Journal of Juvenile Justice, 2*(1), 25–40.

Summers, R. F., Barber, J. P., & Zilcha-Mano, S. (2024). *Psychodynamic therapy*. Guilford Press.

Suomi, A., Evans, L., Rodgers, B., Taplin, S., & Cowlishaw, S. (2019). Couple and family therapies for post-traumatic stress disorder (PTSD). *Cochrane Database of Systematic Reviews, 2019*(12), Article CD011257. https://doi.org/10.1002/14651858.CD011257.pub2

Sussman, M. B. (1995). *A perilous calling: The hazards of psychotherapy practice*. Wiley.

Sussman, M. B. (2007). *A curious calling: Unconscious motivations for practicing psychotherapy*. Jason Aronson.

Sutton, L., Rowe, S., Hammerton, G., & Billings, J. (2022). The contribution of organisational factors to vicarious trauma in mental health professionals: A systematic review and narrative synthesis. *European Journal of Psychotraumatology, 13*(1), Article 2022278. https://doi.org/10.1080/20008198.2021.2022278

Swedo, E. A., Aslam, M. V., Dahlberg, L.L., Niolon, P. H., Guinn, A. S., Simon, T. R., & Mercy, J. A. (2023). Prevalence of adverse childhood experiences among U.S. adults—Behavioral risk factor surveillance system, 2011–2020. *Morbidity and Mortality Weekly Report, 72*(26), 707–715. https://doi.org/10.15585/mmwr.mm7226a2

Swedo, E. A., Pampati, S., Anderson, K. N., Thorne, E., McKinnon, I. I., Brener, N. D., Stinson, J., Mpofu, J. J., & Niolon, P. H. (2024). Adverse childhood experiences and health conditions and risk behaviors among high school students—Youth Risk Behavior Survey, United States, 2023. *MMWR Supplements, 73*(4), 39–49. https://doi.org/10.15585/mmwr.su7304a5

Swenson, C. C., & Schaeffer, C. M. (2018). A multisystemic approach to the prevention and treatment of child abuse and neglect. *International Journal on Child Maltreatment: Research, Policy and Practice, 1*(1), 97–120. https://doi.org/10.1007/s42448-018-0002-2

Szapocznik, J., & Hervis, O. (2020). *Brief strategic family therapy*. American Psychological Association. https://doi.org/10.1037/0000169-000

Szota, K., Schulte, K. L., & Christiansen, H. (2023). Interventions involving caregivers for children and adolescents following traumatic events: A systematic review and meta-analysis. *Clinical Child and Family Psychology Review, 26*(1), 17–32. https://doi.org/10.1007/s10567-022-00415-2

Taft, C. T., Macdonald, A., Creech, S. K., Monson, C. M., & Murphy, C. M. (2016). A randomized controlled clinical trial of the Strength at Home men's program for partner violence in military veterans. *Journal of Clinical Psychiatry, 77*(9), 1168–1175. https://doi.org/10.4088/JCP.15m10020

Tai, D. B. G., Sia, I. G., Doubeni, C. A., & Wieland, M. L. (2022). Disproportionate impact of COVID-19 on racial and ethnic minority groups in the United States: A 2021 update. *Journal of Racial and Ethnic Health Disparities, 9*(6), 2334–2339. https://doi.org/10.1007/s40615-021-01170-w

Taylor, D. (2020). Reflective practice in the art and science of counselling: A scoping review. *Psychotherapy and Counselling Journal of Australia, 8*(1), 1–15. https://doi.org/10.59158/001c.71255

Taylor, R. E., & Kuo, B. C. (2019). Black American psychological help-seeking intention: An integrated literature review with recommendations for clinical practice. *Journal of Psychotherapy Integration, 29*(4), 325–337. https://doi.org/10.1037/int0000131

Teicher, M. H., Samson, J. A., Anderson, C. M., & Ohashi, K. (2016). The effects of childhood maltreatment on brain structure, function and connectivity. *Nature Reviews Neuroscience, 17*(10), 652–666. https://doi.org/10.1038/nrn.2016.111

Tesfai, A., Captari, L. E., Meyer-Weitz, A., & Cowden, R. G. (2023). Coping resources among forced migrants in South Africa: Exploring the role of character strengths in adjustment and flourishing. *International Journal of Environmental Research and Public Health, 21*(1), Article 50. https://doi.org/10.3390/ijerph21010050

Thoburn, J., Hoffman-Robinson, G., Shelly, L. J., & Hagen, A. J. (2013). Clinical practice in family psychology. In J. H. Bray & M. Stanton (Eds.), *Wiley-Blackwell handbook of family psychology* (pp. 198–211). Wiley-Blackwell. https://doi.org/10.1002/9781444310238.ch13

Thomas, K. (2022). Early relational health—A promising approach for equitable systems change in pediatrics: A commentary. *Infant Mental Health Journal, 43*(3), 507–514. https://doi.org/10.1002/imhj.21984

Timm, T. M., & Blow, A. J. (1999). Self-of-the-therapist work: A balance between removing restraints and identifying resources. *Contemporary Family Therapy, 21*(3), 331–351. https://doi.org/10.1023/A:1021960315503

Timshel, I., Montgomery, E., & Dalgaard, N. T. (2017). A systematic review of risk and protective factors associated with family related violence in refugee families. *Child Abuse & Neglect, 70*, 315–330. https://doi.org/10.1016/j.chiabu.2017.06.023

Tomeny, T., Barry, T. D., Fair, E. C., & Riley, R. (2017). Parentification of adult siblings of individuals with autism spectrum disorder. *Journal of Child and Family Studies, 26*(4), 1056–1067. https://doi.org/10.1007/s10826-016-0627-y

Tompkins, T. L. (2007). Parentification and maternal HIV infection: Beneficial role or pathological burden? *Journal of Child and Family Studies, 16*(1), 113–123. https://doi.org/10.1007/s10826-006-9072-7

Toth, S. L., Sturge-Apple, M. L., Rogosch, F. A., & Cicchetti, D. (2015). Mechanisms of change: Testing how preventative interventions impact psychological and physiological stress functioning in mothers in neglectful families. *Development and Psychopathology, 27*(4pt2), 1661–1674. https://doi.org/10.1017/S0954579415001017

Tracey, T. J., Lichtenberg, J. W., Goodyear, R. K., & Wampold, B. E. (2024). Do therapists get better with experience? In F. T. L. Leong, J. L. Callahan, J. Zimmerman, M. J. Constantino, & C. F. Eubanks (Eds.), *APA handbook of psychotherapy: Vol. 2. Evidence-based practice, practice-based evidence, and contextual participant-driven practice* (pp. 255–269). American Psychological Association. https://doi.org/10.1037/0000354-017

Tronick, E., Als, H., Adamson, L., Wise, S., & Brazelton, T. B. (1978). The infant's response to entrapment between contradictory messages in face-to-face interaction. *Journal of the American Academy of Child psychiatry, 17*(1), 1–13. https://doi.org/10.1016/S0002-7138(09)62273-1

Tronick, E. Z., & Beeghly, M. (2011). Infants' meaning-making and the development of mental health problems. *American Psychologist, 66*(2), 107–119. https://doi.org/10.1037/a0021631

Tronick, E. Z., & Gold, C. M. (2020). *The power of discord: Why the ups and downs of relationships are the secret to building intimacy, resilience, and trust*. Hachette UK.

Tryphonopoulos, P. D., Letourneau, N., & Ditommaso, E. (2014). Attachment and caregiver–infant interaction: A review of observational-assessment tools. *Infant Mental Health Journal, 35*(6), 642–656. https://doi.org/10.1002/imhj.21461

Tsvieli, N., Lifshitz, C., & Diamond, G. M. (2022). Corrective attachment episodes in attachment-based family therapy: The power of enactment. *Psychotherapy Research, 32*(2), 209–222. https://doi.org/10.1080/10503307.2021.1913295

Tucker, C., & Smith-Adcock, S. (2017). Theraplay: The evidence for trauma-focused treatment for children and families. In C. Tucker & S. Smith-Adcock (Eds.), *Emerging research in play therapy, child counseling, and consultation* (pp. 42–59). IGI Global.

Tummala-Narra, P. E. (2021). Introduction: Challenges facing racial minority immigrants. In P. Tummala-Narra (Ed.), *Trauma and racial minority immigrants: Turmoil, uncertainty, and resistance* (pp. 3–12). American Psychological Association. https://doi.org/10.1037/0000214-001

Turgeon, J., Milot, T., St-Laurent, D., & Dubois-Comtois, K. (2022). Hostile-helpless states of mind: A scoping review of risk factors, correlates, and consequences. *Infant Mental Health Journal, 43*(4), 597–623. https://doi.org/10.1002/imhj.21994

Tuttle, B. M., Giano, Z., & Merten, M. J. (2018). Stress spillover in policing and negative relationship functioning for law enforcement marriages. *The Family Journal, 26*(2), 246–252. https://doi.org/10.1177/1066480718775739

Ungar, M., & Theron, L. (2020). Resilience and mental health: How multisystemic processes contribute to positive outcomes. *The Lancet Psychiatry, 7*(5), 441–448. https://doi.org/10.1016/S2215-0366(19)30434-1

U.S. Department of Health and Human Services. (1999). *Mental health: A report of the surgeon general*. U.S. Department of Health and Human Services, Substance Abuse and Mental Health Services Administration.

Vaknin, O., & Wiseman, H. (2021). Rescue fantasies in the personal and professional relational narratives of psychotherapists. *Counselling and Psychotherapy Research, 21*(2), 442–447. https://doi.org/10.1002/capr.12362

van den Bos, K., & Miedema, J. (2000). Toward understanding why fairness matters: The influence of mortality salience on reactions to procedural fairness. *Journal of Personality and Social Psychology, 79*(3), 355–366. https://doi.org/10.1037/0022-3514.79.3.355

Van den Eynde, J., & Veno, A. (2013). Coping with disastrous events: An empowerment model of community healing. In R. Gist & B. Lubin (Eds.), *Response to disaster* (pp. 167–192). Routledge. https://doi.org/10.4324/9781315803500-16

van der Kolk, B. (2014). *The body keeps the score: Brain, mind, and body in the healing of trauma*. Penguin Books.

van Dernoot Lipsky, L., & Burke, C. (2009). *Trauma stewardship: An everyday guide to caring for self while caring for others*. Berrett-Koehler Publishers.

van Emmerik, A. A., Kamphuis, J. H., Hulsbosch, A. M., & Emmelkamp, P. M. (2002). Single session debriefing after psychological trauma: A meta-analysis.

The Lancet, *360*(9335), 766–771. https://doi.org/10.1016/S0140-6736(02)09897-5

van IJzendoorn, M. H., Bakermans-Kranenburg, M. J., Coughlan, B., & Reijman, S. (2020). Annual research review: Umbrella synthesis of meta-analyses on child maltreatment antecedents and interventions: Differential susceptibility perspective on risk and resilience. *Journal of Child Psychology and Psychiatry*, *61*(3), 272–290. https://doi.org/10.1111/jcpp.13147

Van Loon, L. M., Van de Ven, M. O., Van Doesum, K. T., Hosman, C. M., & Witteman, C. L. (2017). Parentification, stress, and problem behavior of adolescents who have a parent with mental health problems. *Family Process*, *56*(1), 141–153. https://doi.org/10.1111/famp.12165

Van Parys, H., & Rober, P. (2013). Micro-analysis of a therapist-generated metaphor referring to the position of a parentified child in the family. *Journal of Family Therapy*, *35*(1), 89–113. https://doi.org/10.1111/j.1467-6427.2011.00551.x

Vaughans, K. C. (2016). To unchain haunting blood memories: Intergenerational trauma among African Americans. In J. Salberg & S. Grand (Eds.), *Wounds of history* (pp. 246–262). Routledge.

Velasco, J., Sanmartín, F. J., Gálvez-Lara, M., Cuadrado, F., & Moriana, J. A. (2023). Psychological effects of professional exposure to trauma and human suffering: Systematic review and meta-analysis. *Trauma, Violence, & Abuse*, *24*(3), 1656–1676. https://doi.org/10.1177/15248380221074314

Verbnik, Š., & Možina, M. (2021). Skupni dejavniki v partnerski in družinski tera-piji [Common factors in couple and family therapy]. *Kairos – Slovenian Journal of Psychotherapy*, *15*(1–2), 151–189.

Visser, M., Schoemaker, K., de Schipper, C., Lamers-Winkelman, F., & Finkenauer, C. (2016). Interparental violence and the mediating role of parental availability in children's trauma related symptoms. *Journal of Child & Adolescent Trauma*, *9*(2), 115–125. https://doi.org/10.1007/s40653-015-0071-y

Volkert, J., Taubner, S., Byrne, G., Rossouw, T., & Midgley, N. (2022). Introduction to mentalization-based approaches for parents, children, youths, and families. *American Journal of Psychotherapy*, *75*(1), 4–11. https://doi.org/10.1176/appi.psychotherapy.20210020

Vuchinich, S., Emery, R. E., & Cassidy, J. (1988). Family members as third parties in dyadic family conflict: Strategies, alliances, and outcomes. *Child Development*, *59*(5), 1293–1302. https://doi.org/10.1111/j.1467-8624.1988.tb01498.x

Walfish, S., McAlister, B., O'Donnell, P., & Lambert, M. J. (2012). An investigation of self-assessment bias in mental health providers. *Psychological Reports*, *110*(2), 639–644. https://doi.org/10.2466/02.07.17.PR0.110.2

Walsh, F. (2007). Traumatic loss and major disasters: Strengthening family and community resilience. *Family Process*, *46*(2), 207–227. https://doi.org/10.1111/j.1545-5300.2007.00205.x

Walsh, F. (2012a). Family resilience: Strengths forged through adversity. In F. Walsh (Ed.), *Normal family processes: Growing diversity and complexity* (4th ed., pp. 399–427). Guilford Press.

Walsh, F. (2012b). The new normal: Diversity and complexity in 21st-century families. In F. Walsh (Ed.), *Normal family processes: Growing diversity and complexity* (4th ed., pp. 3–27). Guilford Press.

Walsh, F. (2015). *Strengthening family resilience*. Guilford Press.

Walsh, F. (2016). Family resilience: A developmental systems framework. *European Journal of Developmental Psychology, 13*(3), 313–324. https://doi.org/10.1080/17405629.2016.1154035

Wampler, K. S., Rastogi, M., & Singh, R. (Eds.). (2020). *The handbook of systemic family therapy*. Wiley.

Wampold, B. E., & Imel, Z. E. (2015). *The great psychotherapy debate: The evidence for what makes psychotherapy work*. Routledge.

Wang, M., Liu, S., & Belsky, J. (2017). Triangulation processes experienced by children in contemporary China. *International Journal of Behavioral Development, 41*(6), 688–695. https://doi.org/10.1177/0165025416662345

Wang, M., Sun, S., Liu, X., Yang, Y., Liu, C., Huang, A., & Liu, S. (2024). Interparental conflict and early adolescent depressive symptoms: Parent–child triangulation as the mediator and grandparent support as the moderator. *Journal of Youth and Adolescence, 53*(1), 186–199. https://doi.org/10.1007/s10964-023-01923-2

Ward-Ciesielski, E. F., & Rizvi, S. L. (2021). The potential iatrogenic effects of psychiatric hospitalization for suicidal behavior: A critical review and recommendations for research. *Clinical Psychology: Science and Practice, 28*(1), 60–71. https://doi.org/10.1111/cpsp.12332

Wardoyo, H., Moeloek, N. D., Basrowi, R. W., Ekowati, M., Samah, K., Mustopo, W. I., Nurdjasmi, E., Widyahening, I. S., Medise, B. E., Darus, F., Sundjaya, T., & Pelangi, B. (2023). Mental health awareness and promotion during the first 1000 days of life: An expert consensus. *Healthcare, 12*(1), Article 44. https://doi.org/10.3390/healthcare12010044

Warren, J. M., Halpin, S. A., Hanstock, T. L., Hood, C., & Hunt, S. A. (2022). Outcomes of parent–child interaction therapy (PCIT) for families presenting with child maltreatment: A systematic review. *Child Abuse & Neglect, 134*, Article 105942. https://doi.org/10.1016/j.chiabu.2022.105942

Watson, J. C., & Wiseman, H. E. (2021). *The responsive psychotherapist: Attuning to clients in the moment*. American Psychological Association. https://doi.org/10.1037/0000240-000

Watzlawick, P., Bavelas, J. B., & Jackson, D. D. (1967). *Pragmatics of human communication: A study of interactional patterns, pathologies, and paradoxes*. W. W. Norton.

Weathers, F. W., Blake, D. D., Schnurr, P. P., Kaloupek, D. G., Marx, B. P., & Keane, T. M. (2013a). *The Clinician-Administered PTSD Scale for DSM-5 (CAPS-5)* [Measurement instrument]. https://www.ptsd.va.gov/professional/assessment/adult-int/caps.asp

Weathers, F. W., Blake, D. D., Schnurr, P. P., Kaloupek, D. G., Marx, B. P., & Keane, T. M. (2013b). *The Life Events Checklist for DSM-5 (LEC-5)* [Measurement instrument]. https://www.ptsd.va.gov/professional/assessment/documents/LEC5_Standard_Self-report.pdf

Weathers, F. W., Litz, B. T., Keane, T. M., Palmieri, P. A., Marx, B. P., & Schnurr, P. P. (2013). *The PTSD Checklist for DSM-5 (PCL-5)* [Measurement instrument]. https://www.ptsd.va.gov/professional/assessment/adult-sr/ptsd-checklist.asp

Weerasekera, P. (1996). *Multiperspective case formulation: A step towards treatment integration*. Krieger Publishing.

Weiling, E., Utržan, D. S., Witting, A. B., & Seponski, D. M. (2020). Global mental health, traumatic stress, and displaced families. In K. S. Wampler, M. Rastogi, & R. Singh (Eds.), *The handbook of systemic family therapy* (Vol. 4, pp. 215–241). Wiley. https://doi.org/10.1002/9781119788409.ch9

Wesselmann, D. (2025). *EMDR and family therapy: Integrative treatment for attachment trauma in children*. W. W. Norton.

Wesselmann, D., Armstrong, S., Schweitzer, C., Davidson, M., & Potter, A. (2018). An integrative EMDR and family therapy model for treating attachment trauma in children: A case series. *Journal of EMDR Practice & Research, 12*(4), 196–207. https://doi.org/10.1891/1933-3196.12.4.196

White, K., Rolock, N., Hambrick, E., Bai, R., Bender, A., Evans, K., Diamant-Wilson, R., & Bailey, K. (2023). Longitudinal evaluation of the neurosequential model of therapeutics with adoptive families in Tennessee. *Journal of Evidence-Based Social Work, 20*(6), 1004–1025. https://doi.org/10.1080/26408066.2023.2245819

White, M., & Epston, D. (1990). *Narrative means to therapeutic ends*. W. W. Norton.

Whittenbury, K., Clark, S. L., Brooks, M., Murphy, T., Turner, M. J., & Fawcett, H. (2025). Strengths for helping professionals exposed to secondary trauma: A scoping review. *Trauma, Violence, & Abuse, 26*(2), 251–264. https://doi.org/10.1177/15248380241309371

Widom, C. S. (1989). The cycle of violence. *Science, 244*(4901), 160–166. https://doi.org/10.1126/science.2704995

Williams, J., Riggs, S. A., & Kaminski, P. (2016). A typology of childhood sibling subsystems that may emerge in abusive family systems. *The Family Journal, 24*(4), 378–384. https://doi.org/10.1177/1066480716663182

Williams, L., Edwards, T. M., Patterson, J., & Chamow, L. (2011). *Essential assessment skills for couple and family therapists*. Guilford Press.

Wilson, J. P., & Keane, T. M. (Eds.). (2004). *Assessing psychological trauma and PTSD*. Guilford Press.

Wilson, J. P., & Lindy, J. D. (1994). Empathic strain and countertransference. In J. P. Wilson & J. D. Lindy (Eds.), *Countertransference in the treatment of PTSD* (pp. 5–30). Guilford Press.

Wilson, T. D., & Gilbert, D. T. (2005). Affective forecasting: Knowing what to want. *Current Directions in Psychological Science, 14*(3), 131–134. https://doi.org/10.1111/j.0963-7214.2005.00355.x

Wise, C., & Gomez, J. (2018). The accidental family therapist. *The Family Psychologist, 34*(3). https://www.apadivisions.org/division-43/publications/newsletters/2018/11/accidental-therapist

Wolosky, M. (2022). *Minding the therapist's body: Empathy, interoceptive awareness, and vicarious trauma in psychotherapists* [Doctoral dissertation, Long Island University]. ProQuest Dissertations and Theses Global.

Women of Color Network. (2021). *Domestic violence in communities of color.* https://jbws.org/wp-content/uploads/2021/07/Domestic-Violence-in-Communities-of-Color-compressed.pdf

Worthington, E. L., Jr., Walter, S. L., Schultz, T., McConnell, J. M., Palmer, M. E., Cowden, R. G., & Hill, H. (2024). Treating traumas among Christians in Nigeria: A randomized controlled field study of the healing the wounds of trauma program. *Spirituality in Clinical Practice, 11*(3), 269–283. https://doi.org/10.1037/scp0000368

Wright, A., Reisig, A., & Cullen, B. (2020). Efficacy and cultural adaptations of narrative exposure therapy for trauma-related outcomes in refugees/asylum-seekers: A systematic review and meta-analysis. *Journal of Behavioral and Cognitive Therapy, 30*(4), 301–314. https://doi.org/10.1016/j.jbct.2020.10.003

Wycoff, K. L., & Franzese, B. (2019). *Essentials of trauma-informed assessment and intervention in school and community settings.* Wiley.

Yalom, I. D., & Leszcz, M. (2005). *The theory and practice of group psychotherapy* (5th ed.). Basic Books.

Yehuda, R., Halligan, S. L., & Grossman, R. (2001). Childhood trauma and risk for PTSD: Relationship to intergenerational effects of trauma, parental PTSD, and cortisol excretion. *Development and Psychopathology, 13*(3), 733–753. https://doi.org/10.1017/s0954579401003170

Yehuda, R., & Lehrner, A. (2018). Intergenerational transmission of trauma effects: Putative role of epigenetic mechanisms. *World Psychiatry, 17*(3), 243–257. https://doi.org/10.1002/wps.20568

Zaeske, L. M., Dye, A. R., Spadoni, S., Strothkamp, R., Kane, M. L., Ridgway, K., Dugan, A. J., Patterson, T. P., McEathron, S. R., & Cole, B. P. (2024). Addressing harm from adverse religious/spiritual experiences in psychotherapy: A scoping review. *Practice Innovations, 9*(1), 1–18. https://doi.org/10.1037/pri0000237

Zarling, A., & Russell, D. (2022). A randomized clinical trial of acceptance and commitment therapy and the Duluth model classes for men court-mandated to a domestic violence program. *Journal of Consulting and Clinical Psychology, 90*(4), 326–338. https://doi.org/10.1037/ccp0000722

Zeanah, C. H. (Ed.). (2018). *Handbook of infant mental health.* Guilford Press.

Zhang, H., Hook, J. N., Hodge, A. S., Mosher, D. K., Van Tongeren, D. R., & Davis, D. E. (2021). Religious and spiritual struggles and mental health following a disaster: The moderating role of spiritual fortitude. *Spirituality in Clinical Practice, 8*(4), 268–280. https://doi.org/10.1037/scp0000280

Zumbach, J., Oster, A., Rademacher, A., & Koglin, U. (2022). Reliability and validity of behavior observation coding systems in child maltreatment risk evaluation: A systematic review. *Journal of Child and Family Studies, 31*(2), 545–562. https://doi.org/10.1007/s10826-021-02160-6

Index

G

About the Authors

Shelley A. Riggs, PhD, LP, is a professor at Sam Houston State University, where she is the director of clinical training for the MA program in clinical psychology. In addition to providing direct therapeutic services, Dr. Riggs has been a clinical trainer for 25 years, teaching and supervising both master's and doctoral students at three different universities. Grounded in attachment and systems theories, her research program focuses on the roles of family systems, attachment relationships, and trauma in psychological functioning. Dr. Riggs has authored numerous scholarly publications and currently serves on the editorial boards of the *Journal of Family Psychology* and *Couple and Family Psychology: Research and Practice*. She is the recipient of several awards for teaching excellence, including the Texas Psychological Association's Outstanding Contribution to Education Award. Dr. Riggs served as the vice president for education and is a fellow in the American Psychological Association's Society for Couple and Family Psychology (Division 43), which recognized her with the award for Distinguished Contribution to Couple and Family Psychology in 2021.

Laura E. Captari, PhD, LP, is a staff psychologist and academic researcher at The Albert and Jessie Danielsen Institute at Boston University, and incoming assistant professor in the Counseling, Developmental, and Educational Psychology department at Boston College. In her roles as a psychotherapist, researcher, supervisor, and teacher, she brings a holistic, depth-oriented, and systemic perspective to understanding human experience, suffering, and healing. Dr. Captari's research in psychotherapeutic and community contexts explores the developmental and relational impacts of trauma, disaster, and loss across the lifespan and family system, with particular interest in how culturally embedded strengths and practices can serve as pathways to resilience and flourishing. Her scholarly work also explores novel approaches to address clinicians' risks for vicarious trauma and build professional longevity. Dr. Captari has authored over 50 professional articles and chapters and serves on multiple editorial boards, including *Psychological Trauma: Theory, Research, Practice, and Policy*.

About the Series Editors

Corinne C. Datchi, PhD, ABPP, is a licensed psychologist with board certification in couple and family psychology and a professor and core faculty member of the MA in clinical and counseling psychology in the Department of Psychology at William Paterson University. She was the 2019–2020 president of the Society for Couple and Family Psychology, American Psychological Association (APA) Division 43. Dr. Datchi earned the status of fellow member of Division 43. Her research and clinical practice focus on correctional populations, reentry, problem-solving justice, gender, qualitative research methodology, and the internationalization of research. She has written and published in peer-reviewed journals about family therapy, offender rehabilitation, and qualitative research methods. Her most recent contribution is a volume published by APA in 2022: *Best Clinical Practices for Treating Families in Juvenile and Criminal Justice Systems*. She demonstrates her clinical work with justice-involved populations in the APA video *Working With Couples in the Correctional System*, published in 2022. She is also the coeditor of two volumes published by APA in 2019 and New York University Press in 2017: *Integrative Couple and Family Therapies: Treatment Models for Complex Clinical Issues* and *Gender, Psychology, and Justice: The Mental Health of Women and Girls in the Legal System*.

Anthony Chambers, PhD, ABPP, is the chief academic officer at The Family Institute at Northwestern University. Dr. Chambers is also the director of Northwestern University's Center for Applied Psychological and Family Studies and is a clinical professor in the Department of Psychology. Dr. Chambers is also the past president of the American Psychological Association's Society for Couple and Family Psychology (Division 43), the past president of the American Academy of Couple and Family Psychology (AACFP), and he previously served on the board of directors for the American Psychological Association (APA).

Dr. Chambers received his BA in psychology from Hampton University and completed both his MA and PhD in clinical psychology at the University of Virginia. He completed his internship and postdoctoral clinical residency at Harvard Medical School and Massachusetts General Hospital focused on treating couples and did a second postdoctoral Fellowship at The Family Institute at Northwestern University focused on couple therapy as well as conducting systemically informed research on providing measurement-informed care.

Dr. Chambers engages in scholarly writing, teaching, and public speaking aimed at disseminating the latest knowledge about how to have a healthy relationship. Noteworthy academic achievements include coauthoring *Integrative Systemic Therapy*; coediting the *Encyclopedia of Couple and Family Therapy*; coediting an APA Series on Couple and Family Psychology; and coediting a TFI book series on Integrative Systemic Therapy. He has made frequent media appearances discussing his work with couples, including in *The New York Times*, *Rolling Stone*, *Newsweek*, the Associated Press, and *The Wall Street Journal*.

Dr. Chambers's professional accomplishments have resulted in him becoming a fellow of the APA, a fellow of the AACFP, and a diplomat of the American Board of Couple and Family Psychology. He also serves on the editorial board of the journal *Family Process* and is a former associate editor for the journal *Couple and Family Psychology: Research and Practice*.